...ntum memoriam meorum

BT708P3Y93

BRIDLING OF DESIRE

PAYER PIERRE J

MHC 06/93 35.00

The Bridling of Desir   In

The Bridling
of Desire:
Views of Sex
in the Later
Middle Ages

PIERRE J. PAYER

UNIVERSITY OF TORONTO PRESS

Toronto   Buffalo   London

© University of Toronto Press Incorporated 1993
Toronto   Buffalo   London
Printed in Canada

ISBN 0-8020-2919-1

Printed on acid-free paper

Canadian Cataloguing in Publication Data

Payer, Pierre J., 1936–
   The bridling of desire

   Includes bibliographical references and index.
   ISBN 0-8020-2919-1

   1. Sex – Religious aspects – Christianity – History of doctrines
   – Middle Ages, 600–1500. I. Title.

   BT708.P3 1993   241'.66   C92-095553-8

This book has been published with the help of a grant
from the Canadian Federation for the Humanities, using
funds provided by the Social Sciences and Humanities
Research Council of Canada.

Contents

Acknowledgments

This book would not have been possible without the assistance of several people and institutions. I would like to take this opportunity to thank the Social Sciences and Humanities Research Council of Canada, for a Leave Fellowship that made the initial research and writing possible, and the Research and Publications Committee of Mount Saint Vincent University, which supported me throughout. I have benefited from the comments of the Rev. Leonard Boyle, the Rev. Michael Sheehan, and professors Joe Goering, Philip McShane, and Ken Dewar, who read parts of the manuscript at various stages of writing. Finally, I am most grateful to the librarian of the Pontifical Institute of Mediaeval Studies, who generously made the resources of the library available to me over the years.

Abbreviations

AFP	*Archivum Fratrum Praedicatorum*
AHDLMA	*Archives d'histoire doctrinale et littéraire du moyen âge*
B	Albert the Great, Opera omnia, ed S.C.A. Borgnet
BAV	Biblioteca Apostolica Vaticana
BGPM	Beiträge zur Geschichte der Philosophie des Mittelalters
BGPTM	Beiträge zur Geschichte der Philosophie und Theologie des Mittelalters
C	Albert the Great, Opera omnia, Münster Westf 1952–
CCCM	Corpus christianorum, continuatio mediaevalis
CCSL	Corpus christianorum, series latina
CSEL	Corpus scriptorum ecclesiasticorum latinorum
DTC	*Dictionnaire de théologie catholique*
EETS	Early English Text Society
FS	*Franciscan Studies*
LCL	The Loeb Classical Library
Leonine	Thomas Aquinas, Opera omnia, editio Leonina
MGH	Monumenta Germaniae historica
NE	Aristotle *Nicomachean Ethics*
PEM	O. Lottin *Psychologie et morale aux XIIe et XIIIe siècles* 7 vols
PG	Patrologia graeca
PL	Patrologia latina
RSPT	*Revue des sciences philosophiques et théologiques*
RTAM	*Recherches de théologie ancienne et médiévale*
SFA	*Summa theologica, seu sic ab origine dicta 'Summa Fratris Alexandri'*
ST	Thomas Aquinas *Summa theologiae*
X	Gregory IX *Decretales*

The Bridling of Desire

Introduction

Theologians of the later Middle Ages discussed the nature, purpose, and morality of sexual behaviour in the course of their treatment of a wide range of topics. Few major areas of theological and moral discourse failed to address some facet of sex. Treatments of the virtues, vices, and commandments have subdivisions that consider sex: treatises on the *cardinal virtue of temperance* discuss the need to control lust and unruly sexual desires through the acquisition and exercise of continence and chastity; treatises on the *capital vice of lechery* deal with a whole range of sexual delicts, from the sexual relations of unmarried persons (simple fornication) to bestiality; discussions of lechery are frequently replicated in the consideration of the *sixth and ninth commandments*. Doctrinal tracts on the *sacrament of marriage* contain extensive treatment of sexual matters. Speculative theological discussions of the sacrament of penance show little interest in sex, but their practical counterparts, the handbooks for confessors, demonstrate considerable interest in the correct confession of sexual offences. Theological treatments of *creation* raise the question whether there would have been sexual relations in Paradise before the Fall – a question perhaps strange to us, but one that provided an opportunity to explore what was taken to be the nature of sex in the original divine plan. *Original sin*, its transmission, and the consequent disruptive presence of concupiscence were never discussed without reference to sex. Finally, human existence itself prompted reflection on the most desirable and praiseworthy way of life. This led to placing the state of vowed *virginity* above all other *states of life*, and to requiring *celibacy* of those who served God in the ranks of the higher clergy.

These considerations reflect the simple fact that sex is integral to the human condition. Any attempt to give a realistic account of that condition must provide an account of the role and significance of sex in human existence. It is unlikely that any society has failed to develop institutions to channel sex and procreation, to devise regulations and sanctions aimed at promoting its institutions, and to generate myths, stories, and theories to explain and rationalize its arrangements. Early in its history, Christianity developed such institutions, regulations, and theories.

Flandrin has said that, in regard to the history of marital sexual relations, 'only two [stages] appear essential ... on the doctrinal level: the formation of the traditional doctrine during the first centuries of our era, its radical transformation in the twentieth century.'[1] The claim is substantially correct. Early Christian writers believed that sexual intercourse was naturally oriented to procreation (that is what sex is for), and that it was permissible only within a legitimate marriage. These two beliefs constitute the core of what Flandrin calls the traditional doctrine, for which there was a consensus throughout the Middle Ages.[2] No early authoritative ecclesiastical teaching explicitly enunciates this view, but it is an unstated theological assumption throughout the patristic and medieval periods. Legislation translated the view into regulation, best expressed by the influential Synod of Angers (circa 1217):

In regard to the sacrament of marriage it must be said that every voluntary emission of semen is a mortal sin in both males and females unless excused by legitimate marriage. But faith teaches that sexual intercourse between male and female is excused by a legitimate marriage as long as the union is in the proper manner.[3]

Although this teaching emerged early and was transmitted unchanged, many questions needed answers. What constitutes voluntary seminal emission? What is a legitimate marriage? How can it excuse sexual intercourse? What does 'excuse' mean here? What is the proper manner for sexual relations?

Such questions had to be answered if any sense was to be given to 'the traditional doctrine.' So, although it is correct to say that there was stability in the early teaching, it was a very rudimentary, schematic, and incomplete teaching in need of substantial development. St Augustine worked out its most significant elaboration in the heat of battles, first with the Manichees, who wanted to damn sex and the flesh, and later with the Pelagians, who denied (at least in the eyes of Augustine) the disabling effects of the Fall and original sin.[4] The twelfth-century masters of theology and canon law, however, were the first to provide systematically argued accounts of the origins of sex and of its role in the divine plan for human beings.

Of course, discussions of sex were not the exclusive preserve of theologians and canon lawyers. For example, there were medical and biological treatments that complemented and perhaps even balanced the theological perspective, but the masters of biblical studies, theology, and canon law were the most concerned with providing a correct theoretical view of the place of sex in human existence.[5] The views themselves were not cut from new cloth. They reflect ancient moral beliefs mediated by centuries of life and theological tradition, bearing the stamp of St Augustine's influence. Their formulation, however, was facilitated by the new disciplines of biblical studies, theology, and ecclesiastical jurisprudence.

A vast amount of ancient literature was available by the twelfth century, either in the form of monographs by individual writers or in the form of excerpts in numerous collections containing texts of ecclesiastical law, papal pronouncements, the decrees of church councils, Roman law, patristic literature, and penitential directives. These collections were marked by a singular absence of comment; notwithstanding the inclusion of prologues to some of them, they are no more than compilations, often of apparently conflicting texts.

In the mid-twelfth century there began to emerge a questioning attitude that manifested itself in attempts to make sense out of the inherited texts and to co-ordinate them into systematic accounts. These attempts eventually resulted in the creation of three works whose influence in subsequent centuries was immense – the glossed Bible, the *Decretum* of Gratian, and the *Books of Sentences* of Peter Lombard.[6] The Bible came to bear a gloss consisting of texts selected mainly from recognized patristic sources such as Jerome, Ambrose, and Augustine. This was known as the *Ordinary Gloss*, used later as the standard textbook for biblical studies in the universities.[7]

Ecclesiastical law found a systematizer in a little-known monk named Gratian, who sifted from the tradition a body of texts that became the accepted expression of the law until it was added to in the thirteenth century by Pope Gregory IX. Gratian's work was commonly referred to as the *Decretum*, but the full title betrays the author's true intentions, *The Concordance of Discordant Canons*. He would present apparently contradictory texts on various subjects and offer his own interpretation as to how they ought to be reconciled. This work too became a standard textbook in the ecclesiastical law faculties of the medieval universities.[8]

Theology found its systematizer in Peter Lombard, whose *Books of Sentences* rose above the many theological creations of the twelfth century to become the standard theological text in the university faculties of theology until at least the sixteenth century.[9] Of this work De Ghellinck says, 'It brought what was desired for a long time: a relatively short and precise collection of teachings, without too many extras or digressions, a more or less organic grouping of the enormous mass of material transmitted for a long time from age to age ...'[10]

The *Ordinary Gloss* on the Bible, the *Decretum* of Gratian, and the *Books of Sentences* of Peter Lombard were the standard sources both for texts and for their interpretation. Although never the final word, the interpretations were considered to be presumptively authoritative. Within these works and in subsequent commentaries on the canon law and on the *Sentences* of Peter Lombard there is an internally consistent view of the nature, function, and morality of sex (however much it may be at variance with present-day Western beliefs).

It is important to uncover the guiding principles that led medieval authors to their views of sex, if for no other reason than to avoid the snares of modern misconceptions. There seems to be a conspiracy among contemporary popularizing authors to see the views of medieval writers as the result of the nightmares of fearful, misogynist, guilt-ridden clerics: 'the ecclesiastics who devised these [sexual] codes were, for the most part, not dispassionate philosophers but rather haggard neurotics tormented by a quite obsessive horror of sex.'[11] (One has to wonder about the wisdom of putting the production of sexual codes in the hands of dispassionate philosophers. St Jerome, at least, found a great deal of support in the philosophers for his rather gloomy views of sex and marriage.)[12] Or, more recently, 'Consciously or not, men and women with normal sexual appetites became obsessed by guilt. Sex might <not?> be their only sin, but in the eyes of the Church it was their greatest.'[13] If the theory of sex is to be traced back to St Paul and Augustine, it does not have much chance of representing a balanced view in the eyes of such as Cole: 'They [Paul,

Augustine, Aquinas] were all guilty of male arrogance, to a degree, and were perhaps a trifle afraid of women. Certainly they were afraid of the passion involved in sex.'[14]

One does not have to delve into the psyches of medieval theologians to discover the reasons for their positions on the role and significance of sex in human life. The reasons are readily available in their account of the divine plan of creation. They believed that a chasm existed between the way our human sexual make-up was meant to be in the original order of creation and the way it is now because of the Fall and its inherited consequences, to which we are all heirs through original sin. Failure to appreciate this all-embracing cosmic view leads to misunderstanding of medieval accounts of sex. This misunderstanding is not only apparent in popular writings, but is present in academic accounts of sexual beliefs. In the work by Flandrin referred to above the author says:

> From the second to the twentieth century, then, the seeking of sexual pleasure is vigorously condemned and what we call love remains somewhat foreign to the Christian problematic of marriage. Nonetheless, the latter is granted, sacramentalized, and strenuously defended against those who would only see it as fornication. It is radically differentiated from [fornication] not only by its indissolubility, but by its ends: fornication is the seeking for pleasure, marriage is the duty of procreation. And all seeking after pleasure in marriage makes an adultery out of the union.[15]

Although medieval accounts do not sing the praises of sexual pleasure, with few exceptions do they vigorously condemn it. Fornication is certainly differentiated from marital intercourse, but not on the basis of the seeking of pleasure (in fact, in cases where those living in fornication claim only to aim at the ends that marriage aims at, fornication is still outlawed). 'The too ardent lover of his own wife is an adulterer' was a common saying; but 'adulterer' was never understood to connote adultery in the proper sense of the term (ie, unlawful sexual relations where at least one of the parties is married).[16] Finally, while a link between procreation and sex was always acknowledged, one would be hard pressed to find a belief that in marriage there was a *duty* to procreate. There was a moral duty to be open to the possibility of procreation, but that is quite different from a duty to procreate, which in some cases would have been a duty to do the impossible.[17]

In a study of sin and confession we read: 'In his [Augustine's] view these goods of marriage balanced the objective evil of the sensual act of intercourse.'[18] Evil, yes; but if by objective evil is meant evil in and of itself, evil by nature, then intercourse was decidedly not considered to be an objective evil. As our first chapter will show, 'the sensual act of intercourse' was perceived as a good, flowing from God's good creation and initially lying under the precept to increase and multiply, a precept that was issued by God both before and after the Fall (see, Genesis 1:28; 9:1). It is unlikely that the medieval masters believed God had commanded an objective evil. I have no desire to engage in polemic over the proper interpretation of the late-medieval view of the nature of sex. I mention the above statements simply to suggest that there is ample room for a fresh examination of this view in its theological dimensions.

The following study is organized around three subjects at the heart of the medieval theological teaching on sex. (1) The first might be called 'beginnings': Paradise, the Fall, original sin, and its transmission. In accounts of these matters are to be found the principles underlying later views about the nature and function of sex. (2) Marriage in the present fallen state is not only designed to forward the procreative intentions of God and nature, but also serves as a remedial outlet for those unwilling or unable to abstain from sex. Discussions of marriage trace the permissible limits of sexual intercourse beyond which even marital intercourse was considered immoral. (3) In considerations of the virtue of temperance one discovers how people (married as well as unmarried) were expected to conduct themselves in regard to sex. More significantly, it is in the context of the treatment of this virtue that the ideal of the Christian life is elaborated. This ideal is described in terms of taking a deliberate stand against ever having voluntary sexual experience (ie, in terms of the state of virginity). Temperance moderates unbridled lust by establishing the proper order of reason over passion; virginity is the crowning achievement of temperance.

The elements for a positive account of the nature, function, and morality of sex are present in treatises on Paradise, the Fall, original sin, marriage, and temperance. By a positive account I do not mean a particularly attractive view, but simply one that explains the reality of sex, proposes the legitimate choices open to people in regard to sex, and provides reasons to support the proposals. I shall concentrate on this positive dimension of medieval accounts of sex. This dimension is paralleled in the medieval literature by lengthy treatises on the abuse of sex (the vice of lechery [*luxuria*] and its subdivisions: simple fornication, adultery, incest, violation [*stuprum*], abduction-rape [*raptus*], vice against nature). The theme of lechery does not fit into this study; and even if it did, its discussion would unacceptably enlarge the present volume. It will not be dealt with here, therefore, but will be reserved to a future work on the abuse of sex and on confession, which was seen to provide an opportunity to pick oneself up and continue the battle against the onslaught of lust.[19] Peter the Chanter sounds a common theme when he notes that the fight to safeguard chastity is one met with few victories: 'Among all the struggles of Christians, the greatest are the battles of chastity where fighting is frequent, victory rare. It is truly a great war of continence.'[20] To the extent that the abuse of marital sex is considered to be a form of lechery, some treatment of the vice will be found here. Marital sexual abuses are, however, usually discussed not in the context of lechery but in that of the treatment of marital intercourse.[21]

My title, 'The Bridling of Desire,' captures a common medieval theme.[22] Desire, in the sense of concupiscence, was considered to be the central factor in sex. Absent in Paradise, it was unleashed through original sin and is both the cause of the transmission of original sin and one of its effects. Concupiscence or lust in the parents was considered to be the cause of original sin; in the offspring, it was thought to be the result of original sin. Although marriage was not seen solely as a remedy for concupiscence, this was certainly one of its important roles. Lechery is the wanton expression of unbridled concupiscence; temperance is its measured reining in. As we shall see, the metaphor of bridles and reins is often encountered in the sources.

This is a study of an emerging consensus about what was thought to be the correct theological and moral account of sex. The focus will be on what was arguably the apogee of medieval theology, between the *Summa Fratris Alexandri* (circa 1245) and the *Summa of Theology* of Thomas Aquinas (circa 1272). The texts on which these masters drew take us back to the mid-twelfth century; their influence will take us to the middle of the fourteenth century. So 'the later Middle Ages' of the subtitle covers the period from the middle of the twelfth century to the middle of the fourteenth century. The beginning coincides with the emergence of the principal theological and legal sources.[23] In the thirteenth century, theology came into its own, principally under the influence of three prominent figures, Albert the Great, Bonaventure, and Thomas Aquinas. In this century the ordinary gloss on the *Decretum* of Gratian was completed and the *Decretals* of Gregory IX produced, the latter receiving masterful treatment at the hands of commentators such as Hostiensis in addition to receiving its own standard gloss. In the pastoral field there is first and foremost the impetus given to pastoral concerns by the Fourth Lateran Council (1215). This impetus was perhaps best translated into a learned pastoral literature through the cumulative development from the *Summa* of Raymond of Penyafort through the gloss on Raymond by William of Rennes, to the *Summa for Confessors* written by the Dominican John of Freiburg at the end of the century. The thirteenth century also saw the Latin translation of the complete text of Aristotle's *Nicomachean Ethics* and the creation of the commentaries on that work by Albert the Great and Thomas Aquinas. The immensely popular work by William Peraldus, the *Summa of Vices and Virtues*, was written before 1250.

The choice of where to end the study is perhaps somewhat arbitrary, but not entirely so. By the early years of the fourteenth century the creative force in the development of theology had spent itself, culminating in the commentary on the *Sentences* of Peter of Palude (died 1342), a work widely used in the later fourteenth century and throughout the fifteenth century. Joannes Andreae, the last great medieval commentator on ecclesiastical law, died in 1348. About 1315 the *Summa* of Astesanus of Asti, the Franciscan counterpart to the work of John of Freiburg, was written. The works of these two writers were the main sources for subsequent pastoral manuals. Commentaries from the latter half of the century tended to be repetitious of or at least heavily dependent on those of the preceding period. Proof of this claim is available to anyone who checks the sources of later prominent authors such as Jean Gerson (died 1429), Antoninus of Florence (died 1459), Angelus de Clavasio (died 1495), and Sylvester Prierias (died 1523).

Any discussion that deals with the theology of marital sex in this period must contend with the question of the extent to which it will use the canon law. A recent book by James Brundage demonstrates the extent to which views of marriage and marital sex during our period were influenced by the canon law and its commentators.[24] In fact, the principal theological source, the *Sentences* of Peter Lombard, borrowed extensively from the *Decretum* of Gratian for its texts on marriage. Some theologians were quite aware of this phenomenon and show a sophisticated acquaintance with the canon law (eg, Alexander of Hales, Richard of Mediavilla, Peter of Palude).[25] While canon lawyers and theologians pursued parallel and independent *professional* paths, the textual materials they had at their disposal did not represent two entirely different types of literature. One repeatedly finds the same texts used by both the theologians and the canonists. Sometimes the theologians borrowed directly from Gratian; but it is often the case that the texts entered the mainstream of theology through Peter Lombard, whose treatment of marriage was dependent on Gratian. The theologians and the canon lawyers shared a pool of texts that originated in Gratian's codification of the law and that found a place in the theological literature through Peter Lombard. When I say 'the law' I mean that the texts took on a legal status because of their incorporation into a book of ecclesiastical law, not that they had any peculiarly legal character in themselves. In fact, by far the greatest number of texts in Gratian's treatment of marriage are not from legal sources but from patristic and other ecclesiastical writers, particularly from St Augustine. My use of the canon law will be restricted to the collections of Gratian and Gregory IX, their ordinary glosses, and works by some of the more prominent commentators such as Master Roland, Rufinus, Huguccio, and Hostiensis.[26]

In this sort of study one must choose from a mass of extant original sources, since every writer cannot be examined, much less cited. The choice of sources has been guided by three principles: (1) to give voice to representative exponents of the developing teaching; (2) to ensure a balance between Dominican and Franciscan sources, since these two religious orders represent two different theological traditions, betraying different attitudes to the new learning of the thirteenth century, to the worth of human reason, and to the radical goodness of human nature; (3) to note significant differences of opinion.

Of course, expressions such as 'representative exponents' and 'significant differences' imply evaluative judgments on my part. Short of simply pointing readers in the direction of a well-stocked medieval library, it must be acknowledged that an interpretive study of the kind undertaken here reflects the author's choice of what is worth mentioning, citing, and omitting. It is up to informed readers to judge the wisdom of the choices. I believe that I have captured a consensus of opinion in the medieval writings about sexual matters and that anyone examining the sources of the period will find the same.

The following pages, then, offer my interpretation of the development of late medieval academic beliefs about the nature, purpose, and morality of sex. The development consisted largely in the interpretation of traditional texts and in the assimilation of the interpretation into an overall theological framework. The academic situation at the time might be described as a community of scholars who shared a religious faith and a common morality, who wrote in the conventional form of the medieval question, and who accepted the presumptive authority of certain classes of text. During most of the period, theologians and canonists show a marked preoccupation with the correct interpretation of traditional texts and their integration into consistent positions. After Thomas Aquinas, theologians began to shift their emphasis from textual hermeneutics to a more theoretical exposition of issues. The shift is evident in the commentaries on the *Sentences* by Durandus of St Pourcain and Peter of Palude, which undergo a marked change in literary structure. Objections to the proposed theses are downplayed, the personal conclusions of the authors are highlighted, and reasoning in support of the conclusions replaces the earlier wrestling with received authoritative texts. Furthermore, after Thomas Aquinas there is an increasing tendency to consider his opinions on most subjects, to adopt them, refute them, or modify them. He himself was cloaked with the mantle of authority.[27]

Before leaving the subject of texts and sources, a word should be said about Aristotle and Thomas Aquinas. Aristotle contributed nothing to the actual content of discussions of sexual morality and was even the source of some confusion. He provided much of the conceptual framework for the treatment of most sexual topics, however. For example, his theories of reproduction and generation, of the production and nature of semen, of the inferiority of women, of the nature of virtue and vice, of the conception of temperance, of the centrality of reason, and of the nature of pleasure were adopted by the university masters. The precise contribution of Aristotle to the medieval understanding of sex (in its physical, biological, and moral dimensions) remains an important chapter in the history of ideas that is yet to be written, and it will certainly not be attempted here. It would, however, be a mistake to assume, just because the medieval masters had inherited a morality of sex long before they encountered the substantive works of Aristotle, that Aristotle made no difference. In the matter of sex, his influence was significant in providing conceptual tools to fashion the medieval understanding and to give clarity, precision, and consistency to a traditional biblical and patristic language inappropriate to the language of the schools.

The presentation of the views of Thomas Aquinas poses a problem. The clarity and precision of his expression, his ability to cut to the core of a subject, his immense knowledge and erudition, the balance of his opinions, and his overwhelming influence on subsequent authors tempt one to dwell on his works. I have tried to resist the temptation, presenting the views of Aquinas as part of the general consensus. In regard to the virtue of temperance, however, one cannot avoid according some prominence to Aquinas's views. His account of that virtue completes the development of the concept of temperance and will be used by almost every subsequent writer. In short, I have tried to present Thomas Aquinas in terms of his role in the Middle Ages, not in terms of contemporary assessments of his thought.[28]

There is a considerable body of literature dealing with various aspects of the medieval view of sex and, as the notes and bibliography attest, I have drawn freely on those works. I must note a particular indebtedness to Professor Müller, whose book on the subject of Paradise and marriage provides numerous transcriptions of unedited manuscript material. The subject of marriage is amply treated by numerous authors.[29] No adequate study has been written on the virtue of temperance. I know of no attempt to present a comprehensive picture of the theological views on sex elaborated by the masters of the later Middle Ages. The first volume of Michel Foucault's *The History of Sexuality* (original edition 1976) suggested subsequent studies that would deal with the later Middle Ages, but the second volume (1984) departed from the original plan by turning to the Greeks (volumes 2 and 3). Foucault's death precluded the completion of the fourth volume, which was to deal with the early centuries of the Christian era.[30] One must wonder whether Foucault's decision to focus on the Greek experience was inspired by Nietzsche's observation:

> We take advantage of the freedom to speak about them [the Greeks] in order to be able to be silent about other things – so that these Greeks might themselves whisper something into the ear of the thoughtful

reader. Thus for the modern man the Greeks facilitate the communication of many things which are difficult or hazardous to communicate.[31]

The work of previous scholars facilitates the presentation of the broad-based theological view of sex that was elaborated in the later Middle Ages. If, as Flandrin claims (and he is surely correct), the twentieth century is witness to a radical transformation in sexual values and mores, an understanding of the transformation will be enhanced through an understanding of what is being changed. It is hoped that this study will contribute to that understanding.

A contemporary writer dealing with medieval ideas of sex faces a peculiar problem of language. Treatises entitled 'On sex' are nowhere to be found, nor does one find talk about 'sexuality,' because medieval Latin had no terms for the English words 'sex' and 'sexuality.' In the strictest sense, there are no discussions of sex in the Middle Ages. Whatever one might think of Michel Foucault's overall thesis about the development of the history of sexuality in the West, his claim about the relatively late date for the invention of sex and sexuality is, I believe, of paramount significance. The concept of sex or sexuality as an integral dimension of human persons, as an object of concern, discourse, truth, and knowledge, did not emerge until well after the Middle Ages. Medieval theologians and canon lawyers did not talk about sex as such because they had no language with which to do so. The words 'sex,' 'sexual,' and 'sexuality,' and their counterparts in other European languages, are of relatively recent vintage and have no counterparts in medieval Latin. The adjective *venereus* ('venereal'; substantive *venerea*) is as close as the language came to a general term referring to sex, but its employment is not frequent and it is never used to refer to an object of study. One does not encounter treatises entitled *De venereis* ('On Sexual Matters') in the Middle Ages.[32]

The absence of Latin terms for sex and sexuality points to the absence of corresponding concepts. Sex as a human dimension was not thought about or talked about. Consequently, in theory at least, it should be possible to write about medieval views without ever using the terms 'sex,' 'sexual,' and 'sexuality.' While a purist might be able to do so – and no doubt it would be an interesting experiment in linguistic discipline – it is impractical to attempt to discuss medieval views of sexual matters without using contemporary terminology. In doing so, however, it must be borne in mind that claims made about medieval theories of sexuality are, in fact, contemporary theories. Medieval theologians had theories about the infected nature of the reproductive system, about the legitimate forms of marital intercourse, about the superiority of virginity over marriage, about the sinfulness of homosexuality. Underlying these theories is an account of the Fall and its aftermath that gives them intelligibility. Taking all this into consideration one could plausibly propose a medieval theory of human sexuality, but the theory would be a modern theory about the Middle Ages, not a medieval theory discovered by a modern. The medieval foci of attention were elsewhere. While in practice our contemporary thought patterns make it difficult to avoid the terms 'sex' and 'sexuality,' it is important to bear in mind that they have no linguistic counterparts in medieval Latin or conceptual counterparts in medieval thought.[33]

As a recent author warns:

> To the extent, in fact, that histories of 'sexuality' succeed in concerning themselves with *sexuality*, to just that extent are they doomed to fail as *histories* (Foucault himself taught us that much), unless they also include as an essential part of their proper enterprise the task of demonstrating the historicity, conditions of emergence, modes of construction, and ideological contingencies of the very categories of analysis that undergird their own practice.[34]

While the present study is not a history *per se* but more a history of ideas, this cautionary note applies here as well. Concern should focus on the emergence of the texts, their interpretation, and the construction of views grounded on those interpretations. Of paramount importance are the medieval categories of analysis, not those that a modern writer might bring to the study. Sexuality is decidedly not one of these medieval categories.

This book proceeds on two levels. The text is meant to be intelligible to a moderately sophisticated reader. The notes provide the basic bibliographical information for citations and references. The notes will also be used as a forum for the discussion of points of limited interest. Since the moderately sophisticated reader of today cannot be assumed to read Latin, citations in the body of the book are translated and, unless otherwise noted, all the translations have been made by me. The Latin of translated passages will be given in the notes when the citation is from a manuscript and in cases where the translation itself is thought to be problematic. Although there are English passages without their Latin counterparts, there are no untranslated Latin passages.[35]

Medieval theologians are not well served by English translators. The most readily accessible work in translation is Aquinas' *Summa of Theology*, which was left unfinished and ends before the treatment of marriage. After the death of Thomas Aquinas an effort was made to make up the deficiency by adding a Supplement to the *Summa*. The Supplement was compiled from Aquinas' commentary on the fourth book of the *Sentences* of Peter Lombard. It is a reliable reproduction of the content (not the order of treatment) of the commentary. Reference to the commentary will be followed by reference to the corresponding passage in the Supplement.

The primary and secondary literature that is used in this book requires a consistent method of citation, and the frequent use of the same works requires a set of abbreviations to streamline the notes. The list of abbreviations speaks for itself. However, a word must be said about three matters:

1 The citations of canon law. I cannot improve on the short essay by Professor Brundage and so refer the interested reader to it.[36] I have adapted his system of citations in the following manner:

a) The *Decretum* of Gratian:

   i)   The first part is divided into distinctions and chapters and will be cited thus: D 1.1 (distinction 1, chapter 1).

   ii)   The second part is divided into causae (cases), questions, and chapters and will be cited thus: C 1.1.1 (causa 1, question 1, chapter 1).

   iii)   C 33.3 is traditionally entitled *De penitentia* (*On Penance*) and is divided into distinctions and chapters. It will be cited thus: *De penit* D 1.1 (*On Penance*, distinction 1, chapter 1).

   iv)   The third part of the *Decretum* is entitled *De consecratione* (*On Consecration*) and is divided into distinctions and chapters. It will be cited thus: *De consec* D 1.1 (*On Consecration*, distinction 1, chapter 1).

   v)   Gratian's own comments, which precede or follow the chapters, are referred to as: da (dictum ante, ie, comment before the chapter), and dp (dictum post, ie, comment following the chapter). The reference C 3.4.2, da refers to Gratian's comment before the second chapter of the fourth question of causa 3.

b) Commentaries on Gratian and on other collections of the canon law are usually attached to specific words or phrases. A reference to the *Ordinary Gloss* will be made in the following manner: *Ordinary Gloss* on Gratian, *Decretum* C 1.1.1, ad v *si non gratis datur*.

c) The *Decretals of Gregory IX* are divided into books, titles, and chapters. The work itself is commonly cited as X. A reference to the *Decretals* is made thus: X 1.1.1 (the *Decretals of Gregory IX*, book 1, title 1, chapter 1).

2 Commentaries on the *Books of Sentences* of Peter Lombard are referred to in the standard manner, eg, *In 2 Sent* (*Commentary on the Second Book of the Sentences*). Commentaries on each book are divided into distinctions. Distinctions are usually further divided into questions and the questions into articles, but sometimes the order of questions and articles is reversed (eg, Bonaventure), or there are no questions (eg, Albert the Great), or main questions are subdivided into subquestions (eg, Thomas Aquinas and Peter of Tarentaise). Nothing is to be gained by linguistically noting this variety for each reference; numerical references alone will be used, the first number after 'Sent' *always* refers to the distinction, the subsequent numbers referring to the divisions appropriate to the given work. This internal reference will be followed by a reference to the volume and page number of the edition being used.

3 The *Summa Fratris Alexandri* has a complex internal division. Reference to it will simply be made to the major division into parts (1 [first part]; 1-2 [first part of the second part]; 2-2 [second part of the second part]; 3 [third part]), to the editor's number for the question, then sometimes to the editorial numbering or lettering within the question in order to locate the reference more precisely. This reference is followed by the volume and page number of the Quaracchi edition.

1

Paradise

The scholastic view of the place of sex in human existence comprises several fundamental beliefs: that sexual intercourse was permissible only within a legitimate marriage; that procreation was the primary purpose of marital intercourse; that intercourse was to be regulated according to certain times, places, and conditions of the husband and wife; that virginity was superior to all other states of life. There was considerable hesitation about the moral assessment of sexual pleasure. It was thought that the vice of lechery (*luxuria*) was particularly dangerous, and the difficulties involved in keeping oneself free of its attractions were enormous.

These are some of the main features characteristic of the understanding of post-lapsarian sex. The positions taken in discussions of these features were often consciously elaborated against background beliefs about the way things were meant to be. Theological discussions of marriage, for instance, take for granted a twofold institution of marriage, one before the Fall, one after the Fall:

> The first institution of marriage was effected in Paradise so that there would have been an unstained bed and honourable marriage [Hebrews 13:4] resulting in conception without ardour and birth without pain. The second, to eliminate unlawful movement, was effected outside Paradise such that the infirmity that is prone to foul ruin might be rescued by the uprightness of marriage.[1]

Accounts of the legitimacy of intercourse for pleasure emphasize that ethical problems arise not from the pleasure itself but from the disorder in reason, resulting from pleasure, that is characteristic of intercourse in this fallen state. The pleasure that ties up reason in sexual intercourse is not a moral evil as such, but it is a disruptive consequence of moral evil since it results from the sin of the first parents.[2] The vice of lechery (*luxuria*) is believed to be rooted in the unbridled lust (*libido*) and concupiscence that accompany original sin as a result of the Fall.[3] In all these accounts the Fall and its inherited consequences play an explanatory role.

To gain a balanced view of the medieval theological understanding of the sexual dimension of human nature it is important to explore the answers that were given to the following question: What would have been the case if Adam and Eve had not sinned? Peter Lombard suggests that the undertaking is not a useless endeavour, although some might pursue the question out of idle curiosity.[4] Bonaventure claims that the issue was unavoidable, since Augustine had already raised similar questions.[5]

The question of whether or not there would have been sexual relations in Paradise before the Fall provided an opportunity to explore the original divine plan for sex in the lives of human beings. Taking the lead from Peter Lombard, medieval theologians asked whether there would have been sexual intercourse before sin in the state of nature in its initial institution.[6] The affirmative response and the resulting description of sex in the first state provided a norm and standard for how things were meant to be. As a consequence, it was possible to judge how far the present state of human sex deviated from that norm. To arrive at such an understanding of human nature and of human sex was considered to be a thoroughly theological undertaking, open to believers. Philosophical misconceptions about human nature and sex were frequently attributed to the unbelieving philosophers' lack of knowledge of God's initial plans for human nature in its pristine condition.

Before the Fall human nature was as it was meant to be and so was normative for judgments about what is natural. Albert the Great uses just such a norm to argue that it is not natural to have several wives. He calls the original institution of nature the 'maximally natural.' At the time of the institution it was the intention of nature that one woman would belong to one man. This intention is apparent in Genesis, which says of Adam 'He will adhere to his wife' (Genesis 2:24) not 'wives.'[7] In another place, denying a philosophical claim that reason would have been disordered by sexual intercourse even in the first state, Albert says that the philosophers who made the claim 'only know the state of corrupt nature and not the state of nature in its first innocence.'[8] This view about reason's access to nature implies that the philosophers (meaning the non-Christian Greeks and Arabs) have nothing to teach the medieval theologians about pristine, ordered, human nature in its original constitution.[9] What the philosophers said about nature does not necessarily apply to nature in Paradise.

The concept of the natural is frequently employed by medieval writers in their discussions of Paradise and of sex. They confidently pronounced on what was natural and what was against nature. Sometimes what is natural seems to have been gathered from observation; at other times the natural is not as it appears to be. As we shall see, some eliminatory bodily functions were deemed to be natural in Paradise, others not. Gender differentiation was thought to be natural; spontaneous sexual arousal and nocturnal seminal emission were not. For medieval theologians there is a dimension of the natural perduring as natural from creation through the Fall to the present, and a dimension of the natural coming from the hands of God but appearing now in a corrupted state. (What this corruption consists in will be dealt with in the next chapter.) The implicit epistemological principle that seems to have guided this thinking was that whatever is taken *now* to be imperfect, painful, obscene, or impure would not have been natural in Paradise.[10] Aquinas enunciates the converse of this principle: 'Whatever pertains to the perfection of the human species ought to be attributed to man in the state of innocence.'[11]

GENDER DIFFERENCE

The main question was whether Adam and Eve would have had sexual relations before the Fall. But before that question could be taken seriously, a prior issue required attention: namely, whether gender difference itself was part of the original divine plan. Answers to these questions created a logical imperative to follow through on the discussion, either by pursuing the implications of the answers themselves, or by attempting to explain the contrast between the way things would have been in Paradise and the way they are now.

By the middle of the thirteenth century there was general agreement that before the Fall Adam and Eve embodied human nature as it ought to have been, crowned with certain perfections such as immortality (the ability not to die) and impassibility (the ability not to suffer) that did not pertain to human nature as such but were God's gratuitous endowments. The book of Genesis (1:27) makes it clear that God created Adam and Eve male and female, so gender differentiation would seem to have been intended as a natural feature of the original human condition. Given genders, it follows that sexual intercourse, too, would have been natural, ensuring obedience to the initial divine command that directed the first parents to increase and multiply (Genesis 1:28).

Although such a view was common teaching in the Latin West by the thirteenth century, it had been developed in opposition to a current in Greek theological thinking that was inclined to deny that gender differences were part of the initial divine plan. No one doubted that God created male and female and that this was for no other reason than to provide for generation through sexual relations. But did God initially want it that way? Or did he want things to be otherwise, but foresaw the Fall and made gendered human beings who would reproduce sexually – a manner in keeping with the corrupted state of human nature after the Fall?

These questions suggest a threefold progression: (1) the initial divine plan, (2) the actual state of innocence in Paradise recorded in the book of Genesis, and (3) the state after the Fall. Gregory of Nyssa (end of fourth century), in his *On the Making of Man*, interprets Genesis 1:27 as a record of two moments in the process of creation. The first part of the text ('And God created man in his own image, in the image of God he created him') records the initial divine intention according to which the human person would have been a kind of androgynous being with a spiritualized body, made in the image of God, who is spiritual and genderless. The second part of the text ('male and female he created them') points to the animal body and to gender, which were added because God foresaw that the first parents would sin and so would not be able to reproduce in a spiritual manner. The account in Genesis of the creation of Adam and Eve, then, does not reflect God's initial intention, but records what He did as a result of his foreknowledge of the Fall. Gender differentiation with its attendant ability for sexual reproduction was an act of loving kindness on God's part to save the human race from extinction and to ensure that the number of the elect would be complete. As a recent author puts it, 'without sexual propagation mortal fallen man would have become extinct in Adam and

Eve.'[12] At the resurrection, however, all will rise genderless, and the original intention of God will be realized.[13]

Gregory's *On the Making of Man* was translated into Latin in the sixth century by Denis the Small (Dionysius Exiguus), but the first major use of the work is not found in the West until the eighth century in John Scottus Eriugena's *On the Division of Nature*.[14] Eriugena adopted Gregory's views that sex differences were created as a result of the divine foreknowledge of Adam's sin, and that humans would rise genderless from the dead.[15]

Scottus Eriugena's views on these matters had little immediate effect. At the beginning of the thirteenth century, however, *On the Division of Nature* was being widely enough read for it to be condemned by Pope Honorius III (23 January 1225). In his lectures on the *Decretals of Gregory IX* the canon lawyer Hostiensis says that one of the heresies for which the work was censured was the teaching that humans would rise without sex differences.[16]

John Damascene takes a position similar to that of Gregory of Nyssa. God, foreseeing the Fall, established gender differences and issued the command to increase and multiply in order to save the human race from extinction. The command itself did not necessarily imply reproduction through copulation, however.[17]

In the later Middle Ages John Damascene and Gregory of Nyssa were taken to represent the view that gender differentiation and sexual intercourse were consequences of God's foreknowledge of the Fall, not part of the initial plan. Reference to Gregory is not often encountered, but Thomas Aquinas provides an explanation for how 'ancient teachers' such as Gregory may have arrived at their views. Aquinas suggests that they were so struck by the foulness attaching to sexual relations in the here and now that they assumed that generation in the state of innocence would have been in some other manner. Consequently, they believed that gender differences are a result of God's foreknowledge of the Fall, not part of his original plan. In the judgment of Aquinas such an opinion is unreasonable. God made human beings as higher animals and *as such* they were characterized by gender differences.[18]

John Damascene, as we have noted, raised the question of the reason for gender difference and of the manner by which the human race would have multiplied before the Fall. He says that the command at Genesis 1:28 ('Increase and multiply') does not necessarily connote multiplication through marital copulation. He continues: 'For God was able to multiply this [human] race in another way, if they had observed the commandment unchanged to the end.'[19] The usual response to Damascene is that, while God could have arranged to multiply the human species differently, there is no indication that he did.[20] Albert the Great is prepared to say that such talk about fore-knowledge is a fabrication (*fabula*). If Damascene was referring to the act of intercourse itself and not simply to the absence of concupiscence and foulness, then what he says is false.[21] Genesis nowhere suggests that God's foreknowledge played any role in the creation of gender. So gender differentiation was originally natural and part of the initial divine plan. This is why the theologians offered an affirmative answer to the question whether humans will rise as male and female at the final judgment.[22]

The Latin theological tradition frequently cited Augustine in its defence of the naturalness of gender difference and sexual reproduc-tion. But what became the accepted view did not spring ready-made from the mind of Augustine. Although he was not concerned about the creation of sex differences, he did wonder about the meaning of the command to increase and multiply. As early as his anti-Manichean commentary on Genesis (circa AD 389) he allows for the possibility of a spiritual interpretation of 'Increase and multiply' (Genesis 1:28).[23]

At the beginning of *On the Marriage Good* Augustine avoids ren-dering a definitive opinion on the manner of reproduction that would have been if Adam and Eve had not sinned. He notes that there are different views on the matter that it would take a wide-ranging debate to resolve, but he does record three positions: (1) God could have arranged for reproduction in a way different from sexual coupling; (2) what is written at Genesis 1:28 is to be understood in a figurative sense, referring to mental growth and the increase of virtue; (3) there would have been bodily, sexual reproduction right from the beginning before the Fall. He concludes as he began, confessing that it would be a lengthy undertaking to determine the truth.[24]

At the beginning of his *Literal Commentary on Genesis* Augustine, who is puzzled by how Genesis 1:28 could apply to immortal beings, still seems to allow for a mode of reproduction different from what we know now. In suggesting 'another way,' however, he makes a propo-sal that probably betrays his real concerns, which are not with the mode of pre-lapsarian reproduction but with the quality of that mode:

'Nonetheless, it is possible to say that there could have been another way in immortal bodies so that children would be born out of the affection of piety alone, with no corruptive concupiscence.'[25] If emphasis is placed on the expression 'another way,' then the text could be taken to reflect a view similar to that of Gregory of Nyssa. If emphasis is placed on 'with no corruptive concupiscence,' then the text would be consistent with what will be Augustine's definitive position enunciated later in the commentary: that is, generation through rationally controlled intercourse.[26] Augustine's overriding concern with whether Adam and Eve would have experienced concupiscence and lust (libido) before the Fall suggests that he did not waver about the mode of reproduction; he questioned whether pre-lapsarian intercourse would have been marked by concupiscence.[27]

Whatever the final word on whether there is an evolution in Augustine's views, from the ninth book of the *Literal Commentary on Genesis* his position is clear. Even if Adam and Eve had not sinned, in Paradise they would have reproduced sexually in an honourable marriage without the incentive of lust.[28] As one commentator puts it: 'The "progress", if there is any, of the views of Augustine in relation to previous patristic writers consists in the fact that he surmounted the depreciation of sexuality and understood it as a creation of God, and so a good, *without reference to the sin of the first parents.*'[29] Augustine, so often the whipping boy for what are perceived to be incorrect views about sex, in fact can be seen as successfully challenging and ultimately silencing views that tended to deny the natural goodness of gender differentiation and sexual intercourse.[30]

REPRODUCTION THROUGH INTERCOURSE

Accepting the view that there would have been genders, Peter Lombard initiated a discussion that lasted well into the thirteenth century when he asked whether there would have been sexual relations in Paradise. Before citing Augustine in support of an affirmative answer, the Lombard provides a neat summary of what became the accepted opinion:

> if the first humans had not sinned there would have been carnal union in Paradise without any sin and stain and there would have been an 'unde-filed bed' [Hebrews 13:4] there and union without concupiscence. Fur-

thermore, they would have commanded the genital organs like [they would have commanded] the other organs, so they would not have felt any unlawful movement there [in Paradise]. Just as we move some bodily members towards others, such as the hand to the mouth, without the ardour of lust, likewise they would have used the genital organs without any itching of the flesh.[31]

Later discussions of the situation in Paradise are against the background of three accounts in Genesis: gender creation (Genesis 1:27), the command to increase and multiply (Genesis 1:28), and the statement that woman was given to the man as a helper (Genesis 2:18). After God created male and female (Genesis 1:27) he command them to increase and multiply (Genesis 1:28). To the extent that humans were created as perfect animals (animals divided into genders who reproduce through sexual union) it should have seemed natural for the first humans to reproduce themselves through sexual intercourse. It is the intention of nature to achieve species perpetuity through the multiplication of individuals who exist for a time but whose successive continuity assures the permanence of the species. This is the reason the generative power was given in the first place. Aristotle teaches this and, moreover, he teaches that we approach the perpetuity of divine being through our own reproduction.[32]

This argument, however, applies to individuals who are mortal, who are born and die and so do not remain in perpetuity. The first parents were in no need of perpetuation through species continuity because they were endowed with individual immortality by divine gift. They participated in the perpetuity of divine being through their own immortality, and so there was no need for them to reproduce themselves for the maintenance of the species. Consequently, the generative power in them would have been superfluous. If there was no generative power, there surely could have been no intercourse in the first state. This is a telling argument in which the very rationality of natural philosophy is used against itself, as it were.[33] That is, if the only argument for sexual reproduction is the mortality of individuals, then there would have been no sexual reproduction in Paradise because the individuals there were immortal. Two responses were made to this objection, one from the point of view of the divine intention, the other from the point of view of the implications of the immortality of the first parents for reproduction.

Natural philosophy did not get things quite right. The argument holds for animals below humans. Aristotle's position does not capture the full picture because there is a higher intention for humans that he did not know. According to the intention and ordination of divine providence the generative power was given to humans to complete the number of the elect left incomplete and in ruins by the fall of the angels. This is the principal reason why God made male and female and told them to increase and multiply.[34] Bonaventure adds that God gave the generative power 'on account of the greater union of men so that they would have greater love for one another.'[35]

The objection to sexual relations from the point of view of the immortality of Adam and Eve is found in most theologians of the thirteenth century. The use of the idea that the purpose for reproduction was to fill out the number of the elect seems to be particularly characteristic of theologians who came under the influence of the *Summa Fratris Alexandri*. Albert the Great and Thomas Aquinas provide naturalistic arguments for the claim that in the first state there would have been procreation through sexual relations.

Albert's discussion of the matter is perfunctory, reflecting his belief as stated in the introduction to the treatment of questions relating to the subject of sex in the state of innocence. After listing the questions for treatment, he adds, 'And with regard to all of these matters there is very little doubt.'[36] Albert asks whether there would have been generation in the state of innocence even through sexual union. The answer consists largely of a refutation of the traditional objection taken from Damascene, concluding with a reference to Eve as Adam's helpmate (Genesis 2:18). The underlying argument is based on the fact that God made Adam and Eve with different genders, each of which has a role to play; so, either gender would have been superfluous, or the first parents would have been responsible for generation in Paradise. It is understood that there would have been nothing superfluous in Paradise. Without mentioning him, Albert has in mind the account of sex differences provided by Aristotle in the *Generation of Animals*.[37] The fact that the first parents were immortal in Paradise is not an objection, because they were not naturally immortal. They were mortal in virtue of the principles comprising their nature, and since coitus is an act of that nature there would have been generation through sexual intercourse.[38] Albert had put it succinctly in an earlier work: 'there could have been generation through intercourse before sin, but there would have been conception without concupiscence, pregnancy without hardship, and childbirth without pain.'[39] One should not argue from the immortality enjoyed by Adam and Eve in Paradise to the absence of the need for sexual union to propagate the species. To determine whether there would have been sexual reproduction in Paradise one must consider the nature of the individuals of the human species, not the individuals as they were privileged through grace.[40]

Albert relies on this naturalistic premise: gender differences in individuals who are naturally corruptible have no meaning aside from their orientation to intercourse. He does not mention the need to complete the number of the elect. He does not repudiate the traditional idea of replacing the fallen angels with the number of the elect, but it does not figure in his argumentation for sexual reproduction in Paradise.[41]

Thomas Aquinas approaches the question in two stages without appealing to the need to complete the number of the elect. He first shows the need for generation, and then argues that such generation would have been through sexual intercourse.[42] The necessity for some sort of generative reproduction or multiplication is established on the grounds of the corruptible nature of individuals and the intention of nature for the conservation of the species. He advances Albert's argument by pointing out that in human beings nature does not only intend the serial multiplication of individuals for the conservation of the species. This would be the case if humans were totally corruptible, but they are not. The human soul is naturally immortal. To the extent that individuals have souls, it must be acknowledged that nature also intends the conservation of individuals of the species. (Note that the idea of corruptibility here is a metaphysical not a moral concept. A corruptible nature is one that can break up into its constituent parts and so cease to be as that nature.)

That generation would be through sexual intercourse – the second stage of the argument – follows from the fact that gender differentiation was established by God before the Fall (Genesis 1:27, 2:22)[43] and that humans belong to the class of perfect animals that reproduce naturally through coitus. In fact, coitus is defined as 'the union of male and female for generation.'[44] Procreative finality is built into the very definition of coitus. The whole reason for gender differences is to provide an active principle (male) and a passive principle (female) without which there could not be any reproduction among the higher animals, 'and the natural organs destined for this function are witness to that fact. Therefore, one ought not claim that there would have been no use made of these natural organs before sin anymore than one would make [the claim] for the other organs.'[45] Deformity in sexual relations, which results from immoderate concupiscence, would be lacking in Paradise.

One of the most widely used arguments in support of the claim that there would have been sexual relations in Paradise was based on the theologians' understanding of the reason God had in creating woman. According to Genesis, God created Eve to be Adam's helpmate (Genesis 2:18–20). When Augustine reflected on the nature of this help he could think only of the aid woman provides for generation: 'However, if one asks why there ought to have been this aid there is no other reasonable answer except for the procreation of children.'[46] And, a little farther on: 'If the reason for childbearing is taken away, I find no reason why woman was made as man's helpmate.'[47] The first text found its way into the *Ordinary Gloss* on the Bible; the interlinear gloss comments on 'helpmate' (*adiutorium*), 'woman, to procreate children.'[48] Later medieval theologians make the same point either in general or by quoting Augustine.[49] A male would be better served by the aid of another male in anything else except in the work of generation for which he needs the help of a woman.

SEMEN

Granted the naturalness of gender differentiation and of sexual relations in Paradise before the Fall, problems arose from this very claim to naturalness. Human conception is caused by depositing the man's semen within the woman. The nature of semen was problematic. It was assumed that the human body in its pristine state would have been an efficiently functioning organism without any superfluous elements; but in the accepted Aristotelian view semen was defined as the superfluous residue from food.[50] So it would seem to be unfitting that semen be such a nutritional by-product in Paradise.

In getting out of this conundrum the medieval theologians further expand on their views of the physical constitution of the human body in Paradise. The treatment of semen occasioned the discussion of human waste products generally, applying the principle that present deficiencies and imperfections should not be predicated of the state of innocence. The *Summa Fratris Alexandri* makes an initial distinction between residual superfluity and superfluity arising from impurities.[51] Semen is a residual superfluity only if one considers its relation to the individual. However, semen is not produced for the individual, but has its meaning and intelligibility in its orientation to generation and the conservation of the species. From that angle it is to be seen by no means as a superfluous by-product but as a natural necessity, a sign of the perfecting of nature.[52]

The wider question of waste by-products generally is resolved by distinguishing among kinds of superfluities: (1) those which arise from impurities, (2) those which result from a weakness of the physical retentive system, and (3) those which arise simply from the nature of the food. Wastes that emerge spontaneously, such as nasal mucus and sweat belong to the first category and would not have been in Paradise. Wastes such as faeces and urine that are eliminated through the organ system designed for that purpose belong to the second category and would have been in Paradise without the connotation of uncleanness that attaches to them now.[53] Later theologians resolved the specific problem arising from the definition of semen and the broader problem of waste products in a similar way. Albert adds pollution (spontaneous seminal emission) and menstruation to the category of what would not have been in Paradise, and spit to what would have been in the state of innocence.[54]

The fact that the semen had to be separated off from the man in order for conception to occur in the woman created another problem for the theologians. In fact, the question whether there would have been sexual relations in Paradise is formulated by the *Summa Fratris Alexandri* in terms of this separation: Was the separation of semen possible in the state of innocence?[55] Separation from the male body suggests depletion, imperfection, corruption, and violence (unnaturalness), all of which would have been absent from the first state. But the natural orientation to the reproduction of the species saves the process of seminal separation from any hint of unfittingness. Nature is perfected and completed by the process, which can occur only if semen is separated off from the male. Any depletion that might result is soon restored by the production of new semen out of the digestive process.[56]

Once the basic question of sexual intercourse in Paradise was settled, the medieval theologians were forced to extend their reflections. They were fond of saying that coitus *then* would have been like coitus *now*.[57] But would it? Sexual relations now are marked by intense pleasure; would the same have obtained in Paradise? The sexual process is naturally oriented to reproduction; would the first parents have come together only for purposes of reproduction, and, if so, would a child have been conceived as a result of each union? One of the most exalted states and forms of life now is that of virginity; would virginity have had the same value in the state of innocence, and, if so, how could that be reconciled with the claim that the first parents would have had sexual intercourse even if they had not sinned? Each of these subjects – sexual pleasure, procreative purpose, virginity – as they were conceived in the here and now were amply discussed by the medieval theologians. It is important to understand the conception of their place in the state of innocence, however, since it enlarges the view of the *Idealurmenschensbild* elaborated in the Middle Ages, an image that constituted an ideal and a norm.

PLEASURE

The question of sexual pleasure posed one of the most serious stumbling blocks to the creation of what might be called a realistic sexual ethic in the later medieval period, so it was only natural that when sex in the first state was discussed the question of its attendant pleasure would arise. It was posed in various ways: would there have been intense pleasure in coitus? In the separation of semen would there have been intensity of pleasure? Would there have been titillation? Would there have been the ardour of lust? Would there have been greater pleasure in the act of generation then than now? This last formulation of the question by Peter of Tarentaise captures the underlying preoccupation with the issue.[58]

Peter Lombard's own words and many texts cited from Augustine suggest a belief that there would have been little pleasure in the sexual act in Paradise. The argument is based on the thesis that sexual acts would have been under the control of deliberative reason. The first parents would have been able to command the genital organs just as they would have been able to control other bodily members.[59] An inverse relation is envisaged between rational control and sexual pleasure – the greater the control, the less the pleasure. Augustine argues for such control and notes that it should not be difficult to imagine since even in his own day he knows of people who have extraordinary natural abilities to control some physical functions.[60] The feats that he mentions are at least within the limits of known physiological possibilities, however; his proposals in regard to rational control over the motions of the sex organs would demand a psycho-physical constitution quite different from post-lapsarian experience.[61]

The 'movement' that concerned the theologians was male erection. While discussing the proprieties surrounding sexual intercourse, the *Summa* attributed to Alexander introduces the objection that movement of the genitals and an erection would have been required for the first act of coitus, but this would never have happened before the first sin. The reply is straightforward – 'There would not have been such movements before sin' – and Augustine is enlisted in support.[62] The text from Augustine is the standard text from the literal commentary on Genesis about the ability to control and command the genitals in Paradise.[63] There Augustine says nothing about an erection in the state of innocence, but elsewhere he does seem to suggest that such motion was instituted by God.[64] Albert has no problem with the idea.[65]

One of the difficulties in getting a bearing on the question of whether Adam and Eve would have experienced sexual pleasure before the Fall lies in the ambiguity of expressions used to describe intercourse in that state. In his attempt to distance coitus then from coitus now, Peter Lombard characterizes intercourse in Paradise as being without concupiscence, unlawful movement, the ardour of lust, and itching of the flesh. He then cites Augustine to the same effect, who says that intercourse would be without the itching of pleasure and that 'they would sow without ardour.'[66] These expressions are reminiscent of the language used to describe human affectivity that has been corrupted by original sin and so, strictly speaking, they do not settle the question of whether there would have been sexual pleasure in Paradise. On the one hand, a literal line of interpretation could be taken, concluding from the expressions that there would have been little or no sexual pleasure in Paradise. This would not be inconsistent with the texts. The canonist Huguccio, in comparing the union of the sex organs to the conjunction of two slates, implies that there would have been a lack of pleasure in the original state.[67] On the other hand, a more interpretive approach could be taken, agreeing that there would have been no uncontrolled and immoderate pleasure – no ardour of lust – in the state of innocence, but still maintaining that the ordered, rationally controlled sexual act in Paradise would have been more pleasurable than sexual relations are now. Both approaches to the question were taken.

Most agreed that there would have been some pleasure attached to the act of sexual intercourse, since pleasure is a natural concomitant of the movement of the semen along its proper pathways.[68] (The discussion is virtually always in terms of male pleasure.) Recall that the *Prose Salernitan Questions* incorporates the idea of pleasure into the definition of coitus; this is followed immediately by a question on the reason why pleasure is linked with intercourse. However, whether such pleasure would have been an integral part of intercourse before the Fall is not explored.[69] The *Summa* of Alexander reports two schools of thought: (1) those who claim that there would have been greater pleasure then than now but not immoderate; and (2) those, more in line with the words of Augustine and rational probability (according to the *Summa*), who claim 'that in the separation of semen and the union of the sexes in the time of the institution of nature there would have been pleasure, but moderated and measured pleasure, in line with the demands of human rectitude. Therefore there would not have been as much then as now.'[70]

It is not easy to determine who the proponents of greater pleasure were at this time, but it seems likely that they were in the tradition of the twelfth-century theologian Robert of Melun, who staunchly defended the naturalness of sexual pleasure in Paradise.[71] Albert the Great claims that there would have been greater pleasure, which would have been subject to reason, with the arousal of the members occurring 'as much as, as long as, and when reason wills.'[72] This account certainly affirms the value of sexual pleasure and is grounded in a belief in the unalloyed purity of original nature, which would enjoy a maximum of pleasure in its proper acts.

St Thomas advances the same theoretical account. In the *Summa of Theology* he does not raise the issue of pleasure in Paradise directly, but discusses it when responding to an objection that claims there would have been no union of male and female before the first sin because such union assimilates humans to beasts. In reply he notes that this assimilation results from the lack of rational control over sexual pleasure and from the heat of concupiscence, deficiencies that would have been absent from the state of innocence. He denies the claim of those who say that there would have been less sense pleasure in Paradise; in fact, there would have been more pleasure, because nature would have been purer and the body more sensitive. The desiring faculty, however, would not cling to this pleasure in an immoderate manner against the measure set by reason. The same idea applies to eating. According to Aquinas, a person who eats moderately does not thereby have less pleasure than a glutton. The difference lies in the degree of attachment to the pleasure of eating; the former does not invest his desires in the pleasure of eating as the glutton does.[73] Aquinas maintains that a more perfect and balanced physical constitution shares in a correspondingly greater pleasure. The parallel with eating illustrates the point, although it is arguable that the moderate eater *in eating* enjoys more pleasure than the glutton. Eating is not sex, however, and it may be the case that intense sexual pleasure arises precisely from the ardour of lust and from the mental extasis accompanying it; at least some were of that opinion.

In the view of the *Summa Fratris Alexandri* the intensity of sexual pleasure arises not from the act of intercourse as such but from the consequences of original sin and the loss of control associated with the loss of original justice.[74] The work grants the arguments supporting the view that there would not have been the same intensity then as now. The first argument captures the point: 'The generative power, like other powers, was not disordered in that state. But if pleasure was as intense then as it is now, since now there is disorder in the generative power, particularly in the act of generation because of the intensity of the pleasure, there would have had to be a similar disorder in the generative power then.'[75]

It is unfortunate that Aquinas did not formulate his question in terms of intensity of pleasure, since it would allow for a more exact comparison with the *Summa* of Alexander and with Bonaventure's *Commentary on the Sentences*. In terms of the existence of pleasure, however, there is little difference between the two positions. Both agree that there would have been sexual pleasure in Paradise and that the pleasure would not be like sexual pleasure now, since the latter results from lust and disorder. They differ about the extent of the pleasure in the state of innocence. Aquinas and Albert maintain that there would have been a greater degree of pleasure in Paradise; the Franciscans believe that intense pleasure is a result of original sin, so there would have been less pleasure before the sin of Adam.

The question was still open at the end of the thirteenth century. Richard of Mediavilla reports both views, adding that the position that there would have been greater pleasure in Paradise than now 'seems to many to be more probable.' He does not commit himself, but offers arguments that might be put forward by supporters of each side of the question.[76]

The texts in Peter Lombard that suggest there would have been no pleasure were interpreted to mean that there would be no *inordinate* pleasure. The passages claiming that there would have been command over the genitals similar to command over hands and feet were taken not to suggest that there would have been no pleasure but to emphasize the control that would have been exercised by reason in the first state and the absence of the ardour of lust.[77] Explaining the Lombard's text 'They would conceive without ardour and give birth without pain,' Albert glosses 'ardour': 'However, "ardour" connotes the pleasure that suffocates reason in its act.'[78]

PROCREATION

The ancient tradition that saw sexual intercourse as naturally and exclusively oriented to human procreation is reflected in the response to the question of whether, in the state of innocence, couples would have come together for the purpose of procreation. Actually, two questions were raised in this context: would they have come together only for reasons of procreation? And, would a child have been conceived as a result of each sexual act? Albert answers both affirmatively: 'It must be said that they would never have known each other without the hope and certitude of offspring because every act of coitus would bear fruit in the woman.'[79] In the pristine state of its institution, nothing would have impeded nature from unfolding to its perfect completion. Consequently, the reproductive system would always and only function as it ought.

Again, a new set of objections is raised, stemming from the parallel between sexual nature as it is known now and sexual nature implied by the solution to the question. Since sex is a natural appetite like eating, it would spontaneously arise and seek satisfaction simply as natural desire. Since eating is relatively continuous, semen would be continuously produced, built up, and demand its own release quite independent of the demands of reproduction. Surely, sometimes the woman would be pregnant and the man want to have sexual relations, but this would be contrary to the procreative possibilities of nature at that time.

This range of objections is dealt with extensively in the *Summa Fratris Alexandri*.[80] The reply to virtually all the objections is founded on the conviction that the process of reproduction would have been subject to the control of reason to the most extreme degree: 'When persons suited to intercourse are present, yes even when the genitals are joined together, the generative power would not function without the consent of free choice.'[81] The reproductive system would have been more particularly subject to the rational will than the nutritive system.[82] Sexual appetite would not have functioned as continuously or as frequently as the desire for food. There would have been no unnecessary build-up of semen, but only enough and at the right time for procreative intercourse to occur: 'Adam in that state would have known the power of his own nature and the requirements of food and the time and the hour when he ought to generate. Consequently, he would have lived so modestly and soberly that he would not have been swayed by the superabundance or lack of semen.'[83] Under no circumstance would Adam have wanted to approach his pregnant wife, because that would signal a natural disorder absent from the first state.[84]

VIRGINITY

It must strike one as odd to ask whether virginity would have been maintained in Paradise, in view of the general agreement that there would have been sexual relations in Paradise even if Adam and Eve had not sinned. It struck Albert as being a stupid question, not worth the time to labour over, but since some raised the question, he says he will deal with it.[85] Bonaventure also was not enthusiastic about the question but deals with it because he finds unintelligible some remarks of Augustine claiming that before the Fall a husband would have joined with his wife without any corruption of integrity.[86] Bonaventure adduces this text of Augustine in responding to whether there would have been corruption of integrity in the state of innocence:

The husband, without any seductive stimulus of passion and with peace

of soul and body, would have impregnated the womb of his wife without any corruption of [her] integrity ... Then the male seed could have
been introduced into the womb of the wife with female integrity intact,
just as now, with integrity maintained, menstrual discharge can be
emitted from the womb of a virgin. The same pathway could serve for
the introduction of the former as for the ejection of the latter.[87]

The nature of virginity will be dealt with later in the chapter on
continence and chastity. Here it is simply a matter of determining
whether it was thought that virginal integrity would have been maintained if there had been intercourse in Paradise. The *Summa Fratris
Alexandri* notes three factors that need to be taken into consideration:
(1) physical integrity (intactness of the hymen); (2) the proposal to
safeguard physical integrity; (3) a hatred of all unlawful intercourse.
The first two would not have been maintained in Paradise. The third
would have been, since it cannot be taken away like physical integrity;
it is simply the resolve not to do anything untoward in matters sexual.[88] Albert the Great's solution is straightforward. If the corruption
of integrity means only the opening of the doorways of reproduction,
then virginity would have been corrupted in the first state, barring any
connotation of violence.[89]

Bonaventure follows Albert, except that he has the text of Augustine
to contend with. Bonaventure says that the corruption of integrity
implies three notions: the opening of the doorways (the breaking of
the hymen), passion, which is present as a penalty for original sin, and
unclean pleasure. The first is a matter of nature and would have
occurred if there had been intercourse in the state of nature. The two
other features would not have been found in Paradise because they are
not effects of natural corruption; rather, they are consequences of the
corruption that results from original sin. The Franciscan master does
not respond explicitly to the apparent unintelligibility of Augustine's
remarks but observes that all such objections are to be understood as
claiming that the corruption of virginity implies more than the natural
opening of the reproductive pathways. If Adam and Eve had had
sexual relations in Paradise, there would have been only this natural
opening.[90]

Between the *Commentary on the Sentences* and the *Summa of Theology*,
Thomas Aquinas seems to have changed his mind about the question
of virginity in Paradise. In the earlier commentary he notes that both

physical and mental integrity are required for the perfection of virginity, the former more essential, the latter more esteemed. In every act of intercourse, even in the first state, the physical integrity of virginity would be lost. Mental integrity, which is associated with chastity, is lost through illicit intercourse; in the present state, it is also lost in each act of intercourse because the uncontrolled intensity of pleasure causes reason to be absorbed by the act. Since there would have been neither illicit intercourse nor uncontrolled pleasure in Paradise, mental integrity would have been maintained in the first state; physical integrity alone would have been lost.[91]

In the *Summa of Theology* Aquinas returns to the question of virginity in Paradise. An objection is raised to there being sexual intercourse in Paradise: since coitus would be corruptive of virginal integrity, and there would have been no corruption in the state of innocence, there would have been no intercourse in Paradise. The reply of St Thomas is curious. He does not respond to the specific objection in his own words but quotes Augustine without comment, the same text from *The City of God* that Bonaventure had found unintelligible. In simply citing this text, Aquinas leaves open the possibility that physical integrity would not have been lost. At least it is difficult to square this account with the earlier account in the *Commentary on the Sentences*.[92]

Debates over the nature of the loss of virginity in Paradise continued after Aquinas. The choice was between an opening through a dilation at the time of intercourse and childbirth similar to the opening of the mouth by parting the lips, and an opening through an actual breaking. The former view was an attempt to maintain some kind of physical virginity in Paradise while acknowledging that there would have been sexual relations. The latter view represents the received opinion, which, according to Peter of Tarentaise, is closer to the truth (*verisimilius*).[93]

There is an important issue at stake here touching on the scholastic assessment of sex. The life of consecrated virginity was thought to be the highest attainable form of life for human beings in the present state. Against this background, the crucial question is reflected in the formulation by the *Summa* of Alexander, neither a stupid question nor one asked out of idle curiosity: 'Would continence have been unlawful then?'[94] Would abstinence from sexual relations have had a value in Paradise opposite to what it has now? Would the proposal to remain a virgin be a good to be sought after in Paradise? Theological opinion was entirely negative. The *Summa Fratris Alexandri* is clear: 'However, at that time continence in no way would have been good because it would not have been ordered to the end, but rather it would have deflected from the end because it would have introduced betrayal of God's precept and deformity of his will.'[95]

At the time of creation God placed Adam and Eve under the precept to increase and multiply (Genesis 1:27–8). This precept could not have been carried out without sexual relations, so indirectly God commanded that sexual relations be the norm. Continence in the sense of sexual abstinence and virginity would have been contrary to that command and so would not have been good. Aquinas notes that continence now is praiseworthy because it removes disordered lust. In the state of innocence there would not have been any disordered lust, so continence then would not have been praiseworthy.[96] Sexual relations, under the control of reason and out of obedience to God's command, are not to be considered evils but goods. Abstinence from sex is now a good because it brings with it protection from disorder.

God's command to increase and multiply was not restricted to Paradise and the state before sin. The identical command was reissued after the Fall (Genesis 9:1), but we are no longer subject to it. When was the divine precept relaxed, and when did the value of sexual abstinence and virginity emerge? Albert provides a general principle: the precept was given for a reason; when the reason no longer applied, the precept was relaxed. The reason was the paucity of people. Once this paucity disappeared 'and many were hastening to marry they were absolved [from the precept], rushing together to the fruitfulness of a better life [the life of virginity] on account of a better good which is opposed to the foulness linked to coitus because of sin.'[97] The *Summa* of Alexander sketches a chronology of this relaxation: in the time of the institution of nature, continence was unlawful and not meritorious; in the time of the law of nature and of the written law, continence as a matter of course (*generalis*) was illicit, but dispensation was allowed to individuals; in the time of the law of grace, continence is lawful and meritorious.[98] The *Summa* lists five biblical indicators that show that the command to increase and multiply was gradually relaxed: the virginity of Abel, the virginity of Elias, the virginity of Mary and Joseph and John the Baptist, the virginity of Christ, and the teaching of Christ (Matthew 19:10–11).[99] The second period embraces the time after the expulsion from Paradise and during the era of the Patriarchs in particular.

SEXUAL RELATIONS IN PARADISE?

The questions and answers about sex before the Fall were expressed subjunctively; they deal with what *would have been*. It was agreed that as a matter of fact Adam and Eve did not have sex in Paradise. The first line of Genesis after the expulsion suggested this view: 'And Adam knew Eve his wife who conceived and brought forth Cain' (Genesis 4:1). Peter Lombard, following Augustine, asks why this should have been so, but the later theologians pay little attention to the matter. When the subject is introduced they are content to cite Augustine, adding some legal refinements about the nature of the precept to increase and multiply.[100]

Augustine suggests two reasons why Adam and Eve did not have sexual intercourse in Paradise: because there was no time after the creation of Eve and before the sin, or because God had not yet ordered the couple to do so. God's authority was necessary, since it would not have occurred to them to engage in sexual relations because there was no concupiscence to arouse them.[101] The first parents would have needed a special command over and above the general precept to increase and multiply, since that precept was an affirmative command needing further specification as to time. Augustine's explanation for why God did not give the command comes dangerously close to the Eastern emphasis on God's foreknowledge, an emphasis from which Augustine had apparently freed himself: 'Indeed God did not issue the command because he foresaw the fall of those from whom man was to be propagated.'[102] It is a short step from that view to saying that God had endowed the first parents with genital organs because he foresaw their fall. Augustine seems not to have noticed the apparent inconsistency, perhaps because the comment occurs just about the time he was adopting his final position against those who denied the initial naturalness of gender differentiation and sexual relations in the first parents. The mention of God's foreknowledge is the last sign of Augustine's earlier ambivalence.[103]

Bonaventure raises this issue in his treatment of doubts arising from the text of Peter Lombard. His solution is representative of the later view:

> It must be said that that command [to increase and multiply] was given to the man and to the woman in the state of innocence, but since it was

an affirmative command it did not oblige continuously [*ad semper*] but for
a certain place and time. However, the determination of the time
depended on the revelation of the divine will and because God had not
yet revealed it to them the Master [Peter Lombard] says he had not yet
issued the command.[104]

The scholastics believed that Adam and Eve before the Fall would
have been biologically, physiologically, and psychologically different
from post-lapsarian humans. Eve would not have menstruated and
Adam would never have experienced spontaneous seminal emission.
Excretory functions would have occurred without the foulness and
uncleanness that mark them now. In particular, the reproductive
system would have been completely oriented to its procreative goal
and would function only under the control of reason and will. There
would have been no natural urges or promptings towards sex. Even
the production of semen would have occurred only to the extent that
it was necessary for the act of intercourse, and the timing for the
occurrence of the act would have been known in advance. Since there
were no natural sexual promptings, the initiation of sexual activity
would have had to await a specific divine authorization, which, in fact,
was never given. Consequently, sexual intercourse was first initiated
after the Fall, resulting not from a divine command but from the urges
that were the consequences of the first sin.[105]

This quaint mythology should not be allowed to obscure the positive
achievements that resulted from reflection on the condition of Adam
and Eve in Paradise. Speculation on what would have been the case
had Adam and Eve stood firm led the theologians to two positions
that formed the anthropological foundation of their thinking about
post-lapsarian sex. Gender differentiation between male and female
was considered to be natural and part of the initial creative intentions
of God, not tailored to the state of fallen nature. As a consequence, sex
was believed to be a natural human constituent, willed by God to be
used for the multiplication of the species. The Fall would be seen to
modify the existential conditions in which sex was exercised, but not
its essential naturalness.

In addition to these fundamental views about gender and sex, two
principles guide virtually all thinking about sex in Paradise and will
influence reflections on post-lapsarian sex. First, sex is for procreation;
that is its nature and divinely intended goal. While the principle might

be modified, no modification could ever involve its complete absence. A second might be called the principle of rational control. The exercise of sex is morally upright to the extent that it is subject to the demands of natural reason. Sex in Paradise would have been good and praiseworthy precisely because of the reign of reason there. It is in the destruction of that reign that the Fall is felt most acutely in those born of Adam.

2

The Fall, Original Sin, and Concupiscence

The cover of an edition of Michel Foucault's *The History of Sexuality* is adorned with a reproduction of Albrecht Dürer's depiction of the temptation of Adam and Eve by the serpent. If the scene is meant to suggest that sex was causally influential on the sin of Adam and Eve, the picture is inappropriate from the perspective of medieval theology. If, however, the picture is meant to suggest that the Fall of Adam and Eve had some influence on the status of post-lapsarian sex, then it faithfully represents the views of medieval schoolmen.

Peter Lombard describes the temptation of Adam and Eve in terms that amount to a dress rehearsal for the capital sins (what are usually called the deadly sins today). The devil, who had fallen from his exalted state through *pride*, was *envious* of the happy state of Adam and Eve and set out to drag them down to the level of his own miserable condition. Aware that a frontal attack on the superior intelligence of Adam would likely be unsuccessful, he chose to get to Adam by insinuating himself into the good graces of Eve, who was of a weaker mind. Assuming the shape of a serpent, he approached Eve first by suggesting that she eat the fruit of the tree of the knowledge of good and evil, the fruit forbidden by God.[1] The temptation to *gluttony* got her attention, as it were, in order to tease her with the thought that she could be like God. *Vainglory* led to the belief that indeed she could be like God and that her eyes would be opened with newly acquired divine knowledge. This belief made her *avaricious* for such an exalted position. Eve ate the forbidden fruit against the divine command, which Augustine describes as the easiest of all commands to obey.[2]

In several passages that would be adopted in the later Middle Ages, Augustine presents the unfolding of the temptation from the serpent, through Eve, to Adam as a metaphor for the process of temptation generally. In one of the most popular analyses, the serpent represents suggestion and persuasion, Eve represents the desire for pleasure, and Adam represents rational consent.[3] A similar analysis from Augustine's anti-Manichean commentary on Genesis was adopted by Peter Lombard.[4]

In the course of mentioning the pride and envy of Satan and the temptation to gluttony, vainglory, and avarice, the commentators never suggest that the capital sin of lechery (*luxuria*) was involved. In discussions of the temptation of Eve the theologians did not entertain the possibility of the presence of sexual temptation, and it was never suggested that the sin of Adam was of a sexual nature.[5] In fact, it was the common opinion that, because of the privileged status of Adam and Eve in Paradise, the first sin could have been neither a sin of the flesh nor a minor or venial sin.

In the previous chapter, attention was drawn to the power that reason and will would have had over the reproductive organs in Paradise before the Fall. That power was one manifestation of a harmonious cosmic order in which 'God was first over man and all creatures, man was under God, and the rest was under man.'[6] Alexander of Hales says that such order was the *natural* order of things. However, it is likely that by 'natural' he did not mean 'what pertains to human nature as such'; rather, 'natural' here probably means 'proper,' the order that was part of the original design. Thomas Aquinas notes that if it had belonged to human nature it would be found after the Fall (but it is not found after the Fall). He is insistent that the order was a divine gift: 'In his first institution there was divinely bestowed on man a gift such that as long as his mind was subject to God, the lower powers of the soul were subject to the rational mind, and the body to the soul.'[7] The *existence* of a hierarchized harmony among God, reason, and the lower sense appetites was the result of God's gift. It is not something that is natural to human beings. The *maintenance* of this harmonious order, however, was up to the free choice of Adam and Eve, who had it within their power to destroy the balance; this is the ground of the possibility of the first sin.

To sin venially implies an antecedent state of imperfection. The harmony must already have been broken by a rational and deliberate turning away from God. As a consequence of the will's turning away from God, disruption follows in the other powers of the soul.[8] To sin in the flesh would have been impossible for Adam as long as the original order obtained. Bonaventure notes that the common opinion of his day held that there could be no exit from the original state unless divine justice were condemned, innocence stained, and nature corrupted, all of which could only result from a sin of reason.[9] For Aquinas there could be no rebellion of the flesh against the spirit, and so no disordered desire for an object of the senses, because there was no concupiscence to break out of the order of reason.[10] In the ordered state of innocence there was nothing below reason to draw it away from its submission to God. Reason itself had first to withdraw its allegiance from obedience to God's will, a withdrawal accomplished through pride. Adam's eating the forbidden fruit was the central act of disobedience; it was the effective sin that broke the original harmony and order, thereby introducing sin into the world. It is this that St Paul meant when he said we were all made sinners through the disobedience of one man.[11] The underlying sin was the sin of pride; Adam and Eve disobeyed the divine command through the rational disorder of pride. They desired a spiritual good outside the limits determined by reason.[12]

Although the theologians thought that both Adam and Eve committed the same form of disobedience in eating the forbidden fruit, they did not believe that Eve's pride was the same as Adam's. Eve was thought to have eaten because she really believed that she could become like God; Adam would have liked to become like God, but his superior male intelligence did not allow him to believe it was possible. He ate because he did not want to offend Eve, thinking it an inconsequential minor fault that would be easily forgiven![13] The consequences were disastrous, however, both for the first parents and for their successors.

The first sin was not simply the personal sin of the individual known as Adam. He was understood to represent and to encompass within himself the whole of human nature; he was all of us, and we share a solidarity of human nature with him.[14] In the words of Aquinas, 'All men who are born of Adam can be considered as one man in so far as they come together in the nature that they receive from the first parent.'[15] The individual decision of Adam ruptured the harmony, with consequences not only for him but for all who would share in his nature. Our share in those consequences was called original sin. However conceptualized, original sin was the disruption of the ordered state of innocence, a disruption first visited on Adam and Eve and subsequently on their descendants. Alexander of Hales captures this idea well: 'The perversion of order occurred through man sinning; he refused to be under his superior, and inferiors were not subject to him. Sensuality was not subject to reason since reason was not subject to God.'[16]

Although sex played no part in the temptation to the first sin or in the sin itself, it was understood to manifest itself as an immediate consequence of that sin. While the placement of the Dürer representation mentioned above communicates a somewhat ambiguous message, the artistic creation itself misrepresents the situation. It is clearly meant to depict the temptation scene before the actual eating of the forbidden fruit. Perhaps out of consideration for the sensibilities of his age, however, Dürer covered the genitals of Adam and Eve, and in so doing took away the external symbol of their innocence.

According to Genesis, the first parents were naked and felt no shame before the Fall (Genesis 2:25).[17] Immediately following their disobedience they became aware of their nakedness and covered themselves (Genesis 3:7), which led God to question them about their awareness (Genesis 3:10–11). The immediate manifestation of the effects of the first sin was understood to be felt in the genital area. As Augustine puts it, 'They covered up the shameful parts (*pudenda*), which were the same as before but were not shameful [then].'[18] The disobedience they felt in their flesh was a punishment to match their original disobedience.[19] This was interpreted to mean that the disruption of the initial order was found particularly in a disrupted affectivity, more acutely felt in the power of sex than in other dimensions of sensibility:

When Adam first withdrew from God, his body was also corrupted and not subject to the soul. Sensual motion, infused with the serpent's venom, was so put off track that in its movements it did not obey reason, particularly in regard to sexual pleasures ... For that pleasure moves more than the rest, touch is more sensitive in the area of the genitals, and the transmission of corruption occurs through that area. Consequently, it was

in the motion of the genitals that they [Adam and Eve] were first conscious of their nudity.[20]

To the claim that there is shame in all who have intercourse, even in
married couples, the early Dominican theologian Roland of Cremona
reponds: 'It is true that the shame arises from sin, not that sin is committed then if the intercourse is legitimate, but it arises from the sin of
the first man.'[21] The *Summa Fratris Alexandri* even claims that the use
of the term *pudibunda* (shameful parts) is evidence for the existence of
original sin.[22]

ORIGINAL SIN

The theory of the nature of original sin had an interesting development in the twelfth and thirteenth centuries. Peter Lombard formulated the theory against the background of St Augustine, who had said
that original sin was concupiscence. This became the generally
received view until the early thirteenth century. At that time there was
a return to the theory that had been elaborated in the eleventh century
by St Anselm of Canterbury, who said that original sin was the deprivation of original justice.[23] The emergence of the use of Anselm
occurred about 1225 in Alexander of Hales, John of Saint-Gilles, and
in the collection Douai 434, named after the manuscript in which it is
found.[24] This marked a considerable shift in theory, but in fact little
change occurred because of the reluctance of the university masters to
abandon the language sanctioned by Augustine. Instead of discarding
the old view, the masters distinguished between the *formal* and *material*
elements of original sin. Formally and in its essence, original sin was
taken to be the deprivation and absence of original justice; that is,
God's plan for man if he had stood steadfast in the state of innocence
was abolished, God's gratuitous gifts of immortality and impassibility
were withdrawn, cosmic harmony was shattered, and the future community in the vision of God and friendship with him were rendered
impossible.[25]

For Thomas Aquinas, original justice consisted in an ordered harmony; original sin is a disposition to disorder arising from the dissolution of that harmony.[26] The ordered harmony was the subjection of
the will to God and, since the will is the principal mover of the other
faculties, disorder in all the other powers of the soul followed from

turning away from God.[27] As he says: 'With the dissolution of the harmony of original justice the different powers of the soul were carried off to different [objects].'[28] The privation of original justice by which the will was subject to God is the formal element in original sin.[29]

The tangible effects of the loss of original justice were called concupiscence, the material element of original sin. Through this conception the older theory that saw original sin as concupiscence was incorporated into the new view that conceived of original sin as the loss of original justice. In deference to the tradition, Aquinas says that the disorder of the other powers of the soul 'can be called by the common name "concupiscence".'[30] This concupiscence is a corruption of order found in the physical dimensions of the descendants of Adam. Reflecting a received view of his day, Albert the Great distinguishes between two forms of this corruption. The first consists in defects arising from the very nature of a physical body, such as hunger, thirst, sickness, death. These, he says, the masters call the corruption of passibility – that is, the body is left to take its natural course, which it was exempt from in Paradise through God's special gifts of impassibility and immortality. The second form of corruption is the result of Adam's turning away from the grace of innocence. This is the habitual concupiscence that is spread throughout the bodily organs and that 'the more learned of our day call the corruption of vice.'[31]

It is the view of Dom Lottin that in his later works Aquinas was inclined to see concupiscence simply as an effect of original sin and not a material constituent of it. He adhered to the distinction between formal and material elements out of deference to the tradition. Whether or not this is so, later commentators on the *Sentences* maintained the distinction between formal and material elements.[32]

The term 'concupiscentia' ('concupiscence') had a strong negative connotation for medieval theologians, suggesting disorder, evil, corruption, vice, stain, and blemish. Concupiscence is the basic disorder in the human affective dimensions resulting from the refusal to obey the dictates of right reason. The Lombard's version of Augustine's account was universally accepted: 'Concupiscence itself is the law of the bodily members or of the flesh, which is a certain diseased affection or sluggishness that moves unlawful desire, that is, carnal concupiscence, which is called the law of sin.'[33] Several terms are used to describe original sin as concupiscence, each term suggesting a different facet of the notion. Alexander of Hales glosses the terms: tinder (*fomes*) 'in that it feeds sin'; sluggishness (*languor*) 'in that it hardens in corrupted nature;' tyrant (*tyrannus*) 'in that it highlights the violent domination against right reason'; the law of the members (*lex membrorum*) 'in that it moves the organs themselves in the workings of concupiscence'; the law of the flesh (*lex carnis*) 'in that it excites sense to first movements and reason to consent'; original (*originale*) 'in that the absence of justice derives from the first man'; concupiscence (*concupiscentia*) 'in so far as it is an immediate proneness to the act of concupiscence, as in adults'; concupiscibility (*concupiscibilitas*) 'in so far as it is a remote proneness, as in children.'[34]

All these terms point to what was called a corruption of human nature that stains the race of Adam and that is particularly apparent in the sexual constitution of human beings. Concupiscence is disordered affectivity, the tendency of natural desires and appetites to pursue their own objects in disregard of the proper order of reason. Its natural ground is in the desiring part of the soul, which Albert, following Avicenna, defines as, 'The sense power of the soul whose proper end is the pleasurable found in the senses and it commands movement towards obtaining that pleasure.'[35] The command to movement involved here is through physiological changes that ready the body for the reception of the cognitively entertained pleasure. Albert provides an example of concupiscence for intercourse in the male. The command is felt in the power causing an erection and in the spirits moving semen into the genitals.[36]

The concupiscence that is the material component of original sin must not be confused with the natural concupiscence that is simply the desiring, appetitive aspect of the lower sense part of the soul. Adam and Eve would have had the latter before the Fall to the extent that they would have had natural desires for the pleasures associated with sense experience. As long as the first parents were endowed with original justice, however, these desires would not have been independent of the guiding direction of reason. The removal of original justice left the way open for the lower sense desires to pursue their own objects in disregard of reason's guidance. Both Albert and Thomas provide accounts that distinguish between the natural power of desire and the disordered state of the power. Bonaventure seems simply to understand concupiscence as immoderate desire.[37] The language of desire employed by the schoolmen was rich and varied, not easily captured in English. For example, the two verbs *appetere* and *concupiscere* would both normally be rendered into English by 'to desire.' Albert notes that the first connotes a general inclination of the appetite for its object. *Concupiscere*, however, connotes actively seeking satisfaction in the pleasurable, and enjoyment of the pleasure.[38]

Talk of corruption and concupiscence as the material substrata of original sin should not be understood to imply that human nature was considered to be debilitated in its natural principles as a result of original sin. At least for Aquinas, the corruption involved is that of the divinely bestowed orientation to the *supernatural* goal of beatitude, which transcends human capabilities, and the withdrawal of the gifts of immortality, impassibility, and ordinability of the human powers of the soul. We were created for an end that surpasses our natural powers of achievement, but endowed with the means to ensure its attainment. Through the sin of Adam those means were taken from human nature, the nature that each of Adam's descendants inherits through generation. Human nature is despoiled of its gratuitous endowments and abandoned to its own natural resources: 'Man is left to those goods alone that follow on natural principles.'[39]

It is in this context that one must place remarks about the diminution of the good of human nature and the wounds (*vulnera*) caused by sin. Aquinas proposes three goods of human nature. The first is the constitutive principles of nature along with the properties flowing from them, such as the powers of the soul. This good is neither taken away nor diminished by sin. The natural inclination to virtue is a second good of nature characteristic of rational beings. This good is diminished by sin through impediments to virtue that result from original sin. Finally, the gift of original justice is a good of nature that was completely taken away through the sin of the first parent.[40]

Diminution in the natural inclination to virtue is an effect of the wounds caused by the removal of original justice. These wounds were said to be ignorance (*ignorantia*), evil (*malitia*), infirmity (*infirmitas*), and concupiscence (*concupiscentia*). Through the gift of original justice, reason, which was subject to God, was able to keep proper order in the lower powers of the soul. The removal of original justice left all the powers of the soul destitute of their proper order. This destitution was the wounding of nature. Reason was deprived of an actual orientation to the truth (wound of ignorance), the will was deprived of an actual orientation to the good (wound of evil), and the irascible appetite was deprived of its proper orientation to what is arduous (wound of infirmity), the concupiscible appetite was deprived of its proper orientation to what is pleasurable (wound of concupiscence).[41]

Because of these wounds, human beings are hobbled in the pursuit of their natural inclination to the virtues of prudence (reason), justice (will), fortitude (irascible appetite), and temperance (concupiscible appetite). It should be noted, however, that Aquinas never speaks of an actual deformity as such in post-lapsarian nature. Whether or not one ought to speak here of pure nature, it would seem that in the view of Thomas humans were reduced to their natural state as a result of the Fall, but were not positively debilitated. The tragedy lay in the removal of the props of original justice, not in the reception of actual ontological scars.[42] Human nature after the Fall is pulled in different directions by the powers of the soul that tend to pursue their independent ends in disregard of proper order. Bereft of original justice, the only way to re-establish a semblance of that order is through the acquisition of the natural cardinal virtues. Sex is problematic in this state because of the particularly strong attractions that sexual pleasure has for the desiring faculty of the soul.

Rational control over the desires and appetites of the lower faculties is no longer assured. The attractive pleasures of their objects are constantly pulling us away from rationally ordered desires, particularly in matters of sex. This state of affairs is what is meant by the habitual corruption spread throughout the bodily members. The virtue of temperance, as will be seen, is required to bring order and harmony into the desiring dimension of the human constitution. Temperance is the attempt to re-establish a semblance of the harmony that had been part of original justice and lost through Adam's sin.

SENSUALITY AND FIRST MOVEMENTS

Closely associated with the idea of concupiscence are three notions whose elucidation will help to clarify the sexual aspects of the material component of original sin: sensuality, first movements, lust (*libido*).

In a digression from his discussion of freedom of choice Peter Lombard remarks that while brute animals do not have freedom of choice, 'nonetheless they have the sense and appetite of sensuality.'[43] He then provides the following definition: 'Sensuality is a lower power of the soul giving rise to motion that focuses on the senses of the body; it is the appetite for things pertaining to the body.'[44] On the face of it, this notion seems to refer to what would later be called the sense appetite in medieval psychological analyses. In fact, Albert the Great goes to great lengths to show that sensuality is not a single power or faculty of the soul but embraces the whole perceptive and desiring dimension of the senses. Aquinas identifies sensuality and the sense appetite.[45] But such analyses do not capture the idea of disorder that the term 'sensuality' connotes. Aware of this, the *Summa Fratris Alexandri* raises the question why philosophers never arrived at a knowledge of sensuality. Philosophers dealt with the sense appetite in so far as it was a feature that humans share with other animals, or in so far as it was subject to the persuasion of reason. Sensuality, however, suggests something else – the rebellion against reason arising from the punishment for original sin. Since philosophers did not know about original sin, they could not have known about sensuality.[46] In the felicitous phrase of Michaud-Quantin, sensuality is a theological faculty – that is, a dimension of human affectivity conceived of and discussed by theologians.[47]

As experience teaches, people often have spontaneous inclinations to food, drink, sex, and anger over whose inception they seem to have little or no control. Such are inclinations of sensuality, which were called 'first movements.' Again, the notion of disorder is apparent in the popular definition provided by John of La Rochelle: 'First movement is the movement of sensuality according to the impulse from the tinder [of original sin] tending impetuously to the enjoyment of creaturely pleasure.'[48]

The accounts of sensuality and of first movements are about human desires for material things generally. When the medieval masters inquired about the moral character of first movements, however, they were mainly interested in the first stirrings of sexual inclination, even to the extent of asking whether the first movements towards one's wife were sinful. In some cases, as with Stephen Langton, the question is even restricted to sexual inclinations.[49]

Discussions of the question of the sinfulness of the first movements of sensuality form a curious chapter in the moral psychology of the Middle Ages. On the one hand, there was a clear teaching that located sinfulness in an act of will and reason. On the other hand, there was Peter Lombard's position (which was mistakenly taken to be the view of Augustine) that, although a very light sin, motions of sensuality were nonetheless sinful.[50] This view was in direct opposition to the common teaching about moral imputability. Deman demonstrates the hold that the belief in Augustine's patronage held over medieval thinkers. Albert is explicit: 'But because Augustine expressly says it is a sin, it therefore must be held that sensuality prior to any act of reason is a sin.'[51] The position is entirely the Lombard's, however, and he simply states it, without further explanation. Although there were some dissenting voices, the common view up to Aquinas was that the first movements of sensuality were very minor venial sins. Of the outstanding scholastics of the thirteenth century, Albert alone came around at the end of his life to oppose the common view after realizing that Augustine had not fathered the position.[52]

In order to respect the accepted opinion, the theologians had to find a way to bring the first movements of sensuality under the controlling domain of reason and will. St Thomas Aquinas, whose position remained unchanged throughout his writing career, summarized and codified the tradition. From a psychological point of view he finds a way to impute first movements to rational control and thus to open the way for their moral imputability. An objection is raised based on a frequently used text of Augustine: 'No one sins in regard to what cannot be avoided.' Since sensuality is 'perpetual corruption' as long as we live in this life, it is clear that the disordered movement of sensuality is not a sin.[53] Aquinas acknowledges that 'the perpetual corruption of sensuality' is never eliminated in this life. Although its mere existence is not morally imputable (after baptism), it remains as an active constituent of our make-up and so cannot be avoided as such. The manifestations of sensuality are individualized in space and time, however, and a rational person can in principle escape their serial eruptions by diverting attention to other concerns. For example, when stirred by movements of concupiscence a person might engage in scientific work. To that degree sensuality is avoidable in the concrete and so is brought into the arena of moral assessment. Because of its integral and continuous presence, however, one cannot avoid all movements of sensuality. Aquinas extends his example, noting that the person who turns to scientific speculation to avoid falling into sensual sins may begin to be impressed with the work and be moved to vainglory. The individualized existentiality of the manifestations of sensuality is sufficient ground for Aquinas to claim that sensuality is subject to rational, voluntary control.[54]

The fact that movements of sensuality can be subject to acts of the will still does not provide grounds for arguing the sinfulness of sensuality. Eruptions of sensuality do not necessarily take the course described by Aquinas. It is conceivable that the person in his example successfully diverts attention from concupiscence and simply gets on with the scientific pursuits without further temptation to vainglory. In such a case there would seem to be no room for the imputation of even the slightest sin. He did everything that was humanly possible. The most reasonable construal of the example is surely that the scientist was tempted to sins of lechery and vainglory but did not succumb. In the event that he did give in or go on to dwell on thoughts of vainglory, the fault is in the consent to sins of the flesh or to a vain personal assessment, not in the movements of sensuality themselves. Aquinas was never able to resolve this conundrum.

In the above account, Aquinas uses a formula frequently encountered in discussions of the effects of baptism. Original sin is said to pass away as far as guilt is concerned, but to remain in act ('transit reatu, remanet actu'). The formula, with its roots in Augustine, was universally used to respond to the question whether original sin is taken away in baptism.[55] Guilt, separation from God, and absence of grace are abolished in baptism; concupiscence, tinder, disorder of the flesh, inclination to independent sense desires remain.[56] The features that remain were considered to be punitive consequences of the loss of original justice to which no guilt was attached. Their initial movements pose problems but are not sinful until reason and will combine in rational consent. It is difficult to understand how Aquinas, who provides such a clear analysis of the psychology of the human act, could favour the traditional opinion about the sinfulness of first movements. Perhaps he too was under the influence of the Augustinian patronage of the view. There is no point to extending these remarks further. The traditional view, with increasing dissent, maintained its popularity until the fourteenth century.[57]

LUST AND THE TRANSMISSION OF ORIGINAL SIN

I have suggested that the descendants of Adam who share in human nature were believed to be the heirs to original sin, but this is not entirely correct. The idea of descent from Adam is usually qualified by adverbs such as 'seminally' (*seminaliter*), 'concupiscibly' (*concupiscibil-*

iter), 'libidinously' (*libidinose*). That is, the contracting of original sin does not follow automatically from conception and birth. After all, Christ was conceived and born but did not contract original sin.[58] Sexual intercourse is the agent of transmission, and it is in the context of discussions of the transmission of original sin that the concept of lust (*libido*) is analysed. (Throughout this book, *libido* is translated by 'lust' and *luxuria* by 'lechery.' The difference between the two is significant. Lust is an integral part of the constitution of fallen human nature; lechery is a vice that is freely acquired and for which we are morally responsible. The distinction is usually maintained by medieval writers.)[59] There is in Peter Lombard a text from Fulgentius of Ruspe that sketches the role of lust in human generation. Since marital intercourse is impossible without lust, children who are conceived through intercourse contract original sin. They contract it not from the intercourse as such but from the lust that accompanies all post-lapsarian coitus. This is why David says, 'I was conceived in iniquities, and in sin my mother conceived me' (Psalms 50:7).[60] The text was understood to embrace all conception resulting from sexual intercourse. This forced the theologians to clarify the concept of lust. It is at least possible that some acts of intercourse could occur without any actual feelings of lust, but in such cases original sin would still be contracted.[61]

Discussions of lust owe so much to Augustine that it would be worthwhile, before dealing with the medieval theologians, to turn to some of his accounts. The notion of lust, its relation to original sin and to sin generally, its moral character, and its presence in sexual intercourse before and after the Fall attracted the attention of Augustine on several occasions. *On Freedom of Choice* develops the theme that lust is the cause of all evils and that this lust is cupidity, which ought to be disapproved (*improbanda cupiditate*).[62] Later, he identifies avarice with cupidity and defines cupidity as perverse will (*improba voluntas*), concluding that the latter is the cause of all evils.[63] Augustine never explicitly said that lust is *improba voluntas*, but he implies as much: cupidity is *improba voluntas*, lust (*libido*) is cupidity, so *libido* is *improba voluntas*. Such an association of concepts must have occurred at some point in the tradition, because lust is frequently defined as *improba voluntas*.

Augustine provides a careful analysis of the term 'lust' while discussing the sin of the first parents. He is aware of the classical usage in which the term does not have a predominantly sexual connotation, but points out that the term is also used to describe the craving felt in the genitals: 'Pleasure, however, is preceded by a certain craving that is felt in the flesh as its own desire, such as hunger, thirst, and the desire that is mostly called lust when it affects the sex organs, though this is a general term applicable to any kind of desire.'[64] He means here what might be called felt lust, actual stirrings that prompt sexual desires. In the *City of God*, the term has negative connotations suggesting turpitude, obscenity, shame, embarrassment. These stirrings were aroused by nakedness in Adam and Eve after the Fall, caused embarrassment and shame, and led to their covering themselves out of modesty.

I have already mentioned the different responses given by the early-thirteenth-century scholastics to the question whether there would have been sexual pleasure before the Fall. Associated with this question is the further question whether lust would have been present in the relations between Adam and Eve before the Fall. Obviously, lust in the sense of perverse will would not have been found before Adam and Eve had sinned. Augustine, however, was pushed by his Pelagian opponents to address the possibility of the presence of some kind of morally neutral and ordered lust that would account for sexual promptings even before the Fall. He raised the issue directly and, although the question does not figure in later medieval discussions, it is worthy of mention, since it shows that Augustine struggled with it right up to the end of his life.

Augustine challenged the Pelagians to choose from among four accounts of sexual relations in Paradise: (1) Adam and Eve would have had intercourse whenever they pleased; (2) they would have reined in lust when intercourse was not necessary; (3) lust would have arisen on command of the will when chaste prudence would have felt the need for intercourse; (4) with no lust at all, the genitals would have obeyed the commands of those wishing intercourse without any difficulty in regard to their proper functions, just as the other bodily members perform their own functions. The first two options, he suggests, would be repudiated even by the Pelagians. Of the last two, although Augustine himself prefers the fourth option and admits that the Pelagians would not, he seems to be able to live with the third possibility.[65]

In the last work of his life Augustine returned to the same question, but this time from the point of view of concupiscence. Either concupiscence was not present in Adam before he sinned, or, if it was present in an unalloyed state, it was vitiated in him by sin. If it was present, it was subject to the command of the will before the Fall.[66] In a recently discovered collection of Augustine's letters, there is a letter in which Augustine provides a careful summary of his position on the Pelagian controversy. There the notions of concupiscence for marriage (*concupiscentia nuptiarum*) and concupiscence of the flesh (*concupiscentia carnis*) are contrasted. The former is acknowledged to have had a place in Paradise, the latter not. If one allows that there would have been some sort of concupiscence of the flesh in Paradise, it would not have been like it is now, moving indifferently to lawful and unlawful things.[67]

This possibility of a morally neutral concupiscence or lust subject to the will before the Fall is, as far as I can ascertain, foreign to the later medieval theologians. There is a text in the *Ordinary Gloss* on Gratian, however, that admits the possibility of some sort of sexual excitation in Paradise before the Fall:

> *Without ardour.* For unless man had sinned the union of the genitals would have been as bereft of itching as the union of the other bodily members are [bereft of itching], as if you were to apply a finger to a finger or a hand to a hand. Or, if there were to have been an itching, nonetheless there would have been no sin as there would have been no sin in putting a scabrous hand to the flame.[68]

In the attempt to provide an interpretation of the text of Fulgentius of Ruspe, a threefold conception of lust emerged. There was first of all the generally accepted Augustinian idea of lust as perverse will that precedes every sin actually or dispositively. This is not what is meant when it is said that original sin is transmitted through lust. In fact, Albert and others suggest that it frequently happens that intercourse in marriage occurs without this kind of lust.[69]

The second meaning of lust is variously expressed but comes down basically to the immoderate pleasure that accompanies sexual intercourse, pleasure that some suggest is never or scarcely ever absent. Lust in this sense is not the cause of the transmission of original sin, because it too may or may not be present, is unequal across those who experience it, and is only a sign of a more basic disorder.[70]

The third meaning of lust captures the sense in which lust is said to cause original sin: the lust of the parents causes original sin in the offspring. Albert says that in this third sense lust refers to 'the habitual concupiscence spread in the semen that corrupts the orientation of the bodily organs to the soul in terms of the soul's movement towards what is good.'[71] For Bonaventure it is 'the ruinous (*vitiosa*) corruption that we say is in the semen and even in the generative power outside the act of generation according to which the generative power itself is said to be corrupted and infected.'[72] He adds that conception is never without lust in this sense if it occurs in accord with the law of nature. For Aquinas, it is present like a habit and taken 'for that excessive disorder of the powers, which accounts for the proneness in us to desire in a disordered manner.'[73] In this sense lust is understood to be the cause of original sin in the offspring. For Peter of Tarentaise and Richard of Mediavilla, the third sense of lust refers to the corruption or infection of the power of generation.[74]

This third meaning of lust incorporates the accepted scholastic view that the reproductive system not only shares the corruption common to all the human sense faculties, but is more particularly corrupted or, as they said, infected. Sometimes the infection is claimed to characterize the reproductive system alone, sometimes the whole appetitive dimension, and Aquinas extends it even to the sense of touch.[75] The underlying idea in these texts corresponds to the idea of infectious disease – a disease that people not only have themselves, but can pass on to others.

In accounts of the infectious nature of semen a comparison with the transmission of leprosy is often encountered. The reproductive system was designed in the service of nature to conserve the species through reproduction of other persons. This particularly applies to male semen. Since it is the active ingredient in generation, the infection is said to be located there. It is not that the semen was thought to possess some particularly bad or dirty positive quality; rather, it is said to be infected because it is the agent or vehicle of the transmission of original sin. Likewise, in the case of leprosy the semen was believed to be not itself leprous but a carrier of the disease – virtually or potentially leprous and so able to cause the disease in the offspring. An additional feature that justified seeing an extreme degree of corruption in the sex organs was their further remove from the control of reason over the human faculties. As the *Summa Fratris Alexandri* puts it: 'In this power there is less obedience and greater repugnance in its movements in respect to a well disposed reason, for willy-nilly indecent and shameful motion arises.'[76]

The unfolding of the process does not concern us directly but might be briefly summarized: the fetus was thought to be initially begun through the workings of infected male semen on the material matrix of the woman; the result is corrupted, disordered flesh; each soul is created unblemished by God and infused into the body; it is only on contact with the corrupted body that the soul can be said to contract original sin – privation of the original justice that Adam lost, and concupiscence, which constitutes the material substratum of original sin. The overall medieval thinking about these matters is succinctly expressed by Peter Lombard:

> While before sin man and woman could come together without the incentive of lust and the fire of concupiscence, and there would have been 'an undefiled bed' [Hebrews 13:4], the flesh was so corrupted in Adam through sin that after sin there could not have been carnal union without lustful concupiscence that is always a disability [*vitium*] and even a fault unless it is excused by the goods of marriage. So the flesh formed into the body of a child is conceived in concupiscence and lust. Whence the flesh, which is conceived in corrupt [*vitiosa*] concupiscence, is itself polluted and corrupted. Through contact with it the soul, when infused, contracts a stain by which it is polluted and becomes blameworthy – a stain, that is, which is the disability of concupiscence, which is original sin.[77]

This extreme realism in the account of the connection between sexual reproduction and original sin is confirmed in answers given to the question whether a person conceived by some miracle asexually (from a finger or from a piece of flesh, for example) would contract original sin. Because the body was formed from corrupt flesh, the person would suffer the penalties attached to original sin such as hunger, thirst, sickness, disease, and death. But because it was not generated through infectious sexual intercourse, the medieval thinkers were agreed, the formal element of original sin would not be contracted. It would be interesting to hear what these theologians would say about the modern possibilities created by advances in genetic engineering.[78]

I have been concerned to provide a summary of some common views about the relationship between original sin and sex found in the writers of the thirteenth century. The discussion of original sin continued in the schools and erupted at the end of the century into a full-blown debate between those who wanted to return to a more purist Augustinian position (identifying original sin with concupiscence), and those who wanted to develop the Thomistic possibilities further, viewing concupiscence as merely a consequence of original sin, a position that Dom Lottin believed represents Aquinas' theoretical inclination. These later developments do not change in any fundamental way the conviction that sex and original sin were interrelated.[79]

BROKEN REINS

Medieval theological views of sex are the intellectual, dialectical elaboration of a shared mythos of truly cosmic proportions. Divine creation, Paradise, the Fall, and original sin are the principal themes of the story that the scholastic masters believed they could read in the Bible and in its Augustinian commentaries. Sex was a central feature of creative providence operating in concert with nature to multiply individuals of the human species and, in the view of some, to fill up the number of the elect. Sex was meant to have a functional role subject to the divine plan, entirely under the control of rational will, and to be deployed for purposes of procreation. This is the way human sex was meant to be – reined in by the twin leashes of God's design and rational control – not a hard-fought control against a recalcitrant force but a tranquil disposition of harmonious order. Sex in Paradise would have been like a well-behaved horse, obedient at every turn to its master.

Adam's tragic fall brought all this to an end. His legacy to us of original sin ensures that sex as it is can never be as it ought to have been. That will always remain, perhaps, a distant ideal impossible of complete realization because of the impossibility of eliminating lust. In fact, it was believed that the very nature of marriage changed after the Fall to accommodate the new situation in which sex found itself. Because of the disruption of the controlled harmony in which reproduction was subject to reason and reason to God, sex is no longer comparable to a well-behaved horse; it is now more like a wild horse that has broken its reins, running amok, unleashed, in feverish frenzy.

> For now that power [sex] has largely abandoned the command of reason while reason has lost the bond and tether of original justice through which it issued orders to the lower powers. Therefore, with its reins slackened, that power plunges with all its force and inclination into pleasures that are offered to it, not because of the intensity of the moving power but because of the defect of the restraining power. So the point under discussion should be understood in comparison with a sexually stimulated [*lascivus*] horse who runs more swiftly and impetuously after its harness is broken than when it is harnessed and held back by the horseman, although the horse does not have any more power.[80]

This unruly aspect of sex is an integral, material concomitant of original sin that remains even after baptism. Very much like a frenzied horse, it will lead to self-destruction unless brought under control and reined in; but a horse, even when bridled, must have some outlet for its energies. There was a recognition of the need for general, overall control on the one hand, and for some outlet on the other. The former could be achieved through the virtue of temperance, the latter through marriage, which was seen as the sole context for permissible sexual expression. It is in the treatment of marriage that the most concentrated discussion of legitimate sexual behaviour is provided.

3

Marriage and Sex

In Paradise, Adam and Eve would have carried out the divine command to increase and multiply (Genesis 1:28) undisturbed by passion, lust, or concupiscence. Nature, biology, physiology, and psychology would have been marshalled at the right time for sexual union in order to ensure generation and only to ensure generation.

After the sin of Adam and Eve and their ejection from Paradise, sex took on a new dimension as a consequence of original sin. It was seen to have become one of the most rebellious and recalcitrant elements in the human psycho-physical constitution. It no longer functioned within the integral harmony of the original divine plan but tended to follow the impulses of passion, lust, and concupiscence. This state of affairs raised problems for any view that saw marriage simply as the framework within which human beings would promote the multiplication of the species through the reasoned deployment of sex. The challenge to medieval thinkers was to elaborate a view of marriage and sex that took account of the plan for Paradise, on the one hand, and of post-lapsarian human beings in the real world of fallen nature, on the other. The challenge was met, resulting in numerous treatments of marriage and marital sex based largely on the accounts of Gratian and Peter Lombard.[1] Of course all treatments lay under the considerable influence of Augustine, who had risen to the challenge, particularly in his debates with the Pelagians. His solutions were never far from medieval attempts to provide a systematic account of marriage. The extent of the influence of Augustine will be endlessly disputed. For good or ill, however, there can be no doubt that it was overwhelming on medieval conceptions of marriage and the place of sex within marriage, apparent both in the canon law and theology.[2]

Almost every topic in medieval discussions of marriage has a sexual dimension to it, from the nature of the consent required for a valid marriage to the duties and obligations that arise from a valid marriage. A traditional question asked throughout the period is, 'Does intercourse pertain to the integrity of marriage?' One of the basic duties (dealt with in the following chapter) is 'to pay the debt' (*reddere debitum*), meaning to respond to a request by one's spouse for sex. Since marriage was acknowledged to be the sole context for legitimate sexual relations, it is in treatises on marriage where one encounters accounts of the requirements for proper sexual behaviour, accounts that became progressively more complex with the development of a casuistry of sexual behaviour. This and the next two chapters will present the thinking that underlay the conception of the legitimacy of marital sex and the constraints that were imposed on its enjoyment. That conception was elaborated both on the level of the nature of marriage and intercourse taken objectively (chapter 3), and on the level of the subjective intentions of those engaging in marital sexual relations (chapters 3 and 4).

This chapter deals with marriage and sex in general – with those aspects of marriage that were believed to ground the legitimacy of sexual relations and to give them their morally upright character. The relevant aspects are noted in treatments of the *institution* of marriage, its *naturalness*, the *goods* of marriage, and how the goods *excuse* marriage. The treatment of the general moral character of intercourse is, in the first instance, grounded in the conception of the radical goodness of marriage.

However good marital sexual relations were conceived to be in the abstract, it is people who engage in such relations, people who were expected to respect the conditions for the goodness of intercourse and to reflect those conditions in their subjective intentions. From the thirteenth century, theologians and canonists distinguished four intentions or reasons (*causae*): (1) to have children, (2) to pay the marriage debt, (3) to avoid fornication, (4) to satisfy lust or for the sake of pleasure. The first two reasons were generally believed to provide at least prima facie moral legitimacy to sexual relations in marriage; the last two posed problems that were never satisfactorily resolved in the Middle Ages.

Admittedly, this treatment results in a one-sided picture of marriage, omitting much that is positive and ennobling like the love, respect, and friendship that were meant to characterize the union. It is not as if ideas that were firmly associated in the thought of medieval writers are being forcefully or artificially separated, however. One looks in vain for a developed account of the relationship between love and sex in medieval accounts of marriage. Furthermore, although the discussion of marital sex does not provide a complete picture of marriage, it by no means exaggerates a subject that was peripheral to medieval thought. Sex was not peripheral to the subject of marriage; it was central to the treatment of almost every facet of marriage.[3]

THE TWOFOLD INSTITUTION OF MARRIAGE

In a celebrated section of his *Decretum* (*Causa* 32), Gratian explores the nature of marriage from the point of view of the motivation for getting married.[4] One of the questions that he poses is whether a woman who marries for reasons of incontinence alone can be called a wife. The problem is set out in scholastic fashion, beginning with the claim that a woman is not really a wife who is taken solely for reasons of incontinence, because marriage was instituted by God for the sake of procreation, not to satisfy lust. Texts from Ambrose and Jerome reinforce the claim that union to satisfy lust and not to procreate offspring creates fornicators, not spouses.[5] These objections suggest that if marriage is now as it was meant to be in the state of innocence, there is no room for those who marry under the impulse of sexual drives. There are sexual drives independent of procreative motives, however, and since marriage is the only legitimate context for sexual outlet, marriage must be somewhat different now than it was originally meant to be. Marriage now must in some way accommodate those drives.

The response to the problem is found in a classic *dictum* of Gratian that brings together many of the themes and sources that will be commonplace throughout the Middle Ages.[6] Gratian proposed two institutions of marriage that came to be known as marriage *ad officium* and marriage *ad remedium*. The source for the two expressions is probably Augustine's claim that 'what is a service for the healthy, is a remedy for the sick.'[7] The first institution was in Paradise where there would have been honourable marriage, and an unsoiled marriage bed (cf Hebrews 13:4), conception without ardour, and birth without pain. The absence of ardour or lust in Paradise has been discussed in the first chapter. Aside from some difference of opinion about the intensity of sexual pleasure in Paradise, it was universally accepted that there would certainly have been no undue ardour.

Gratian's statement about the first institution receives further clarification from canonists and theologians. Master Roland specifies that the first institution was for the propagation of the human race *alone*, the technical expression for which is *ad officium* in the words of Peter Lombard, an ellipsis for *ad officium naturae* ('in the service of nature').[8] Before the sin of Adam, marriage was a matter of precept that was to hold until the requisite multiplication of the species was reached. The Lombard suggests that this precept held even after the Flood, which almost exterminated the human race. The implication is that sexual relations in marriage under a precept were good, since God would never bind people to do evil.[9] The procreative purpose of sex was central to its proper understanding. It linked sex now with God's original design, with the way things would have been in Paradise (and for the descendants of Adam and Eve if there had been no sin). As we shall see, procreation was tied to one of the goods of marriage, constituted a legitimating reason for sexual relations, and established the naturalness of marriage and coitus. Of course, refinements were made in the conception of the intention of procreation, but in its broad outline it was relatively unproblematic. Its absence posed problems; its presence resolved most problems.

The second institution was effected outside Paradise 'to eliminate unlawful movement ... so that the infirmity that is prone to foul ruin might be rescued by the uprightness of marriage.' Master Roland speaks of 'the depression of unlawful movement,' Peter Lombard of 'the avoidance of unlawful movement'; and Raymond of Penyafort, using an expression of the Lombard, says that the second institution was 'in order that the vice of the flesh might be restrained.' The technical phrase is *ad remedium*, an ellipsis for *ad remedium concupiscentiae* ('as a remedy for concupiscence').[10]

Marriage took on this remedial function after the Fall. In spite of some early views to the contrary, however, it was not as if marriage before the Fall or after the Flood was in the service of nature, but now was exclusively a remedy. Its remedial character was grounded in its orientation to serve nature in procreation. One might say that marriage was *ad remedium* to the extent that the *ad officium* aspect was at least minimally respected. As Albert the Great puts it, '[Marriage] is principally *ad officium* in which service is found a remedy against the wound

that occurred as a result of sin.'[11] Marriage as remedy is not independent of the procreative finality of marriage and ought never to be
intentionally separated from that finality. There may well be *de facto*
reasons why the finality cannot unfold to its natural fruition in generation, such as the age of the woman, existing pregnancy, or sterility.
In such cases, as will be seen, the remedial nature of marriage is
sufficient to justify sexual relations, to provide a curative outlet for
sexual passion.

The language of healing and medicine is reminiscent of similar
language used to describe the function of confession. Interestingly, St
Jerome, whose description of penance as the second plank after the
shipwreck of the Fall was a commonplace in the Middle Ages, also
describes marriage as a second plank.[12] Another ancient saying associated with the medicinal role of penance was, 'Contraries are cured
by contraries.'[13] Pride is cured through humility, avarice through
generosity, lechery through mortification of the flesh. If marriage is a
medicinal remedy, then it too must cure through contraries, driving
out sickness and morbidity in the way humility drives out pride and
mortification drives out lechery. Albert does not deny the medicinal
character of marriage, but he notes the unique nature of the disease it
is meant to heal. The infirmity of concupiscence is not like other infir-
mities, since it is not entirely driven out by the remedy of marriage.
Concupiscence is like a chronic disease rooted in corrupt human
nature, so the medicine can have only limited effects. It can dispel
vices that may have arisen from concupiscence, stabilize the orders of
nature and grace from being subverted by morbidity, and alleviate the
sickness that is an inevitable punitive concomitant of original sin even
after baptism.[14] It should be noted that the healing effects of matrimony are not simply the result of the fact that marriage offers an
outlet for natural sexual inclinations. First and foremost it is the grace
of the sacrament of matrimony through which, according to Aquinas,
'[Concupiscence] is repressed in its root.'[15]

The teaching on the twofold institution of marriage provided an
account that accommodated the sexual proclivities of post-lapsarian
human beings. It broke the link between marriage, sex, and procreation that was believed to be characteristic of the state of innocence.
Although procreation was never entirely eliminated, the positive and
exclusive intention to procreate was no longer seen to be a necessary
condition of marriage and intercourse. Gratian is unequivocal about

this: 'Therefore, given that they are admonished to return to the natural use because of incontinence, it is clear that they are not commanded to join together solely for the procreation of children.'[16]

THE NATURALNESS OF MARRIAGE

Both the early decretists and the theologians followed the lines of development laid down by Gratian and Peter Lombard in regard to the twofold institution of marriage.[17] Implicit in this view was the perception of marriage as an integral dimension of the natural order, since the state of innocence was the state of pristine, uncorrupted nature. However, this implication was late in being drawn out and was not adequately discussed until the thirteenth century.

William of Auxerre was one of the earliest to raise the question of the naturalness of marriage, or more precisely, to ask whether marriage pertains to the natural law. His concern is with marriage as a monogamous union characterized by the obligation of mutual sexual fidelity of the spouses. He approaches the subject first by dealing with an issue that might be seen to damage any claim to naturalness for this type of marriage, namely, the anomalous examples of Old Testament figures in polygamous unions. His guarded response ('without prejudice to a better opinion') is not matched by his bald assertion that monogamy is a matter of natural law. He goes on to explain that the biblical examples do not undercut his position because they are simply examples of divine dispensation for reasons dictated by the circumstances of the times.[18] William's argument that 'one woman is to be of one man' establishes a connection with natural law straightaway, although the connection is not immediately apparent, since William makes the link with natural law without citing his sources. According to the first argument, it is a directive of natural reason that, 'You shall not do to another what you do not want done to yourself.' This is, of course, another way of saying, 'Therefore, whatever you wish that men do to you, do to them' (Matthew 7:12). The connection with natural law lies in the fact that this text is used by Gratian and Peter Lombard as an illustration of the natural law.[19] William then applies the idea to marriage: 'No husband would want to divide his flesh with many. Therefore, he ought not divide his flesh with many women.'[20]

Two other arguments trade on the movement from what was considered to be natural to natural law. Turtle-doves tend to be monogamous and consequently observe a kind of chastity similar to what is required of humans. If some animals do this naturally, there is all the more reason for it to be expected of humans; so monogamy is of the natural law. Finally, William argues from the epigram 'The voice of all is the voice of nature.' Since all say monogamy is good, it must be the voice of nature, so it must be by natural law.

Assuming these arguments, William advances an answer to the question whether marriage pertains to the natural law. A threefold distinction is made in regard to the extension of the natural law. *Most universal* natural law applies to all things and is a remote ground for any union, since nothing is completely unrelated to other things. *More universal* natural law is what dictates to all animals. To the extent that marriage consists in the union of male and female, it is of the natural law since this is what the natural law dictates to all animals. This is an allusion to the Roman Law (*Digest*) definition 'Natural law is what nature has taught all animals,' and to the inclusion both by the Roman Law and by Isidore of the union of male and female among the teachings and dictates of natural law.[21] The third type is called *special* natural law, characterstic of those with the use of reason. William grounds the fidelity required of married people in this aspect of the natural law, concluding: 'So, it is a matter of special natural law that one woman be of one man.'[22]

Thomas Aquinas follows William of Auxerre in his own account of the naturalness of marriage.[23] One of the striking features in his account is the absence of appeals to theological sources. The authorities cited prior to the solution to the question are a Roman law definition of natural law as the union of male and female, and Aristotle's claim that man is naturally more a marrying animal than a political animal. The conclusion from both is that marriage is natural.[24]

The natural is either what results of necessity from the principles of nature (such as the fact that the constitutive principles of heavy bodies necessarily cause them to fall downward when they are unimpeded), or what nature inclines to but which is perfected through the mediation of the will (such as the acts of the virtues. We are not virtuous by nature, but nature inclines us to virtue that we can choose to acquire through our own human actions). Marriage is natural in the latter sense. Natural reason inclines both to the principal end and to the secondary end of marriage. The principal end is the good of offspring, including procreation, rearing, and fostering 'right up to the perfect state of man, as man, which is the state of virtue.'[25] This idea is fundamental for St Thomas Aquinas, who makes it do yeoman duty in grounding the goods of offspring, fidelity, and indissolubility.[26] The secondary end of marriage is mutual service. The argument concludes: 'whence nature moves so that there will be a union of man and woman; marriage consists in this.'[27]

Aquinas has no trouble with the idea of the twofold institution of marriage. To the extent that marriage is ordered to the procreation of children, it was instituted before sin; to the extent that it provides a remedy for the wound caused by sin, it was instituted after sin 'in the time of the law of nature' (the time between the expulsion from Paradise and the law of Moses). Actually, Thomas suggests a fivefold progressive institution: before sin (in the service of nature); in the time of the law of nature (as remedy); in the law of Moses that specified the monogamous nature of post-lapsarian marriage; in the New Law when marriage represents the union of Christ and the Church; and in the civil law that determines the amenities following from marriage.[28]

THE GOODS OF MARRIAGE

The idea that intercourse is evil 'unless excused by the goods of marriage' is fundamental to the theory of marriage and sex in the Middle Ages. As noted in the introduction, one of the earliest legislative expressions of this view is found in the synodal statutes of Angers (circa 1217) that note, 'that every voluntary emission of semen is a mortal sin in both males and females unless excused by legitimate marriage.'[29] John Pecham offers a similar rule in his instructions on the sacraments for ordinary parish priests: 'Every commingling of man and woman that the goods of marriage do not excuse is forbidden by the same commandment.'[30] These pastoral regulations are expressions of theological and canonical teachings that provided for their theoretical underpinning.

There was a stock list of *ad hominem* arguments drawn from the Bible that were used to show that marriage must be good. Peter Lombard, for example, proposes several: the institution of marriage in Paradise (Genesis 2:24); the presence of Christ at the marriage feast of Cana and the working of his first miracle there (John 2:2–10); the command to remain married 'except in the case of fornication' (Matthew 5:32; 19:19); Paul's statement that a virgin does not sin if she marries (1 Corinthians 7:28). Besides, marriage would not be a sacrament if it were not good.[31] Peter Lombard and William Peraldus advance these arguments in an attempt to confute heretics, a preoccupation in accounts of the goodness of marriage. Of course, such *ad hominem* arguments may very well persuade the faithful, but they prove nothing against the heretics. It is not that Christ's presence at Cana, for example, made marriage good; rather, his presence there is a sign that marriage must be good, otherwise he would not have graced it with his presence. An independent argument was required to establish the goodness of marriage in the first place. Such an argument was found in St Augustine's theory of the goods of marriage.

At the end of the fourth century St Jerome wrote a vitriolic attack against a lapsed monk named Jovinian who claimed that there was no difference between the state of virginity and the state of marriage.[32] One of the results of Jerome's spirited defence of the superiority of virginity was an at best grudging acknowledgment of the goodness of marriage. Although Augustine shared Jerome's views about the superiority of virginity over marriage, he seems to have felt that Jerome went too far in his defence of virginity and came close to denying the goodness of marriage. In response Augustine wrote *On the Marriage Good* in an effort to provide a more balanced view of the goodness of marriage.[33]

Augustine bases his account of the goodness of marriage on the idea of goods in general. There are some goods given by God, such as wisdom, health, and friendship, that are to be pursued for their own sakes. There are others such as teaching, food, drink, sleep, marriage, and intercourse, that are necessary for something else. He then matches up the two sets: teaching is necessary for wisdom; food, drink, sleep are necessary for health; marriage and intercourse are necessary for the association of friendship.[34] Things that are given for something else have no intrinsic goodness; they are good to the extent that they are used for what they were given for. A person who uses them other than in the service of what they were instituted for sins, sometimes venially, sometimes mortally (*damnabiliter*).

Marriage and intercourse belong to the class of goods that are oriented to something else and so are only good to the extent that the orientation is respected. As Augustine says, 'Marriage is good in everything that is proper to marriage.'[35] There are two things proper to all marriages; three proper to the marriage of Christians. Procreation and a chaste fidelity are common to all nations; Christian marriage adds inseparability to those common goods. Together they constitute the three goods of marriage, called by Augustine *proles* (offspring), *fides* (fidelity), and *sacramentum* (inseparability).[36] One of Augustine's more frequently cited accounts of these goods is in his *Literal Commentary on Genesis*:

> In fidelity the focus is on the exclusion of intercourse with another woman or man outside the marriage bond. In offspring the focus is on loving reception, kind nurture, and religious upbringing. In the sacrament the focus is on the inseparability of marriage, and [on the requirement] that a man or woman, if dismissed, does not join with another for the sake of offspring. This is the rule of marriage by which the fruitfulness of nature is crowned, or the depravity of incontinence is regulated.[37]

Fides is a good that imposes the obligation of mutual sexual fidelity on the parties to a marriage. Those who marry must respect this value and not commit adultery, which is a sin against fidelity. To commit adultery is not destructive of the marriage, however; it does not annihilate the union between the partners. *Proles* is a good that imposes on the married partners the obligation to be open to conception and not to interfere positively with the reproductive process in order to try to avoid conception. Simply to practise contraception, however, is not destructive of the marriage. Both fidelity and offspring are moral values that may or may not be respected by married people. Although conscious, deliberate acts against fidelity and offspring within an established marriage were not considered to be destructive of the marriage, a pact to eliminate them from a marriage *about to be entered into* was quite another matter. Such a pact was considered to be a defect in the consent that was required to effect any marriage and so would undercut the possibility of entering into a legitimate marriage. *Sacramentum* as a good does not refer to the idea that marriage is one of the seven sacraments. It refers to the idea that *a consummated marriage* between Christians is a sign of the union between Christ and the Church, with the consequence that such a marriage cannot be dissolved.[38]

The medieval masters discussed the goods of marriage at some length, particularly under the rubric of their excusing function.[39] The goods are said to excuse marriage and to excuse intercourse within marriage; questions are raised about the necessity of the presence and the possibility of the absence of the three goods.

Marriage itself is excused because in its very nature it is constituted by the goods of marriage. These goods are characteristic of marriage *ad officium* so that it would even be correct to say that marriage before the Fall was excused. It is precisely because of this that marriage is able to be a remedy. According to Albert, the goods are effected by marriage in so far as marriage is *ad officium*, and they are annexed to it in so far as it is *in remedium*.[40] Marriage rescues concupiscence through the goods that it has from the first institution, 'and they make it morally upright (*honestum*) even after concupiscence enters the scene.'[41] For Aquinas the goods of marriage compensate for the loss incurred in marriage – the disturbance of reason and the tribulation of the flesh. The choice to marry receives its correct ordering from the goods of marriage, and the consequent union is made morally upright (*honestetur*) thereby.[42]

In these accounts the goods of marriage are often made to converge with the naturalness of marriage by mapping them onto the levels of natural law. In this way it was possible to argue that the goods of marriage were grounded in the natural law and were manifestations of nature: offspring pertains to the animal level of the union of male and female; fidelity is a dictate of the first level of natural reason; inseparability is a dictate of the highest level of natural reason.[43] Bonaventure argues that the command to increase and multiply is itself a precept of nature.[44]

In addition to the ideas of marriage as remedy and marriage as a condition in need of excuse, there is the idea of marriage by way of indulgence; but the interpretation and application of this third idea are not at all clear. The notion of remedy and excuse are not co-extensive. Marriage and intercourse are excused to the extent that they are justified and made morally upright by their intrinsic finality, by their orientation to goods that are intrinsic to their nature. This is characteristic of marriage and marital sexual relations both before and after the Fall. To the extent that it provides a bulwark against concupiscence, all marriage after the Fall is a remedy in its very institution. To say that marriage or intercourse is granted by way of indulgence raises the question whether the indulgence characterizes all marriages and intercourse after the Fall in the way that marriage as remedy is characteristic of such marriages. Perhaps the notion of indulgence is meant to apply only to marriage and intercourse under certain conditions. In the Middle Ages the idea of indulgence is dealt with in two contexts: in general discussions of the nature of marriage and of the moral character of intercourse; and in discussions of the third reason for intercourse (to avoid fornication). Since even the general discussions frequently appeal to the third reason, my treatment of marriage and intercourse that are granted by way of indulgence will be undertaken in connection with the discussion of the third reason.[45]

CONTRACEPTION

The goods of offspring and fidelity provide principles for an understanding of three subjects that I would like to touch on briefly: contraception, impotence, and sterility.[46] Peter Lombard concludes his discussion of the legitimate motives for marrying with, 'So those who come together for intercourse alone are called spouses as long as they do not avoid the generation of offspring by some evil ruse.'[47] This is followed by a text that John Noonan calls the medieval *locus classicus* against contraception and abortion that censures those who procure sterilizing or abortifacient potions.[48] Peter Lombard's remark is primarily about a deliberate intention, made prior to or even as a condition of marrying, to have sex but to avoid offspring. Such an intention undercuts the intrinsic finality of intercourse in marriage, and so would render the consent null and void.

While not destroying a marriage already entered into, contraceptive practices in the sense of deliberate actions to avoid conception while having sex were direct attacks on the primary purpose of marriage and coitus and so were considered to be seriously immoral acts. The means might be the ingestion of potions thought to have sterilizing effects, blocking the entry of semen, or the external application to the genitals of substances believed to be sterilizing. The methods might also involve modifications in the act of intercourse itself, such as withdrawal or, as Robert Grosseteste puts it in speaking about extramarital relations, behaviour in an unnatural manner or not in the proper place, 'lest their iniquity be detected.'[49] Whatever the means, such activity is directly against the openness required by the good of offspring. When potions are used there is the additional possibility that they will be abortifacients, thus compounding the offence with homicide if the conceptus was ensouled. The danger of an unwitting abortion may explain the harsh penance recorded in a confessional collection attributed to Robert Grosseteste: 'If a woman drinks or makes something so as not to conceive she shall do penance for five years.' Albert the Great recommends the imposition of a heavy penance for the use of potions in order to deter their future use.[50]

IMPOTENCE

The response to the question whether an impotent person can marry appeals to a radically physicalist sense of the openness required of the good of offspring. Impotence or the impossibility of having sexual relations 'is a defect (*vitium*) of the spirit, of the body, or of both whereby one is impeded from mixing carnally with another.'[51] Impotence was considered to be an impediment to marriage, not because the act of intercourse pertains to the essence of marriage but because the possibility of intercourse pertains to its essence. The possibility is a necessary condition for effective marital consent because, as Aquinas notes, in matrimony each gives to the other the power over their own bodies in respect of copulation.[52] An impotent person does not have the proper goods to give, if you will, and so is not in a position to marry. It should be noted that talk of impotence is always talk about union, commingling, and coitus, not about seminal emission or ejaculation. The concern is simply with the ability to achieve vaginal penetration. I note this because of the way Noonan describes impotence: 'the inability to ejaculate semen into the vagina, or inability to receive ejaculated semen.'[53] While not necessarily inaccurate, the description is misleading, because even if there is no semen and so no ability to ejaculate semen, that inability would not constitute impotence.[54]

The concern was with impotence *antecedent* to the expression of marital consent (not necessarily known antecedently): a marriage is entered into and the impotence is discovered afterwards. Impotence that might occur *consequent* to a valid consummated marriage had to be accepted and lived with. Antecedent impotence rendered the putative marriage null and void. It frustrated the contractual nature of marriage, the good of offspring, and the remedial function of marriage. The question was whether in such a case the people involved could marry others after separating from each other. In resolving that question several distinctions were made. Generally speaking, male impotence was called frigidity; female impotence was apparently seen to be constituted exclusively by vaginal tightness or constriction (*arctatio*).[55] Impotence was either natural or accidental: natural in the sense of a given fact about the constitution of some adult individuals as such, or natural in terms of age or sexual immaturity; accidental in the sense of being the result of some external force such as castration. The principal form of accidental impotence was believed to be caused by sorcery (*maleficium*); as far as I can make out, it was males who were usually spoken of as being the victims of *maleficium*. Both natural and accidental impotence could be temporary or perpetual.

Discussions of impotence could become quite complex, as is evidenced in the twenty-five questions raised by John of Freiburg in its regard.[56] This is not the place to enter into the twists and turns of these discussions. Some general principles may be noted, however. The presumption was that people are not impotent; impotence had to be demonstrated. Generally speaking, marriage was null and remarriage not permitted in the case of perpetual natural impotence. The idea here is that such impotence adhered to persons, no matter who their non-impotent spouse might be. Of course a person's frigidity could be the psychological result of his abhorrence of his wife and so assimilable to accidental and temporary impotence. Likewise, a woman's tightness might be specific to a particular male or be correctable through surgery or exercise. Such questions were grist for the casuistry of impotence.

In cases of temporary impotence, the marriage was considered to be null, but the impotent person could remarry with the disappearance of the impotence. The obvious case is when impotence is a result of sexual immaturity because of age; it is simply a matter of waiting to grow up and mature. The case most frequently discussed is that of impotence resulting from sorcery. The idea here is that *this* man is hexed in regard to *this* woman, but not necessarily in regard to another woman.[57]

Two epistemological problems were endemic to discussions of impotence – the determination of perpetuity and the determination of sorcery as the cause. Assuming that people are not naturally impotent, if impotence were discovered the understanding was that the couple would apply themselves to try to have intercourse. If after three years nothing had changed, the impotence was assumed to be natural and perpetual. The marriage would be declared null through judicial process on the word of the spouses whose word was to be confirmed by acquaintances ('by the seventh hand').[58] In this case the non-impotent person could remarry after the declaration.

If remarriage was to be allowed, the presumption of natural, perpetual impotence had to be removed in favour of impotence as a result of sorcery. This could be done only through experience that could show that, although the man was impotent in regard to his wife, he was not impotent *tout court*. If this were established, then the man could remarry, since the assumption was that he was hexed only in regard to the one woman.[59]

STERILITY

The common understanding was that sterility did not constitute an impediment to marriage. The same physicalist understanding of the good of offspring is operative here as in the discussion of impotence. Since sterility did not remove the possibility of intercourse and was not a deliberate act to frustrate procreation, the marriage of the sterile could still serve as a legitimate remedy for concupiscence. A twelfth-century commentary on St Paul even advises marrying a sterile woman rather than a fertile woman if she is seen to provide a more agreeable remedy for incontinence.[60]

It is not clear how one is to know whether a woman is sterile except, for example, in the case of a widow who has had sexual relations over some time and not borne children, or in the case of one beyond childbearing age. Certainly, the usual situation would be one in which the sterility becomes apparent after a marriage. In fact, age would be the only certain indicator of sterility, and the marriage of old people was never prohibited. While continence was encouraged for such marriages, it was not required.[61]

Aside from cases of women beyond their childbearing years, sterility and its perdurance would not be known with any certainty. If discovered (in the sense that pregnancy did not follow intercourse over time), sterility did not constitute grounds for separation or remarriage. There is also the element of medical and biological ignorance. Speaking about abnormal menstrual flow (sometimes called continuous flow), which was generally believed to be a cause of sterility, Aquinas says: 'Some women in their youth are sterile and are fertile with the passage of time, and vice versa.'[62] Nor does sterility provide grounds for taking a consort in order to have children through her in spite of the (apocryphal) scriptural text 'The sterile woman who has not left seed on the earth will be cursed.'[63] The curse was not understood to be levelled at some personal fault of the woman; it consisted in the shame and lack of respect resulting from being infertile. The shame was to be borne and did not constitute a reason for separation or a justification for the husband to go outside the marriage alliance in order to procreate children.[64]

The good of offspring and the mutual sexual obligation each spouse owes to the other require as a minimum the possibility of physical union in order to enter into a marriage. It is for this reason that the discovery of antecedent impotence provides grounds for declaring a marriage null and the discovery of sterility does not. While a sterile marriage cannot be said to be open to offspring except in the most extended sense of 'open,' it does provide a remedial outlet for sex and so is consistent with the second institution of matrimony. Where there is the possibility of physical union, the good of offspring requires at least the negative position that, in entering into a marriage, procreation not be intentionally ruled out, and that in marital sex no positive contraceptive intervention be taken to avoid conception.[65]

THE MANNER OF INTERCOURSE

Before dealing with the moral character of sexual relations a word should be said about the manner itself of the behaviour. Implicit in all medieval discussions of intercourse is the understanding that there is a natural and morally correct way to have sex. There are two dimensions to this natural way that might be called the basic form, on the one hand, and the position, on the other. The fundamental requirement of the basic form is that intercourse must be vaginal intercourse. This is a necessary condition of all morally correct sexual relations, since only in this way can coitus respect the natural procreative finality of sex. The natural position is what is sometimes referred to today as the missionary position, the woman lying on her back with the man lying on top, facing her.[66]

The sketch of such an account was already in Augustine, who distinguishes between acting contrary to nature and acting in line with the natural use but slipping in regard to the manner of its execution (defective in its mode). To act contrary to nature is described in a formula adopted in the later Middle Ages – to use a bodily member (or vessel) not granted by nature for such use. I assume this is a reference to oral and anal sex.[67] Augustine does not expand on what he means by natural use that is defective in its mode, but he was understood to refer to sexual positions.[68]

Various distinctions were made in an attempt to capture the difference between infringements against the basic form and those against the natural position or manner. One of the clearest was made by William Peraldus, who distinguished between acting against nature in terms of the substance of the act (non-vaginal intercourse) and in terms of the manner of the act (intercourse not in the missionary position):

> The fifth species [of lechery] is the sin against nature, which occurs in two ways. For sometimes it is against nature in terms of the manner as when a woman mounts or when this act is done in a bestial manner but in the correct vessel. But sometimes it is against nature in terms of the substance when someone procures and consents to semen being spilled elsewhere than in the place deputed by nature.[69]

Mention of the proper form and position for sexual relations is encountered frequently in the later Middle Ages; Albert the Great raises the issue explicitly in a separate question. Although the text of Peter Lombard provides grounds for introducing the question, Albert's reason for dealing with the matter is quite practical. Before offering his account he excuses himself on the grounds that he is compelled to treat such 'foul questions' because of his confessional experience.[70] Confessors were forced to touch on the question of proper sexual behaviour because of the requirement that each mortal sin was to be confessed in its full specification. Priests were caught in a dilemma of needing to know whether married people observed the correct forms, on the one hand, and of wanting to avoid informing penitents of novel ways to have sex, on the other. The passage just cited from Peraldus continues: 'There is to be great caution in speaking and preaching about this vice and in asking questions about it in confession so that nothing is revealed to men that might provide them an occasion for sinning.'[71] Manuals of penance attempted to chart a middle course by advising confessors to be cautious in inquiring about the issue, but, if the evidence suggested they should, to pursue the questioning to determine whether there was an infringement of the correct form.

Albert first approaches the question from the point of view of the possibility of acting against nature with one's own spouse. His concern is whether any form of behaviour is intrinsically a mortal sin. As long as the proper vessel is respected then nothing that a husband does with his wife is in and of itself a mortal sin. The implication is that non-vaginal intercourse is against nature and intrinsically mortal. That matter is disposed of rather swiftly. Albert's principal interest is in the subject of sexual positions, which he introduces in this way: 'it seems that none of the things a husband does with his wife, as long as the proper body or vessel is respected, is in and of itself a mortal sin. But there can be a sign of deadly concupiscence when, for instance, the manner that nature determines through the arrangement of the members is not enough for them and they engage in the ways of brute animals.'[72] The correct sexual position is known from the placement of the sexual organs, and in this way nature itself teaches the proper manner so as to ensure conception.[73]

The importance of Albert's formulation of the first question becomes clear in his discussion of sexual positions. As long as there is vaginal intercourse, deviations from the natural position are not intrinsically mortal sins. Consequently, there could be reasons to justify positions other than the missionary position. Such deviations are graded from the least serious (couples on their side) through sitting and standing, to the most serious that Albert describes as being done *retrorsum*, in the manner of mules. This latter is intercourse from the rear, described in the older penitential literature as being *retro*, in a doglike fashion.[74]

It goes without saying that deviations from the norm were believed to be wrong, particularly when used to achieve variety or novel pleasures in intercourse. By the time of Albert's writing, however, the view had been well established that in some circumstances necessity might require couples to take sexual positions other than the one taught by nature. The two most frequently discussed cases were when physical obesity did not allow the natural position and when there was danger of smothering the fetus in the advanced stages of pregnancy. The received view, with which Albert agrees, allowed deviations in such cases.[75]

Curiously, in his grading of deviations from the natural position Albert does not mention one that seemed to have been viewed with particular horror – the reversal of the missionary position. For Peraldus such reversal is not conducive to the proper emission and reception of semen.[76] This reason does not explain the particular animus with which the position was viewed. That explanation (referred to by Peraldus in the passage just mentioned) is found in Peter Comestor's account of the Flood. Peter cites a work attributed to Methodius in which the Flood is said to be sent by God in response to increasingly serious sexual offences. One of those offences was that women were so crazed that they misused men by mounting them.[77]

Aquinas, echoing Albert, summarizes the matter:

Use of a spouse is against nature when it bypasses the proper vessel, or the proper manner instituted by nature in terms of the position. The first case is always a mortal sin because offspring cannot result and so the intention of nature is totally frustrated. In the second case it is not always a mortal sin, as some say, but can be a sign of deadly concupiscence. Sometimes it can even be without sin when the disposition of the body does not allow the other way [the position instituted by nature]. Otherwise, the gravity is in proportion to the distance from the natural manner.[78]

THE MORAL CHARACTER OF MARITAL RELATIONS

The moral character of marital sexual relations was discussed from three points of view. There is, first, the general question of their goodness or badness, which is, in effect, whether considered in and of itself sexual intercourse within marriage is always evil and a sin. This perspective focuses on the act itself in abstraction from agents with actual intentions. A second approach to the question of the moral character of marital intercourse considers the subjective reasons for having sex. Granted that marital sex is not evil in and of itself, does its upright exercise depend on having special subjective intentions? Are there right-making intentions and wrong-making intentions? These questions are answered in a general way by the traditional account of the four reasons for having sex: to have children, to pay the debt, to avoid fornication, and to gain pleasure. Once the discussion of subjective intentions was launched, there arose a need to consider the concrete circumstances of human living. This raises a third set of questions that focused on the myriad particular situations in which married people actually have sexual relations – a casuistry of sex, if you will.

For Thomas Aquinas the general question of the sinfulness of what he calls 'the marriage act' is settled by his account of the naturalness of marriage. Following his treatment of the preceptive character of marriage he asks: 'Is the matrimonial act always a sin?' The query is set against the background of Peter Lombard's reference to heretics who condemn marriage and its use. Aquinas himself has in mind the Cathar or Albigensian heresy with which his own Dominican Order had been grappling for so long.[79] The beginning and end of his solution leave no doubt as to Aquinas' preoccupations in this question. He begins with the *assumption* that corporeal nature has been established by a good God, and follows his conclusion with, 'unless it is posited, according to the insanity of certain ones, that corporeal things were created by an evil God.'

Between these allusions to Catharism, Aquinas presents his reasoning. On the assumption that corporeal nature has been established by a good God, it cannot be said that things pertaining to the conservation of corporeal nature, things to which nature inclines, are universally evil. Since nature inclines to the procreation of offspring whereby the species is conserved, it cannot be said that the act by which offspring are procreated is universally unlawful in the sense that it is impossible to establish a virtuous mean in the act of procreation.[80] Unlike adultery, which is universally unlawful and so can have no virtuous mean, marital sex allows for the possibility of a virtuous mean, the virtue of 'marital chastity.'

Aquinas is making a very limited claim here *about what can and cannot be said*: If you suppose (ie, assume, posit, grant, say, affirm, or claim without proof) that the truth of 'corporeal nature was instituted by a good God' then it is impossible to say (ie, without contradiction) that 'those things that pertain to the conservation of corporeal nature and to which nature inclines, are universally evil.' In other words, one cannot (logically cannot) say, 'A good God made corporeal nature' and 'All arrangements to which nature inclines for the conservation of that nature are evil.' Since intercourse is one of those arrangements, one cannot say, 'All sexual intercourse is unlawful.' The logical point allows the possibility for *some* marital intercourse not to be sinful. This is the possibility explored in questions such as: 'Can the matrimonial act be excused by the aforesaid goods so that it is not a sin?'

or 'Can the matrimonial act be excused even without the goods of marriage?'[81]

The subject of the moral character of marital sex in general was approached from various points of view: Is it good? Is it bad? Is it a sin? Is it meritorious? Is it excused by the three goods?[82] The first line of defence of the moral uprightness of marital sexual relations is provided by the theory of the goods of marriage.[83] Intercourse was said to be excused by the goods of marriage, not in the sense that intercourse in and of itself was considered evil, but that it *would be* evil unless marked by the right circumstances that are constituted by the goods of marriage.[84] Aquinas notes that the only difference between marital sex and fornication is that the former is characterized by the goods of marriage.[85]

The accepted view is that the goods of offspring and fidelity are the only ones with sexual implications.[86] There is a sense in which this is true, but also a sense in which it is not. In terms of the subjective reasons for intercourse, the good of sacrament or inseparability is not counted as a legitimate reason for sex. That is, one is not morally permitted to have sexual relations 'for the sake of the sacrament.'[87] From another point of view, however, the good of sacrament is precisely what makes the essential difference between marriage and fornication and constitutes a necessary condition for licit sexual relations. As accounts of fornication point out, a man and woman might very well agree to live together and to be open to having children. Such an arrangement, no matter how faithfully carried out, would not legitimate their sexual relations because it lacks a crucial effect of marital consent, namely, inseparability, the good of sacrament. This good is not a function of their intentions but a structural feature of the institution of marriage itself over which the contracting parties have no control. Willy-nilly, to consent to marry is to be inseparably united until death once the marriage is consummated. It is the indivisible union that provides the possibility for morally upright sexual relations. Lacking that, the firmest resolve to live faithfully together cannot justify non-marital sex. So, although the good of the sacrament is not counted as a proper reason for sexual relations within marriage, it is the condition for the possibility of all legitimate sexual unions. This is applicable to intercourse *ad officium* and *ad remedium*, whether before the Fall or afterwards. As Peter of Palude says: 'However, it [coitus] is excused through the circumstances that constitute it to be an act of marriage and these circumstances are the goods of offspring, fidelity, and sacrament. By means of them the carnal act, *even in the time of innocence* was rendered good.'[88]

By way of objection, it is sometimes claimed that in the present state intercourse can never be good because it is always accompanied by lust, which is an evil, and reason is disturbed to the point of suspension by the pleasure associated with intercourse. The responses to these two objections are standard. The lust in question is an inescapable constituent of fallen human nature, and its evil is a punitive residue of original sin (*malum poenae*), not an evil that can be imputed to the persons themselves (*malum cuplae*). Consequently, the mere presence of lust has no bearing on the moral character of the act of intercourse.[89] Of course lust is not a neutral ingredient of the human constitution. While its presence alone in the act of intercourse does not make that act sinful, its promptings might very well lead to actions that are sinful. But that is a different matter, affecting not the nature of the act but the subjective intention of the agents.

The objection from the point of view of the disruptive consequences of intercourse on reason is often made against the background of the description by Augustine of the absorption of reason by coitus. Augustine's observations are made in the context of remarks on St Paul: 'He who fornicates sins against his own body' (1 Corinthians 6:18). His comment is in terms of the effects of fornication, but these effects were not understood to be peculiar to fornication. They were characteristic of sexual intercourse generally. In other types of crime we are free to turn our minds to other things, but 'in the act and at the time of fornication the mind [*animus*] is not free to think of anything else. The whole man is so absorbed by it in his body that his mind cannot be said to be his own but at once the whole man can be said to be flesh "with the spirit departing and not returning" [Psalms 77:39].'[90] This view coincided neatly with a similar view found in Aristotle: 'Pleasures are a hindrance to prudent deliberation, and the more so the more enjoyable they are; for instance, sexual pleasure: no one could think of anything while indulging in it.'[91]

The response to this objection appeals to the institutional nature of marriage. All agree that reason is absorbed by the pleasures of intercourse in the present state and that during the act one has no discriminatory control over rational thought. But a proper marriage and respect for the goods of marriage establish a radically correct orientation and disposition of the partners. The temporary suspension of conscious participation in that orientation during acts of intercourse is not sufficient to make the act itself wrong, any more than the suspension of reason while sleeping makes sleeping wrong. The moral issue does not arise because of the pleasure or the intensity of the pleasure but from the motivation, intention, and manner of seeking the pleasure. St Thomas Aquinas, for instance, says: 'However, pleasure that occurs in the matrimonial act, although the most intense in terms of quantity, nonetheless does not exceed the limits set to it by reason prior to its inception.'[92]

Granted a proper marriage, the goods of offspring and fidelity excuse sexual relations within a union that is confirmed by the good of sacrament. This is the basic structure of Christian marriage. Of course, since it is individual married people who have sexual relations, they must appropriate into their own lives the goods of offspring and fidelity and manifest them in their sexual acts. It is possible, in other words, to act sinfully in the context of a proper marriage. The goods of marriage excuse individuals only to the extent that the goods become concrete expressions of the reasons or intentions that the married partners have in their sexual behaviour. The analysis of the moral character of sexual intercourse must take into account not only the goods of marriage but the reasons, intentions, and purposes of individuals in acting. This was done by the scholastics in their accounts of the *causae* of coitus – the subjective intentions of people engaged in sex, that for the sake of which they act. Peter Lombard's account of the conditions under which the goods excuse intercourse is developed through an appeal to what would become the standard four reasons for sexual relations.[93]

4

Legitimate Reasons for Marital Relations

Discussions of the morality of marital relations invariably deal with the different types of reason or intention of the husband and wife for engaging in intercourse. Such reasons are usually signified by the term *causa* ('by reason of,' 'for the sake of'). While both Gratian and Peter Lombard mention different kinds of intention, neither proposes a systematic account of intentions. The tendency of their commentators, however, was to provide just such accounts, which were meant to be all-inclusive. Two sets were current up to about the mid-thirteenth century.

REASONS IN GENERAL

One division of intercourse subsumed the reasons under terms that primarily connoted the moral character of the relation. Although there were slight variations in the terminology, the division was usually into three types. There were, first, the correct and upright intentions whose presence made intercourse sinless. These were, at least, the intention of procreation and the intention of 'paying the debt.' I say 'at least' because there was some debate over whether intercourse to avoid incontinence ought to be included. The terms used for this first type of intercourse were 'legitimate' (*legittimus*), 'conjugal' (*coniugalis*), or 'licit' (*licitus*). The second type of intention was less than ideal but saved intercourse from being seriously sinful. St Paul was understood to have had this sort in mind when he spoke of conceding marriage 'on account of fornication' (1 Corinthians 7:2). The conditions as expressed by the Lombard are: 'When there is an absence of the good of offspring but with fidelity respected, [coitus] for the sake of incontinence is not excused to the extent that it is faultless, but the fault is venial.'[1] The terms for this type of intercourse are 'fragile' (*fragilis*), 'carnal' (*carnalis*), or 'permitted' (*permissus*). Finally, there are improper reasons that render marital intercourse mortally sinful. They are usually connected with pleasure or embrace a whole set of circumstances of time, place, the condition of the woman, and the manner and position in which intercourse occurs. The term used for this type of sexual relation is 'impetuous' (*impetuosus*).[2]

Although in use for a century or more, this division did not win the day. Concurrent with it was another division that was more descriptive of the intentions themselves. This division was elaborated in reference to Gratian's account of the twofold institution of marriage. Although the decretists did not show much interest in developing the notion of the two institutions, they discussed the implications of the text for the morality of marital sexual relations. Rufinus, an early commentator on Gratian, notes an apparent conflict between Gratian's remarks and other texts in the *Decretum* that seem to contradict the position of Gratian. To resolve the conundrum, Rufinus proposes a division of intercourse to show that the problematic texts are to be interpreted as applying not to coitus in general, but to particular types.[3]

He first divides coitus into spontaneous intercourse and intercourse that is demanded by the debt. The latter is not sinful.[4] Spontaneous intercourse is further divided into what is according to the natural use and what is against nature. The latter is an enormous crime.[5] Intercourse according to the natural use is divided into three types: (1) for the sake of offspring, which is sinless; (2) for the sake of [avoiding] incontinence, which is a venial sin; (3) for the sake of satisfying lust, which is said to be a mortal sin.[6] A similar approach is taken by the canonist Huguccio in his commentary on Gratian's *dictum* and by the *Ordinary Gloss* in its commentary on the canon immediately following the *dictum*.[7] These later discussions subsume the intention of paying the debt under reasons connected with the natural use. In this way they end up with four reasons. Raymond of Penyafort, a consummate canon lawyer, provides a summary of these four reasons:

These goods have the power to excuse from sin if, respecting the fidelity of the marriage bed, spouses come together for the sake of children. Consequently, note that 1) sometimes spouses commingle for the sake of [*causa*] having children, 2) sometimes for the sake of paying the debt, 3) sometimes for the sake of [overcoming] incontinence or of avoiding fornication, 4) sometimes for the sake of satisfying lust. In the first and second case there is no sin, in the third there is venial sin, in the fourth there is mortal sin.[8]

In spite of some difference of opinion about the moral evaluations stated in this text, by the middle of the thirteenth century the division itself was generally accepted. While commenting on Raymond of Penyafort's account, William of Rennes notes that the masters are accustomed to distinguish only four reasons. I assume the masters here are the canon lawyers and theologians whose fourfold distinction can be traced back from the *Ordinary Gloss* on Gratian, through Huguccio, to Rufinus.[9] The meaning, application, and moral evaluation of each of these reasons have their own problems that will be dealt with in this and the next chapter.[10]

FOR THE SAKE OF OFFSPRING

The least problematic of all the reasons for intercourse is that of offspring, that is, marital intercourse for the sake of, for the purpose of, with the intention of having children. Raymond is content to cite the authority of Augustine: 'Conjugal union for the sake of generation is without fault.' If there could be no such union without sin, God would never have issued the command to increase and multiply after the Flood (Genesis 9:1), since at that time (after the Fall) couples could never have had sexual union without carnal concupiscence.[11] The principle was clearly expressed by Gregory the Great: 'So, legitimate carnal union ought to be for the sake of offspring, not pleasure, and for the sake of creating children, not of satisfying vices.'[12]

Intercourse for the sake of offspring exemplifies everything that is good about sexual relations. It coincides with the original divine plan for marriage that was designed to be in the service of nature (*ad officium*); it respects the natural orientation of the reproductive organs towards generation; it corresponds with the good of offspring. This last, however, must be properly understood. The good of offspring was never envisaged simply as the physical reproduction of children; in fact it has little to do with successful reproduction at all: 'Again, note that the good of offspring does not mean offspring itself, which is sought sometimes for reasons of hereditary succession, but it is the hope and desire for offspring in order to bring them up religiously. Many have offspring who do not have the good of offspring.'[13]

Positively, this good implies an active openness to conception, informed by the intention of rearing the children in the ways of God. Negatively, it implies that nothing be done intentionally that would impede the natural process of generation, since such an impediment would be inconsistent with the requisite desire and hope. Marital intercourse for the sake of offspring, meeting the demands of the good of offspring, would be excused from any fault. In fact, it would be an act of the virtues of piety and religion, since its aim is to bring children up with an eye to the worship of God (ad cultum Dei).[14]

Albert the Great believes that marital intercourse for the sake of offspring, when nature and virtue unite in the sex act, is a good act exemplifying the original design of God for sex in marriage. Marriage is substantially ordered to the service of nature and so cannot be said to be conceded or to be granted by way of indulgence without qualification. It is conceded to cover intercourse that is moved by lust (ad remedium). Sexual relations for the sake of offspring, out of marital fidelity, or to pay the debt are in no need of indulgence. Whether the idea of concession comes into play depends on the reason and motive accompanying the sexual act.[15] Thomas Aquinas is of the same view.[16] However, in his earlier commentary on the Sentences he introduces a refinement that clarifies his understanding of the concept of the good of offspring. Nature is oriented to offspring in the order of creation, so to bring one's intention in line only with the intentionality of nature is to remain in a realm where intercourse cannot be undertaken without sin. The intention of nature must actually or by way of habit be referred 'to the intention [of having] offspring in so far as it is the good of the sacrament.' The 'good of the sacrament' here connotes not the sacramental character of marriage but the idea that marriage is a sign of the union between Christ and his Church, exemplified in all legitimate marriages between baptized partners. Offspring are brought under the good of the sacrament when the intention of having children is referred beyond the natural reproduction of the species to embrace a reference to God and education in the ways of God. Aquinas is quick to add, however, that this is not because the motion of nature in this case is evil, 'but that it is imperfect unless it is oriented to a further good of matrimony,' meaning the good of the sacrament.[17]

In the previous text from Aquinas, mention was made of intention 'actually or by way of habit.' This is a commonplace distinction among medieval writers. An actual intention is one that is consciously and explicitly formulated, governing the execution of an act. Someone, seeing a hated enemy, says, 'I am going to kill him,' takes aim and shoots him to death. In this case he shoots him with the actual intention of killing him. An habitual intention is not quite so clear-cut, nor is it always easy to determine its presence. It begins as an actual intention at some point. A judge, for instance, might take an oath expressing his intention to uphold the constitution and the laws of the land. He then goes on to perform his functions as a judge, perhaps for thirty or forty years, without ever again expressly formulating that intention. His actions, judgments, and decisions, however, show him still to have the original intention and to be acting under its influence. Unless there is evidence to the contrary, one assumes that a person continues to perform a class of actions over time *with* the intention that was actually made when that class of actions was first undertaken.[18]

There was a tendency to require that the intention of offspring be in the forefront as an actual intention if it was to render the intercourse sinless, virtuous, and meritorious. Bonaventure hints at this when he says that sexual relations for the sake of offspring can be without any fault 'if the intention lasts from beginning to end so that the mind is not deflected to something else; but this is extremely difficult.'[19] Aquinas says that 'to the degree that they [the goods of fidelity and offspring] are *in actual intention* they make the marriage act morally upright (*honestum*) in regard to the two goods that are concerned with that act.' Peter of Tarentaise adds that where there is another motive the act is not entirely excused.[20] In the fourteenth century, Durandus of St Pourcain and Peter of Palude seem to require the same degree of intentionality, although they do not use the language of 'actual' intention. Durandus speaks of the act being *ordered* to the principal end (offspring); Peter of Palude speaks of its being *principally intended*: 'Nonetheless, it must be realized that whenever procreation of offspring is possible, which is the principal end, unless it is principally intended the act is always disordered and vitiated because it is not performed as it ought when it is not performed for the purpose for which it was instituted when that is possible.'[21]

At the level of theory, then, the reason for intercourse 'for the sake of offspring' can be realized in its fullest sense only when it is expressed in actual intention. An habitual intention is not enough. The implication is that marital sexual relations at the existential level of operation would probably be frequently at least slightly disordered and so mildly sinful. This suggests that the theory of sexual relations in marriage had not progressed much beyond an ancient view, attributed to St Augustine, which classed sexual relations that were unaccompanied by the desire for offspring (*excepto desiderio filiorum*) among the class of minor sins.[22]

Another possibility is that intercourse for the sake of offspring was not considered the only intention able to legitimate sexual relations. Perhaps there were other reasons sufficiently powerful not only to excuse the act but to render it immune to the need for concession or indulgence. In fact the *Ordinary Gloss* on the text just cited comments on the word 'desire': 'add "and for the sake of paying the debt,"'[23]

THE MARITAL DEBT

Discussions of the conjugal debt (*debitum coniugale*) are cast in the legal terms of justice and mutual rights, using what one author calls a 'debt model.'[24] Debts are owed, or paid; sometimes payment is asked for, sometimes it is demanded; sometimes payment is made, sometimes it is withheld. Nothing is gained by fudging the matter through translations that attempt to take the edge off this analogy with the world of finance. Consequently, the usual Latin terminology will be translated as follows: *debitum* as 'debt'; *reddere debitum* as 'to pay the debt'; *exigere debitum* as 'to demand the debt'; *petere debitum* as 'to ask for the debt'. The last two expressions are ellipses for 'to demand payment of the debt' and 'to ask for payment of the debt.'[25]

To analyse sexual relations in terms of the marital debt does not reduce those human relations to justice and obligation, nor does it imply any denial of love, friendship, and mutual affection. However, a debt owed in justice is one thing; love is quite another. To mix the two distorts the medieval conception of marital sexual relations in the name of what one writer calls 'a real *translation*.' He says of Aquinas, 'Because of our dichotomous dissociation of justice from love we do wrong to translate the expression [*redditio debiti*] as "paying one's debt." A real *translation* is called for, and "rendering a due love" comes nearer St. Thomas' meaning ...'[26] No textual evidence is offered for this interpretation, nor could any be forthcoming. Such an interpretation would be difficult to reconcile with some of the ideas traditionally associated with the teaching on the debt. For instance, what could be made of the idea that one could vow not to ask for the debt, or that a sexless marriage by mutual consent is a desirable arrangement? Would this mean that a marriage without due love was being recommended? To stray from the debt-justice model would make nonsense out of this aspect of the teaching.[27]

Generally speaking, marital relations for the sake of paying the debt were considered to be sinless, and to be meritorious and an exercise of the virtue of justice for those in the state of grace. The view was grounded on the formidable authority of St Paul and St Augustine. To support his position Raymond of Penyafort contents himself with citing Augustine: 'Augustine, "Pay the debt. Even if you do not demand, pay. God will count it for your perfect holiness if you do not demand what is due you, but you pay what is due your wife."'[28] No further comment is made, nor does William of Rennes add any gloss to this text. However, the idea had been developed earlier by Raymond in his discussion of the effects of marriage, two of which are the power each marriage partner has over the other's body, and the mutual compulsion each lies under to pay the debt to the other. These effects emphasize two different facets of the marital sexual relationship, and both are rooted in the text of St Paul that underlies this whole doctrine: 'Let the husband pay the debt to his wife, and the wife also in like manner to the husband. The wife does not have power over her own body, but the husband; likewise, the husband does not have power over his own body, but the wife [1 Corinthians 7:3–4].' The interlinear gloss at the beginning of the fourth verse clarifies the relationship between the two verses by glossing with a 'because' (quia); that is, the debt can be demanded because each has power over the other's body.[29]

Mutual power over each other's body and the obligation of the debt ground the fidelity each owes to the other, making of adultery a sin of injustice. Both prevent either spouse from entering religion or practising continence without the consent of the other. These effects come into play after a consummated marriage, that is, after the first act of intercourse of a properly contracted marriage. This teaching was in potential conflict with another widespread teaching. After the expression of marital consent and before the marriage was consummated, there was a legally sanctioned possibility for either spouse to enter religious life within two months after the marriage ceremony.[30] One would think that decisions about entering religion would have been made before a marriage and that if they had not been made the two-month period after the expression of consent would not be likely to make much difference in practice. It is conceivable, however, that parental pressures could be sufficiently strong to force a marriage, but that the married state itself provided the independence from parents to satisfy a desire to enter religion. Whatever the realities of the situation, it was possible for either to enter religion under such circumstances. The potential for a conflict of rights was present if the desire to enter religion was entertained by only one spouse.

On the one hand, each had the right to ask for sex and the duty to pay the debt when asked. On the other hand, each had the right to enter religion within a two-month period prior to consummation. Did this latter give the right to refuse to pay the debt for two months after the expression of consent? There is really no conflict of rights here. The ecclesiastical law was understood to give to each, after the expression of consent, a two-month period for further deliberation about entering into religious life. With this came the right to refuse a request for sex, a right that was considered to override the right each had over the other's body. This means, as Aquinas notes, that the initial transfer of sexual rights in the marital consent is not absolute but is under an implied condition that one of the spouses does not 'fly off to the fruits of a better life' within the allotted time. Neither is bound to pay the debt immediately after the marriage has been contracted.[31]

What if the wife decides to avail herself of the ecclesiastical right to enter religious life and refuses the debt when asked, only to have the marriage consummated by force? Such a case was posed by William of Rennes in his gloss on Raymond of Penyafort. Given that the woman protests that she wants to enter religion, is she still free to enter? William says that this is a *questio dominicalis* (a disputation held on Sundays in lieu of lectures) about which there are different opinions. Much earlier, Alexander of Hales had introduced the question and indicated a difference of opinion among unnamed authors. Alexander says that marriage is to be considered consummated and the husband is not to be thought of as having raped his wife; William of Rennes says that the wife cannot contradict her husband. Neither author allows the wife to enter a monastery if she was forced to submit to intercourse.[32] Bonaventure too considers the marriage in such a case to be consummated because the intercourse took place within marriage and is grounded in voluntary consent (meaning consent to the marriage). Consequently, the intercourse is to be judged as being voluntary. He then adds, but does not elaborate: 'Furthermore, the very concept of consent implies liberty, but bodily union does not [imply liberty] in the same way.' In the sense that marriage gives power over one's own body to the other, the statement is true enough; but Bonaventure here countenances force even in the face of the legal right the woman has to enter religion within a stated period of time.[33] In the case of force these authors acknowledge the priority of the rights and obligations attached to the marital debt over the right to enter religion.[34]

The theory of the debt is clear enough in the abstract. It implies a right to ask for sex and an obligation not to deny the one who asks. As such it provides grounds for the mutual sexual fidelity of the spouses. Furthermore, the sexual rights created by the marriage bond are equal rights; the man, who in every other area of medieval life enjoyed superiority because of his maleness, was not considered to have any more rights or to be advantaged or superior in matters relating to the conjugal debt. This equality obtained only in sexual matters, however. A gloss on Gratian is quick to point this out. The text of Gratian enunciates the general, unconditional statement: 'With us, what is not permitted to women is equally not permitted to men, and the same servitude is considered under equal conditions.' It is glossed: 'In regard to paying the debt and observing fidelity, but not in other things.'[35]

This gloss expresses the generally held view of theologians and canonists after Gratian and Peter Lombard.[36] Aquinas, however, in responding to the question whether the husband and wife are equal in the matrimonial act, seems to depart from this view by distinguishing between equality of quantity and equality of proportion. Equality of quantity is absolute equality or sameness; a pound of butter is equal to a pound of gold *in weight*. Aquinas rules this sort of equality out of marriage completely; but it seems that this is precisely the sort of equality accorded to the marriage debt by the tradition. He is clear, however, that in regard to equality of quantity, 'the husband and wife are not equal in marriage, neither in the conjugal act in which what is more noble is due the husband, nor in regard to the administration of the home, in which matter the wife is ruled and the husband rules.'

Equality of proportion is found between two ratios of the same species, such as double to double. The relation of ten to five is equal to the relation of four to two; they are both related as two to one. How is this to be translated into marriage terms? The common species or idea here is spousal responsibility. The man (10) is superior to the woman (4), but his responsibilities (5) are greater than the woman's (2). To the extent that the man is bound to the responsibilities of man (10/5) and the woman to the responsibilities of woman (4/2), they are proportionally equal. So, for Aquinas, the equality of husband and wife in regard to sex is the same as the equality in regard to the running of the house, which is certainly not the equality suggested by the theory of the debt.[37]

I suspect the reason Aquinas took the position he did was because he was focusing on the inequality in the sexual act itself, in which the male was thought to be the active force, the female the passive force; but both are acting in the proper manner designed for each. Furthermore, the question is asked in terms of the matrimonial *act*, not from the legal point of view of equal rights to the marriage debt, although Aquinas applies his view to the subject of the debt. Albert, on the other hand, distinguished between paying and demanding the debt (equals) and the act of generation (unequals). Perhaps Aquinas had not read his master closely enough here.[38]

The equality in question must be seen in the context of the moral structure of marital sexual relations viewed from the standpoint of justice. Particular sexual acts were seen to be initiated by one who asks (*petere*) or demands (*exigere*). The response is invariably conceived as payment. The husband and wife have equal *rights* to ask or demand, and both lie under the *duty* to respond when asked. The relation might be seen as one in which each holds against the other a demand note that can be called up at any time. The right is rooted in the power each has over the other's body; the duty is correlative to that right. As already noted, the authority for this conceptualization is found in the medieval reading of St Paul's instruction to the Corinthians (1 Corinthians 7:3–4) about the relations of husbands and wives. Commentators emphasize the prescriptive, obligatory nature of the duty to respond sexually when asked. A twelfth-century commentary on Gilbert de la Porrée states the case succinctly: 'once the union is entered into, each, willy-nilly, is bound by the necessity of precept to pay the debt to the one making the demand.'[39]

While there was an acknowledged requirement to pay the debt, neither spouse was considered under a duty or obligation to ask for sex, and so either could vow not to ask, although neither could unilaterally vow continence.[40] To ask for sex is a right, and no one is bound to use a right that has been granted him for himself alone.[41] There was, however, a middle ground between the situation in which sex was explicitly requested and the situation in which it was not sought at all. Sometimes a request or demand may not be explicit but may be signalled. In such a case the signs ought to be picked up by a sensitive spouse. This might be called an interpretive demand that required a response. Aquinas insists that while indeed it is better to be continent, it is stupid presumption to insist on continence in the face of indicators signalling a desire for sex in one's spouse. This teaching about the need to be open to the signals of sexual desire is invariably presented along gender lines; the wife gives the signs, the husband is to be sensitive enough to interpret them. Aquinas offers the reason: 'For the husband, because he has the more noble part in the conjugal act, is naturally more disposed than his wife not to be ashamed to ask for the debt. Consequently, the wife is not bound to pay the debt to her husband who does not seek it in the way the husband [is bound to pay it] to his wife [who does not seek it].'[42]

Of course, as with any general rules governing free behaviour, the requirement to pay the debt was subject to the possibility of paying it, or, in the words of Albert the Great, the debt is to be paid 'according to opportunity and ability.'[43] He poses the case in which the debt cannot be paid because of frequent intercourse or because of other exercises (such as physical hardship or inability because of exhaustion). The exercises he mentions are likely penitential exercises of fasting and vigils. If the inability has arisen from the marriage itself, then there is no requirement to pay the debt; sexual obligations have been satisfied. It is evident from the reason he gives that Albert is thinking of male inability. The husband is not bound to immoderate intercourse. The wife should be satisfied in such circumstances, and if she is not she shows herself to be more a prostitute than a wife.[44] If the inability arises from a cause other than marriage, it is either from a legitimate cause or an illegitimate cause. If from a legitimate cause, then he is not bound to pay the debt 'because God made him unable.'[45] If from an illegitimate cause, then the husband is in the wrong. Should his wife seek sexual gratification elsewhere, the resulting sin is in some way to be imputed to the husband unless he repents and tries to assure his wife's continence.[46] This is reminiscent of a text in Gratian: 'If you abstain without your wife's agreement you give to her a license to fornicate and her sin will be attributed to your abstinence.' The 'license' is interpreted as 'occasion' and the commentators make it clear that in such a case the wife is still bound to observe chastity. Should she commit adultery, however, the husband is partially responsible and cannot use her fall into adultery to dismiss his wife by appealing to the New Testament permission to dismiss one's spouse 'on account of fornication' (Matthew 5:32).[47]

Aquinas introduces a condition on the requirement to pay the debt that subordinates the conservation of the species to the conservation of the individual. The physical well-being of the individual is not to be risked in the service of the generation of offspring. There is always the implied condition that 'the husband is bound to pay the debt in contexts that look to the generation of offspring, *saving, nonetheless, the prior integrity of the person.*'[48] The condition is usually worded in an androcentric manner, envisaging danger to the husband's health should he pay the debt. Peter of Tarentaise speaks of imminent bodily danger; Richard of Mediavilla of notable prejudice to one's own bodily well-being.[49]

In registering his agreement with these views about sex and the safeguarding of health, Durandus of St Pourcain differentiates between 'remaining at the level of general terms' and 'descending to a particular case' (in this instance, whether a healthy spouse is bound to pay the debt to a marriage partner with leprosy).[50] This is just one of a variety of cases found in the casuistry of the marital debt that developed in the Middle Ages. It was inevitable that a casuistry would emerge from reflection on marital sexual relations because of the tension between the almost absolute rule requiring payment of the debt, on the one hand, and the ancient traditions requiring sexual abstinence under particular circumstances, on the other. While the rule would modify many of the traditional prohibitions, these same traditions would force exceptions to the rule.

The teaching on the obligatory nature of the requirement to pay the debt when asked was initially formulated as an unconditioned general rule: 'According to the apostolic words, even if the husband wished to be continent and you [the wife] refused, he is bound to pay the debt to you and God will impute it to him as continence if he cedes not to his own but to your infirmity lest you fall into adultery.'[51] The *Ordinary Gloss* is quite explicit: 'because the one on whom the demand is made is bound to pay the debt at any time whatsoever.'[52]

This unconditional statement of the teaching on paying the debt is characteristic of some early theological formulations. Peter Lombard himself says that, 'although the debt is always to be paid to one who asks, it is not permitted to ask on any day whatsoever.'[53] Robert of Flamborough enunciates a relatively unconditional principle: 'I believe, however, that wherever and whenever a demand is made on you, you are bound to pay unless you can peacefully avoid it.'[54] The Dominican theologian Roland of Cremona says bluntly that a married person can never sin in paying the debt, 'since it is an act of justice.'[55]

Such general formulations are quite misleading. There was a prima facie right to ask for payment of the debt, and there was a prima facie duty to pay the debt. That much is clear and is reflected in a twelfth-century gloss on Peter Lombard that claims that Peter Lombard is 'proposing the general rule (*regulam generalem*)' of paying the debt. In the fourteenth century, Peter of Palude says that it must be held as a rule (*pro regula*) that the debt must be paid.[56] In both cases, however, reference is also made to conditions on the general rule, the earlier author recording the view of a certain Master Odo who had said that payment of the debt is not obligatory on the days of solemn fasts; Peter of Palude mentions the proper time and place. These riders are a recognition that the descent to particular cases will modify the general rule. Consideration of the circumstances of time, place, and the physical condition of the spouses raised numerous questions about the legitimacy of asking for sex and the duty to respond to the request.

Medieval authors had various ways of categorizing the circumstances to be taken into account when assessing sexual behaviour, but there is considerable agreement even across academic disciplines. The canonist Sicard of Cremona, writing at the end of the twelfth century, says that the conjugal act can be immoderate from five points of view: time, mental attitude, place, condition [of persons], manner.[57] In one of his pastoral writings, Robert Grosseteste presents in schematic form what are considered 'to stand in the way of asking for the debt: incest, time, place, sacred place, sacred object, status [of persons], reason.'[58]

The theological *Summa* attributed to Alexander of Hales notes the conditions that can make the conjugal act mortal or venial: pleasure, unnatural manner, prohibited time, forbidden place, and with a woman near pregnancy or at the time of menstruation.[59] Assuming that the intercourse is in the natural manner, the act can be disordered from the point of view of the end, the manner, the place, the time, and the person.[60]

It is considerations such as the above that gave rise to the casuistry of the marital debt. Problems arose with regard the permissibility of asking for payment of the debt and the obligation to pay when asked. The treatment of these questions was not occasioned simply by the abstract consideration of sexual behaviour in particular circumstances. It was required by the confrontation between the theory of the marital debt elaborated after Gratian and Peter Lombard and ancient Christian traditions that proscribed sex at certain times, such as during feasts and fasts, in certain places such as in a church, a cemetery, or in public, and with a wife who was pregnant or menstruating. Such proscriptions had grown and multiplied over centuries independent of any explicit theory of marital intercourse.

The tradition is most clearly seen in the penitential literature that originated in Ireland in the sixth century and was still current in the manuals for confessors of the later Middle Ages.[61] But while the penitentials provide the clearest examples of proscribing sexual intercourse under certain circumstances, they are not the earliest witnesses to the belief that occasional sexual abstinence was required of married couples. Numerous texts transmitted by Gratian in this regard antedate the penitentials.

A version of Peter the Chanter's *Verbum abbreviatum*, which stipulates that spouses 'not mix together throughout the whole of Advent and Lent and on Sundays and feast days,' reflects almost a millennium of ecclesiastical tradition.[62] Over time the various prohibitions had become so numerous that Robert of Courson dubs as semi-heretics those who preach sexual abstinence for almost every day of the week, supporting their admonitions with pious reasons: not on Thursday because the Lord was captured that evening, not on Friday because he suffered on that day, not on Saturday because that day was given over to the Blessed Virgin. In this way they disallow intercourse for almost the whole week and as a consequence they strive to destroy marriage indirectly.[63]

TIME

The evolution of a reasoned, systematic approach to the law and theology of marriage required that the question of sexual relations during the traditional prohibited times be addressed. The times themselves fall into several broad categories: times of private, personal prayer implied by St Paul's admonition: 'Do not defraud one another except perhaps for a time with mutual consent to provide leisure for prayer' (1 Corinthians 7:5); times associated with the liturgical year, such as Advent, Lent, Pentecost, feast days, vigils, and fast days; before and after the reception of the eucharist. In addition, an ancient requirement that newlyweds abstain from sex for several days after their marriage and the general prohibition of intercourse while doing penance found their way into the ecclesiastical law.

In the introduction to Causa 33 Gratian asks: 'Can one pay the marriage debt at the time of prayer?' When he comes to that question, however, he does not repeat the original formulation; he simply launches into the discussion in language more general than the first form of the question: 'However, blessed Jerome in a sermon writes that at the time of prayer one is not permitted to give oneself to any form of marital action [intercourse] ...'[64] The *Ordinary Gloss* accounts for the change from the original question by noting that there is no doubt about the question in its original formulation since the debt is to be paid whenever it is asked for.[65]

A number of texts in Gratian lay down the rule that at certain times there are to be no sexual relations between a husband and his wife. Cumulatively, the times mentioned in these canons represent a substantial number of days in a year, particularly when the details of general references to feast days and fast days are expanded. The actual periods mentioned in Gratian are the following:

– time of prayer in general (33.4.1; 33.4.12)
– the eucharist (33.4.1). This canon requiring sexual abstinence before communion is complemented by a later canon stipulating abstinence 'three or four or seven days' before communion.[66]
– 'the days of the birth of the Lord or other feasts' (33.4.2)
– fast days (33.4.3, rubric)
– feast days and processional days (33.4.4)
– processional days and fast days (33.4.5)
– while performing one's penance (33.4.6).

Commentaries on Gratian provide some indication of their understanding of the general references to times of prayer, processional days, feast days, and fast days. Huguccio understands the expression 'time of prayer' to refer to formal periods of prayer in church 'such as Lent and the established fasts and the vigils of the saints, Sundays, and all other feasts.'[67] Processional days were the rogation days on the feast of St Mark (25 April) and the days before the Ascension.[68] For feast days the *Ordinary Gloss* refers to a lengthy ninth-century tabulation of liturgical celebrations 'to be announced to the laity.'[69] This was meant to be a model that could be adapted to particular dioceses; it concludes 'and other feast days that individual bishops in their own dioceses celebrate together with the people.'[70] Neither Huguccio nor the *Ordinary Gloss* on Gratian expands on the mention of fast days. Huguccio does mention 'the times of established fasts' (*tempora statutorum ieiuniorum*), however.[71] It would not be unreasonable to expand the reference with the aid of the early-thirteenth-century Synod of Paris that commanded the observance of 'the established fasts' (*instituta ieiunia*): Lent, ember days, vigils, Fridays.[72]

The accumulated periods for sexual abstinence catalogued by Gratian correspond to the regulations found in the penitential tradition of his day. Gratian bypassed this tradition in the sources he chose to adduce, however, largely restricting himself to citing Jerome, Ambrose, and Augustine.[73] One of the advantageous consequences of using these ancient sources was the absence of specific penances attached to the non-observance of the regulations. This made the task of interpretation easier than if the commentators had had to deal with the wide variety of penances levied against those who were remiss in regard to the requirements of periodic sexual abstinence.[74] Although Gratian ignored the penitential sources, the authorities he adduced supported the regulations found in those sources. Gratian's commentators were left with the task of providing some guidance as to the proper interpretation of the regulations.

All the time periods proposed for sexual abstinence were resolved in the same way. The distinction between demanding and paying the debt was central to the interpretation. The regulations were understood to be binding on the initiation of sex during the prohibited times, that is, it was forbidden to ask for or demand the marital debt then. If it was demanded, however, the other spouse was to pay, the one making the demand being understood to have sinned venially and the one paying remaining sinless. This solution of Huguccio seems to have been adopted by later canonists and theologians. Huguccio notes that even the intention of procreation does not absolve from venial sin the one who asks at prohibited times.[75] The position of the *Ordinary Gloss* is not entirely clear to me, but it appears to agree with Huguccio's position. Commenting on the same phrase as Huguccio, it notes a diversity of opinion about whether it is licit to demand the debt at times of prayer. Some, following the canons of Gratian, say that one ought not to have sexual relations with his wife at the time of prayer. Others understand the canons to be a matter of counsel. The gloss instructs the reader to take a middle course. Sometimes it is a matter of precept not to have intercourse, sometimes it is a matter of counsel. It is a precept not to know her for the sake of pleasure. It is a counsel when one wishes intercourse for the sake of offspring or to avoid fornication.

All this applies to the one making the demand.[76] If it were a true counsel then there would be no sin. In a comment on the first canon in regard to the reception of the eucharist, however, the *Ordinary Gloss* speaks of sinning *in exigendo* (demanding), but not *reddendo* (paying). In regard to another regulation on the reception of the eucharist the gloss says that it is not a matter of precept.[77] It seems that by 'precept' the *Ordinary Gloss* means 'under penalty of mortal sin' and by 'counsel' it means 'under penalty of venial sin.' At least this interpretation would reconcile some of the different comments of the *Ordinary Gloss*.

There are two versions of a canon in Gratian that, I think, would be more the object of curiosity than serious legal concern. In one version (D 23.33) newlyweds are directed to remain virgins on the night of the day they receive the marital blessing. In the other version (C 30.5.5) they are directed to remain in that state for two or three days. The *Ordinary Gloss* says that both canons are proposing a counsel.[78]

In dealing with the question of periodic abstinence from sexual relations Peter Lombard depends entirely on Gratian for his sources.[79] This ensured that later theologians would comment on the subject. Their interpretations coincide with the canonistic commentaries on Gratian. As Alexander of Hales puts it: 'The married are bound not to ask at certain times. Nonetheless, if asked they are bound to pay.'[80] Bonaventure seems to be alone in the view that 'it scarcely happens that on the principal days there is no grave sin.'[81]

In addition to a concern with the regulations themselves, the theologians show an interest in providing an explanation for the teaching. In their view it is not simply a matter of positive ecclesiastical law; the time prohibitions are rooted in the subjective psychological requirements of prayer and worship. In order to pray properly and fruitfully one must be in the proper frame of mind to focus on spiritual things. Sex is antithetical to such high-minded pursuits and so is incongruous with the psychology of prayer. This account is particularly prominent in Albert the Great.[82] In regard to abstinence during feast days Albert says: 'We ought always to hold ourselves worthy and therefore to make ourselves free from embraces that weigh the mind down from being able to rise to heavenly things.'[83] Aquinas reflects the same belief: 'Since it [coitus] weighs down reason because of carnal pleasure, it renders man inept for spiritual things.'[84] Underlying this discussion is a sermon of Augustine alluded to already in which he speaks of man's being absorbed by the flesh in intercourse.[85] Huguccio uses this text of Augustine to interpret a passage in Gratian already encountered in connection with the question of the meritorious nature of marital relations.[86] Gratian's introductory remark leaves no doubt as to the meaning: 'However, the presence of the Holy Spirit is not given at the time when conjugal acts are undertaken.'[87] The absence of the spirit is first interpreted using the sermon of Augustine. The contemplation of higher things is blocked because the whole man is absorbed by the flesh and is totally in the service of carnal concupiscence.[88]

The carnal nature of sexual relations, compounded by lust and concupiscence, is incongruous with the psychological state required for prayer. As a consequence, periodic sexual abstinence is necessary to dispose one properly for prayer and spiritual exercises. This is not to denigrate intercourse, but simply to acknowledge its distracting effects.[89]

The basic expectations reflected in the penitential tradition were left untouched by the canon lawyers, theologians, and pastoral writers of the later Middle Ages. A lengthy list of periods of sexual abstinence remained; the consensus was that at such times neither married party was to request sex. The theory of the marital debt permitted the one who was asked to accede to the request, but the one initiating the request was held to be guilty of venial sin.

PLACE

Neither Gratian nor Peter Lombard raises the question of demanding or paying the debt in a consecrated place, such as a church or cemetery. It is asked explicitly by Huguccio and the *Ordinary Gloss* on Gratian, and theologians at least mention the subject.[90] The common opinion follows Huguccio in distinguishing between ordinary and extraordinary circumstances, but does not follow him entirely in his solution. According to Huguccio, as long as another place is available it is a mortal sin to ask for and to pay the debt in a church.[91] All agree with this position. It is sinful because the holiness of the place is incongruous with such actions when other places can equally well be found. Furthermore, there is also a danger of causing scandal.

In this connection reference is sometimes made to canonical texts requiring that a church be reconsecrated when polluted by 'someone's seed.'[92] In spite of the generality of the expression, however, it is usually interpreted to refer to sexual acts that are themselves sinful, such as adultery, fornication, or violation of a virgin, and that render the act a sacrilege.[93]

Huguccio says that if another place is not available it is wrong to ask that the debt be paid, but if asked for payment is to be made. Such a case could arise during a war, when people might be confined in the church building for a lengthy period of time.[94] The element of necessity requires new principles to deal with sexual proclivities during a period of confinement. The subsequent tradition generally took a more lenient line than Huguccio, absolving from mortal sin both the asking and the paying of the debt at such a time. The holiness or the concern with the purity of the place is not meant to be a snare for souls.[95]

CONDITION OF PERSONS

A third set of questions arose from the consideration of certain physiological conditions of persons. One class comprising three cases is of ancient origin, found in the penitential literature from the sixth century, but by no means restricted to it. This class concerns specifically female conditions: pregnancy, the period after birth, and during menstruation. A fourth, although not entirely unknown to the tradition, is discussed more frequently from the thirteenth century – the question of sexual and cohabitational rights and duties when one of the partners to a marriage is a leper. A common thread running through all four cases is concern for the normal, healthy conception and development of the child.

Intercourse during pregnancy is in conflict with a purely procreational view of marital relations. It conflicts with the first institution of marriage, the natural finality of coitus, the principal end of marriage, and the good of offspring. The conflict here does not arise from impropriety and incongruity but from the physical impossibility of conception by a pregnant woman. It is a useless undertaking, in the words of William of Auvergne.[96] This idea is behind the list of prohibitions from Ambrosiaster introduced with, 'If a wife is taken because of the procreation of children, then it seems that not much time is granted for its use ...'[97] Two of the items on the list are 'by reason of what has been conceived' (during pregnancy) and 'by reason of what has been born' (after pregnancy). This view is sometimes reinforced with two nature analogies. Animals do not continue having sex after the female has conceived, and humans ought to be able to improve on animal behaviour.[98] A farmer does not sow over a field that has already been seeded.[99]

The justification of intercourse during pregnancy rested on the remedial nature of marriage. The marital debt could be asked for with the obligation to pay it, or there could simply be a need to avoid seeking satisfaction outside the marriage union. This seems to have been the understanding of the *prima facie* rights involved in the case considered simply as one marked by the impossibility of procreation. The gloss of Gratian measures pregnancy from the time there is movement in the womb and counsels sexual abstinence from that time.[100]

The problem posed by pregnancy was not simply that it made procreation impossible. After all, sterility and old age raised the same issues and were resolved using the argument from the remedial nature of marriage. The physical health and safety of the fetus was also an issue, and this became more central to discussions of the legitimacy of intercourse during pregnancy. This concern was already suggested in an important text of Jerome first incorporated into the canon law by Gratian: 'Certainly those who say they have been joined with wives to procreate for the sake of the republic and the human race ought at least to imitate cattle. After the womb of their wife has swelled they should not destroy the offspring, nor present themselves to their wives as lovers but as husbands.'[101]

It was believed that intercourse during pregnancy harmed the fetus because of the 'excessive and frequent oppression and pounding.'[102] Oppression could arise from what was called the natural coital position; the pounding, I assume, refers to the act itself. Both concerns apply when the pregnancy is well advanced, the fetus is developed, and birth is near at hand. It is such a case that an early thirteenth-century confessional manual has in mind in its directive to a confessor who is to ask the husband: 'Have you approached a pregnant woman? I ask this because many little ones are enfeebled then, are oppressed, and become epileptics.'[103] Jacques de Vitry adds a spiritual note. Not only is the offspring killed but it is deprived of baptism and its soul is taken from God.[104]

Concern was also expressed about the beginning of the pregnancy. The theological view depended on a text of the Arabian philosopher Avicenna, who noted that the motion and pleasure associated with intercourse could cause the womb of a pregnant woman to reopen, with the danger of the expulsion of the recently formed fetus.[105] Albert claims that the danger is present during the first four months 'before the embryo has taken root.'[106]

Concern with the health and even life of the fetus introduces an added dimension to the prohibition of intercourse during pregnancy. But the theologians did not draw from this any hard and fast rule about not asking for or paying the debt at that time, nor did they see the possible danger as creating an absolute prohibition under penalty of mortal sin. The issue was resolved in terms of the calculation of probabilities, and so thrown back on those having sexual relations. If there was thought to be a high probability of danger to the fetus, then intercourse was considered to be a mortal sin because it would be against the good of offspring.[107]

Albert the Great notes that some say that a pregnant woman abhors intercourse, more if the conceptus is male than if it is female. But Albert's empirical cast of mind goes with the reports of the women themselves who 'say that they get greater pleasure out of intercourse when pregnant than when not pregnant.'[108] The practical conclusion is that a pregnant woman has the added pressure to restrain herself from asking for sex when she is pregnant: 'Therefore, because of the fear created by the great danger [to the fetus], she should rein herself in; but if she avails herself of coitus she does not sin mortally.'[109]

The list of prohibitions attributed to Ambrose mentions 'by reason of what has been born,' adding, 'according to the law,' an allusion to the Biblical regulation of purification after childbirth.[110] The Old Testament regulation makes no mention of sexual abstinence during the post-partum period, but in the calculation of the period of uncleanness reference is made to menstruation. The Christian prohibition of intercourse during the period of purification was based on an analogy with the prohibition of intercourse during menstruation, for which there are biblical prescriptions. In both cases it is a matter of impurity arising from blood; this is why the periods after pregnancy and menstruation are sometimes discussed together.

There are several issues involved in the treatment of the post-partum period: church entry, reception of the eucharist, nursing, and intercourse. The last two are connected in the literature, although it appears that the medieval authors were somewhat at a loss to understand the mention of nursing. All these matters are touched on in the central text in this regard, the response of Pope Gregory I to Augustine of Canterbury. The following question is addressed by Gregory: 'After she has given birth, after how long a time can she enter a church and after how long a time can her husband be joined to her in carnal copulation?'[111]

Gregory distinguishes between the two issues. Church entry and the reception of the eucharist are permitted right after birth if the woman wants to do so; but if she does not her devotion is not to be censured. The Old Testament purification regulations are understood to have been abrogated, and this was to be the official Church position, proposed by Nicholas I to the recently converted Bulgars, incorporated into the canon law by Gratian, and reiterated by Pope Innocent III and incorporated into the *Decretals*. The reiteration of the freedom of church entry seems to have been required in an effort to combat a contrary popular custom that was resistant to official ecclesiastical teaching.[112]

Intercourse, however, was not permitted after childbirth before weaning, or before the mother was purified. It is clear from the text of Gregory that the times are related – the newborn is not to be given over to a wet-nurse until after purification.[113] The reason for requiring sexual abstinence after childbirth seems to be connected with blood taboos and a fear that, if the woman conceives again in the interim, the fetus will be deformed in some way. The Synod of Angers requires such abstinence but imposes a mild penance of ten days for infringement.[114] In an instruction to confessors, Robert of Flamborough is clear about the reason for the regulation. The confessor is to ask whether the man has approached a woman who is menstruating, pregnant, or not yet purified, 'because when conceived during menstruation or before purification lepers, epileptics, and those with other disabilities are wont to be born.'[115]

The reason for the requirement to nurse the baby is not clear, and Gregory gives no reason for censuring the practice of wet-nursing.[116] The *Ordinary Gloss* on Gratian notes that if the milk is not drawn off the mother will get sick. Much later, Astesanus simply notes that a mother ought to nurse her offspring. Abstinence after childbirth provides for that because it ensures that the milk will not dry up, which would happen if she were to have sexual relations and become pregnant.[117]

The moral position regarding this type of intercourse was not widely discussed but, when it was addressed, the common view was that one is not to ask, but if asked the debt is to be paid.[118] Peter of Palude notes that the regulation is one of moral uprightness not strict necessity, so that to ask is only a venial sin. In the case where the woman is ill after delivery, however, and there is fear of death or even of aggravating the illness from the intercourse, it would be a serious offence to ask.[119]

Aside from a passing mention in Gratian, neither Gratian nor Peter Lombard explicitly addresses the question of sexual abstinence during menstruation.[120] This is surprising because the prohibition of sexual relations during menstruation is consistently found in the penitential literature and has, of all the regulations of sex, the clearest biblical grounding. One is not to approach a menstruating woman (Leviticus 18:19; Ezechiel 18:6), and if one has sex with her he is considered unclean for seven days (Leviticus 15:24). Another regulation directs that both be removed from the population and killed (Leviticus 20:18). Belittling comparisons are made with the napkin used for menstruation (Esther 14:16; Isaiah 64:6).

The biblical tradition was confirmed and reinforced by folklore and superstition. Pliny details both the negative and positive wonders associated with menstrual blood. Although Pliny does not link negative effects on the offspring with intercourse during menstruation, one can understand how readers of Pliny might have made the connection. Speaking of spontaneous flow during pregnancy Pliny says: 'Hence when this flux occurs with women heavy with child, the offspring is sickly or still-born or sanious ...'[121] A man risks disease and death if he has intercourse with a menstruating woman during an eclipse or when there is no moon.[122] A smear of the blood or even stepping over it can cause a miscarriage.[123] The works of Pliny were known to the West, and some of his accounts about menstrual blood entered through Solinus, whose material about menstruation was used by Isidore in his *Etymologies*.[124] Although Solinus and Isidore do not relate the effects of menstrual blood on intercourse or the fetus, they do note its negative effects on other living things. Rufinus picks up on these references from Solinus to confirm the view of the unclean nature of the blood.[125]

The principal patristic text in regard to intercourse during menstruation is found in Jerome's commentary on the book of Ezechiel (18:6) where he details the dire effects of such behaviour:

'And he shall not approach a menstruating woman' [Ezech 18:6]. Each month women's heavy and sluggish bodies are revealed in the flow of unclean blood. If a man has intercourse with a woman at this time the fetuses that are conceived are said to draw on the defects of the semen. The result is that lepers and those with elephantiasis are born from the conception. The corrupted blood causes the foul bodies in both sexes to degenerate with deformity of the members in number and size.[126]

After noting that there are appointed times for marital intercourse he continues:

Therefore, the wife should beware lest perhaps, overcome by the desire for intercourse, she conceals [her menstruation] from her husband, and the husband should beware that he does not bring force to bear on his wife thinking that the pleasure of marriage ought to be available to him at all times. This is why Paul says, 'Let each know how to keep his vessel in holiness and purity' [1 Thessalonians 4:4]. In the *Sentences* of Sextus the Pythagorean it is well said, 'The too ardent lover of his own wife is an adulterer.'[127]

The prohibition of intercourse during menstruation was based both on the uncleanness associated with the blood and on the danger to the fetus. Rufinus says that pleasure is to be restrained not only because of the uncleanness of the blood but also to avoid the conception of a defective fetus.[128]

Because of the danger attendant on such intercourse, the biblical prohibitions were viewed as moral and not simply a ceremonial or juridical requirement for the Jewish people. That is, they applied to the Middle Ages as well as to Old Testament times. The nature of the rule, however, needed clarification. Huguccio supplied a complex argument based on a point of law. One can be promoted to ecclesiastical office if not stained with crimes that are punished by death in the Old Testament. Crimes so punished are not venial sins but mortal and, since intercourse with a menstruous woman is punished by death (Leviticus 20:18), it too is a mortal sin. If a man asks for sex, knowing his wife is having her period, it is a mortal sin; if the wife refuses the request it is not a sin, and vice versa. If the one asked suspects that refusal will lead to sexual delicts in the one asking, however, he or she can accede to the request.[129]

As in other areas of sexual morality, the view of Huguccio defines a rigorist position. The *Ordinary Gloss* on Gratian understands the prohibition to be a counsel, which usually means that its infringement does not involve a mortal sin. William of Rennes takes a middle course. He presents the two views and comments that Huguccio's position is truer and more in line with the authorities. This view is not to be insisted on, however. Absolution is not to be denied to those who, in confession, refuse to promise to be continent at this time.[130]

Theological opinion held that the prohibition of intercourse during menstruation is a moral precept (not simply a purity taboo) and so to ask knowingly is a mortal sin unless the gravity of the offence is diminished for compensatory reasons, such as to avoid adultery.[131] Danger to the fetus is central to these accounts. This is shown in the discussion of the permissibility of intercourse with a woman who experiences what was called a continuous flow (not the usual periodic menstrual flows). Intercourse was permitted then because it was believed that a woman was sterile during such times.[132]

Peter of Palude breaks with much of the traditional view regarding intercourse during menstruation by casting doubt on its two foundation stones. He denies that the Levitical precept is moral; it is juridical and so does not hold for Christians of the fourteenth century. He also suggests that there is considerable lack of certainty whether a woman will conceive during her period and, if she does conceive, whether the conceptus will be leprous or deformed. He also argues by analogy from the view about sexual relations between lepers (which will be taken up in the next section). He brings the whole discussion together by way of a conclusion (*epilogendo*) in five points. The upshot is that intercourse during menstruation is never a mortal sin.[133]

The issue of the fear of leprosy where no leprosy is actually present arises in several areas of discussion about sex. We have already seen the contexts in which the fear that leprosy would be contracted by the fetus leads to the regulation of sexual relations. According to Peter of Poitiers, leprosy is not widespread among Jews because they observe the menstruation regulations.[134] Leprosy is proposed as one of the reasons for staying away from prostitutes because it is easily contracted through intercourse. It may not be visible in the prostitute, but if she has contracted it, it grows in her and is easily caught from her.[135] Even simple sexual over-indulgence can result in leprosy.[136]

Such fears were compounded when leprosy was known to be present in one of the spouses in a marriage. The situation was complicated because the provisions for segregation enunciated in the third Lateran council (1179) were in conflict with the requirements of cohabitation that were part of marriage and the obligation each spouse had to the other to pay the debt when asked.[137] Further, the fear of leprosy arose both in regard to the fetus and the healthy party. These concerns regarding married people who had leprosy were late in being considered in the canon law. One of the first pronouncements was made by Pope Alexander III after the *Decretum* of Gratian. Alexander's position was incorporated into an early compilation of the law after Gratian, and from there was taken over into the *Decretals* of Gregory IX.[138] In general, it was held that consequent leprosy can justify the dissolution of an engagement pact but not an existing marriage.[139] Whatever the living arrangements of the married, the healthy spouse must provide care and the necessities of life for the leprous partner.[140]

My concern here is with the question of cohabitation and the debt. Alexander III is clear about the debt: 'If it happens by divine judgment that a husband or wife should become leprous and the sick demands the carnal debt from the healthy, what is demanded is to be paid on the basis of the general precept of the apostle. No exception is found to that precept in the present case.'[141] Such an unnuanced position required some honing. Of course there was always the option of mutually agreed-upon continence, a choice recommended by Albert the Great, for instance.[142] A common view emerged. Because of the danger of infection from association, the spouses were not forced to cohabit, but the healthy person was to dwell nearby. The debt was to be paid sometimes since it would be unreasonable to require abstinence. Occasional contact is not likely to cause leprosy except in the case of the advanced stages of the disease. And this regardless of danger to the offspring, since, as the theologians generally held, it is better to be born a leper than not to be born at all.[143]

The generally accepted view was worked out by canonists and theologians. Durandus of St Pourcain records this view and notes that there is no truth to it except on the supposition that there is imminent danger of infection. This is an empirical question whose answer must be sought from the medical doctors. The doctors say that there is danger of infection and the danger is greater for the healthy man than for the healthy woman, particularly in regard to the worst species of leprosy (leonina). Since the risk is greater for the healthy husband than for the healthy wife, he has greater scope to refuse his wife than she him.[144]

One of the principal challenges facing the schoolmen of the thirteenth century was to evaluate the ancient regulations that severely restricted permissible times for marital sexual relations. Their achievements lie in two advances over the tradition. First, under the influence of the theory of the debt, they reduced to matters of counsel virtually all the old prohibitions relating to liturgical feasts and fasts and to specific days of the week. Observance of many of the ancient controls on sexual expression might be the heroic thing to do, but it was not seen to be mandated under penalty of serious sin. Second, they were inclined to require a rationale for other types of prohibition, particularly for those that today we might call purity taboos. There was an increasing unwillingness to ground the prohibition of intercourse during menstruation, for example, simply on its perceived impurity. In most of these cases a harm principle is adduced to justify restrictions on sex, harm to the husband, or to the wife, or to the fetus. In addition, appeal was sometimes made to medical opinion to determine whether in fact there would be harm.

Measured against the unnuanced restrictions of earlier ages, which, as we have seen, were deplored by Robert of Courson, the scholastic rethinking of the tradition marks a considerable advance in the development of Western ideas of marital sexual relations. One does not detect a similar development in what I have called the problematic reasons for marital intercourse.

5

Problematic Reasons for
Marital Relations

In contrast with the reasons just examined, the third and fourth reasons for having marital sexual relations posed problems. It was a matter of the correct interpretation of the need to avoid incontinence (the third reason), and the proper moral assessment of coitus for pleasure (the fourth reason). That the motive of pleasure should be problematic is not surprising given the Christian-Stoic suspicion of pleasure. That motive would always be a stumbling block. The interpretation of the third reason, however, is puzzling since it seems to fly in the face of the conception of marriage as a remedy for concupiscence.

BECAUSE OF INCONTINENCE

The third reason for marital relations is expressed in various ways: 'because of incontinence,' 'to avoid incontinence,' 'to restrain incontinence,' 'to avoid fornication.'[1] These expressions appear to suggest a situation of sexual arousal and desire, and the eruption of concupiscence and lust that can occur in either spouse (but is usually discussed from an androcentric point of view). The kind of intercourse that follows is described by Rufinus as 'spontaneous,' I assume in the sense that the arousal simply happens and achieves an outlet through marital relations. Huguccio, in an attempt to distinguish between the third and fourth reasons, clarifies the ideas through a distinction between being hindered by pleasure, and anticipating or getting a head start on the pleasure. In the former case one is, if you will, the victim of the arousal; in the latter one works at it by provoking it 'with one's hands, or thought, or by using heat [meaning hot liquids] and incentives so that a person will be up to having more intercourse with his wife.'[2]

This distinction is clear in terms of the *causes* of the states of arousal, but in terms of the motives of the person acting on those states it would appear that in both cases the behaviour is for pleasure. The distinction was maintained because the third reason covered more than the case of an aroused person who had sex to avoid incontinence.

The state of arousal resulting from the spontaneous eruption of sexual desire is conceived of as one that has the possibility of leading to illicit sexual behaviour. Marital sex is available to avoid that immoral behaviour, and so the usual formulation of the third reason: 'to avoid fornication.'[3] In its straightforward sense, the third reason would seem to embrace a large part of the normal experience of married people who had sex because they were sexually aroused. There should not be any problem with the moral assessment of coitus for that reason. Nevertheless, the third reason was not interpreted in a straightforward sense.

The *apparent* connotation – the straightforward sense, as it were – of expressions of the third reason is that the one aroused seeks a sexual outlet with his partner to avoid fornication in himself. An examination of the different accounts of the moral assessment of intercourse to avoid fornication, however, indicates that the differences arose because the expression was understood to apply to two different situations. In the one case the partner who is not aroused initiates sex with the one aroused in order to safeguard that person from illicit unions, or accedes to the request by the aroused person to help that person in their state of arousal. In the second case, it is the sexually stimulated person who initiates sex for his own benefit. A third case, to be examined later, envisages a man who has no immediate sexual desires but who foresees that he will have to be in a compromising situation in the future. To lessen the danger he has sex *now* to avoid fornication *then*.

There was no unanimous agreement about the morality of marital sexual relations in order to avoid fornication, but generally speaking it was considered to be a venial sin. One would think otherwise, given the theory of marriage as remedy. What is it that marriage is supposed to provide a remedy for if not the spontaneous eruption of sexual desire as a result of the presence of concupiscence and lust? One could also argue for the legitimacy of intercourse in such a context on the basis of a literal reading of St Paul who says that spouses can be had 'on account of fornication' (1 Corinthians 7:2) and that if people are not going to be continent they should marry (1 Corinthians 7:9). After counselling sexual abstinence for a while in order to leave time for prayer, Paul advises a return to sex in case Satan tempts them because of their incontinence (1 Corinthians 7:5). On the face of it, Paul appears to have no problem with marriage and sex as means of avoiding illicit sexual unions and out of consideration of people's weakness; he makes no mention of sin in this regard. However, he does make it clear that his preference is for virginity (to be as he is, 1 Corinthians 7:7) and that he is not ordering people to marry but is speaking 'secundum indulgentiam' (1 Corinthians 7:6). One of the sources of the belief that intercourse to avoid incontinence or fornication is a sin is to be found in the interpretation of the latter phrase ('secundum indulgentiam').

Paul is understood to be *conceding* marriage and intercourse, but not to be issuing a command or order.[4] Early commentaries emphasize the contrast between what Paul wants and what he allows, or between the advice he gives in order to eliminate fornication and his not closing the door to those striving for a better life (the life of virginity).[5] This idea is captured in a twelfth-century definition proposed by Robert of Melun: 'Indulgence is the concession of a laxer state of life through which what would be illicit and a sin unless it were in that state is made licit, for the carnal commingling of a man and a woman would be a sin if they did not take on the status of being spouses.'[6] Gilbert of La Porrée links the need for the concession both to the inescapable presence of a nature depraved by the disobedience of its genital organs and to the occurrence of arousal that leads to sex for reasons other than procreation.[7] Paul was understood to be granting a lesser good (marriage and intercourse) than what he himself would like to see chosen. However, that is not how the indulgence text was read by Peter Lombard, who provided the generally accepted interpretation of 1 Corinthians 7:6

I have been talking about the text of Paul as if it solely read 'secundum indulgentiam.' But Augustine used another text that was a decisive factor in seeing a venial sin in coitus to avoid fornication. With few exceptions, Augustine used a text that read 'secundum veniam,' that is, 'by way of forgiveness.' For Augustine, Paul was saying, 'I say this by way of forgiveness, not by way of command.' Since it is faults that are forgiven, it follows that whatever it is that Paul has in mind must be evil and wrong. What he has in mind, according to Augustine, is marriage and intercourse severed from their procreative purpose and moderating the infirmity of concupiscence. What is granted to husbands and wives to avoid fornication is conceded by way of forgiveness, not commanded. 'Evidently when he offers forgiveness he is implying there is fault.'[8] Whether Augustine himself means fault in the sense of personal and blameworthy sin is an open question that need not concern us here.[9]

Medieval writers understood him to mean a venial sin, but then had to specify more clearly what it was that was sinful and granted by way of indulgence. It is not an exaggeration to say that St Paul was read in the 'indulgentia' text but understood according to the 'venia' reading. This is clear in a text of Gregory the Great that was used to justify the choice of the lesser of two evils:

> When Paul saw incontinent people in the Church he conceded the minimum so that they would turn away from the maximum, saying 'However, on account of fornication let each man have his own wife' [1 Corinthians 7:2]. And because spouses only commingled without fault when they did so to raise up children, not to expend their lust, in order to show that what he had conceded was not without fault (although minimal) he added, 'But I say this by way of indulgence, not command' [1 Corinthians 7:6]. What is pardoned and not commanded is not without vice. Indeed he saw sin, which he foresaw could be indulged.[10]

Peter Lombard provided the conceptual framework within which the idea of indulgence was discussed. First, he contrasts marriage in its first institution with marriage in its second institution. Marriage in its first institution both in Paradise and after the Flood was under the precept to increase and multiply (Genesis 1:28; 9:1); the precept lasted until the human race was sufficiently numerous. After the requisite number was reached the precept ceased. Then marriage was granted by way of indulgence; that is, it was no longer a matter of divine command but rather of voluntary choice. We learn this from Paul who teaches that marriage was granted to the human race to avoid fornication. Since to choose to marry is not to choose better things (virginity) marriage acts as remedy but lacks any reward.[11]

Peter Lombard distinguishes two sorts of indulgence, that of concession and that of permission. Marriage and marital intercourse solely for procreation were granted by way of concession. Intercourse beyond the necessity of procreation on account of incontinence was granted by way of permission. In the latter there is some slight fault but it is readily forgivable. Such intercourse is not commanded or conceded but permitted.[12] Peter Lombard's interpretation is contrary to a plain reading of Paul in the text the Lombard had. I suspect he was influenced by texts of Augustine that speak not of Paul's conceding or granting an indulgence but of his conceding or granting forgiveness.[13] The distinction was accepted. Marriage as a state less excellent than virginity was conceded and this was announced by Paul. Intercourse not for procreation or to pay the debt was permitted out of consideration for human weakness. It was saved from serious sin by the good of marriage. It is this type of coitus that is in need of indulgence, not marital relations *tout court*.[14]

The moral assessment of marital relations that were undertaken because of incontinence or to avoid fornication required an analysis of the meaning of the expression and a determination of its range of application. Raymond's unnuanced claim that intercourse for those reasons was a venial sin was not acceptable. When the reason is stated without qualification, it is safe to assume that the case envisaged is that of a sexually aroused person initiating sex so as to avoid going outside the bounds of marriage. There are early indications, however, that the reason was not exclusively understood in that way. Master Roland, for instance, amplifies the expression by applying it to wives, and the canonist-theologian Omnebene speaks of 'his own fornication or his wife's.'[15]

This was an important distinction, since much was made to hang on it in morally assessing intercourse to avoid fornication. Philip the Chancellor was one of the first authors of the thirteenth century to draw out the differences between the two senses. It is one thing to have sex to escape one's own incontinence, quite another to approach one's spouse lest she commit fornication. (I say 'she' because the discussion is usually conducted in those androcentric terms.) To ask in the former case is a venial sin; to ask in the latter case is no sin but an act of justice and fidelity.[16]

The distinction and the moral evaluation of each of its members was generally accepted throughout the thirteenth century. Lack of sinfulness in having sex to avoid one's own fornication is encountered in some early writers and the fact is registered by a gloss on Gratian that notes that the reason given for the position is 1 Corinthians 7:2. The early Dominican canonist and moralist Paul of Hungary explicitly aligns himself with the opinion recorded in the gloss.[17] This opinion had little chance of winning the day, however, since the opposite view was adopted by the major mid-century commentators on the *Sentences*. Albert the Great uses the old Augustinian argument that whatever is granted by way of indulgence (permitted) is directed against sin.[18] Bonaventure provides a reason that is adopted by Aquinas and Peter of Tarentaise. To have sex to avoid falling into fornication is a venial sin because it indicates the presence of a certain *superfluity*. That is, intercourse in that case does not fall under the reasons that could justify coitus, and so the passions are allowed to seek an outlet in a context that is not justified. Intercourse is superfluous because there are non-sexual ways to control one's urges.[19]

This is a revealing position. In effect these major theologians reduce the remedial character of marital intercourse to offering a remedy to one's spouse but not to availing oneself of the remedy for oneself. That this was the understanding is made clear by Richard of Mediavilla, who asks whether intercourse for reasons other than paying the debt or for offspring is always sinful. One of the objections to an affirmative answer is that marriage 'was not only instituted for the generation of offspring but also to avoid fornication.' According to Richard the objection holds as far as avoiding fornication in another (a matter of faithfulness to the contract) but not in oneself, 'because it is not using her according to the judgment of reason that dictates that he ought not to use her except on account of the good of offspring or fidelity.'[20]

The position went unchallenged throughout the thirteenth century but was directly opposed by Durandus of St Pourcain. After accurately reporting the prevailing opinion, he denies that in intercourse to avoid fornication in oneself there is a superabundance of passion such as to be a vice since it subverts reason. In the case in point the situation is quite the reverse since such intercourse is a demonstration of an act of reason prompting the repression of passion lest passion lead to sin. So one can hold with probability the view that seeking to avoid fornication through marital coitus is not a sin. Coitus is not intrinsically evil and it is ordered to a proper end, that of marital fidelity. To protect oneself from adultery is to protect the marriage.[21]

A third case envisaged a situation where sex in the present is not the issue. Here we have a literal application of the idea of avoiding fornication. The question is whether a man foreseeing that he will be absent from his wife for a time can have sex now so as to avoid temptation and a possible fall later. Alexander of Hales had raised the point and replied that such a reason is not sufficient to clear sex from venial sin because other means are available.[22]

Raymond of Penyafort says the third reason for intercourse is 'because of incontinence or to avoid fornication.' In his gloss William of Rennes notes that these disjuncts are not necessarily synonymous. Acting 'because of incontinence' can be understood as seeking a sexual outlet because of arousal, which would be a venial sin. 'To avoid fornication' could be understood to apply to one who has sexual relations to avoid falling into sin, but not to seek pleasure. Of this last William says, 'and then perhaps there is no sin.' He backs away from that suggestion because it would imply five reasons for intercourse, and the masters traditionally acknowledge only four, equating coitus on account of incontinence and coitus to avoid fornication.[23]

This failure of nerve is not shared by Peter of Palude, who attempts to reconcile the traditional view with the suggestion of William of Rennes. In a lengthy discussion Peter presents the case of a man who has intercourse now so as to avoid adultery or worse in the future. He could avoid sin through repression or flight or by ensuring he does not talk alone with a woman. Knowing this, he still prefers intercourse now because it is the most pleasurable means to the desired end. In such a case there would be venial sin because of a superabundance of pleasure, since there is a conscious choice for pleasure that absorbs reason. It is sinful because of the choice of an inappropriate means. If the traditional view has in mind that case, then it is true.[24]

There is another possibility. The man knows that he will have to talk with a woman for some time in a secret and suspicious location, and from experience he also knows that he will be tempted. Likewise from experience he knows that if he has intercourse before going on his journey he will be 'cooled off' sufficiently to safeguard himself from being vulnerable to temptation. In such circumstances pleasure does not move the man but the rational calculation that having coitus now is the best way of avoiding sin on the trip. In such a case there is no sin because of the fidelity to the marriage bond, even if offspring is not hoped for.[25]

The interpretation of the third reason for marital relations offered by the major theologians of the thirteenth century flies in the face of the obvious sense of the idea of marriage as remedy for concupiscence, the straightforward meaning of 'to avoid fornication', and a literal reading of St Paul. If, as would seem to be the case, much of the sexual behaviour of married people was prompted by this reason, then the received opinion would relegate that behaviour to the realm of sin. Not serious sin, but sin nonetheless. Like the common view about the sinfulness of the first movements of sexuality, this is yet another example of a medieval view lying under the heavy weight of Augustine's tutelage. One would like to think that, had Aquinas completed his *Summa of Theology*, he would have cast off that weight and embraced the view of his younger confrere, Paul of Hungary.

INTERCOURSE TO SATISFY LUST OR FOR THE SAKE OF PLEASURE

There is no reason not to accept the word of William of Rennes, writing about 1241, when he claims that the masters of his day commonly accepted four reasons for marital sexual relations, the fourth of which was to satisfy lust or for the sake of pleasure. However, at least up to that date an equally common account divided coitus into conjugal, fragile, and impetuous. There is a rough parallel between intercourse to satisfy lust and what was called impetuous coitus, since both cover cases of marital sexual relations that fell outside the range of justifying reasons. This type of intercourse is unproblematic to the extent that it was conceived to be always sinful; problems arise from two quarters – the reason why it is sinful, and the circumstances that differentiate between its being venially sinful or mortally sinful.

The treatment of impetuous coitus was developed early and established the background against which the fourth reason was frequently interpreted. The jumping-off point for both approaches is a text of Peter Lombard, 'However, when these goods are absent, namely fidelity and offspring, it does not seem that intercourse is defended from being a crime. Whence in the *Sentences* of Sextus the Pythagorean we read, "Every too ardent lover of his own wife is an adulterer."'[26] In the older accounts the Lombard is understood to be referring to impetuous intercourse, and the text of Sextus was illustrative but of secondary significance. Since later accounts give more prominence to the Sextus text, the examination of the text will be postponed.

The criminal nature of impetuous intercourse meant that it was illicit, prohibited, and mortally sinful. But what was impetuous intercourse? As a category it was a catch-all for cases that were understood to be seriously sinful, but a consistent position emerged about what those cases were. In an early commentary on the Lombard's *Sentences* four forms of impetuous intercourse are proposed: (1) to love one's wife as a prostitute by snatching pleasures from her; (2) to have sex during pregnancy; (3) to have sex during the times set aside for prayer; (4) to use a bodily organ not meant for that use.[27]

This is a rather mixed bag combining types of sexual relations that were not treated under the same rubric by later masters. The first form attempts to get at the requisite psychological attitude of a husband towards his wife and establishes a line of development that will be used in interpreting the fourth reason. The second and third forms touch on cases usually dealt with under the debt and, as we saw, were not generally viewed as being mortally sinful. The fourth form is what will be known as intercourse against nature. John of La Rochelle includes the regulation against intercourse in a holy place and adds the menstruation prohibition to that of coitus during pregnancy, in this way constituting five modes of impetuous coitus. He prefaces his account with a definition of impetuous relations, which, he says, are those 'arising from lust alone that transcend the bounds of uprightness and reason and so are always mortal.'[28] This account was incorporated into a brief explanation of the ten commandments written for ordinary parish priests.[29]

Discussions of marital relations from the point of view of the fourth reason (to satisfy lust or for the sake of pleasure) is not inconsistent with the account from the point of view of impetuous coitus.[30] The tendency was to formulate the account in terms of a general principle, however, and not in terms of a taxonomy of cases. The distinction between coitus on account of incontinence (or to avoid fornication) and coitus to satisfy lust (or for the sake of pleasure) was established before Huguccio, but he provided a differentiating principle that captured an important idea. After presenting the four subjective reasons for intercourse Huguccio adds:

> And note the difference between these two cases when, that is, a husband mixes with his wife because of incontinence, or to give an outlet to pleasure and to satisfy lust. In the first case he is overtaken by pleasure and wishes rather to sin in these circumstances than to commit fornication. In the second case he anticipates the pleasure and provokes it with his hands or in thought or by using hot [liquids] and incentives so that he will be more able to have intercourse with his wife.[31]

A more abstract principle was current at the time of Huguccio and it would become the generally accepted touchstone in accounts of the fourth reason. It was occasioned by a text invariably associated with the motivation of lust and pleasure: 'Whence in the *Sentences* of Sextus the Pythagorean we read, "Every too ardent lover of his own wife is an adulterer."'[32] In Peter Lombard this passage is followed by a text attributed to Jerome, frequently referred to as *origo* from its first word.[33] This *origo* text is central in discussions of the interior dispositions required of married people in their sexual relations. There is scarcely an author who discusses the subject who does not at least allude to the *origo* text or to the Sextus passage.[34] Aside from the mention of Sextus, there is no indication that this passage is, in fact, excerpted from a literary pastiche carefully constructed by Jerome using a now lost work by Seneca on marriage.

In the course of describing the evil effects love can have, Jerome provides an example from Seneca of a man virtually driven to madness out of love for his wife. Gratian's excerpt begins with the last part of Seneca's description. In the original, *origo* simply refers to the beginning of the man's love. In its excerpted form it was interpreted to mean the origins or proper reasons for love and marriage.[35] As it appears in Gratian, the text comprises four parts: two from Seneca, which are separated by an excerpt from Sextus, and Jerome's final remarks.[36] The text begins with a passage from a fragment of Seneca: 'Indeed the beginning of the love was upright but its growth was deformed. However, it does not matter how upright the cause may be of someone's insanity.'[37] The Sextus text is then cited: 'Whence Sextus in the *Sentences* says, "The too ardent lover of his own wife is an adulterer."'[38] Jerome then adds another piece from a fragment of Seneca:

> In fact all love of another's wife is shameful, as is the excessive love of one's own. The wise man ought to love his wife with judgment, not affection. The impulse of pleasure does not reign in him nor is he borne headlong to intercourse. Nothing is more foul than to love one's wife as if she were an adulteress.[39]

The passage concludes with Jerome's own words:

> Certainly, those who say that they are joined to their wives and procreate

children for the sake of the republic and the human race should at least imitate cattle and, after the belly of their wife has swelled, not destroy the children. Nor should they exhibit themselves to their wives as lovers but as husbands.

The point Jerome wants to make is that uprightness in marital relations requires that they be under the control of reason. The emphasis is on judgment, discretion, reason – the measured character of sex that is demonstrated by the wise man who is in control of and is not controlled by his emotions. A sign of this control is the respect a husband will have in abstaining from sexual relations during the time of his wife's pregnancy.[40] This is in contrast with adulterous relations that respect no bounds but follow the lead of passion.

The text of Sextus came to symbolize this way of thinking and to have an independent life of its own. It became a moral trope summarizing the medieval judgment on seriously improper, excessive, or deviant marital sexual relations.[41] Because of the text's popularity, its history is somewhat complex. I would like to digress a bit to comment on that history before taking up its meaning and use by the canon lawyers and theologians after Gratian.

It is known with a considerable degree of confidence that the text itself is from a Greek collection of gnomic sayings by a man named Sextus. The collection was in existence at least at the time of Origen. It is likely that it was non-Christian originally, but in its extant form the collection has been reworked by a Christian compiler. Rufinus of Aquileia translated the sayings into Latin about AD 400, and in his preface he reinforced what seems to have been a general belief that the Sextus in question was Pope Xystus II (257–8). Jerome vehemently denied the ascription to the martyr-pope, opting rather for the ascription to a pagan Pythagorean philosopher called Sextus.[42]

Jerome cites the Sextus passage in question on two occasions, the first time in his *Adversus Iovinianum*, which was written prior to the Rufinus translation, the second time in his commentary on Ezechiel well after the translation of Rufinus had appeared. The first translation is that of Jerome himself and even after Rufinus Jerome continued to adhere to his own translation, giving little quarter to that of Rufinus. To the extent that the works of Jerome were known to the Middle Ages, the Sextus text would have been available, nested in the *Adversus Iovinianum* and the commentary on Ezechiel. In addition to the two *ardentior* forms of the text in Jerome, there was a third version commonly used in the twelfth century that substituted *vehemens* for *ardentior*. By the middle of the twelfth century the text could be found in all three of the basic academic texts, the *Decretum* of Gratian, the *Sentences* of Peter Lombard, and the *Ordinary Gloss* on the Bible.

In summary, the three versions of the Sextus text current in the later Middle Ages were:

1 'Hence, Sextus says in the Sentences, "The too ardent lover of his [own] wife is an adulterer."' ('Unde Sextus in Sententiis: "Adulter est" inquit, "in suam uxorem amator ardentior."')[43]

2 'It is well said in the sentences of Sextus the Pythagorean, "The too ardent lover of his own wife is an adulterer."' ('Pulchre in Sexti pythagorici sententiolis dicitur: "Adulter est uxoris propriae amator ardentior."')[44]

3 'Every vehement lover of his own wife is an adulterer.' ('Omnis vehemens amator propriae uxoris adulter est.')[45]

The idea that one can have sufficiently improper sexual relations with one's wife for the behaviour to be dubbed adultery is not restricted to the text from Sextus. In the *origo* passage itself, the second fragment from Seneca on marriage concludes with a statement reiterating Sextus: 'Nothing is more foul than to love one's wife as if she were an adulteress.'[46] The idea is clear in an authentic work of Seneca: 'If one sleeps with his own wife as if with another's he is an adulterer although she is not an adulteress.'[47] More significantly, the same idea is found in Augustine. Arguing that lust can be blameworthy even in marriage, Augustine cites a text from a now lost work of Ambrose (*On Philosophy*): 'Is not the man who is intemperate in marriage none other than a sort of adulterer of his wife?'[48] Even by the fourth century the idea that one could be in some sense an adulterer of one's own wife was associated with Sextus, Xystus, Jerome, Augustine, and Ambrose; it is therefore not surprising that in the later Middle Ages one finds the Sextus text attributed to a number of authors. This is no doubt a measure of its penetration into the common conceptual framework.[49]

Neither the decretists nor the theologians seriously entertained the belief that there could be adultery in the strict sense between a husband and his wife. They saw in the Sextus text a comparison with adulterous relations. A man could act like an adulterer (*more adulteri*) even in regard to his own wife.[50] Initially, the interpretation tended in the direction of clear, verifiable types of behaviour, but a more general covering principle gradually emerged. The principle is enunciated as early as Master Roland. A man is too ardent when he is so moved to have sex that even if this woman were not his wife he would be resolved to have sex with her. In one formulation or another that became the standard interpretation of the Sextus text in the decretists.[51]

The theologians shared this interpretation. Albert the Great raises the question as to the meaning of the Sextus text. His response points to a further distinction elaborated by the theologians: '"Too ardent" indicates ardour that exceeds the concession and uprightness that are to characterize marriage.'[52] Marriage carries its own imperatives and does not give a licence for completely unbridled sex. Husbands having sexual relations must bear these imperatives in mind, otherwise they are no better than adulterers or those who frequent prostitutes. Adultery and prostitution are marked precisely by a disregard for the requirements of marriage. Not to care whether or not this woman is one's wife signifies that one lacks the requisite interior orientation demanded of a husband, and in that sense he can be said to be using his wife for his own selfish ends. An early-thirteenth-century confessional manual captures the idea well: 'The vehement lover of his own wife is an adulterer and sins gravely, particularly if he approaches his wife with indifference without respect for the marriage bond, and irreverently as if she were another's.'[53]

Albert's idea about exceeding the allowable concession and uprightness of marriage was captured in a distinction between intercourse with one's wife *within* and *outside* the bounds or limits of marriage.[54] Marriage was seen to establish limits to marital relations. Sex that respected the goods of offspring and fidelity, the reasons of procreation and paying the debt, and the natural manner was understood to be within the limits. At best it was good and meritorious, at worst it was venially sinful. Sex that did not respect those boundaries was understood to be outside the limits of marriage and mortally sinful. The standard formulaic explanation for sex outside the limits was sex with one's wife regardless of whether she was one's wife.[55]

This interpretation of the Sextus text provided a solution to the problem of coitus for pleasure. The subject of pleasure is never far from discussions of the legitimacy and morality of marital relations. Among the theologians, the question of pleasure is found in three principal contexts:

1 In explicit questions about the morality of intercourse motivated by lust, concupiscence, or pleasure.[56]

2 In the question whether coitus can be excused in the absence of all the goods of marriage. Peter of Tarentaise, for example, formulates the question in general terms ('Whether without these goods it [intercourse] would always be a mortal sin'), but the beginning of the discussion is cast in terms of lust ('It seems that intercourse to expend lust is always a mortal sin').[57]

3 In all questions that explore whether coitus can be sinless. Invariably in such questions there is a battery of objections stipulating that since intercourse is necessarily accompanied by lust, concupiscence, and pleasure it can never be entirely sinless.[58]

Some of this discussion has the tenor of a schoolroom exercise, particularly in regard to the view that intercourse is always sinful because of the sheer presence of lust and concupiscence. The theology of original sin had a ready answer to this objection. Although lust and concupiscence are inescapably present even after baptism, they are not present as items of personal, individual sin but are the remnants and reminders of our origin in Adam. Of course they *incline* towards sexual acts, but such an inclination is not of itself sinful. Sin arises from what is made of the inclination, how it is directed and channelled.[59]

Even after such objections are disposed of, however, there still remained a need to address the question of pleasure. Just as the Sextus text provided a link between the theologians and canonists, so too in the matter of pleasure there was a link between them through a text common to both Gratian and Peter Lombard. In this case, however, there was a difference. Peter Lombard made little of the Sextus text, being content to cite it in support of the assertion that intercourse without the goods of fidelity and offspring is criminal. He deals with the text on pleasure in formal scholastic fashion, in the course of which he develops a position on the morality of intercourse for pleasure. The text in question, a lengthy excerpt from Pope Gregory's response to Augustine of Canterbury, is used by Gratian in the context of his treatment of the times of abstinence required of married couples.[60]

Neither in the original nor in Gratian is the subject of pleasure the purpose of the remarks. In the original, the account is in response to the question whether after intercourse, as soon as a man has washed, he can enter a church or even receive communion.[61] The response provides one of the earliest sustained comments on the subject of sexual pleasure.[62] Gregory notes that the ancient Roman practice was to wash after intercourse and to refrain from entering a church for a time. He hastens to add that this is not said to dub marriage a fault; 'but because the licit commingling of a spouse is not possible without carnal pleasure he must refrain from entering the sacred place because the pleasure itself is in no way possible without fault.'[63]

Legitimate intercourse is to be for the sake of offspring, not for pleasure. In terms of the main question, Gregory distinguishes between those who have intercourse to create children, not because they are carried away by a desire for pleasure, and those dominated by pleasure, not the love of procreation. In the first case, church entry and the reception of communion are left to the judgment of the husband. In the second case 'the spouses have something to deplore in their union.'

Huguccio draws two conclusions from the text of Gregory. Distinguishing between intercourse and its exercise, he notes that intercourse itself is not a sin, but the emission of semen in its exercise is invariably accompanied by a certain itching of the flesh and pleasure. The itching and the pleasure are sins, although very minor (*venialissimum*).[64] It is because intercourse cannot be exercised without sin even by a holy man that Christ did not wish to be born through the normal way of coitus.[65] Whatever might be thought of the position, Huguccio's conclusion seems to be consistent with the text of Gregory.

The same cannot be said of the second conclusion Huguccio draws. Gregory had said that intercourse was to be in the service of procreation, not out of a desire for pleasure. When pleasure dominates, the spouses have something to deplore in their union. Huguccio takes this to refer to the fourth reason for intercourse (to satisfy pleasure), which, he says, is a mortal sin.[66] The *Ordinary Gloss* on this passage is largely taken up with reporting the views of Huguccio. On the subject of intercourse where pleasure dominates, it records the position of Huguccio but adds, 'According to us it is not mortal in this case but venial and he [Gregory] indicates this when he says that "they deplore."'[67]

Here the gloss goes some way towards resolving the ambiguity in its previous formal account of the fourth reason, which is given in terms of Huguccio's distinction between being overtaken by pleasure and actively provoking it. It reports Huguccio's view that in the latter case there is mortal sin, but adds that others (including the gloss itself?) hold that intercourse for pleasure is a venial sin. It is said to be mortal in the case of marital relations in the manner of adultery, or as an exhortation to continence, or when it is against nature 'because then he [the husband] sins mortally according to everyone.'[68]

By the early thirteenth century, then, the canon law on intercourse for pleasure represented two opposed positions: that of Huguccio, who held such behaviour to be a mortal sin; and that of the *Ordinary Gloss*, which seemed to take the view that intercourse simply for pleasure (without further aggravating factors) was a venial sin. The blunt statement of Raymond of Penyafort that intercourse for the sake of pleasure is a mortal sin follows Huguccio.[69] William of Rennes, after noting that Raymond is following Huguccio, presents a position more in line with the *Ordinary Gloss*, that such coitus is a venial sin as long as the order of nature is maintained.[70] This view can be granted for spouses who have sexual relations out of mutual fidelity. In virtue of the right each has to the body of the other, they would not act in such a way unless they were joined in marriage.[71]

The theologians were no more successful than the canonists in resolving the moral conundrum posed by the case of coitus for the sake of pleasure. They were clearer, however, and in some cases discussed the question formally at some length, taking the opportunity provided by Peter Lombard's account. The rubric to that account captures its theme: 'That not all pleasure of the flesh is a sin.'[72] The Lombard imagines a person claiming that all carnal concupiscence and pleasure in intercourse is evil and a sin because it is disordered and arises out of sin. He agrees that concupiscence is always evil because it is foul and the punishment for (original) sin. He interprets the claim that pleasure cannot be without sin as applying to intercourse when the good of offspring is not present; in that case the pleasure is not sinless. The Lombard concludes his remarks with the observation that there is scarcely anyone who at least sometimes does not have marital relations outside the intention of procreation.[73]

This account of Peter Lombard makes a point that Huguccio seems to have ignored. The mere presence of pleasure is not evil. (This point has already been seen in the chapter-one outline of the medieval discussion about whether Adam and Eve would have felt pleasure before the Fall.) The account begins with the claim that all carnal concupiscence and pleasure are evil and sins. The response does not continue to deal with both together; it grants that concupiscence is always evil, but not always a sin. It then deals separately with pleasure, noting that neither sexual nor non-sexual pleasure is a sin unless it is immoderate. One kind of immoderate pleasure is pleasure taken in intercourse that is not informed by the procreative intention.

The question of the morality of sexual pleasure is pervasive in accounts of marital relations. The accounts of Bonaventure and Aquinas determine the prevailing view. The basic account is that of Bonaventure, whose presentation Aquinas follows closely. Two opinions regarding pleasure are advanced, the first unacceptable, the second acceptable. The unacceptable position holds that to seek pleasure as one's final end (that is, to have sexual relations *for* pleasure) is always a mortal sin; to take pleasure in intercourse when having sex for some other prime reason is a venial sin; to tolerate the pleasure but to take no delight in it is the mark of perfection.[74]

Although they agree on the details of this opinion, they disagree in their assessment of it. For Bonaventure it is probable but too harsh, since couples are allowed to be playful and to take pleasure in sex as long as it is with marital affection.[75] According to Aquinas the first opinion cannot stand because it conflicts with a fundamental Aristotelian principle. The moral assessment of pleasures follows the moral assessment of the acts that they accompany; 'So since the matrimonial act is not intrinsically (*per se*) evil, to seek pleasure will not always be a mortal sin.'[76] The central question for both authors is whether *seeking* pleasure in marital relations is a mortal sin, since there seems no doubt that it is at least a venial sin. Prima facie it is not a mortal sin in terms of the principle of whether the husband would go ahead and have intercourse with this woman even if she were not his wife. If he attends to his wife as his wife, he acts within the limits of marriage and so sins only venially. If, however, he would have sexual relations with her even if she were not his wife, then he is seeking pleasure outside the bounds of the goods of marriage; he is the too-ardent lover, and so sins mortally.[77] For the period covered in our study, I am aware of only one author who questions the possibility that sexual relations for pleasure between a husband and wife are a mortal sin. After faithfully presenting the view of Aquinas, Durandus of St Pourcain adds: 'In regard to its being a mortal sin, I do not see that a mortal sin is present there since it is not contrary to any precept that orients us to God or neighbour.'[78]

The principle used by Bonaventure and Aquinas was adumbrated by Master Roland in the mid-twelfth century. It is surely safe to assume that it was meaningful to its users and played a role in their understanding of marital sexual relations. Unfortunately for us, no author who applies the principle expands on its meaning beyond linking it with the kind of sex found in adulterous and meretricious relationships or, as in early accounts, with empirically verifiable infractions, such as unnatural sex or sex at prohibited times. What is at stake, it seems to me, is the desire to make the point that marriage requires a type of interior psychological orientation between spouses. In our contemporary language, marriage does not permit one to use one's spouse purely as a sex object. The authors in question are contributing, in the words of Noonan, 'to a development of personal values in marriage.'[79]

While recognizing that the principle can be seen as a defence of 'personal values in marriage,' Noonan emphasizes its impractical character and cites a remark of Antoninus of Florence to that effect. In his presentation of cases of marital sex that are mortally sinful Antoninus enunciates the principle: 'If he relates to her with such inordinate affection in the conjugal act that if she were not his wife he would still do this carnal act with her or with another,' adding 'but it is difficult to discerne and to know this.'[80] In one place Noonan refers to the principle as requiring 'a deliberate act of abstraction from actual circumstances' and in the next sentence as a 'hypothetical test so unlikely to be of practical use.'[81] It does not require an act of abstraction nor is it a hypothetical test, since it never was meant to be of practical use. The principle was a theoretical elaboration by academics in their attempt to describe an abusive kind of marital sexual relationship in which the driving force of sex is allowed unbridled play in disregard of the correct limits set for the relationship. As a guide for a confessor in determining the sinfulness of marital sexual acts, the principle of course is useless. Earlier in his confessional manual, Antoninus of Florence had acknowledged as much: 'Nonetheless one can know his wife with such a degree of lust that it would be a mortal sin as when he knows her as if she were not his wife. Regarding such acts there is no need for the confessor to know whether they are mortal or venial because frequently there is no need for the penitent to know it.'[82]

This is reminiscent of a similar point made by Robert of Courson at the beginning of the thirteenth century, when the theory of the four reasons was beginning to solidify. It is objected against the theory that ordinary simple men (*vulgari*) attend to none of the reasons, but approach their wives out of habit. They attend only to the fact that they are married or that one wishes to have sex with the other. The implication is that they do this legitimately without concern for any of the reasons. Robert claims that Augustine (under whose patronage the theory was placed) did not deny that there were more than the four reasons. He adduces as an example the above case:

> when a simple man who is not bound to know the heights of the law approaches his wife, that is, he simply approaches her without tending more to one end than to another. But he approaches his wife as his wife, wishing to use her as his own. The laity are not to be judged as worthy of condemnation because they have a great love to hold their wives or because they approach them frequently.[83]

This common-sense awareness of how people actually live their sex is characteristic of the early Parisian school of moralists, but is understandably absent from the theoretical concerns of the later university commentators on the *Sentences* of Peter Lombard. It will resurface with the emergence of a distinct moral theology in the fifteenth century. Whatever one might think about the magisterial pronouncements on the three goods of marriage and the four reasons for intercourse, it must be borne in mind that absent from such a view was a conception of sexuality as a positive, integral component of a person's psychological make-up. As Michel Foucault has shown, sexuality is a relatively modern invention, and to use such a notion to judge medieval views of marital sex would be anachronistic at best.

The thinking examined in the last three chapters has been concerned with two basic issues: the purpose and the morality of coitus. The purpose was seen to reside in the socio-biological teleology of human reproduction. The biological and psycho-emotional structure of human beings are manifestations of a natural orientation to the procreation and the social and religious rearing of children. The natural finality of reproduction is not towards mere physical conception and birth but towards the full flowering of human beings in the ways of God. This teleology requires an institutional determination or specification of the progenitors in the interests of the offspring. It was believed that for Christians the correct institutional arrangement was that of indivisible monogamous marriage.

The general morality of coitus was a matter of conforming behaviour to the natural finality of reproduction in the proper institutional setting. This theory was elaborated within the conceptual framework provided by the ideas of the twofold institution of marriage, the three goods of marriage, and the four reasons for coitus. The whole discussion is set against the background of a theological anthropology of the Fall, original sin, lust, and concupiscence.

Granting these basic positions, it seems that this first sophisticated reflection on sex in the West since Augustine could boast some achievements. Aside from a humane modification of ancient coital regulations and an understandable concern with the possibility of physical harm as a result of intercourse under certain circumstances, far more ontologically significant positions were established. The radical goodness of gender differences, coitus, and marriage was clearly affirmed. The disruptive presence of lust and concupiscence was acknowledged, but was never seen morally to mar the otherwise correct enjoyment of intercourse in marriage. While sexual pleasure was to be subordinated to the values of marriage, the pleasure itself was not seen to be an evil but a natural good reinforcing the natural finality of reproduction.

By the end of the thirteenth century there was in place a theology of the impersonal natural forces of reproduction that were thought to be immune to deliberate interference. In the theory of the remedial character of marriage, however, both canon lawyers and theologians implicitly recognized a value in intercourse independent of the possibility of procreation. That is why they could say that intercourse in the case of sterility, or old age, or during pregnancy was morally acceptable. It apparently did not occur to anyone to argue that since it was permitted to use nature in circumstances in which nature was incapable of culminating in conception, it might be permissible to render nature incapable of conception through deliberate contraceptive techniques. Noonan's *Contraception* is an eloquent record of resistance to such an argument, a resistance that continues in the official Roman Catholic teaching to this day.

I am not aware of any evidence showing that married people in the Middle Ages actually believed and observed this teaching about the inviolable link between intercourse and procreation when conception was possible. We know more about attitudes towards the link between intercourse and marriage. There is considerable evidence of widespread belief that what was called simple fornication was either sinless or at most a venial sin.[84]

6

The Virtue of Temperance

There is a radical dislocation in the human constitution resulting from original sin, a tendency for desires to rebel against reason in the pursuit of their own independent ends. This lack of harmony is particularly true of sexual desire, symbolized in the absence of rational and voluntary control over the genitals. The challenge and imperative for everyone born after Adam is to attempt to re-establish and maintain rational control over the lower appetites, under God. Although this would seem to call for general treatises on proper human sexual behaviour, none is to be found, probably because the linguistic and conceptual tools were not available. Of course, there are many discussions of marriage and the proper limits of marital sexual relations. However, not all marry. Marriage may very well be the only legitimate outlet for sex, but is it the most preferable way of life? Is the complete renunciation of sex a more commendable way of life? If so, why? These are some of the issues that one might expect to be addressed in a medieval treatise on proper sexual conduct.

Although such treatises did not exist in the Middle Ages, there were treatises on the virtue of temperance that afforded the opportunity to address the question of sex from a general, positive point of view. General, in the sense that they do not focus exclusively on the specific range of allowable marital relations; positive, in the sense that they provide accounts of preferable ways of choosing and acting where sex is concerned (rather than focusing only on how not to act, which is dealt with in discussions of lechery). Treatises on temperance did not deal solely with the sphere of sexual behaviour, but sex constitutes a major area of their concern. What is at issue is a *virtue*, an habitual disposition to act out of choice in a morally upright manner. Temperance is the key to re-establishing and maintaining at least a semblance of the original harmony, particularly in regard to sexual behaviour.

Although they did not recognize the cause of the lack of harmony in human nature, pre-Christian philosophers recognized the *fact* and insisted that there is a proper order and balance that must obtain in human affairs. Perhaps they might even have agreed with St Paul: 'But I see another law in my members fighting against the law of my mind and captivating me in the law of sin that is in my members' (Romans 7:23). Proper order, balance, and rule are established through the acquisition of the virtue of temperance, the account of which was a non-Christian philosophical achievement that entered the Middle Ages through two principal channels – Stoic (particularly the works of Cicero), and Aristotelian. Aristotle's initial account of temperance, however, was unknown before the Latin translation of the first three books of the *Nicomachean Ethics* at the beginning of the thirteenth century; his full account was not known until the completion of the translation of the entire *Nicomachean Ethics* about the middle of the century. Cicero was the principal source for conceptions of temperance up to the thirteenth century.[1]

In this chapter I shall deal with the conception of the virtue of temperance and with the development of treatises on temperance that culminated in the account by Aquinas. The following chapter will single out for particular consideration the three parts of temperance that were traditionally associated with the moderation of sexual behaviour – continence, chastity, and virginity.

CONCEPTIONS OF TEMPERANCE

At the risk of some over-simplification, it might be said that a broad and a narrow conception of temperance competed for acceptance throughout the Middle Ages. The broad conception corresponds to Cicero's ideal of the balanced, moderate Roman gentleman with a cultured sense of shame who incorporates the values of moral uprightness (*honestas*) and decorum or propriety (*decor*). This is the ideal of human excellence in those areas in which human nature differs from the rest of animal nature, often expressed in the proverb 'Nothing in excess.'[2] Through temperance, measure and moderation are established across the whole area of human affairs, certainly including sex, but embracing much more, including eating, dress, gait, language, and human interrelations.

This broad notion of temperance, which embraces almost the whole sphere of moral uprightness, was adopted early in the Christian era and adapted by Ambrose to the ideal of ministers of the Church.[3] It is evident in Isidore of Seville, who describes temperance as 'a measured style of life in every word and work'; it is the companion of a sense of shame, guards the rule of humility, preserves peace of mind, embraces continence and chastity, fosters propriety and uprightness, restricts desire through reason, represses anger, and does not requite insults.[4] Alcuin, too, associates temperance with a measured style of life and with the ideal of nothing in excess: 'Temperance is the measure of the whole of life keeping man from excessive love or hate; it tempers all the varieties of this life with considered care.'[5] In the twelfth century, St Bernard reflects the same view: 'So it seems to me not entirely absurd to define temperance ... according to the words of the philosopher, "Nothing in excess"'.[6] Temperance imposes measure on justice; its function is none other than to prevent anything immoderate.[7]

The moderation of sexual inclinations and appetites was just one of the numerous functions of temperance in this Stoic conception, and does not stand out in any particular way. There is also a narrower conception of temperance that tended to restrict the field of the virtue to acts of eating and drinking, on the one hand, and to sexual behaviour, on the other. Through temperance, moderation was established in the two most basic drives of our animal, sensual nature – self-preservation and the preservation of the species. The emergence of this view is particularly evident at the end of the twelfth century and in the first decades of the thirteenth. It occurred under the influence of a Christian reading of Cicero and was powerfully reinforced by Aristotle's account of the virtue. In the end, Aquinas integrated the broad and narrow conceptions into a complex view marking the culmination of the development of the idea of temperance.

Medieval accounts focused on three subjects: the conception or definition of temperance, its psychological setting, and its parts. Cicero set the theme and orientation of the discussion on all three counts; if we might apply the remark of Alfred North Whitehead about Plato to Cicero's account of temperance, we can say that subsequent discussions of the virtue are a series of footnotes to Cicero.[8]

Cicero provided the standard definition of temperance: 'The firm and moderate domination of reason over lust and other improper impulses of the mind.'[9] All the features that would become central to the concept of temperance are present in this definition. The active feature is that of dominion, rule, lordship, domination. In his *De officiis* Cicero develops this idea against a psychological background that dovetailed with the Aristotelian analysis of temperance. There are two powers of the soul, desire and reason; temperance is the establishment of proper order between the two. Desire pulls hither and yon, reason clearly teaches what is to be done and avoided. This can only happen if reason leads the way and desire follows. This is the proper order that ought to obtain between reason and desire; in its absence we will act blindly, fortuitously, in a flighty and negligent manner, without moderation or a sense of shame.[10]

There is no suggestion in Cicero that lust (*libido*) has any particular sexual connotation, but this should not be taken to imply that he had no concern with sexual matters. There are a few passages in Cicero's *De officiis* that relate to subjects with sexual connotations: human superiority over beasts and the need to control pleasures (1.30.105–6); the lust of youth (1.34.122); the impropriety of lechery in the elderly (1.34.123); parts of the body whose sight is ugly and foul, whose functions are all right, but which should not be spoken of openly (1.35.126–9).

Appetite embraces lust and other improper impulses. Once Cicero's use of the term 'lust' was adopted into a Christian conceptual framework without any further specification, it could be understood to refer to nothing else but sexual drives. This point was explicitly made by Saint Augustine in his careful analysis of the term in the *City of God*.[11] The language of Cicero would have suggested to a medieval reader the broad sweep of the idea of the Fall, lust, concupiscence, and first movements. Isidore speaks of temperance as that by which lust and concupiscence are bridled; the twelfth-century *Epitome* of Hermannus speaks of temperance as the power of bridling unlawful movements, a theme common throughout the period. William of Auxerre says that temperance 'tames the rebellion of the flesh and holds back its unlawful movements.'[12] Restraining, taming, bridling, reining in connote the central idea of temperance with its roots in Stoicism.[13]

Similar connotations are encountered in specifically theological contexts. There is a popular definition of temperance in the *Ordinary*

Gloss on Matthew 15:38: 'Temperance is the restraining of desire from things that give pleasure in a temporal manner.'[14] In the same vein, the definition of temperance chosen by Peter Lombard is also from Augustine: 'Temperance consists in the coercion of depraved pleasures.' Curiously, although this definition is the only one proposed by the Lombard in the *Sentences*, it receives little attention in the thirteenth-century treatises of Philip the Chancellor and Albert the Great, and is virtually ignored by later commentaries.[15]

THE PARTS OF TEMPERANCE

In addition to providing a definition of the virtue, Cicero also bequeathed a basic division of temperance. He divides temperance into three parts or subvirtues: continence (*continentia*), clemency (*clementia*), and modesty (*modestia*). Continence governs the field of desire; clemency regulates the unreasonable hatred a superior might have for an inferior; and modesty provides that sense of shame that safeguards moral uprightness and authority.[16] The division reflects a broad conception of temperance, but when adopted into a Christian framework it is not difficult to see how continence and modesty, with their sexual connotations, would encourage a narrowing of the conception of the virtue.[17]

Cicero's account was supplemented by Macrobius, who divides temperance into nine parts: modesty, sense of shame (*verecundia*), abstinence, chastity, uprightness (*honestas*), moderation, frugality (*parcitas*), sobriety, purity (*pudicitia*).[18] In contrast with Cicero, Macrobius does not bother to define the members of his division. While one might think that this omission on the part of Macrobius would have resulted in a confusing welter of definitions, in fact the definitions provided by the celebrated twelfth-century *Teaching of the Moral Philosophers* (*Moralium dogma philosophorum*) were generally accepted as standard. Beginning with Cicero's definition of temperance, this work adopts the Macrobian division, defining each item on the list and illustrating each with quotations from such classical authors as Horace, Cicero, Juvenal, Persius, Terence, Seneca, and Ovid. Chastity is omitted, perhaps because it is thought to be covered by purity or because of its specifically Christian association.[19]

Initially, the adoption of the divisions of temperance found in Cicero and their association with those of Macrobius contributed to the early popularity of a broad conception of the virtue in which sexual concerns were subordinate to the idea of a generalized moderation. The different functions of temperance and the virtues associated with it in Isidore have already been noted. A specifically sexual orientation is not found in his account. Continence and chastity are not singled out for particular mention; nor do they hold pride of place. In some passages Isidore discusses continence and chastity independently of temperance, and in a work on ecclesiastical and liturgical duties he provides three chapters on virgins, widows, and the married, three states of life defined in reference to sex that were to become important elements in later scholastic treatments of temperance.[20] In his work on the virtues and vices, Alcuin witnesses to this broad conception in which sexual concerns are not prominent. Chastity is dealt with separately in the course of a treatment of assorted virtues unrelated to temperance.[21]

Some of the early divisions in twelfth-century authors reflect this same approach, including within themselves elements that would become extraneous to the conception of temperance. Abelard, in addition to frugality, chastity, and sobriety, includes humility and meekness.[22] In a text found among the works of Hugh of St Victor (*On the Fruits of the Flesh and the Spirit*) one finds: contempt of the world, silence, and compliance, in addition to fasting and sobriety. The idea of discernment (*discretio*), which was frequently associated with temperance in the early tradition, is included here among the companions of temperance.[23] A measure of the lack of a settled division is also evident in the association of the virtues governing sex with the theological virtues of faith (chastity and continence), and hope (modesty)![24] Gradually, however, the divisions of Cicero and Macrobius came to assume a privileged position in the conceptualization of temperance, and that development was accompanied by a narrowing of the scope of the virtue to matters of food, drink, and sex. Cicero's continence and modesty had clear sexual connotations. Most of the parts proposed by Macrobius lent themselves, under the influence of a Christian reading, to an association with food (abstinence, moderation, frugality, sobriety) and sex (modesty, sense of shame, chastity, purity).[25]

In the twelfth century two developments occurred in the thinking about the parts of temperance associated with sex that would remain more or less stable. First, the field of sex was divided into two broad areas: that of sexual inclinations and desires (subsumed under the idea of lust), and that of peripheral externalities that sometimes are signs of lust, such as gestures, words, ornament, and dress. The relevant parts of temperance in this regard were continence, chastity, purity, modesty, and sense of shame. There was considerable vacillation about continence, since the term was sometimes used to refer to the abstention from all unlawful things, and sometimes taken to refer to a general virtue, with chastity and purity as subspecies.[26] Chastity is invariably associated with the rational control of lust.[27] Purity is said to embrace both sexual impulses and their signs.[28] Modesty and sense of shame were said to govern the external signs of lust.[29] Chastity and continence were seen to be concerned directly with sexual feelings and lustful drives; purity both with lust and its signs; modesty and sense of shame with the peripheral areas of gestures, speech, attire, and gait.

The second development stemmed from the tendency to differentiate states of life in terms of the choices people make about participation in sexual experience. First, there was an association, probably by way of an aside, of particular virtues with different classes of people. Chastity is related to virgins, and purity is related to matrons. (It is not clear to whom the term 'matron' refers, but I suspect it is meant to cover the class of mature widows.)[30] This association opened the door for the incorporation into the scheme of the parts of temperance of an ancient tradition that divided the states of life along sexual lines. In this development, not only was an additional division introduced into the parts of temperance but a hierarchized value system was also incorporated into the framework. A text of Hugh of St Victor is an early witness to this occurrence. In a work long attributed to Hugh but probably by Conrad of Hirsau, affliction of the flesh ('by which the seeds of a lascivious mind are suppressed by discrete punishment') is listed as a companion of temperance.[31] In what is claimed to be a genuine work of Hugh (*Scala celi*), the following account of affliction of the flesh is provided: 'Affliction of the flesh consists in three things: in labour, in abstinence, in continence ... Continence is threefold: conjugal chastity, purity of widows, virginal integrity.'[32] This division of continence is a specifically Christian element whose source is found in a tradition of biblical interpretation that associated the married, widowed, and virginal states of life with the thirtyfold, sixtyfold, and hundredfold rewards of the parable of the sower (Matthew 13:8 and 23).[33]

Alan of Lille incorporated this threefold division into his account of the virtue of temperance as a subdivision of chastity. Alan speaks of the virginal state, the continence of widows, and conjugal purity. The first restrains the movements of carnal concupiscence so that it does not fall down the slippery path of the flesh. The continence of widows is the renunciation of all sexual experience after having had the experience. Conjugal purity frees carnal union from fault through the sacrament of matrimony.[34]

A comparison of the terminology of the *Scala celi* and Alan's *On the Virtues and Vices* shows that no settled definitions for continence, chastity, and purity had been agreed on by the end of the twelfth century. Hugh speaks of conjugal chastity, Alan speaks of conjugal purity; Hugh speaks of the purity of widows, Alan speaks of the continence of widows. Neither uses a virtue term in reference to virgins. Chastity is used in a sexual context by both authors and will continue to be used with an exclusively sexual connotation. The term continence often has a sexual connotation but was also taken to mean abstaining from any illicit behaviour. Alan reflects the usage recorded in the efforts of Papias (circa 1050) to define the two terms. Papias associates chastity with incorruption of the flesh and continence with renunciation of sex after corruption, but then reports another view that associates chastity with spiritual marriages and continence with virgins.[35] The adjective *castus*, he says, comes from castration, but afterwards the ancients agreed that it could be used to refer to those who had promised perpetual abstinence from lust.[36] His account of *continentia* is consistent with his first account under chastity, but when he comes to the term *continens* he notes the wider connotation: 'The continent person ... not only in chastity after corruption but from every vice.'[37]

Prior to the thirteenth century, accounts of temperance consisted largely of definitions and lists of the parts into which the virtue was subdivided. With William of Auxerre, Philip the Chancellor, and Albert the Great, treatises emerged that dealt with the virtue in a more discursive manner. No doubt, this occurred as a result of the development of theology generally. In regard to the virtue of temperance, however, the evolution was enhanced by the translation into Latin of the third book of Aristotle's *Nicomachean Ethics*, which provided the first critical account of the virtue in the West. In the thirteenth century, academic and non-academic treatises on the virtues were written. The learned, academic treatises, taking a theoretical, analytical approach, developed in three stages: (1) the early summas of William of Auxerre and Philip the Chancellor, followed by the *Sentence* gloss of Alexander of Hales, and culminating in the *De bono* of Albert the Great; (2) the period of the *Sentence* commentaries of Albert, Bonaventure, and Thomas Aquinas; (3) the *Summa of Theology* of Thomas Aquinas, which marks the culmination of the development.

A recently published list of incipits of works on the virtues and vices is convincing evidence of the immense number of non-academic treatises on the virtues from the thirteenth century on and suggests that any attempt to categorize them would be a futile undertaking. The virtues are dealt with in manuals of penance, such as those of Paul of Hungary and Robert Grosseteste, and in the popular theological compendium of Hugh of Strasbourg; Aquinas's *Summa* treatment of temperance is found virtually unchanged in the fourteenth-century *Speculum morale* attributed to Vincent of Beauvais.[38]

One of the most outstanding non-academic works is the *Summa of the Vices and Virtues* of William Peraldus. This summa is a schematic treatment of the vices and virtues, prepared for preachers and confessors; it is written almost in point form, with each point supported by illustrative texts from the Bible, ecclesiastical authors, and moral authorities such as Cicero and Seneca. It is likely that the temperance preached from the pulpit or recommended in the confessional was more often that of Peraldus than that of the university masters.

The *Summa* of Peraldus is often cited as a single work and was probably meant to be so by its author. The treatise on the virtues (written about 1248), however, appeared twelve years after the treatise on the vices. If the number of surviving manuscripts is a measure of a work's success, then the hundreds of extant manuscripts confirm the judgment that 'few works in the whole history of literature knew such a brilliant success' as the work of Peraldus.[39] He wrote outside the university context, making little use of the academic treatises current in his day.[40] More to the point, in the words of Dondaine, 'Peyraut [Peraldus] is, in the middle of the thirteenth century, an exceptional witness to a Christian moral theology essentially traditional and Latin.'[41] Traditional in values, outlook, perspective, and in his thorough grounding in the Bible and its gloss; Latin in his recourse to the great authorities of the Western Church: Ambrose, Jerome, Augustine, and Gregory the Great. To these Christian sources must be added the Latin Seneca, whose name is frequently invoked by Peraldus.[42]

What contributed to the huge success of the work of Peraldus was probably its practical, pastoral orientation and its schematic structure. It does not engage in debate and argumentation to resolve conceptual questions or matters of substance. The whole approach to the vices and virtues assumes that there is a common heritage about these matters that the author marshals in the service of those who have care of the Christian life, particularly preachers and guides of conscience.[43]

The treatise on the virtue of temperance by Peraldus is a complete presentation of what was thought to be the traditional, proper, and preferred Christian approach to sexual behaviour. It is a positive rounding out of the picture sketched in the earlier treatment of lechery, which deals with the abuses of sex. After giving the reasons for dealing with temperance before fortitude, Peraldus outlines his approach: (1) meanings of the term temperance; (2) its description; (3) its commendation; (4) its parts. In treating the parts of temperance Peraldus draws on the divisions of Cicero and offers numerous reasons meant to dissuade the reader from the love of pleasures. After the division into continence, clemency, and modesty, the work falls into two sections, the first dealing with pleasures of the senses under the general rubric of sobriety, which covers the field of eating and drinking, the second with the pleasures of touch under the general rubric of continence, which covers the field of sex. Continence is further subdivided according to the three states of virginity, widowhood, and marriage, with a treatment of clerical chastity added after widowhood.[44]

ARISTOTLE

The thirteenth century inherited a substantial body of writings on the virtue of temperance in which the definition of Cicero and the divisions of Cicero and Macrobius were central. This whole tradition, as with so many other received views, was subjected to critical scrutiny by the masters of the thirteenth century with the aid of recently acquired Aristotelian learning. The details of the entry of the Latin translations of Aristotle's *Nicomachean Ethics* are complex and need not be recorded here.[45] The entry occurred in two stages. From the beginning of the century to about 1246, there was available a Latin translation from the Greek of books 2 and 3 (*Ethica vetus*), book 1 (*Ethica nova*), and some fragments of book 7. By 1246–7, there was available a translation by Robert Grosseteste of the entire Greek text of the *Nicomachean Ethics* along with a translation of the Greek commentaries accompanied by Grosseteste's notes, which were largely of a lexicographical character.

What this meant, in effect, was that by the beginning of the century Aristotle's general theory of virtue (book 2) was accessible, along with his treatment of the virtue of temperance.[46] In spite of its lack of a specific definition, the Aristotelian discussion of the virtue made an important contribution to the medieval understanding of temperance. Aristotle restricts the field of temperance to the pleasures of touch (*tactus*) and taste (*gustus*) in so far as taste is conceived as a form of touch. Taste refers to eating and drinking; touch to sexual relations.[47] This position reinforced and sanctioned the narrowing of the field of temperance that is apparent in Alan of Lille. The function of temperance is to achieve a rational, virtuous mean in the pleasures that humans share with other members of the animal kingdom and to keep humans from becoming enslaved by bestial, animal pleasures. Although every virtue is a mean between excess and defect, Aristotle notes that it is scarcely human for people to be defective in the pursuit of pleasure; it is unlikely that humans will be found to choose to renounce all pleasures of taste and touch (the vice of insensibility).[48]

This, then, is the basic Aristotelian framework within which thirteenth-century treatises on temperance were written, up to and including the *De bono* of Albert the Great. Aristotle's views dovetailed surprisingly well with the traditional Stoic-Christian position on the virtue, posing no serious challenge and requiring few modifications. The seeds of a problem were present, however, in Aristotle's general theory of virtue. Virginity might not square well with the view that virtue is a mean, with the implication that the conscious renunciation of all voluntary sexual pleasure was a vice rather than a virtue. This question will become acute later in the century. An incidental inconvenience, which posed no serious problem but clearly puzzled Philip the Chancellor and Albert, was the language of the Aristotelian treatment. The Latin word for temperance is *temperantia*, a term used by both Stoic and Christian authors. The Greek used by Aristotle for what I have called temperance is *sophrosune*, the vice of excess is *akolasia*. Robert Grosseteste translates these terms by *temperantia* and *intemperan-*

tia; in the earlier *Ethica vetus*, they are translated as *castitas* and *incontinentia*, respectively. Medieval writers certainly believed that the last chapters of the third book of the *Nicomachean Ethics* were about what they understood to be temperance. So why the use of *castitas*, a term traditionally understood to have an exclusively sexual connotation? In response, Philip the Chancellor is led to present a fascinating discussion of why the moral philosopher uses only one term (*castitas*) to talk about temperance, while the theologian uses two (*sobrietas* and *continentia*). Albert does not deal with the question extensively, but he does attempt to explain how different terms highlight different aspects of the virtue of temperance.[49]

The translation of the complete text of the *Ethics* contributed further to an understanding of the Aristotelian view of the virtue of temperance on three counts: (1) the lengthy discussion of moral weakness in book 7 (chapters 1-10) sheds more light on the precise nature of temperance, the field of temperance, and its relation to what is called continence; (2) the relation between prudence and temperance is clarified (NE 6.5, 1140b12–20); (3) two accounts of the nature of pleasure are provided (NE 7.11–14 and NE 10.1–5). Another benefit arising from the translation of the complete text was the initiation of a long tradition of commentaries on the *Nicomachean Ethics*. The ink was barely dry on Grosseteste's translation when Albert the Great wrote an *ad litteram* commentary with questions that perhaps was never surpassed in scope, clarity, or erudition. Gauthier claims that it is the best of the medieval commentaries.[50]

One serious problem arose with the translation of the complete text of the *Ethics*. The seventh book has to do with moral weakness and self-restraint, translated by *incontinentia* and *continentia* respectively. The problem resulted from Aristotle's claim that *continentia* is not a full-fledged virtue like temperance. What is an intellectual culture nourished on the idea that *continentia* is a virtue and a part of temperance to make of such a claim? As we shall see, it was disturbing to at least some in authority.

EARLY THIRTEENTH-CENTURY ACCOUNTS

Three of the major academic treatises in the first half of the thirteenth century share a narrow view of temperance, with most of their discussions divided between the virtues governing eating and drinking on the one hand, and those related to sex on the other. Furthermore, William of Auxerre, Philip the Chancellor, and Albert also agree in dividing the sexual component according to the three states of virginity, widowhood, and marriage. In each case considerable space is devoted to the discussion of virginity; widowhood receives some mention; and the extent of the treatment of marital chastity is determined by the overall plan of the particular work. Marital chastity received more substantial treatment under the virtue of temperance if the author did not discuss the sacrament of matrimony elsewhere. William of Auxerre, who deals with marital sex in the context of marriage, does not discuss marital chastity in his account of temperance. Albert has a short article on continence in marriage, no doubt because he had already dealt with marriage in his *De sacramentis* and intended to deal with the question in his *Commentary on the Sentences*. On the other hand, Philip the Chancellor, who does not deal with the sacrament of matrimony, provides a detailed discussion of marital sex in his treatise on temperance, very much as William Peraldus did.[51]

In his discussion of the definition of temperance, Albert concentrates on the definitions of Cicero and the *Ordinary Gloss* on Matthew 15:38, offering what amounts to lengthy literal commentaries on each. His concerns are twofold: to co-ordinate and reconcile the definitions he found in Philip the Chancellor, and to specify the precise nature of the virtue. Albert accepts the Aristotelian position that the field of temperance is that of touch and taste. Temperance is the virtue of the concupiscible appetite. It regulates sensual, animal desires, that is, lust, in the sense of a tendency to turn towards created, temporal, changeable values. The definition of Cicero is the best because it captures everything necessary for a knowledge of the virtue: the act (dominion, domination), the mean (moderation), the dimension of the difficult (firm), the specific matter (lust), the general matter (other unlawful movements).[52]

Albert highlights the special need for temperance because of the particular difficulty the human animal has in controlling the base drives of his lower nature. For Aristotle, virtue has to do with what is most difficult; where there is no specific difficulty there is no particular virtue.[53] Difficulty arises for humans from the pleasurable drives towards eating and sex that are integral to human nature and shared with other animals. This is not a matter of external dangers threatening from other sources but one of innate inclinations that cling to our very bones, as it were. They cannot be fled, avoided, or borne with fortitude, as can life-threatening situations for which we have no appetite or desire. A firm restraint is called for to keep us from the abasement to which our cattle-like nature (*pecorina natura*) inclines.[54] The main source of difficulty, needing a special virtue, is the area of touching having to do with sexual pleasures, which is even located in a special place (the genitals). Chastity is the ultimate virtue of temperance because its matter is ultimate in the order of difficulty and its lack (lechery) is ultimate in the degree of harm, since lechery assimilates us to brute animals.[55]

If domestic animals are to be of any use, they must be bridled and reined in. The definition of temperance from the gloss on Matthew 15:38 highlights this notion of constraint: 'Temperance is the reining in of desire from those things that please in a temporal manner.' Reins and bridles are not bonds holding back altogether, but are means of directing, ruling, and containing a horse so that it walks on the right road. Temperance is compared to reins in this sense. Albert suggests that the equestrian metaphor is particularly apt because concupiscence, which temperance restrains, flourishes more particularly in horses than in other animals.[56] Much of this does not differ from Aristotle's account of temperance. The difference between Aristotle and the medieval masters lies not so much in their descriptions of the human condition as in their explanations of its origin. Belief in a fallen nature informed the medieval accounts of temperance, as is apparent, for instance, in both Philip the Chancellor and Albert.

In providing an explanation of his conception of the parts of temperance, Philip ties the division directly to the consequences of original sin. Through the sin of the first parents, corrupted flesh contracts fluxibility, corruption, and the desire for self-transcendence (*superpositionis sue appetitus*). Fluxibility manifests itself in the wearing away of the body, producing the drive to eat and requiring the virtue of sobriety; the desire for self-transcendence is manifested in our wanting to get ahead of others, producing a tendency to quarrels and to inflicting injuries and requiring clemency.[57] The fluxibility and corruptibility of the flesh expose us to harm from the elements, and nudity itself poses problems, leading to the requirements for dress, as in the first parents, for which there is modesty to control the use of dress and ornament.[58]

Because we who were created immortal are now mortal and corruptible (that is, we die), we cannot maintain ourselves in existence.

Consequently, we have a powerful desire to maintain ourselves by the multiplication of the species, a desire that is manifested through the generative power of reproduction. Continence is necessary to control and moderate the vehemence of this sexual appetite.[59]

Philosophers have no concern with original sin and its effects; theologians must take this dimension into account. The philosopher simply has an eye on sensual acts whereby the person can be said to corrupt his own nature; the theologian, however, has an eye on nature itself that corrupts persons and their operations. That is, as a consequence of original sin, persons are corrupt prior to any free acts on their part, and so the theologians consider not only actual sin (sin resulting from free will), but also original sin (inherited without any concurrence from the individual's free will).[60]

Albert, too, appeals to the state of fallen nature in his account of the virtue of temperance. In commenting on the expression 'other unlawful impulses,' Albert notes that these are not just any impulses but those that draw us suddenly out of a desire for pleasure. They do not arise from nature *tout court*, nor are they to be attributed to vice, since there is no vice in a temperate person. But there is a corrupt nature in every temperate person, whose concupiscible powers, the *sancti* say, are both corrupted and infected. This nature cannot be eliminated or wiped clean, but it can be controlled through the habits of the virtues.[61]

This conditioned optimism is noted later by Albert when he responds to an objection posed from the point of view of the Fall, original sin, and concupiscence. In his account of chastity, which he defines as a pure and upright disposition of the whole body to tame the furies of vices, the objection is raised that it is futile to speak of such a virtue because the presence of sensuality makes subjection impossible. He responds:

> concupiscence with its fury can be tamed so that it is humanized, so to speak, but not thoroughly. What is tamed is removed from frenzied impulse, but the brute [in it] remains; what is humanized embraces human nature from the point of view of discretion and meekness. This is the case with concupiscence which, indeed, is restrained from wild furies, but cannot be abstracted from its bruteness.[62]

Albert synthesizes these ideas in his explanation of why a special reward is allocated to virginity:

we must bear in mind how, when Adam first withdrew from God, his body was also corrupted and not subject to the soul. Sensual motion, infused with the serpent's venom, was so put off track that in its movements it did not obey reason, particularly in regard to sexual pleasure ... For that pleasure moves more than the rest, touch is more sensitive in the area of the genitals, and the transmission of corruption occurs through that area. Consequently, it was in the motion of the genitals that they [Adam and Eve] were first conscious of their nudity. Therefore, those organs in particular are not subject to reason. So discipline and the cultivation of continence and the repression of the thorns in sexual matters demand more labour.[63]

Finally, in his later commentary on the *Nicomachean Ethics*, Albert develops the discussion of Philip the Chancellor about the different points of view that are possible in regard to the focus of temperance on the pleasures of eating and sex. The question suggests that the pleasures of touch with which temperance is concerned are not centred in determined parts of the body (the organs of taste and the genitals). Albert replies that temperance is indeed concerned with pleasure in those two parts because they are the most powerful and in them the principal bridling virtue has its function. The natural philosopher, the theologian, and the moral philosopher have their own explanations for the power of these particular pleasures. According to the natural philosopher, nature places the greatest pleasure in taste and sex in order to ensure its own preservation and conservation in the individual and in the species. 'However, according to the theologian, the reason is because those parts are more corrupt than the other parts because the first sin was committed by the act of eating and is transmitted by the act of generation.' According to the moral philosopher, the power of the pleasures arises from their innate character, which is tied to the conservation of nature through food and sex (*venerea*).[64]

Human animal nature in its drive towards the preservation of the individual and the conservation of the species is encouraged and enticed by powerful reinforcing pleasures that constantly threaten to unseat it from the balance that ought to obtain between reason and desire. This threat arises from the radical disruption introduced into nature and history by original sin. According to Cicero, the guidance and direction, the taming and bridling are the result of the domination or lordship of reason (*rationis dominatio*). For some cause of which I am unaware the Ciceronian definition of temperance that Albert uses in the *De bono* omits the term *rationis*.[65] One can only imagine the direction Albert's careful analysis and word-for-word commentary on Cicero would have taken if he had used the correct definition. Although not beginning with Cicero, Thomas Aquinas focuses almost entirely on the need for proper *rational* order in our affective life and locates the need for temperance squarely in our rational and animal nature.

THOMAS AQUINAS

By the time of his *Summa of Theology*, Thomas Aquinas was freed from concordist preoccupations with texts that characterize the accounts of temperance in Albert the Great. There are no lengthy discussions of the various definitions of temperance that would have been current in Aquinas' day; in fact, nowhere in his account of temperance does Aquinas even offer a definition of temperance, perhaps because Aristotle offers none.

The treatise of Aquinas on temperance in the *Summa of Theology* (2-2.141–70) is complex, the result of his resolve to bring together related themes under each of the virtues. He believes this to be a more comprehensive and useful approach. The matter of morality is reduced to the virtues (to which are annexed the corresponding gifts of the Holy Spirit), the opposing vices, and the negative and affirmative precepts concerning each virtue. In this way no moral matter is overlooked.[66] Since no gift of the Holy Spirit corresponds to temperance, the treatise falls into three major divisions: temperance itself (and its opposing vice); the parts of temperance (and their opposing vices); the precepts of temperance. A measure of the scope of the treatise is seen in the relating of the opposing vices to the parts of temperance. One of the most traditional accounts of vice was under the rubric of the seven capital sins (pride, lechery, gluttony, anger, envy, avarice, sloth). Of these Aquinas deals with *four* in his treatise on temperance: pride (opposed to humility), lechery (opposed to chastity), gluttony (opposed to sobriety), and anger (opposed to meekness). Furthermore, his treatment of pride occasions the treatment of the sin of the first parents.[67] In Aquinas there is a return to a broad conception of temperance with due emphasis on eating, drinking, and sexual relations. This conception results from Aquinas' division of the virtue into its constituent parts.

From the time of Cicero, parts, companions, auxiliary virtues, or followers had been associated with the virtue of temperance, usually without any effort made to clarify the nature of the relation of the parts to temperance itself. Alan of Lille, without developing the idea further, suggests that the parts are powers or potentialities through which temperance is able to operate. Philip the Chancellor provides bases for the division of temperance into sobriety, chastity, and modesty, but does not have a theory of parts as such. Albert the Great returns to the divisions of Cicero and Macrobius, reducing the latter to the former and adopting the threefold division of chastity into the states of virginity, widowhood, and marriage, which he correctly claims to be a division of the *sancti*, that is, the ecclesiastical tradition. In addition to this material division of temperance, Albert does have an inchoate formal theory of parts as such; but it is not developed, nor does he highlight its use in dividing the cardinal virtues into parts.[68]

Thomas Aquinas has a formal theory about the parts of virtue that he applies in the division into parts of each of the cardinal virtues. There are three kinds of parts: integral, subjective, and potential. Integral parts are those that must concur for the perfect act of the virtue in question; they are necessary conditions for a cardinal virtue to be a full-fledged virtue.[69] To be an integral part of virtue is to be a part in the way that walls, roof, and foundations are parts of a house.[70] An integral part is not necessarily a virtue itself but may simply be a condition or state grounding the virtue.

The subjective parts of a cardinal virtue are closer to an ordinary idea of a part; they are the different species of the virtue in the way that ox and lion are parts of animal.[71] The subjective parts as species of a genus are the class embracing individuals as the ultimate realization in the real world of the genus, which, as such, is not in the real world. There are no animals in reality over and above the specific members (cats, dogs, oxen, lions, elephants, etc.) of the genus or class. Aquinas is claiming that there is no prudence, justice, temperance, or fortitude that is possessed by virtuous people over and above the subjective parts of those classes of virtue. To be temperate is to possess the different specific virtues into which temperance is divided.

'Potential parts of any virtue are said to be annexed virtues that have an orientation to some secondary acts or matter but that do not have the total power of the principal virtue.'[72] They are secondary virtues that operate like the principal virtue but do so in regard to other related material objects in which there is not the same degree of difficulty.[73] The example offered is that of the nutritive and sensitive aspects of the soul, each of which is a manifestation of the virtuosity of the form but neither of which manifests the full power of the soul.[74]

Aquinas uses this account to categorize the parts of each of the cardinal virtues. In the *Summa of Theology* he begins with three divisions of temperance: those of Cicero and Macrobius, which we have already seen, and the division from *On the Passions* that was attributed to Andronicus of Rhodes (austerity, continence, humility, simplicity, adornment, good order, self-sufficiency).[75] The result of the application of the theory of parts to temperance might be set out schematically as follows:

Quasi-integral parts
   verecundia (sense of shame; ST 2-2.144)
   honestas (uprightness; ST 2-2.145)

Subjective parts
Re food:
   abstinentia (abstinence; ST 2-2.146)
   ieiunium (fasting; ST 2-2.147)
Re drink:
   sobrietas (sobriety; ST 2-2.149)
Re sexual pleasures:
   castitas (chastity; ST 2-2.151)
   pudicitia (purity as pertaining to chastity; ST 2-2.151.4)
   virginitas (virginity as part of chastity; ST 2-2.152)

Potential parts
   continentia (continence; ST 2-2.155)
   clementia et mansuetudo (clemency and meekness; ST 2-2.157)
   modestia (modesty; ST 2-2.160)
   (Species of modesty)
   – *humilitas* (humility; ST 2-2.161)
   – *studiositas* (studiousness; ST 2-2.166)
   – re external actions of the body (ST 2-2.168)
   – re external ornament (ST 2-2.169)

Thomas introduces three terms into this division not found in his sources: *fasting* as an act of abstinence (*ST* 2-2.147); *virginity* as a part of chastity (*ST* 2-2.152); and *studiousness* (*studiositas*, meaning controlled intellectual curiosity) as a species of modesty (*ST* 2-2.166).[76]

The subjective parts of temperance reflect a narrow conception of the virtue, focusing as it does on eating/drinking (abstinence and sobriety) and sex (chastity and purity). In this Aquinas is in agreement with his immediate predecessors and with Aristotle. The relegation of continence to a potential part is a considerable departure from tradition and probably reflects an Aristotelian influence (to be examined in the next chapter).

Aquinas approaches the concept of temperance with a single-minded concern for the rational nature of human beings. Concupiscence and pleasures arising from the passions are threats to reason, and so there is a need for control over passion. At the centre of his thought is a text from the *Divine Names* that he uses rather freely. According to Dionysius, the evil of the soul is to be outside reason. While Aquinas is not unfamiliar with this account, his use of the idea is frequently couched in positive terms about the good of man, and sometimes the accounts are combined: 'the good or evil of man is to be in accord with reason or outside reason.'[77]

The good, the goal, the end of human activity is to act in accordance with reason, but in order to do that the inner forces that conspire against reason must be curbed, bridled, and brought to heel. Generally speaking, it is human virtue that inclines to what is in line with reason;[78] the virtues are conservative of the human good in so far as through them 'the passions are moderated lest they lead man away from the good of reason.'[79] Specifically, concupiscence implies an impulse to what is pleasurable, and this impulse requires bridling, which pertains to temperance.[80] Temperance is a special virtue in so far as it restrains the appetite from the things that are particularly alluring to man and contrary to reason;[81] these are what are lowest in man, squaring with his bestial nature.[82]

The particularly enticing desires and appetites are those of touch, as Aristotle had said. Whatever passion impels us against reason must be repressed through temperance.[83] In his account of the cardinal virtues in general, Aquinas offers this description: 'Temperance is a disposition of the spirit that imposes measure on certain passions or operations lest they be borne beyond what is due.'[84] He does not expand on what this 'due' is, but it seems to be the good of reason. What is this good of reason according to which man must act if he is to be true to his being? The good of reason is that the order of reason be honoured and observed; that is what is due:

> The principal order of reason, however, consists in the fact that it orders things to an end and the good of reason consists in this order above all, for the good implies the concept of an end, and the end itself is the rule for things ordered towards the end. But all pleasures that enter into human use are ordered to some necessity of this life as to an end. Therefore, temperance takes the necessity of this life as the rule for the pleasures that it uses; that is, it only uses them as the necessity of this life requires.[85]

This text goes some distance towards specifying the formal notion of the good of man: good of man = to be according to reason = the order of reason = the use of pleasures as necessity requires. What is this necessity? In this text Aquinas does not spell out what the necessity of this life requires, beyond distinguishing between necessity as that without which a thing is unable in any way to be, and that without which a thing is unable to be in a fitting manner.[86] From other passages, however, it is clear that the first necessity refers to the necessity related to the conservation of human life, either in the species or in the individual. For the conservation of individual life, food is required, to which there is attached an essential pleasure rooted in our nature to ensure its use. For the conservation of the species, the use of woman (intercourse) is required, to which there is attached a corresponding pleasure.[87]

Temperance, then, pertains to the areas of human life in which the pleasures of the sense of touch are bound to what relates to the integrity of that life, either in the individual or the species, 'as are the pleasures of food and sex.' Taking a leaf from Aristotle (and Albert), Aquinas notes that there is no special virtue for the other senses because they are not vehement (that is, there are no vehement pleasures associated with them) and so do not present any particular difficulty.[88]

Sex is oriented to the conservation of the species. The right exercise of sex and the proper enjoyment of its pleasures are ruled and governed by the requirements of the conservation of the species. What these requirements are must be further specified (in the account of marriage),[89] but the relationship among sex, procreation, and conservation of the species is clearly established. Since all are sexed, all must be temperate, channelling sex correctly through the appropriate virtues. It must be remembered, however, that in a medieval view of things sex differs from eating in one important respect. Everyone eats, and so temperance operates in a sphere in which natural inclinations to eat and drink obtain some satisfaction. It is a matter of establishing correct moderation in what has to be done. This model does not apply to sex, which is the exclusive preserve of married people. Within marriage it is a matter of correctly moderating sexual behaviour; outside marriage it is a matter of total restraint and repression.

7

Continence, Chastity, and Virginity

In spite of efforts to sort out the vocabulary of the virtues that were particularly concerned with sexual matters, the terms *continentia* (continence) and *castitas* (chastity) continued to lack determined and settled definitions. Philip the Chancellor, for instance, raises the question of the proper usage of these terms as well as of the term, *pudicitia* (purity). It is clear from his analysis that the words were sometimes used interchangeably and resisted mutually exclusive definitions. The meanings reported by Papias are characteristic of thirteenth-century usage: *continentia* connotes self-restraint in general, but is often used with a marked sexual reference; *castitas* connotes restraint from illicit sexual behaviour; *pudicitia* connotes areas tangential to sex such as touches, looks, and kisses, but it is sometimes taken to be synonymous with chastity. Philip the Chancellor reports several uses of the term *pudicitia*. Later in the century St Thomas Aquinas, who attempts to distinguish between chastity and purity so carefully, has to admit that 'sometimes, nonetheless, the one is used for the other.'[1] Although chastity will be the focus of this chapter, a word must first be said about continence whose connection with temperance antedates even Christian reflection on the virtues.

CONTINENCE

The concept of continence had a long history from its initial association with temperance by Cicero. It is a member of virtually all major divisions of temperance and is central to many divisions of the late twelfth and early thirteenth centuries, often being used interchangeably with chastity. Eventually, however, chastity won the day as the virtue concerned with sexual feelings and desires. One of the reasons why 'continence' lost out to 'chastity' as the preferred term for the virtue covering sexual matters was undoubtedly the connotation of general restraint traditionally associated with the term. Another reason may have been Robert Grosseteste's use of the Latin *continentia* to translate a key Aristotelian term in the seventh book of the *Nicomachean Ethics*. The seventh book provides an account of *enkrateia* and *akrasia*, translated in Latin as *continentia* and *incontinentia* respectively. The account is a complex effort on the part of Aristotle to show the difference between virtuous and vicious persons in matters of temperance, on the one hand, and their near neighbours, who were said to be continent and incontinent persons, on the other.[2]

Temperance and continence are both concerned with pleasures of taste and touch, and they lead to the same way of acting in regard to these pleasures. In the view of Aristotle, however, there is a profound difference between the two. The temperate person is one who not only intellectually judges rightly and as he ought in regard to the pleasures of taste and touch and acts accordingly, but has no desire to act otherwise. The continent person knows how he ought to act and acts accordingly, but his desires and passions pull him to act in wrong ways in regard to the pleasures of food, drink, and sex. He has depraved desires and to that extent he is not virtuous:

> the temperate man, as well as the self-restrained [continent] is so constituted as never to be led by the pleasures of the body to act against principle. But whereas the self-restrained man has evil desires, the temperate man has none; he is so constituted as to take no pleasure in things that are contrary to principle, whereas the self-restrained man does feel pleasure in such things, but does not yield to it.[3]

The continent are on the road to virtue but not yet virtuous.

Through this account by Aristotle a new conception of continence is introduced that undercuts the tradition that saw in continence a valued virtue and ideal of sexual behaviour. Initially at least, the Aristotelian account posed no substantive problem. Albert shows no concern with the concept in his commentary on the *Ethics*, but accepts the new usage in its own context, as does Aquinas in his commentary. Neither confronts Aristotle with the tradition.[4] In other works, Aquinas does confront the Aristotelian meaning of continence with other meanings that make of continence a virtue, even the supreme manifestation of temperance in virginity. In Aristotle's sense, continence lacks a certain degree of perfection and to that degree is not fully a virtue. As Aquinas notes, continence is 'a certain imperfect [element] in the genus of virtue.'[5]

Neither Albert nor Aquinas registers any particular concern with the alternative sense of continence introduced by the *Nicomachean Ethics*, but more literalist minds could well take offence at this apparent attack on a Christian ideal. As Gauthier says:

> To say, for example, that continence is not a virtue was to enunciate an evident truth for one familiar with the Aristotelian theory. On the other hand, for one who only knew of the continence of which theology had traditionally spoken, it would have been to break openly with the Christian ideal. The conflict is not imaginary; on 7 March 1277 it culminated in the condemnation of the proposition, 'Quod continentia non est [*add* essentialiter] virtus.' ['That continence is not essentially a virtue.'][6]

The condemnation seems to have been aimed at those who accepted the Aristotelian view that continence did not measure up to the requirements of a full-fledged virtue. To the extent that Aquinas accepts the account of Aristotle, he would come under the censure. Albert, too, comes under the censure in his commentary on the *Ethics* and might even have been its chief target, since he explicitly denies, without further distinction, that continence is essentially ('secundum essentiam') a virtue.[7]

There may very well have been other reasons for the condemnation of the proposition about the virtuous nature of continence, and there may have been arguments in some quarters (as Raymond Lull suggests there were) that continence frustrated the natural end of procreation.[8] The parallel with Aristotle's view is too exact for it not to have been the main focus of the censure, however. Aquinas' usage shows him to be comfortable with the different meanings of *continentia*. I have some difficulty with Gauthier's suggestion that Aquinas took over the Aristotelian account. He certainly incorporated it at *ST* 2-2.155.1 (Gauthier's reference), but he did not claim that it was the only possible meaning. In fact, in a later discussion of the essence of religious life, Aquinas asks whether not perpetual chastity but perpetual continence is required for the religious state. It is clear from his affirmative reply that he is not using 'continence' in the Aristotelian sense.[9]

Some later commentaries on Aristotle from the Arts Faculty after 1277 accepted the view of the *Ethics* without further ado.[10] In this they were no different from the commentaries of Albert and Thomas, if perhaps less prudent, given the time of writing. John Buridan is more circumspect in his *Questions on the Ethics* when he asks whether continence should be called a virtue. He argues that it ought to be, because Cicero treats it as a part of temperance and it is placed by Seneca among the cardinal virtues; but he notes that Aristotle says it is not a virtue. Buridan recalls the various traditional uses of the term and enunciates the Aristotelian meaning, concluding, 'And it is in this sense that I accept the term in the present question.'[11] Other condemnations in regard to sexual matters are far more substantive than the essentially verbal dispute about continence. This one arose from a literal reading of Aristotle and from neglecting to attend to the careful distinctions in meaning made by Aquinas.

An important point was missed by Albert, Aquinas, and John Buridan in their commentaries on the seventh book of the *Ethics*, although Aquinas perhaps sensed the point. For a Christian writer viewing human beings in the actual state of fallen nature, Aristotle's account of continence comes much closer to an account of the virtuous person struggling with concupiscence, lust, and sexual inclinations than his claims for the temperate man who is unperturbed by such appetites and passions. Aristotle's temperate man has more in common with Adam before the Fall than with the sons of Adam. Aquinas hints at this when he compares Aristotle and the desert fathers: 'Indeed, others say that continence is that whereby one resists depraved desires that exist vehemently in him. It is in this way that the Philosopher takes continence in *Ethics* 7 and continence is also taken in this way in the *Conversations of the Fathers*.'[12] Aquinas' account of temperance in itself and of chastity, with its insistence on controlling, repressing, and bridling, is much closer to the Aristotelian account of continence in the seventh book of the *Ethics* than to the idealized view of temperance in the same book. In an un-Aristotelian observation, Philip the Chancellor says that temperance does not guarantee that passions do not arise, but that they do not gain the upper hand:

First of all animal motions surge up, then are bridled, and domi-

nation over them follows from habituation ... Thus we concede that
the act of bridling is midway between domination that precedes and
domination that follows. However, domination must be understood
in this way – not that motions do not surge up, but that when they
do emerge they are not consented to.[13]

Bonaventure notes that the definition of temperance used by Peter
Lombard is given from the point of view 'of the state of fallen nature
in which depraved pleasures arise and are bridled by the virtue of
temperance.'[14]

CHASTITY

The term for the control of genital sex that seems to have won the day
was 'chastity,' reflected in the usage of Aquinas who says that chastity
is 'a certain special virtue, having special matter, namely the desires
for pleasures that are in sexual matters.'[15] It is ordered to the reproductive power in reference to the principal pleasures of intercourse
itself.[16] There is need for a special virtue because sexual pleasures are
more vehement than others, are more oppressive of reason than the
pleasures of eating, and so are in special need of bridling and castigation.[17] The association of chastity with castigation made by Aquinas
is a curious throwback to an older translation of Aristotle. Aquinas
begins the treatment of chastity with the remark 'the word "chastity"
is taken from this that through reason concupiscence is castigated and
bridled in the manner of [dealing with] youths as is clear from the
Philosopher in the third book of the Ethics.' In the translation com-
mented on by Aquinas, however, there is no mention of castitas or
chastisement, and the etymological point made by Aristotle does not
work in Latin. It worked for the Ethica vetus, which does not have the
term temperantia but uses castitas to translate sophrosune.[18]

Purity is a subjective part of temperance that refers to the pleasures
surrounding intercourse, such as are in kisses, touches, and embraces,
and so has a special relation to chastity.[19] The root of the word pudicitia is pudor (shame), so purity should govern the area in which shame
is particularly felt – the area of sexual acts, where shame is felt to such
an extent that it is present even in conjugal relations, which are embel-
lished with the moral uprightness of marriage. The reason for this is
because the genitals are not obedient to reason in the way other bodily

members are. Chastity has reference to sexual acts themselves; purity to sexual signs such as impure looks, kisses, and touches.[20] In apparent contradiction with the theory that would have the subjective parts of virtue being specific virtues, Aquinas claims that purity is not a distinct virtue from chastity but expresses a certain circumstance of chastity. If it is not a distinct virtue, what is it? Aquinas does not say. Richard of Mediavilla modifies this view somewhat when, agreeing that it is not a distinct virtue, he claims that purity pertains to the essence of chastity, or at least to its completion. One who is perfectly habituated to safeguard the good of reason in regard to sexual matters will be thereby habituated to safeguard the good of reason in regard to embraces and kisses.[21]

For Aquinas chastity has one subspecies, virginity, which shall be taken up below. From his earliest writing, Aquinas resisted the traditional threefold division of chastity (or continence) into that of virgins, widows, and the married. He gives no special weight to the forms chastity must take according to the states of life of those who must exercise the virtue, except for virginity, which he claims to be a virtue. In this he is at variance with his academic predecessors of the thirteenth century and with the subsequent pastoral and moral tradition. The reason for his position seems to be that Aquinas could not find anything in widowhood or in marriage to specify further the general virtue of chastity in order to generate virtues distinct from chastity. In explaining his position, Aquinas suggests an interesting view of chastity. In the question whether virginity is a virtue, the objection is raised that virginity is divided over against widowhood and conjugal purity. Since the latter two are not virtues, virginity is not a virtue either. His reply:

> Conjugal chastity is praiseworthy from this alone that it abstains from
> illicit pleasures and so has no particular excellence over and above common chastity. Widowhood, however, surely adds something over and
> above common chastity but does not attain perfection in its field, namely
> the complete immunity from sexual pleasure. Only virginity does that.[22]

The implication here is that chastity is not, in its perfection, a matter of chastisement, control, and bridling of sexual pleasures, but of total abstinence from them. Consequently, except for virginity, which manifests the perfection of chastity, the states of life that demand different kinds of chastity hold no particular interest for Aquinas. One might have expected closer scrutiny of these states in a moral treatise that claims to go beyond the universal language of morality.[23] It might be argued that to do so is not the job of a theological treatise of the sort Aquinas is writing, except that he himself suggests that particular moral consideration can be taken of 'the special states of man, for example when it deals with subjects and overseers, those in the active and contemplative lives, *and certain other differences* among men.'[24] The differences in the states of chastity did not count sufficiently to prompt Aquinas to give them particular consideration.

This failure in Aquinas to deal with the states of chastity results in the absence from his treatise of a rich tradition that saw in chastity an excellence to be encouraged, promoted, and safeguarded in accordance with the chosen life-style of Christians, whatever it might be. Alexander of Hales sees in the three states the ways that are open for Christians to repair the corruption and infection in the concupiscible appetite resulting from original sin. Through grace one is raised to one of the states of continence suitable to one's particular life.[25] Concern with the different states of chastity is found in later pastoral works that frequently depend on the threefold division of chastity into virginity, widowhood, and marriage. The fourteenth-century English vernacular *Book of Vices and Virtues* says that there are seven branches of the tree of chastity, which are 'the seven staates of men and wommen that ben in this world.'[26] These are: the general state of what might be called secular virgins (no vows), unvowed seculars who had lost virginity, the married, widows, virgins proper, clergy, and religious. The mention of each state occasions a short treatise on the way of life in question from the standpoint of sex. The *Speculum morale*, falsely attributed to Vincent of Beauvais, after a presentation of chastity and purity, which is simply an excerpt from Thomas Aquinas, runs on immediately with the very unthomistic, 'We ought to realize that chastity is divided into virginal, that of widows, and conjugal.'[27]

In all those who comment on the threefold state of chastity, the term 'widow' is retained, no doubt out of consideration for traditional usage.[28] But since the division into states is meant to embrace everyone, the term cannot be strictly interpreted. If it were, the class of people who were never married but who had sexual experiences would not be included in the division. Consequently, it was understood that the three states of chastity are: (1) those who never have and who propose never to experience sex willingly (virgins); (2) those presently unmarried who have experienced sex willingly and who propose never more to experience it ('widows'); (3) those who are married and who legitimately exercise their rights to sex.

VIRGINITY

The emphasis on virginity, as not only a desirable state but one preferable to all others, is an invariant tradition from early Christianity through the Middle Ages, supported by St Paul's advice to fathers: 'So he does well who joins his virgin in marriage, and one who does not so join her does better' (1 Corinthians 7:38). The writings of Tertullian (died circa 225) and Cyprian (died 258) lavish high praise on virginity and are harbingers of the flood of writings on the subject in the late fourth and early fifth centuries in both East and West. These latter set the tone for the subsequent tradition in the Latin Church, and it is to them that the medieval masters turn for their authorities on virginity.[29]

If treatises on marriage demonstrate the difficulty Christianity had with the exercise of sex, treatises on virginity demonstrate where its heart was in regard to sex. The doctrine of virginity is a touchstone of the Christian perception of the value of sex for post-lapsarian existence. The term 'doctrine' is used advisedly here because the preeminence of virginity and its superiority to marriage were cast in doctrinal terms as a result of Jerome's fierce battle with Jovinian. Jovinian is listed among the heretics by Augustine, whose work on heresies taught the Middle Ages about the varieties of heresy.[30]

Theology, canon law, exhortatory treatises on the virtues, and sermons reflect a continued interest in the subject of virginity in the later Middle Ages. What the later commentaries lack in flair and rhetoric (characteristics of the fourth- and fifth-century treatises), they make up for in clarity, precision, and critical appreciation.[31] Academic discussions of virginity focused on five issues: (1) the nature of virginity; (2) the conditions under which virginity can be truly said to be lost; (3) whether virginity is a virtue; (4) the relative value of virginity vis-à-vis other states, particularly marriage; and finally, (5) the heavenly rewards to be bestowed on virgins.

The most popular definition of virginity was provided by Augustine: 'However, virginal integrity and immunity from all intercourse through devout continence is an angelic sharing and the *exercise (meditatio) of perpetual incorruption in corruptible flesh.*' The underlined words were taken to constitute the definition itself, but because of a linguistic development in regard to the term *meditatio* and a misreading of the text of Augustine the more common medieval version would read: 'Virginity is the perpetual meditation on incorruption in corruptible flesh.'[32] In the explications of this definition and in the efforts to explain the essential nature of virginity, it is apparent that virginity is perceived to be much more a state of mind than a state of body.

Of course the word itself connotes freedom from ever having had sexual relations and, at least in women, the physical integrity presumed to persist from such freedom. Normally this would be the case. But there are cases in which physical integrity would be lost and we would not want to say that virginity was lost, or in which women could have sexual experience and retain physical integrity and we would want to say that virginity was lost. Then there is male virginity, which has no meaningful physical integrity associated with it. It must have been considerations such as these that led many medieval writers to distinguish among types of virginity in order to highlight the virginity that has moral and spiritual worth. Albert's views are helpful here, since he directly addresses the question of what virginity essentially (*substantialiter*) consists in.

Albert distinguishes four types of virginity. First, there is the innate virginity of infants before the age of rational, intelligent control over their behaviour. Second, there is the innate virginity that is safeguarded and protected but without a religious vow of continence. The third type of virginity is innate, safeguarded, and dedicated to God through a vow or a firm proposal. Finally, there is innate but foolish virginity, which is of two kinds: venal virginity under the cloak of piety, and virginity that retains its physical, innate quality but exhibits itself in the attire and outward manner of prostitutes. According to Albert 'only the third virginity is worthy of praise although the first and second have bodily fairness.'[33] There are three characteristics of virginity in the fully moral sense of the term: integrity from birth, resolve to safeguard that integrity, and the directing of that resolve to God. These features belong to the ideal type, but are not necessary conditions, since physical integrity may be lost but virginity retained.

In his introduction to the question about the corruption of virginity or the conditions under which it can truly be lost, Albert says that consideration ought first to be given to what is substantially constitutive of virginity, 'and then from that it will be known what corrupts it.'[34] He repeats his earlier description of virginity and provides a careful analysis of its meaning. 'Virginity ... is integrity of the flesh witnessing to incorruption of the mind.'[35] Integrity of the flesh does not mean freedom from every form of lesion, since a virgin can be wounded in her pudenda by a sword or a stick without the integrity being hurt. He then explains the sort of incorruption he has in mind: 'However, the incorruption is said to be from the actual and complete pleasure of concupiscence [arising] from the will in operation, or consenting, or not dissenting, or not denying the preliminaries to the extent possible.'[36] By complete pleasure is meant the pleasure in the act that is comparable to the pleasure in intercourse (orgasm?), but note that Albert does not say that there has to be sexual intercourse, just a comparable amount of pleasure. Such pleasure corrupts the body through the corruption of vice, not simply through passion over which one might not have any control. For virginity to be lost through a finger, hand, piece of wood or any other instrument, the will must be *operative* in those using such things to touch or to bring pressure on the interior nerves of the genitals to such a degree that the complete pleasure of intercourse follows. This can be through *consenting* to homosexual experience (*sodomia*), heterosexual experience, or bestiality. *Not dissenting* is found in those who do not cry out, presumably when they are being sexually attacked. *Not denying* is found in those who do not always take an opposing position in heart and body, so that even if they cannot defend the body they at least keep the heart from the desire for pleasure.[37]

The essence of virginity is located squarely in the will and has nothing necessarily to do with the presence or absence of physical lesion in the genitals. Confirmation of this is offered when Albert notes that since virginity is the same in men and women when it comes to merit and reward, it must be the same in what can corrupt it. 'But since it is impossible to assign a way that a male is corrupted through a division [of the flesh], division of the body is not even corruptive of virginity in a female.'[38]

This account is designed to obviate a conception of virginity that would locate its essence in a requirement of physical intactness. One must wonder whether Albert's insistence on actual and complete pleasure, which appears to be what today would be called orgasm, does not go too far the other way. Imagine a case in which a woman had up to a point in time retained her virginity in Albert's full sense of the term. At some later point, overcome by temptation, she stimulates herself clear-headedly and willingly, but no pleasure ensues. According to his definition, integrity of the flesh is maintained because actual and complete pleasure does not accompany her action. But surely this integrity does not attest to incorruption of her mind, and it would seem that one would want to say that she had chosen to abandon her virginity.

In his *Commentary on the Sentences*, Aquinas closely follows Albert's account of virginity, but there, and more clearly elsewhere, he provides clarification that avoids the difficulty we noted in Albert's focus on complete pleasure. A way out of the problem is suggested in Aquinas' description of a virgin as a person 'who chose incorruption, which is the material element in virginity, that he never lost and intends to have and to conserve.'[39] The choice was made (the past) and the incorruption was never lost (past and present), and he intends (present) to have and conserve it (the future). In the case I just proposed, the choice was made and the incorruption never lost, but the intention is changed and so to that degree the person, on the account of Aquinas, cannot be said to be a virgin.

In sexual pleasure there are three things to be considered: (1) the rupture of the virginal seal on the part of the body; (2) the resolution of semen causing sense pleasure on the part of the union of body and soul; (3) the proposal to attain to such pleasure on the part of the soul alone. Virginity is the state that distances itself from these three factors. Physical integrity has an incidental (*per accidens*) relation to virginity, normally accompanies it, but is not necessarily present. Sexual pleasure is the material factor or substratum of virginity; that is, it is in regard to pleasure that one makes oneself a virgin, a position coinciding with that of Albert. Aquinas adds a third element that is formal and perfective, however – the proposal to abstain from sexual pleasure forever. The resolute will never to experience sexual pleasure must be present in a virgin.[40] The perfect state of virginity requires the concurrence of all three elements, but the absence of the first and second does not necessarily destroy the state. In the case proposed above, the woman was no longer formally a virgin because of her will for pleasure, but I believe Aquinas would have to say that because she did not experience the pleasure she wanted she did not lose her virginity in a material sense. Consequently, she can repent, confess, and recoup her virginal state.

Before discussing the moral value of virginity, a word must be said about the conditions under which virginity can be lost. This question, which had received considerable attention from Gratian, was systematized in the pastoral summas of John of Freiburg and Astesanus. The issue was not one of purely academic curiosity or speculative interest, but was prompted by institutional requirements. Albert is reluctant to talk about masturbation in this context, but says that 'on account of the evil of the day it is necessary to introduce [such] foul questions.'[41] The evil of the day is likely the fact that such acts were being performed; but why the necessity? Later, in the article on the veiling and consecration of virgins, he reveals the reason for introducing the issue: 'the evil of the day and *the insistence of those who want to be veiled* excuse the foulness of the question.'[42]

The overriding principle is the spiritual, voluntary nature of virginity, which cannot be taken away against one's will or outside of one's will. Gratian is concerned with rape-abduction (*raptus*); he believes that virginity is not necessarily destroyed through rape. A text from the Office of St Lucy is used by several authors who discuss the matter. In the version of Gratian, Lucy says: 'If you force me to be violated unwillingly my chastity will be doubled into a crown.'[43] Any deliberate act intending the loss of physical integrity or sexual pleasure that successfully reaches completion was considered to result in the loss of virginity, both materially and formally. Virginity could never be regained. Purely mental acts can result in the loss of formal virginity, but there seems to have been general agreement that true penance can repair the damage, incorruption can be recouped, and the rewards of virginity reaped. Other cases are mentioned that involve violence against the will (rape), prepubescence, natural occurrences (continuous menstrual flow, nocturnal pollution), or occurrences outside the will (violation while drunk or asleep or by an incubus). In all these cases virginity was considered not to be lost.[44]

The position in regard to rape is a conclusion consistent with the principle of the free, spiritual nature of virginity, but actually establishes only a general presumption in favour of the perdurance of the virginal state. When it came to the consecration of a virgin who was raped, however, there was a reluctance to act on this presumption.

Rather, a presumption in favour of the strength of the sexual pleasure was endorsed. Astesanus, provides the reason:

> The genitals are quite compacted with nerves and so touching them causes titillation and consequently inclines to pleasure. This attracts consent or at least hinders a person from entirely taking a contrary position. Therefore, since complete dissent cannot be clear to the Church, it was established that such women humbly abstain from consecration.[45]

Finally, the firm resolve to distance oneself from every deliberate sexual experience is not an end in itself, nor does it confer any particular moral value. The precepts of moral uprightness do not demand virginity from those who want to be morally good. Virginity is essentially a religious state in which the firm resolve to abstain from sexual pleasure gains value from the ordering of that resolve to God: 'The proposal of perpetual abstinence from sexual pleasure is what is formal and perfective in virginity, and this proposal is rendered praiseworthy from the end, namely to the extent that it is made to establish freedom for divine things.'[46]

The question of moral value is closely linked with the question of the virtuous character of virginity. This was complicated by considerations arising from the Aristotelian definition of virtue. At one level, whether virginity is a virtue or not can be seen as an issue of semantics with nothing substantive hanging in the balance. If sufficient specificity of matter, excellence, and difficulty is perceived, then virginity will be called a separate virtue in its own right, a subspecies of chastity. This is the position taken by Aquinas in opposition to St Albert, who denies that virginity is a virtue but claims that it is something more excellent than virtue, since virtue is a matter of precept but virginity is not.[47] Aquinas sees in the abstention from all sexual experience a degree of excellence sufficient to constitute a special virtue. He does not find in conjugal chastity or widowhood a similar specificity of excellence over and above the general virtue of chastity and so refuses the status of special virtue to these two states.[48]

Authors after Aquinas tend to take a middle position. They do not want to deny that virginity is in some sense a virtue, but they are reluctant to endow virginity with the status of a special virtue. The solution of Richard of Mediavilla charts a course between these two tendencies:

It [virginity] is not a virtue essentially distinct from conjugal chastity for both determine the will to what right reason directs in regard to what must be observed in sexual pleasures. But virginity determines the will more perfectly in this regard than conjugal chastity. Whence, virginity adds a state of perfection over and above conjugal chastity and so they seem to differ as imperfect and perfect virtues, which are not essentially distinguished.[49]

In addition, there is another much more substantive issue, querying not whether virginity is a virtue or something better but whether it is a virtue or something worse. Before dealing with the question whether virginity is a virtue, Aquinas asks whether it is illicit, Peter of Palude asks whether it is licit and a good in its own right, and John Buridan asks whether virginity is a virtue or a vice.[50]

Two considerations lie behind the question of Aquinas, one specifically theological, the other specifically philosophical. The former arises from the precept to increase and multiply (Genesis 1:28), which was part of the original plan of creation. Virginity seems contrary to that directive. The place of virginity in the present state of fallen nature has been touched on already in the first chapter, where it was noted that in Paradise marriage and procreation would have been superior to virginity, while the opposite is the case now.[51] Aquinas does not refer to such considerations when discussing whether virginity is licit, but contents himself with noting that the obligation of procreation applies to the class of humans, but not distributively to each member of the class. For the precept to be met it is enough that a sufficient number procreate. Besides, there is a need for the spiritual growth and progress that are provided by those who abstain from procreation and give themselves over to divine contemplation for the enhancement and salvation of the whole human race.[52]

The second main consideration prompting the question of whether virginity is licit arises from Aristotle's conception of the nature of moral virtue. Virtue is a mean between the extremes of excess and defect, which constitute the vices opposed to virtue. Virginity, in its complete renunciation of all sexual pleasures, would seem to be a departure from the mean of temperance and so a vice. As Aristotle says: 'He that indulges in every pleasure and refrains from none is intemperate; and he who flees all pleasures is a boor and insensible.'[53]

Raising the question whether virginity is licit could well have been prompted purely by intellectual curiosity and the challenge of confronting Aristotle's doctrine of the mean with a Christian moral value that traditionally was considered to be a virtue although, apparently located at one of the extremes. There was more to it than that, however, a fact suggested by the condemnation in 1277 of the proposition 'That perfect abstinence from the act of the flesh corrupts virtue and the species.'[54]

Hissette wonders whether the censors in their haste attributed to Siger of Brabant the very objections he himself raised and refuted, or whether they simply condemned dangerous theses of Aristotle. I suspect neither is the case, since Siger's views on virginity are completely orthodox and Aristotle does not broach the question of virginity.[55] Aristotle's doctrine of the mean could, however, be taken to imply that virginity was a vice against the virtue of temperance and, as Gauthier suggests, virginity would also have been in conflict with Aristotle's imposition of legislation requiring marriage for the good of the polis.[56] It is likely that the condemnation envisaged conclusions that were, or could be, drawn from Aristotle. Gauthier provides some evidence that the philosophical conclusion that virginity was a vice was actually drawn in the thirteenth century. He cites a text of Bonaventure, who reports that the doctor of Frederick II saw in the Aristotelian doctrine of insensibility the condemnation of virginity. If a commentary on Aristotle reflects actual conditions, then the question whether virginity is a virtue was debated and positions contrary to accepted theological views about virginity were held:

In regard to the second question there are diverse opinions but it is true according to our faith and the truth that it must be posited [habet poni] that virginity is a virtue since: virgins are rewarded; reward, however, is given to virtue; therefore, etc. But as to what is to be said according to the Philosopher [Aristotle], some say that according to the Philosopher virginity is not a virtue because virginity is complete abstinence from everything sexual, and therefore, as they say, it pertains to a certain insensibility, namely, that one is not inclined in any way to such pleasures. But in truth this is not held by the Philosopher, therefore I say to the question that according to faith and truth, and it can even be held according to the Philosopher, that virginity is a virtue.[57]

This is not the place to engage in the debate over the view that the

Averroists in the Faculty of Arts at Paris defended their speculation on the basis of a doctrine of double truth: that is, that something could be true in philosophy but false for the faith or vice versa. I encountered a text from the early fourteenth century, however that shows the extent to which an inference of Aristotelian views could be drawn in sexual matters that was entirely contrary to the established Christian position. In questions appended to his commentary on the Pseudo-Boethian *De disciplina scolarium*, William of Wheteley (active 1309–16) asks: 'Now the question arises whether lechery would benefit a student.' He leaves no doubt that he has in mind intercourse and perhaps even masturbation (*emissio seminis*). He replies in the affirmative, as long as it is done in moderation. Such a response is consistent with the Aristotelian doctrine of the mean, but one could not imagine a more unorthodox reply.[58]

In spite of the possibility that there may have been voices raised against the virtuous character of virginity, theologians and commentators seemed to rush to the defence of Aristotle. The defence was made on the ground that the doctrine of the mean must be taken not in a purely quantitative way but in a formal, rational way, and that virginity meets the requirements of rationality. Bonaventure parodies a quantitative interpretation of Aristotle, noting that chastity surely does not require finding the mid-point between intercourse with no woman and intercourse with all women. Virtue is not a matter of a material mid-point, but of the manner in which acts are performed.[59] Aquinas, no doubt sensing the import of Aristotle's views on insensibility, alerts the reader in his *Commentary on the Ethics* that such views do not mean that virginity is a vice. First, because virginity is not the abstention from all pleasures (only sexual), and second, because the abstention from sexual pleasures is done according to right reason. A balanced and rational position is taken on the circumstances of adopting the proposal of virginity, so that the choice is made as it ought to be, in accord with right reason.[60]

Elsewhere he states in what the rationality of virginity precisely consists. Following Aristotle, he notes that there are three human goods: external goods such as riches, the goods of the body, and the goods of the soul, among which the goods of the contemplative life are greater than those of the active life. There is a rational ordering among these goods, so that the renunciation of lower goods for the benefit of higher goods is not a vice but is in accord with right reason. Devout (*pia*) virginity abstains from sexual pleasure (a good of the body) to leave more room for divine contemplation (a higher good), so virginity, rather than being a vice, is praiseworthy.[61]

Not only is virginity laudable, but it is the preferred state, superior to all other states of life. The pre-eminence of virginity over marriage was never seriously doubted by the medieval masters, as is apparent in their responses to the standard question whether virginity is better than marriage. The arguments used to support the view that marriage is inferior to virginity are of two types, appealing either to the nature of perfect continence in this life, or to the special rewards bestowed on virgins in the hereafter. Such rewards are of two kinds – the hundredfold fruit of chastity that is greater than the sixtyfold of widows and the thirtyfold of the married, and the coronet (*aureola*) reserved for martyrs, virgins, and preachers of the word of God. I shall expand on these subjects later, but first a word must be said about what is perhaps the reason why the superiority of virginity was never doubted. To suggest otherwise was to fall into heresy, the heresy of Jovinian. Both Albert and Thomas Aquinas refer to the 'heresy of Jovinian,' Albert probably drawing on Augustine's work *On Heresies* that taught the Middle Ages about heresy, Aquinas drawing on the *Book of Church Teachings* attributed to Gennadius of Marseilles. Writing at the end of the fifth century, Gennadius says: 'To equate marriage with consecrated virginity is not the work of a Christian but of Jovinian.'[62]

Although Augustine (died 430), who was nearing the end of his life when he wrote *On Heresies*, could say that the heresy of Jovinian was extinct at the time of writing, it was very much alive in the last decade of the fourth century. Little is known of Jovinian and what is known must be gleaned from the writings of his opponents, as is so often the case with heresiarchs. Unfortunately, information about Jovinian must be drawn almost entirely from Jerome, who was no disinterested critic of error but a brilliant if acerbic satirist, who gives no quarter in his attacks on Jovinian.[63]

Jovinian was a monk who defected from his religious way of life, preaching his views in Milan and Rome. If he had been nothing more than a disaffected religious gathering around himself a few like-minded followers, it is unlikely he would have caused the stir he did. In fact, he attracted the attention of four of the great ecclesiastical luminaries of the day: Pope Siricius, Ambrose, Jerome, and Augustine, each of whom felt compelled to write against him. The serial chronology of the whole affair is clear enough, but the precise dates of the writings of the first three are unclear. It is uncertain whether Jerome's *Against Jovinian*, which is the most sustained attack, was written with the knowledge that Pope Siricius and Ambrose had written against Jovinian.

Jerome's recent biographer suggests that Jerome had received the writings of Jovinian at about the same time (early 393) that Siricius and Ambrose were denouncing him and that he wrote his own work ignorant of their condemnations. The reason he offers is that Jerome would have cited Siricius and Ambrose if he had known of their writings. While Kelly's chronology is acceptable, or at least there is nothing clearly against it, his reason for Jerome's silence is not. The tract against Jovinian is an independent work in which Jerome displays his personal, rhetorical skills, biblical knowledge, and acquaintance with secular literature. He shows no interest in appealing to ecclesiastical authorities to prop up his case. In the justification and defence of his work that he wrote to Pammachius almost immediately after *Against Jovinian*, however, Jerome does show a desire to defend himself by appealing to authority, even citing Ambrose. If Jerome had known of the specific censures of Jovinian by Siricius and Ambrose it is likely that he would have cited them in his letter of justification, but he does not. It is reasonable to assume that he was ignorant of them then, and so he was ignorant of them at the time of writing the earlier *Against Jovinian*.[64]

Jerome reports four errors of Jovinian, the first of which is of interest to us. It is the one that disturbed Jerome the most and to which he dedicated most of his refutations. According to Jerome, 'He [Jovinian] says that virgins, widows, and married women who were once washed in Christ, are of equal merit if they do not differ in other works.'[65] Note that Jovinian does not condemn virginity, and so Jerome's tract is not a defence of virginity *per se*; it is, rather, a tract on the *superiority* of virginity over marriage. If the two states are of equal merit, it is likely that young girls would be less inclined to embrace virginity; there would be no particular reason to do so, and Jovinian's preaching would probably have the effect of turning their minds away from virginity to marriage. Even professed virgins of mature age were said to have married after hearing Jovinian.[66]

Jerome attacks Jovinian on two fronts. First, he undertakes an exhaustive survey of the whole Bible in order to show the weakness of

Jovinian's appeal to the support of biblical examples. The centrepiece of this section is Jerome's lengthy commentary on St Paul (1 Corinthians 7) in which he shows that for Paul, and so for Christianity, virginity is to be preferred to marriage because it is superior to marriage. Jerome's arguments, sometimes terribly weak when he tries to engage in logic, reinforce the *leitmotiv* of the first book, which is summed up in his application of the parable of the sower (Matthew 13:8, 23) to the three states of virginity, widowhood, and marriage.[67]

Contrary to a view noted in the first chapter, Jerome puts much store in the idea that Adam and Eve were virgins in Paradise and had intercourse only after sinning and being ejected from the Garden; what things would have been like if they had not sinned no one knows (246A, 263A). A comparative note runs through his remarks: he accepts marriage but prefers virginity (223B); Christ loves virgins more because they spontaneously offer what is not commanded (238C); the difference between marriage and virginity is the difference between not sinning and acting well or between the good and what is better (243B); John the Evangelist remained a virgin and *therefore* was loved more by the Lord (258B). In sum: 'Now I will just say this, as virginity alone without other works does not lead to salvation, so all works without virginity, purity, continence, chastity are imperfect (281C).' One of the most well-known texts is Jerome's 'Marriages fill the earth, virginity [fills] paradise' (246B).

If Jerome had stopped after his extended survey of the Bible he would have left to posterity a plausible case for the superiority of virginity over marriage, and one that, though somewhat grudgingly, acknowledges the legitimacy and fundamental goodness of marriage. He notes from the very beginning of his treatise:

> Nor do we, following the teaching of Marcion and Manichaeus, disparage marriage; nor, deceived by the error of Tatian the prince of the Encratites, do we think all intercourse impure ... We are not ignorant of 'Honourable marriage and immaculate bed' [Hebrews 13:4]. We read the first command of God, 'Increase and multiply and fill the earth' [Genesis 1:28]; but we accept marriage in such a way that we prefer virginity, which is born of marriage.[68]

Jerome goes on to enlist secular literature, his second line of attack, to show that Christianity was not alone in its high regard for virginity

(1.41–9; 282B–96A). This section is an interesting display of Jerome's knowledge (direct or borrowed) of classical literature, the cumulative effect of which is a treatise not so much on the superiority of virginity as on the inferiority and even undesirability of marriage. In spite of his earlier protests to the contrary, Jerome's rhetoric in this section carries him to the verge of condemning marriage. This last part of the first book of *Against Jovinian* would provide much ammunition for those medieval writers who wrote tracts on the dire evils and burdens of marriage. Perhaps Augustine has this part of Jerome in mind when giving his reason for writing *On the Marriage Good*: 'particularly since Jovinian could not have been opposed by praising marriage but by demeaning it, for this reason I issued that book whose title is, *On the Marriage Good*.'[69]

There is no indication of an influence from Jerome's *Against Jovinian* until the twelfth century, when many texts on virginity and marriage were incorporated by Gratian into the *Decretum*. These texts reinforce the view of the superiority of virginity and give it some legal status. The manuscript evidence suggests that *Against Jovinian* was far more influential in the later Middle Ages than it was in the centuries immediately following its publication. Its point was grasped, however, and is evidenced in the medieval references to the heresy of Jovinian.[70]

To argue the case for the superiority of virginity on the basis of the rewards due it is surely to put the cart before the horse. The value of virginity does not arise because of the rewards that will be given to it in the future; rather, the rewards are granted because of its value here and now. So the principal arguments must rest on the very nature of virginity itself. The picture that emerges portrays an interesting reflection of the medieval view of continence and, as was suggested already, is a touchstone of the medieval view of the value of sex in human lives.

Virginity is the abstinence from voluntary sexual experience over all time frames (past, present, and future) and with all persons.[71] This total and complete abstinence was perceived to be a value and to mark the highest, best, and most perfect expression of the virtue of chastity. Albert says that the most perfect virtue is found in those who are continent always and entirely.[72] When married people have intercourse they are not practising continence except in an incidental way (*secundum quid*); they are not continent always, but only at the times established for prayer.[73] Perfect continence in sexual matters is really total abstinence. For Aquinas, sex is seen as an enemy, so the most perfect kind of victory and the most splendid is never to give in to the enemy.[74] With sex, even legitimate sex, comes a certain corruption no matter how it is done. For Bonaventure marriage incurs this corruption; virginity bestows beauty and so 'virginity is to be preferred to conjugal chastity because in the latter there is foul corruption, in the former, however, is holy incorruption.'[75]

In his later treatment in the *Summa*, Aquinas claims that the superiority of virginity can also be proved by rational argument. Divine goods are more potent than human; the goods of the soul are to be preferred to the goods of the body; the good of contemplation is to be preferred to the good of the active life. On all these counts virginity is on the side of the higher good, marriage on the side of the lower good; so without any doubt virginity is to be preferred to marriage.[76]

In the fourteenth century, Durandus of St Pourcain and Peter of Palude add to their use of Aquinas the note that the superiority of virginity is valid for the modern age (*pro statu moderno*). I doubt that they are speaking about their own contemporary age. They likely have in mind the objection that virginity cannot be superior to marriage since it was not the state designed for Paradise in the original plan. They may also be thinking of a much-cited text of Augustine: 'there is no inequality in the merit of continence in John who never experienced marriage, and in Abraham who gave rise to children.'[77] This text is frequently adduced against the claim that virginity is superior to marriage. Alexander of Hales and Albert make an important point in this regard when they note that the question of the superiority of virginity is a matter of comparing *states*, not persons. The text of Augustine speaks of two people who may be equal in merit. Individuals in an inferior state may be superior in merit to tepid and lukewarm people in a superior state. While states of life have a fixed ordering of value (and a fixed ordering of reward), Albert says that persons are related as those who exceed and who are exceeded, thus cutting across boundaries of status. That is, among individual persons there is a hierarchy of merit that does not necessarily correspond to the hierarchy of states in which those persons exist. The failure to recognize the difference between states and persons was the reason that Jovinian fell into error.[78]

If John and Abraham are to represent states, then some other argument must be found for the superiority of virginity. It might be found in considerations of history. One cannot legitimately compare virginity now to marriage at the time of the patriarchs without taking into consideration the differences in the divine plan for the two stages of history. To try to do otherwise is to try to compare apples and oranges; it can be done, but the basis of the comparison must be clear. Bonaventure distinguishes between the time of the law (Old Testament) and the time of grace (after Christ) and notes that, if the two states are compared within the same order of time, then marriage was superior under the law, virginity is superior under grace, when fruitfulness of the womb is not required but 'holiness and incorruption and purity of mind.' If the two states are compared across orders of time then there is no basis for comparison; but marriage is the best state under the law, virginity is the best state under grace.[79] This reply seems too good to be true, however, and in fact it becomes contaminated by the master's preference for virginity in an absolute sense (shades of Jerome's lauding the virginity of Adam and Eve). In the view of some, Abraham was considered to be a closet virgin, somewhat reluctantly procreating under the divine command but in his heart of hearts yearning to abstain from sex. As Aquinas says: 'However, Abraham was so mentally disposed that he was prepared to observe virginity if the time was right.' Or, in the words of Bonaventure: 'It would have been the easiest thing for him, as a most temperate man, completely to abstain from a woman.'[80]

Although pointing to the rewards of virginity does not establish its superiority, it is a strong *ad hominem* argument for the fact of its superiority. In the developed theology of the thirteenth century, two classes of reward were recognized: general and special. General reward was the substantial reward each received in proportion to his degree of charity at the time of death. This would be expressed in the crown (*aurea*) bestowed on all who die in charity. In addition to this crown there were two special subsidiary rewards, called coronets (*aureolae*) and fruits (*fructus*), that were reserved for special classes or states of persons. Coronets were for martyrs, virgins, and preachers; fruits were bestowed on virgins, widows, and the married. Virginity stands to gain in the two categories of special reward.[81]

The idea of the fruits of chastity, based on a spiritual interpretation of Matthew 13:8, 23, is an ancient tradition that recognized a graded reward to be bestowed in proportion to the distancing from sexual experience: a hundredfold for complete sexual abstinence, sixtyfold for those who had had sexual experience but who resolved to remain without it in the future, and thirtyfold for married people whose lives are inextricably bound up with sex.[82] Two questions arose in regard to the fruits of chastity: Why does this virtue deserve such a special reward? And what is the precise significance of the numbers 100, 60, and 30? The latter question led to complex and varied answers that cannot be adequately treated here. An outline of the development will have to suffice.

Jerome was the first to explain the significance of the numbers through a reference to the ancient method of counting on the fingers. Jerome, who simply alludes to the method, must have presupposed an understanding in his readers:

> The thirtyfold refers to marriage, for the very union of the fingers, like an embrace and a tender kiss, portrays husband and wife. The sixtyfold refers to widows since they were placed in difficulty and tribulation. Their repression is signified by the upper finger ... Finally, the number one hundred (reader, take careful note) is transferred from the left to the right hand, a circle is made with the same fingers, but not on the same hand, which were used to signify the married and widows, signifying the crown of virginity.[83]

The thumb and index finger of the left hand were brought together in such a way as to form opened lips for the number thirty and flattened together to form sixty. The hundreds begin on the right hand, with one hundred formed like ten on the left, the right index finger curved to touch the middle joint of the right thumb, thus making a circle.[84] Reference to Jerome (through the Venerable Bede) continues to be encountered in the thirteenth century, even prompting two disputed questions from Henry of Ghent.[85]

Bede's account was somewhat primitive, however, and probably had no relevance at the time. Consequently, efforts were made to find significance in the numbers themselves. It was not understood to be a matter of giving the numbers significance but of finding it, of extracting it, as it were, from the very nature of the numbers 100, 60, and 30. In defence of his own account, Albert says: 'And this is Bede's reasoning and it is good enough, but the first [Albert's own] are more in accord with the nature of numbers.'[86]

The idea of the three fruits was a given. The task was to provide appropriate reasons for its suitability and for its exclusive application to chastity. The agricultural metaphor was central here.[87] The most obvious material substratum in human beings is the flesh. Growth, development, and flourishing of the human person mean the growth of the seed of the word of God or of grace working in that person. Growth and development will occur to the extent that the flesh and concupiscence are controlled. Sex is the most fleshy, the most disturbing element in the human constitution, holding us back from full spiritual development. The subjection of sex has special significance for this development, so there should be a special relishing of the delights that come with its accomplishment. This relish is the fruit of chastity, proportioned to the success of the subjugation. As Aquinas says: 'So the more someone, drawing away from the flesh, is turned to spirituality, to that degree there is greater fruit of the word of God in him.'[88] Since virginity is at the very horizon of carnality and spirituality, it represents the most complete subjection of the flesh and so deserves the greatest of the fruits, the hundredfold.

The main connotation of fruits is the notion of relish and the enjoyment of the results of one's labour in cultivating the flesh so it can nourish the seeds of spirituality. The achievements of this labour can also be looked at from another point of view, in which the placid agricultural metaphor gives way to a military metaphor of war and victory. A farmer's harvest, except in the direst of circumstances, is not seen as a victory over the soil. However, the achievement of virginity in subjugating sexual desire is viewed as a victory, as meriting a special glory. This is the coronet that is due the special victories of virgins over the flesh, of martyrs over death for Christ, of preachers over the enemies of the faith: 'The coronet is a certain privileged reward corresponding to a privileged victory ... In the fight against the flesh he obtains the most powerful victory who completely abstains from sexual pleasures, which are the main ones in this genus [the flesh]. Therefore, a coronet is due virginity.'[89] Since neither widowhood nor marriage represents complete victory over the flesh, neither merits a special reward.

In regard to the coronet due to virginity there is an interesting split between the *Ordinary Gloss* on Gratian and the theologians. It has to do with the question whether a virgin who has lost physical integrity against her will but who remains a virgin in the formal sense will receive the coronet reserved for virgins. Everything we have seen the theologians say about the spiritual, voluntary nature of virginity would suggest that the theological opinion would favour an affirmative reply. The *Ordinary Gloss*, however, in several passages denies the coronet to violated virgins.[90]

Virginity represents the perfection of chastity, which is one of the main parts of the virtue of temperance. Chastity here means abstinence. Within the context of marriage, as we have seen, chastity has a different role to play but one that is no less a manifestation of the virtue of temperance.

Conclusion

For the first time since Augustine a comprehensive view of what we call sex was provided in the Latin West in the two hundred years surveyed in this book. The treatment of sex was comprehensive in its coverage and was integrated into an overall theological synthesis. Important discussions of different facets of sex are encountered in accounts as diverse as those of creation and the Fall and of heaven and its rewards. A systematic theology was created that included within its range of interests accounts of the nature, purpose, and morality of sex in all its dimensions. It was these accounts that were diffused through legislation, confessional manuals, pastoral instructional handbooks, and sermons.

In the core ideas there was a high degree of consensus if not unanimity among the theologians. Such agreement should not be surprising given the fact that the views were elaborated by men who shared a common faith and morality, who read the same texts, and who wrote in the same milieu following the same academic conventions. If they had had the concept and language they might have said something like, 'Sex is a natural, impersonal biological force with an inherent teleological orientation to the conservation of the species.' Lacking that conceptual and linguistic tool, they spoke instead of what nature intended for sexual intercourse (*coitus*, *concubitus*). Their conception was both teleological and instrumentalist. Coitus was inherently teleological and was to be used as the instrument for reproducing the human species. Sexual pleasure was a natural concomitant of intercourse in order to ensure its deployment.

The finality of sexual relations did not end with conception or even birth. Nature intended not only the procreation of offspring, but also their proper rearing and education. This goal required the management of nature within a determined institutional arrangement that would be conducive to the correct upbringing of children. It was thought that indivisible monogamous marriage created the best conditions for the procreation and education of children and for the provision of their future needs.

Nature was thought to be not only indicative of what is but normative of what ought to be, embodying, as it were, a sexual hypothetical imperative: if one wants to engage legitimately in sexual relations, then one must do so within the institutional context of marriage, honour the physiological requirements for procreation, and respect the subordinate, ancillary function of pleasure in the overall scheme of things. To abide by these requirements would be to act in a morally correct manner. To have sex when not married or with someone other than one's spouse, to have homosexual or non-vaginal relations, or to have sex simply for pleasure is to depart from the conditions set by nature and so to act in a morally improper manner.

The moral ideal was that people bring themselves into line with natural teleology by appropriating it into their subjective intentions. That is, it was desirable that in having sexual relations people actually intend what nature intends, in the way nature intends, and with a proper attitude towards pleasure. Beliefs about sex were grounded in a teleological view of nature that supported the superstructure of the institution of marriage.

Since nature was the good creation of a good God, the fact of sex and its correct use and enjoyment were thought to be goods. If human beings were to act in accord with the sexual hypothetical imperative they would act in accord with God's intentions. This is the way things would have been had Adam and Eve not sinned. Reason would have recognized both the teleological and functional nature of sex. There would have been nothing to deflect reason from the proper control of sexual intercourse. Adam and Eve did sin, however, and as a consequence lust (*libido*) was unleashed into the human condition.

Belief in the presence of lust accounts for the shape of almost every position that was taken on sexual topics. Lust marks the divide between pre-lapsarian and post-lapsarian human nature. Its absence in Paradise would have ensured the rational and harmonious deployment (*usus*) of sex in the service of God's will through the natural reproduction of the species. Its presence after the Fall guarantees that such deployment, if possible at all, can only be won with great effort. Lust accounts for the transmission and perpetuation of original sin. Marriage is no longer simply in the service of nature, but is a remedy for lust and concupiscence. Lust is the reason for the irrational effects of pleasure, pleasure which itself was initially designed to be in the service of nature, to encourage and reinforce natural inclinations to reproduction. Temperance is a central moral value now because of the difficulties inherent in post-lapsarian passion – there would have been no need for temperance in Paradise. The worth of virginity is not accounted for because of its inherent value, but because it represents the ultimate, difficult victory over the disruptions of lustful passion.

This lust is not something that may or may not be present in human beings. It is integral to the present state of human nature, bred in the bones if you will. It is the permanent and pervasive tendency of sensual desire to pursue its own animal ends in disregard of the dictates of natural reason. It constantly threatens to subvert that reason, particularly through sexual desires and appetites. While it can be controlled, channelled, and bridled, it can be neither eliminated nor escaped. After all is said, lust is perhaps simply the human condition stripped of the divine aid of original justice that was believed to have been granted to ensure proper balance for human beings, existing as they do on the horizon of carnality and spirituality. That seems to be the implication of Aquinas' claim that, as a result of the first sin, human beings were abandoned to the natural principles of their nature.

While this view of sex and the human condition was integral to faith and theology, it was not the pure invention of Christian thinkers. Foucault has shown that such a view of human passion and desire was prevalent in antiquity: sex was to be bridled within the limits of a procreative teleology and the institutional forms of marriage.[1] To borrow a term from Foucault, it might be said that for the medievals it was the presence of lust in post-lapsarian human beings that was the cause of the *problematization* of sex.

In comparing Graeco-Roman and Christian views of sex Foucault says, with perceptive insight, 'While the experience of sexuality, as a singular historical figure, is perhaps quite distinct from the Christian experience of the "flesh," both appear nonetheless to be dominated by the principle of "desiring man."'[2] He goes on to ask: 'What were the games of truth by which human beings come to see themselves as desiring individuals?'[3] That is, what are the rules and principles that lead to conceiving of human beings as characterized, perhaps dominated, by the force of desire?[4]

In the Middle Ages the games of truth were played out in the mythology of Paradise and the Fall, in the theology of original sin and lust, and in part, too, in the rhetoric of wild horses and broken reins, corruption and infection. The sexual truth about human beings was not only that they were desiring animals, but that they were lustful animals – naturally lustful in spite of the rhetoric of corruption. After all, Adam's sin did not transform desire into something else called lust. It caused desire to be desire without the restraining tether of original justice. The most recalcitrant was sexual desire, which constantly threatens to subvert reason and to assimilate human beings to brute animals.

The rules of the game of truth about sexual desire were set in the lecture halls of theology and canon law, and communicated from the pulpit and in the confessional. The games were also played out in the lives of people who were offered the one choice between marriage and sexual abstinence. It seems, however, that people in the later Middle Ages had their own rules for the game of simple fornication. (The adjective 'simple' was used to differentiate this type of sexual offence from other types.) From Bartholemew of Exeter in the twelfth century to John Bromyard in the fourteenth century, there is considerable evidence to indicate that the official rules about the sinfulness of heterosexual relations between unmarried and otherwise unattached people were rejected. This was not simply a matter of behavioural deviance from the rules. It was a matter of *belief* in another set of rules that did not hold fornication to be a sin. As Aquinas says: 'Note that although some believe adultery is a sin, nonetheless they do not believe that simple fornication is a sin.'[5] Widespread belief in the sinlessness of simple fornication suggests that the truth about sex was not solely produced by the orthodox rule-makers.[6]

A fundamental difference between antiquity and the later Middle Ages was that the latter allowed for no moral ground between marrying and the complete renunciation of sex. Whatever the *ideals* of pre-Christian thought, there was always moral room for the personal appropriation of genital sex for one's own pleasure and satisfaction and as a mode of expression of human relations. A return to such a view could only occur as the result of a complete breakdown in the intercourse-procreation-marriage connection. I suppose the history of the so-called sexual revolution is the history of that breakdown, following on the emergence of the perception of sex and sexuality as personal values. The culmination of the revolution is seen in the ideas of a morally neutral sexual orientation and sexual preference resulting from a reconceptualization of the very idea of nature itself, which the scholastics saw as underlying and dictating the moral links between sex and procreation and sex and marriage. Interestingly, Aquinas had the idea of sexual orientation, which, he said, was *connatural* to individuals. Some men (ie, males) become habituated to taking pleasure in intercourse with men. Such behaviour is natural for those individuals, but unnatural in terms of human nature. The behaviour results from a breakdown (corruption) of the natural principles of the species. An individual's connaturality is not determinative of the morality of behaviour. That is determined in reference to specific human nature.[7]

Nature, intercourse, marriage – these are the fundamental concepts out of which the medieval masters forged their views of sex in the smithy of Augustine. The core of those views was as applicable to Adam and Eve in Paradise as to their descendants after the Fall. It was the presence of lust that required a reshaping of the basic ideas so as to bring them into line with the actual state of what those same masters were accustomed to call a corrupted and infected nature.

I believe it could be legitimately claimed without exaggeration that everything that has been examined in this book was seen by the medieval theologians and canonists as an extended gloss on the frequently encountered admonition and warning:

> Let marriage be honourable in all and the bed undefiled, for God will judge fornicators and adulterers [Hebrews 13:4].

The Twofold Institution of Marriage

The following *dictum* of Gratian encapsulates the main tenets of the medieval teaching on marriage, tenets which would be the cornerstone of theological discussion throughout the period covered in this book. This appendix is arranged in the following manner:

A English translation of the *dictum*
B Latin text of the *dictum*
C Annotations
D Latin text of the commentary of Huguccio on the *dictum*
E Latin text of the *Ordinary Gloss* on the *dictum*.

Numbered annotations in parentheses are identical in the English and Latin texts of Gratian and may be found following the Latin text of Gratian.

It is the practice of commentaries on Gratian to employ abbreviated references with incipits in their work. I have not reproduced these references in Huguccio and the gloss. Modern references are in square brackets in the texts of Huguccio and the gloss.

A Gratian *Decretum* C 32.2.2 dp (English Translation)

The response is as follows: The first institution of marriage was effected in Paradise such that there would have been 'an unstained bed and honourable marriage' [Hebrews 13:4] resulting in conception without ardour and birth without pain (1). The second, to eliminate unlawful movement, was effected outside Paradise such that the infirmity that is prone to foul ruin might be rescued by the uprightness of marriage (2). This is why the apostle, writing to the Corinthians, says, 'On account of fornication let each man have his own wife and each woman her own husband' [1 Corinthians 7:2] (3). It is for this reason that the married owe a mutual debt to each other and cannot deny each other. So the apostle says, 'Do not defraud one another except perhaps by consent for a time in order to give yourselves [more readily] to prayer. But return to it again lest Satan tempt you. [However, I say this] on account of your incontinence' [1 Corinthians 7:5] (4). Therefore, given that they are admonished to return to the natural use (5) because of incontinence, it is clear that they are not commanded to join together solely for the procreation of children. Yet marriage is not to be judged evil on that account, for what is done outside of the intention of generation is not an evil of marriage, but is forgivable on account of the good of marriage which is threefold: fidelity, offspring, and sacrament (6).

B Gratian *Decretum* C 32.2.2 dp

'His ita respondetur: Prima institutio coniugii in paradyso facta est, ut esset immaculatus thorus, et honorabiles nuptiae [Hebrews 13:4], ex quibus sine ardore conciperent, sine dolore parerent (1). Secunda propter illicitum motum eliminandum extra paradysum facta est, ut infirmitas, prona in ruinam turpitudinis, honestate exciperetur coniugii (2). Unde Apostolus scribens ad Corinthios ait: 'Propter fornicationem unusquisque suam uxorem, et unaqueque virum suum habeat' [1 Corinthians 7:2] (3). Ex hac itaque causa fit, ut coniugati se sibi invicem debeant, nec se sibi negare possint. Unde Apostolus: 'Nolite fraudare invicem, nisi forte ex consensu, et ad tempus, ut [expeditius] vacetis orationi, et iterum revertimini in id ipsum, ne temptet vos sathanas. [Hoc autem dico] propter incontinentiam vestram' [1 Corinthians 7:5] (4). Qui ergo propter incontinentiam in naturalem usum (5) redire monentur, patet, quod non propter filiorum procreationem tantum misceri iubentur. §.1. Non tamen ideo nuptiae malae iudicantur. Quod enim preter intentionem generandi fit, non est nuptiarum malum, sed est veniale propter nuptiarum bonum, quod est tripertitum; fides videlicet, proles, et sacramentum (6).

C Annotations

(1) See *Ordinary Gloss* on Genesis 2:18 (Lyra 1.76); from Augustine *De Genesi ad litteram* 9.3 (CSEL 28.1, 271). The allusion to the Epistle to the Hebrews is in Augustine. See Lombard *Sent* 2.20.1.3 (1.428).
(2) See *Ordinary Gloss* on Genesis 2:18 (Lyra 1.77); from Augustine *De Genesi ad litteram* 9.7 (CSEL 28.1, 275). See Lombard *Sent* 2.20.1.3 (1.428).
(3) 1 Corinthians 7:2 figures prominently in debates over the morality of marital relations 'to avoid fornication.' See above, ch 5.
(4) 1 Corinthians 7:5 figures prominently in the discussion of the marital debt. 'Expeditius' ('more readily') is not in the Vulgate; 'hoc autem dico' ('however, I say this') is transposed from 1 Corinthians 7:6. See above, ch 4.
(5) Note the interpretive exposition of St. Paul – the couples are to return to the *natural* use of marriage.

(6) See *Ordinary Gloss* on Genesis 2:18 (Lyra 1.77); from Augustine *De Genesi ad litteram* 9.7 (CSEL 28.1, 275). For the goods of marriage see above, ch 3.

D Huguccio *Summa* on Gratian, *Decretum* C 32.2.2, dp (Admont, Stiftsbibliothek 7, ff 369va–370ra)

/369va/ *His ita*, v. *sine ardore*. Si enim homo non pecasset talis esset coniunctio genitalium membrorum et ita sine fervore et pruritu volu<p>tatis [ms: voluntatis] sicut est aliorum membrorum coniunctio. Sic /369vb/ enim membrum membro sine pruritu carnis coniungeretur sicut aliud membrorum alii membro vel tabula tabule coniungitur.

eliminandum: id est, coercendum.

extra paradisum facta: id est, ostensa esse facta, vel in scriptis redacta.

prona: ut [Gratian *Decretum* C 20.3.2].

exciperetur: id est, excluderetur a fornicatione.

suam uxorem: per hoc excluduntur concubine. Non enim simpliciter dixit suam sed addit uxorem. Et similiter per hoc excluduntur illi qui uxores ducere non possunt ut sunt monachi, devoti, et clerici in sacris ordinibus constituti et ceteri qui sibi preiudicium fecerunt. [There follows an explanation of the last remark.]

revertimini: consilium est quo ad exigendum, preceptum quo ad reddendum.

in idipsum: id est, in carnalem usum.

quod enim: verba sunt Augustini introducta a magistro. sed ut melius intelligantur hec verba et duo sequentia et capitula eis contraria assignata notandum quod vir connuscetur uxori quatuor de causis, scilicet causa prolis, causa reddendi debitum, causa incontinentie, causa exsaturande libidinis vel explende voluptatis.

Cum causa prolis tunc ipse coitus nullum peccatum est veniale vel mortale. Immo si fiat ex caritate meritorius est vite eterne. ut [Gratian *Decretum* D 13.4, § 4; D 25.3, dp § 7].

Idem est ex toto cum causa reddendi debitum ei commiscetur ut [Gratian *Decretum* C 33.5.1].

Item cum causa incontinentie tunc ipse coitus veniale peccatum est et venialiter vir peccat ut hic et in proximo sequenti cap. [Gratian *Decretum* C 32.2.3] et [C 27.2.10; C 33.4.7].

Cum vero causa explende libidinis sive voluptatis tunc ipse coitus mortale peccatum est et mortaliter vir peccat ut [Gratian *Decretum* C 32.7.11] et prox. c. Sed sive coitus sit peccatum sive non, nunquam tamen fit sine peccato quia semper fit et exercetur cum quodam pruritu et quadam voluptate. Nam in emissione spermatis semper subest quidam fervor, quidam pruritus, quedam voluptas que sine culpa esse non potest, ut [Gratian *Decretum* C 33.4.7; C 27.2.10; C 32.2.4; C 32.1.11; D 5.1].

Et hec quidem dicta sunt cum vir miscetur uxori ordine nature nam si contra naturam semper mortaliter peccat et gravius cum uxore quam cum alia et gravius est puniendus ut [Gratian *Decretum* C 32.7.11].

/369vb/ Et nota differentiam inter illos duos casus scilicet cum commiscetur vir uxori causa incontinentie vel causa explende voluptatis et exsaturande libidinis.

In primo casu prevenitur a voluptate et potius vult sic peccare quam fornicari. In secundo prevenit voluptatem et provocat eam manibus vel cogitatione vel utendo calidis et incentivis ut plus cum uxore coire valeat. Quidam tamen dicunt quod in his duobus casibus coitus est tantum veniale peccatum et venialiter tantum peccat vir sive causa incontinentie sive causa exsaturande libidinis commisceatur uxori ut [Gratian, *Decretum* D 25.3, dp alias]

Si ergo alibi videtur dici quod mortaliter peccet vel dicitur ad exortationem continentie et in detestationem criminis adulterii, vel intelligitur quando contra naturam coit ut [Gratian *Decretum* C 32.7.11], vel quia ad modum adulterii agit sicut adulter ardet in adulteram, sic iste in uxorem propriam [Gratian *Decretum* C 32.4.5]. Sed non discedo a verbis capitulo a prima distinctione et dico quod sequens cap. intelligitur de coitu incontinentie et congrue intelligitur de coitu exsaturande libidinis sicut iam patebit.

Hec autem verba Augustini intelligitur de coitu incontinentie et exponuntur sic. Illud quod fit preter intentionem igitur id est coitus qui fit causa incontinentie tantum et ita fit preter intentionem generationis non est malum nuptie id est propter nuptias quasi quod est malum et culpande, vel non est malum nuptiarum id est propter nuptias quasi quod est malum non provenit nuptiis id est non sit malum est hoc quod legittime sunt coniuncti illi quorum est malum.

sed est veniale: non ponit illud /370ra/ genus peccati sed negatione intelligitur.

veniale: id est non mortale, id est ad mortem eternam non imputabile scilicet tale quale non esset coniugium.

non tamen: per ipsum coniugium sed per auctorem qui ita instituit et voluit.

propter nuptiarum bonum: Transitive potest intelligi quia per bona coniugii excusatur coitus coniugalis. Sed ego intelligo intransitive id est propter nuptias que sunt bonum ut [Gratian *Decretum* C 27.1.41] et tunc sequens quod facit simplicem relationem. .q. et bonum nuptiarum est tibi id est bonum coniunctorum nuptiis est tripertitum. De hoc triplici bono plene invenies [Gratian *Decretum* C 27.2.10].

E *Ordinary Gloss* to Gratian *Decretum* C 32.2.2, dp

His ita respondetur: Hec est secunda pars questionis, in qua dicitur quod matrimonium bis fuit institutum sive permissum. Primo in paradiso propter sobolem tantum. Secundo extra paradisum propter sobolem et propter infirmitatem carnis vitandam, quia bonum matrimonii tripertitum est, scilicet fides, proles, et sacramentum. Io. de Fan.

Casus. In hoc .§. Gratianus duas distinguit institutiones matrimonii. Unam que fuit ante peccatum et causa sobolis procreande. Et aliam que data fuit post peccatum et facta fuit causa fornicationis vitande. Quod probatur auctoritate apostoli dicentis: 'Propter fornicationem,' etc. Unde qui sic coniuncti sunt, continere non possunt nisi de communi consensu. Quod probatur similiter auctoritate apostoli. Unde qui propter fornicationem vitandam coniuncti sunt, debent coniuges appelari. Et ad hoc probandum inducit sequens ca.

excipitur: id est excluditur a fornicatione.

facta: Solo consensu, ut et nunc, et instituit dominus matrimonium ex eo quod mulierem fecit, dicendo illi quod uxor Ade esset futura.

sine ardore: Nisi enim homo peccasset ita sine ardore et pruritu esset genitalium coniunctio, sicut est aliorum membrorum, veluti si applices digitum digito, vel manum cum manu. Vel si esset pruritus, non tamen esset peccatum, sicut non esset peccatum manum scabiosam mittere ad ignem.

eliminandum: id est coercendum.

facta est: id est, ostensa facta, alias in paradiso etiam secundo facta est, sed quero per que veba, vel quando.

coniugii: Sed hodie sacerdos diaconus magis punitur si contrahat quam si fornicetur, ut [Gratian *Decretum* D 27.16].

unusquisque: Qui per votum sibi non preiudicabit [Gratian, *Decretum* C 27.1.40].

nolite: [Gratian *Decretum* C 30.1.3]

usum: id est carnalem usum.

veniale: id est, dignum venia, id est ad mortem non imputabile [Gratian *Decretum* D 13.2, § 4], [C 32.4.12], contra [D 25.3., dp, § 4]. Arg. contra [C 33.4.7], dic ut no infra ca prox

quod: Simplex est relatio.

tripertitum: id est, bonum nuptiale est triplex: id est coniunctorum nuptiis bonum est triplex.

William Peraldus on Temperance

William Peraldus *Summa de vitiis et virtutibus*, *'De temperantia'* (Schlägl, Stifts-bibliothek 12, ff 248ra–263va; = S) See, G. Vilhaber *Catalogus codicum Plagen-sium (Cpl.) manuscriptorum* (Linz 1918) 18.

William Peraldus wrote (circa 1248) his treatise on the virtues some twelve years after his treatise on the vices and so was able to benefit from the sub-stantial academic treatments provided by Philip the Chancellor and Albert the Great. The following sketch outlines the major articulations of his work, which, in his own words, is divided into four parts. Peraldus does not provide any further divisions of his treatise. Although the manuscript I used divides the work into chapters, I have not followed the chapter enumeration, but have used Roman numerals to indicate the major fourfold division. Subdivisions within the fourth part are indicated in brackets preceded by the corresponding Roman numeral. Frequently the author indicates the plan he intends to follow in regard to subsections of the treatise. These plans have been reproduced in the outline.

OUTLINE

Prologue
  A Reasons for treatment of temperance before fortitude (S 248ra–va)
  B Plan (S 248va)
'Temperance will be discussed in this way: (I) first, the different senses of the term temperance will be assigned; (II) second, its descriptions will be pres-ented; (III) third, what pertains to its commendation; (IV) fourth, the parts of temperance will be dealt with.' ('De temperantia vero hoc modo dicetur: [I] primo diverse acceptiones huius nominis temperantia assignabuntur; [II] se-cundo descriptiones eius ponentur; [III] tertio ea que pertinent ad eius com-mendationem; [IV] quarto agetur de partibus temperantiae.' [S 248va])

I The Term Temperance, Three Senses (S 248va)
    Temperance in general
    In regard to deviant impulses of mind
    In regard to pleasures of the senses
II Descriptions of Temperance (S 248va–vb)
    A Definitions (S 248va–vb)
        1 Cicero *De inventione*
        2 Cicero *De officiis*
        3 Augustine *De moribus ecclesie*
        4 Macrobius
        5 Augustine *De libero arbitrio*
    B 'Modus' 4 senses (S 248vb)
III Commendation of Temperance (S 248vb–249ra) (8 points made)
IV Parts of Temperance (General)
    A Cicero *De inventione* (S 249va)
        1 Continence
        2 Clemency
        3 Modesty
    B Continence (brief) (S 249va)
        1 Desire for pleasures
        2 Desire for riches
    C What Dissuades from Love of Pleasures (S 249va–250va) (12 points made)
(IV.1) Clemency (S 250va–251va)
    Definitions
    Re Kings and Prelates
    Twelve Points Inciting a Prince to Clemency (S 250vb–251va)
(IV.2) Modesty (S 251va–252vb)
    Definition
    Discussion
(IV.3) Temperance in regard to Pleasures of the Senses
    General (S 252rb-va)
        Taste, the object of sobriety
        Touch, the object of continence
Plan
'Among the virtues that pertain to the pleasures of the five senses, first we shall take up sobriety, second, continence, third we will touch on the type of temperance that concerns the pleasures of the other three senses.' ('Inter virtutes vero pertinentes ad delectationes quinque sensuum primo prosequemur de sobrietate, secundo de continentia, tertio tangemus de illa temperantia que est circa delectationes aliorum trium sensuum.' [252va])
(IV.4) Sobriety (S 252va–254va)
    The term (4 meanings)

Commendation
Duties of sobriety
Question: whether any excess destroys sobriety
(IV.5) Continence (General) (S 254va–vb)
Several kinds
Re sex organs
Parts
  Conjugal
  Virginal
  'Vidual' (widows)
(IV.6) Virginity (S 254vb–258vb)
Plan

'Of these three species of continence, virginal continence, which is before the others in time and dignity, will be spoken of first in this way: first, the ways the term virginity is taken; second, a description of virginity will be adduced and explained; third, its commendation will be pursued; fourth, the things that virgins must particularly fear; fifth, the triple coronet.' ('Inter has vero tres species continentie primo dicetur de virginali que ceteris prior est et tempore et dignitate de qua hoc ordine dicetur: primo ostendetur quot modis nomen virginitatis sumitur; secundo descriptio virginitatis ponetur et exponetur; tertio commendationi eius insistetur; quarto de hiis que specialiter virginibus sunt timenda; quinto de triplici aureola.' [S 254vb])

The term (4 senses) (S 255ra)
Description
 Commendation (S 255rb–256vb)
What must be feared by virgins
Triple coronet (S 257vb–258vb)
(IV.7) Chastity in General (S 258vb–259vb)
Types
  Any continence
  Widows
  Ministers of the church
Commendation of chastity (meant to refer to widows) (S 258vb–259rb)
Chastity of the ministers of the Church
General
Why fitting (S 259va–vb)
(IV.8) Conjugal Chastity (S 259vb–263ra)
Plan

'The treatment of conjugal continence follows. In its regard, first the error of those who condemn marriage will be destroyed; second, matrimony will be commended; third, how marriage is to be contracted will be shown; fourth, because conjugal continence should abstain from unlawful carnal behaviour

and engage in lawful behaviour, what carnal behaviour is lawful, what unlawful will be shown.' ('Sequitur de continentia coniugali circa quam primo des-
truitur error ille qui matrimonium dampnat; secundo matrimonium com-
mendabitur; tertio ostendetur qualiter sint matrimonia contrahenda; quarto
quia continentia coniugalis abstinet a carnali opere illicito <et> utitur licito
ostendetur quod opus carnale sit licitum, quod illicitum.' [S 259vb])

Destroy errors of those condemning marriage (S 259vb–260va)
Commendation (12 points) (S 260va–261rb)
Way of Contracting Marriage
Licit and Illicit Intercourse (S 261va–262ra)
Requirements for Meritorious Intercourse (S 262ra–rb)
Requirements for Inseparability
(IV.9) Temperance in regard to Other Senses (S 263rb–va)
Sight, Hearing, Smell

Notes

INTRODUCTION

1 Flandrin 'La doctrine chrétienne du mariage' 101
2 This was undoubtedly the orthodox view. However, from the twelfth century on there was a widespread belief that heterosexual intercourse between unmarried and otherwise unattached consenting adults was not seriously sinful. See: 'For example, there are some stupid priests – priests in name only – who believe that simple fornication is a venial sin, that is, for an unattached man to sleep with a woman who does not have a husband.' (Verbi gratia, sunt quidam fatui sacerdotes tantum nomine qui credunt simplicem fornicationem esse veniale peccatum, scilicet solutum hominem dormire cum femina que non habet virum.) Peter the Chanter *Verbum abbreviatum* BL Add MS 19767 f 154v. See a sermon of Maurice of Sully: 'quar il dient desque le hom n'a feme, ne la feme segnor, n'est pas pecies dampnables se il gisent ensamble.' Sermon on the Twenty-fourth Sunday after Pentecost in Maurice of Sully *Maurice of Sully and the Medieval Vernacular Homily* 169. See below, Conclusion n 6.
3 Synod of Angers n 129 in Synodal Statutes (French) ed Pontal 232–4. Pontal refers to the statutes of the Synod of Angers as the 'Synodal of the West' because of their influence on subsequent European diocesan statutes down to the Council of Trent.
4 See Peter Brown 'Sexuality and Society in the Fifth Century A.D.' 49–70; and his *The Body and Society.*
5 There is the well-known treatise on intercourse by Constantinus Africanus, *Liber de coitu.* See Thomas Benedek 'Beliefs about Human Sexual Function in the Middle Ages and Renaissance'; Thomasset 'La représentation de la sexualité et de la génération dans la pensée scientifique médiévale'; Jacquart and Thomasset *Sexuality and Medicine in the Middle Ages.*
6 For a useful account of the scholarly atmosphere of the time, see Rouse and Rouse *'Statim invenire.* Schools, Preachers, and New Attitudes to

the Page'; Leclercq 'The Renewal of Theology'; Häring 'Commentary and Hermeneutics'; Kuttner 'The Revival of Jurisprudence.'

7 Of the gloss on the Bible, Beryl Smalley says: 'From about the middle of the twelfth century, a glossed Bible normally contains the same set of prefaces and glosses, that is to say, the *Gloss*. There are variations from copy to copy in detail, but no large-scale changes or additions are made ... From Paris the *Gloss* was spread throughout Latin Christendom and accepted as the standard work' (Smalley 'The Bible in the Medieval Schools'). Smalley also notes that 'the early printed editions are not very different from the manuscripts' (*The Study of the Bible in the Middle Ages* 65).

8 For Gratian see: Kuttner 'The Father of the Science of Canon Law' and his *Harmony from Dissonance*; Noonan 'Gratian Slept Here.'

9 See De Ghellinck *Le movement théologique du XIIe siècle* 213–77; Delhaye *Pierre Lombard* 19–21. For recent discussion of the Lombard and his work see the latest edition *Sententiae* vol 1 Prolegomena (Rome 1971) and vol 2.1*–87* (Rome 1981). In the latter volume (19*) the editors refine their dating of the publication of the *Sentences* to 'the scholastic year, 1157–58.' For theological collections of the twelfth century see Cloes 'La systématisation théologique pendant la première moitié du XIIe siècle,' in particular 278–80. The basic guide to the theology of the period is Landgraf *Introduction à l'histoire de la littérature théologique de la scolastique naissante*.

10 De Ghellinck *Le movement théologique du XIIe siècle* 244

11 Taylor *Sex in History* 72.

12 See Jerome *Adversus Iovinianum* 1.47–9 (PL 23.288–96); Bickel *Diatribe in Senecae philosophi fragmenta*; Delhaye 'Le Dossier anti-matrimonial de l'*Adversus Jovinianum*.'

13 Tannahill *Sex in History* 161; the sense of the cited passage seems to require my addition of <not>. Whatever the Church's view of sexual sins, if there was such an official view at this time, one can find abundant evidence that those who raised the question of the comparative gravity of sins rejected the idea that sexual offences were the worst. This sort of ignorance of what medieval views actually were is pervasive. Barbara Tuchman seems to equate sex and sin (*A Distant Mirror* 211). In an account of medieval deviants we read that 'Carnal pleasure was, in the opinion of the Church, an invention of the Devil, the direct result of Man's Fall from Grace and a mortal sin' (McCall *The Medieval Underworld* 179).

14 Cole *Sex in Christianity and Psychoanalysis* 91

15 Flandrin 'La doctrine chrétienne du mariage' 101–2

16 See ch 5 for a discussion of this saying.

17 See Cohen *Be Fertile and Increase*.

18 Tentler *Sin and Confession on the Eve of the Reformation* 168

19 See Payer 'Sex and Confession in the Thirteenth Century.'

20 'Inter omnia christianorum certamina maiora sunt castitatis prelia, ubi

frequens pugna et rara victoria. Est vere magnum bellum continentie'
(Peter the Chanter *Verbum abbreviatum* in BL Add MS 19767 f 178v).
According to Baldwin this manuscript belongs to a family of manuscripts representing a reorganization of the *Verbum abbreviatum* from
the early thirteenth century (see Baldwin *Masters, Princes and Merchants*
2.253–5). Müller (*Paradiesesehe* 152 n 79) cites this text from a manuscript of the same family (Munich, Clm 17458). The text is from
Caesarius of Arles (Sermon 41, CCSL 103.181) but was usually attributed
to Augustine in the Middle Ages and is found among the works of
Augustine (Sermon 293 n 2 [PL 39.2302]). See *SFA* 2-2, n. 621 (3.602);
Aquinas *ST* 2-2.154.3, ad 1. This view is echoed by John Bromyard in
the fourteenth century: 'But this safeguarding of chastity is extremely
difficult ... it is almost a miracle, for it is a greater miracle to uproot the
tinder of lechery from the flesh than to expel unclean spirits from the
bodies of others' (Bromyard *Summa praedicantium* 'Castitas' 1.109ra); see
Bromyard *Summa praedicantium* 'Bellum' 1.96rb. According to Isidore,
the human race is subjected to the devil more through the vice of
lechery than through any other sin (see Isidore, *Sententiae* 2.39.21
[PL 83.642]); *SFA* 2-2 n 621 [3.602]).

21 See the treatment of *luxuria* by Aquinas *ST* 2-2.153–4. I have omitted a
treatment of clerical celibacy as such, since this was a matter of the
positive law of the Latin Church. However ingeniously medieval
writers sought to justify celibacy, they were well aware of the legitimacy of a married clergy from their knowledge of Greek Christianity.

22 See Baldwin 'Five Discourses on Desire.'

23 'Twelfth-century scholarship is characterized by the effort to gather,
organize, and harmonize the legacy of the Christian past as it pertained
to jurisprudence, theological doctrine, and Scripture. The products of
this effort, the *Decretum*, the *Sentences*, and the Ordinary Gloss to the
Bible, were in existence by about 1150' (Rouse and Rouse '*Statim
invenire*. Schools, Preachers, and New Attitudes to the Page' 201).

24 Brundage *Law, Sex, and Christian Society in Medieval Europe*

25 Paul Fournier presents Peter of Palude as a theologian and canon lawyer in 'Pierre de la Palu' 37.39–84.

26 The name 'Master Roland' refers to the author of the commentary on
Gratian who has traditionally been identified with Roland Bandinelli,
who became Pope Alexander III. This identification can no longer be
sustained; see Noonan 'Who was Rolandus?'; Weigand 'Magister
Rolandus und Papst Alexander III.'

27 The impact of Aquinas on the evolution of theology in the late thirteenth and early fourteenth century is difficult to detect in the absence
of critical editions. In terms of the treatment of marriage in the *Sentences*, for example, the only reliable editions in existence are those of
Peter Lombard, the gloss of Alexander of Hales, and the commentary
of Bonaventure, all written before the commentary on the *Sentences* by
Aquinas.

28 For the views of Aquinas on sex and an appreciation of his thought, see Fuchs *Die Sexualethik des heiligen Thomas von Aquin*. The views of two other Dominicans are worthy of note: Brandl *Die Sexualethik des heiligen Albertus Magnus*; Doherty *The Sexual Doctrine of Cardinal Cajetan*. No similar work exists for any major Franciscan writer.

29 The recent book by James Brundage on sex and the law is a particularly helpful addition to the literature on marriage: see *Law, Sex, and Christian Society in Medieval Europe*.

30 See Foucault *The History of Sexuality 2. The Use of Pleasure* and *The History of Sexuality 3. The Care of the Self*.

31 Nietzsche *Human, All-Too-Human* vol 2, First Section, 218, cited in Nietzsche *Philosophy and Truth* xli

32 See Foucault *The History of Sexuality 1. An Introduction; The History of Sexuality 2. The Use of Pleasure* 3–7. I touch on this point in my 'Foucault on Penance and the Shaping of Sexuality.' The Latin word *sexus* means 'gender' and nothing more. It is misleading to use a claim such as 'gender [*sexus*] is common to man and other animals' (Aquinas, *ST* 1.92.2 obj 1) as if it were a claim about sex as the term is used today. Fuchs seems to do this in his account of the views of Aquinas on sex (*Die Sexualethik des heiligen Thomas von Aquin* 42 n 31). I encountered a text that defies translation in terms of gender but makes sense if translated in terms of genital sex. In the account of the term '*castus*,' the *Catholicon* differentiates between chastity (*castitas*) and continence (*continentia*). The former is incorruption of one's own body (ie, absence of sexual experience), the latter 'est post corrupcionem sexui abrenunciatio.' It would make no sense to translate 'sexui abrenunciatio' as 'the renunciation of gender.' The only intelligible translation of the text is 'the renunciation of sex after corruption.' See Balbus *Catholicon* sv *castus*. It is likely that other examples of a non-gender meaning of *sexus* can be found. While such a meaning is an aberration from ordinary usage, it witnesses to a very early linguistic openness of the term for gender to embrace the idea of sex.

33 See Quentin Skinner: 'What then is the relationship between concepts and words? We can scarcely hope to capture the answer in a single formula, but I think we can at least say this: the surest sign that a group or society has entered into the self-conscious possession of a new concept is that a corresponding vocabulary will be developed, a vocabulary which can then be used to pick out and discuss the concept with consistency' ('Language and Social Change' 120).

34 Halperin 'Is There a History of Sexuality?' 273 (author's emphasis). See Padgug 'Sexual Matters.'

35 The first appendix is an exception to this general rule. It includes two untranslated Latin passages, one from the canonist Huguccio, the other from the *Ordinary Gloss* on the *Decretum* of Gratian. These texts are translated in the body of the book whenever they are cited, however.

36 Brundage 'Appendix: Medieval Canon Law and Its Sources'

CHAPTER 1: PARADISE

1 Gratian *Decretum* C. 32.2.2, dp (for the entire passage see Appendix 1
  A: English translation, B: Latin text); see Peter Lombard *Sent* 4.26.2.1
  (2.417); Raymond of Penyafort *Summa* 4.2.5 (513–14); Bonaventure *In 4
  Sent* 26.1.1 (4.661–3); Thomas Aquinas *In 4 Sent* 26.2.2 (*ST* Supplement
  42.2). Peter of Palude (*In 4 Sent* 26.1.3 [ff 138va–vb]), writing during the
  first quarter of the fourteenth century, follows the canon lawyer
  Hostiensis (*Summa* 4.2.8 [ff 195ra, 196vb, 206rb]) in his account of the
  twofold institution – a sign perhaps that the question had lost theological significance by that date.
2 Thomas Aquinas *ST* 1-2.34.1, ad 1; see Aquinas *In 4 Sent* 31.2.3 (*ST* Supplement 49.6).
3 Most definitions of lechery suggest some relationship with lust or concupiscence: *Summa sententiarum* 3.16 (PL 176.114); Alan of Lille *De
  virtutibus et vitiis* (Lottin ed PEM 6.75); SFA 2-2, n. 623, arg. 1 (3.604);
  Albert the Great *Summa theologiae* 2.122.1.1 (B 33.394); Thomas Aquinas
  De malo 15.1 (Leonine 23.270); John Bromyard *Summa praedicantium*
  'Luxuria' 1.457ra.
4 Peter Lombard *Sent* 2.19.1.1 (1.421): 'quae non inutiliter sciuntur, licet
  aliquando curiositate quaerantur'
5 See Bonaventure's remark in the context of the question whether virginity would have been maintained in Paradise (below, n 86). Albert
  the Great is reluctant to take up questions about the way things would
  have been before the Fall either because there was little doubt about
  the answers (see below, n 36) or because he believed the questions to
  be stupid (see below, n 85). He takes them up out of regard for the
  theological practice of his contemporaries.
6 See Peter Lombard *Sent* 2.20.1.3 (1.427–8); this is the context in which
  later commentaries on the *Sentences* discuss the matter. The theological
  summa prepared under the direction of Alexander of Hales, which is
  not a commentary, provides the most thorough treatment of the subject. See *Summa Fratris Alexandri* 1-2, nn 495–8 (2.698–711). Some of the
  more frequently used expressions to refer to the period before the Fall
  are: *in statu innocentiae* ('in the state of innocence'), *in statu illo* ('in that
  state'), *tunc* ('then'), *in paradiso* ('in Paradise'), *in paradiso terrestri* ('in
  the earthly Paradise'), *in statu naturae institutae* ('in the state of the
  institution of nature'), *in statu ante peccatum* ('in the state before sin'), *in
  primo statu* ('in the first state'). For a well-documented presentation of
  medieval accounts of the original state in Paradise see Köster *Urstand,
  Fall und Erbsünde* 11–95.
7 Albert the Great *In 4 Sent* 33.2, in contrarium 1 (B 30.291); 'maximally
  natural' translates the Latin *maxime naturale*. See X 4.19.8. According to
  Bonaventure, nature was more perfected (*perfectior*) in the state of innocence than it is now (*In 2 Sent* 20.1.1 [2.478]).
8 Albert *In 2 Sent* 20.2, ad 4 (B 27.343)

9 See Vincent of Beauvais 'De errore philosophorum circa conditionem generis humani (On the error of philosophers concerning the condition of the human race)' *Speculum naturale* 30.11 (Douai 1624) 1.2219, and 'Cur ad huius scientiae veram notitiam philosophi non pervenerunt? (Why did philosophers not arrive at true knowledge of this science?)' *Speculum doctrinale* 17.2 (Douai 1624) 2.1550–1. For the term 'philosopher,' see M.D. Chenu 'Les "philosophes" dans la philosophie chrétienne médiévale' and his *Toward Understanding St. Thomas* 138.

10 Alexander Neckam provides an account of the sweeping deleterious effects of the Fall throughout the whole of nature. See his *De naturis rerum* 2.192 (349–54). According to Peter Lombard (*Sent* 2.15.3 [1.401]) animals were created harmless, but became harmful because of the sin of the first parents. According to Albert (*In 4 Sent* 26.7 [B 30.106]), the occurrence of excessive vaginal extension or tightness in women is not natural but a result of original sin.

11 Aquinas *In 2 Sent* 20.1.1

12 Ladner 'The Philosophical Anthropology of Saint Gregory of Nyssa' 2.854

13 Gregory of Nyssa *De hominis opificio* 16–17 (PG 44.177D–192A). See Floeri 'Le sens de la "division des sexes" chez Grégoire de Nysse; Ladner 'The Philosophical Anthropology of Saint Gregory of Nyssa' 2.831–65; Jeauneau 'La division des sexes chez Grégoire de Nysse et chez Jean Scot Erigène' 36–46; Pagels *Adam, Eve, and the Serpent* xxv; Peter Brown *The Body and Society* 294–5. Müller (*Paradiesesehe* 13–16) outlines Gregory's views. For a general treatment of the theme see Moorehead 'Adam and Eve and the Discovery of Sex.'

14 Eriugena did not use the translation of Denis the Small (PL 67.347–408) but apparently made his own translation of Gregory. See Cappuyns 'Le "De imagine" de Grégoire de Nysse traduit par Jean Scot Erigène.'

15 For a summary statement of his views see John Scottus Eriugena *De divisione naturae* 4.12 (PL 122.799A); on the resurrection: 'For in the resurrection gender will be taken away, nature will be made one, and there will be only one man (*homo*) just as it would have been if he had not sinned' (*De divisione naturae* 5.20 [PL 122.893C]). For Eriugena's views on sex differences see Stock 'The Philosophical Anthropology of Johannes Scottus Eriugena' 41–5; Allegro *Giovanni Scoto Eriugena II* ch 20 'Maschio e femmina' 99–105; Jeauneau 'La division des sexes chez Grégoire de Nysse et chez Jean Scot Erigène' 46–54.

16 See *Chartularium universitatis Parisiensis* 1 (1200–86) ed Denifle and Chatelain 106–7 n 50. The editors cite Hostiensis, who says that the third heresy for which the work was censured claimed 'that after the consummation of the world there will be integration (*adunatio*) of the sexes, or there will be no gender distinctions' 107 n 1. For the condemnations of Eriugena, see Cappuyns *Jean Scot Erigène* 248–51.

17 John Damascene *De fide orthodoxa* 97.2 ed Buytaert (367–8). This work of Damascene was translated into Latin in the twelfth century.

18 Aquinas *ST* 1.98.2; the reference to Gregory is not found in Aquinas' earlier treatment of the question of sexual reproduction in Paradise (*In 2 Sent* 20.1.2). See Richard of Mediavilla *In 2 Sent* 20.1.1 (2.251).

19 'Poterat enim Deus et alio modo genus hoc multiplicare, si mandatum usque in finem observassent intransmutatum' (John Damascene *De fide orthodoxa* 97.2 ed Buytaert 368).

20 *SFA* 1–2 n 495, contra 2 (2.699); Albert the Great *In 2 Sent* 20.1, obj 2 (B 27.341) and *In 4 Sent* 26.6, obj 2 (B 30.104); Bonaventure *In 2 Sent* 20.1.1, sed contra 2 (2.478); Aquinas *In 2 Sent* 20.1.1, obj 1; Peter of Tarentaise *In 2 Sent* 20.1.1, obj 2 (2.168)

21 Albert *In 2 Sent* 20.1, sol, and ad 2 (B 27.342)

22 See Peter Lombard *Sent* 4.44.1.2 (2.516–17); Aquinas *In 4 Sent* 44.1.2 (1) (*ST*, Supplement 81.1) and *In 4 Sent* 44.1.3 (3) (*ST* Supplement 81.3). And see Augustine *The City of God* 22.17 tr Green 280–5.

23 For an account of this matter in Augustine, see Müller (*Paradiesesehe* 19–32); the notes in Augustine *La Genèse au sens littéral en douze livres (VIII–XII)* 516–30; Schmitt *Le mariage chrétien dans l'oeuvre de saint Augustin* 83–105; Clark '"Adam's Only Companion"' 143.

24 Augustine *De bono coniugali* 2.2–3 (CSEL 41.188–90)

25 Augustine *De Genesi ad litteram* 3.21 (CSEL 28.1, 88)

26 In these remarks I follow the suggestions in the notes in Augustine *La Genèse au sens littéral en douze livres (VIII–XII)* 518–21.

27 See ch 2 for a treatment of Augustine's concern with the possibility of the presence of concupiscence and lust in Paradise before the Fall.

28 See Augustine *De Genesi ad litteram* 9.6 (CSEL 28.1, 271–2); *The City of God* 14.22 tr Levine 374–7; *De nuptiis et concupiscentia* 2.13.26 (CSEL 42.279); *Contra secundam Iuliani responsionem imperfectum opus* 5.14 (PL 45.1444). See Clark '"Adam's Only Companion"' 143–6.

29 Augustine *La Genèse au sens littéral en douze livres (VIII–XII)* 523 (my emphasis). For an excellent study of Augustine's views about sex and perceptive comment on the secondary literature see Lodovici 'Sessualità, matrimonio e concupiscenza in sant' Agostino.' For a later medieval reflection of Augustine's position see Grosseteste *Hexaëmeron* 245.

30 Passages reflecting Augustine's earlier doubts are not often encountered in the Middle Ages; Müller (*Paradiesesehe* 21 n 10) cites an eleventh-century commentary on Genesis: 'Children would have been born to them [first parents] solely through the affection of pious charity, with no carnal concupiscence.' And see *SFA* 1–2 n 498, obj 7 (2.708) citing the same text of Augustine in which the possibility of reproduction through 'the affection of charity' is proposed as an alternative to the apparent necessity of intercourse. The references to charity are from a variant reading of the same text cited above as 'out of the affection of piety.' See Augustine *De Genesi ad litteram* 3.21 (CSEL 28.1, 88).

31 Lombard, *Sent* 2.20.1.3 (1.427–8)

32 See Aristotle *Generation of Animals* 2.1, 731b31-5.

33 See SFA 1-2 n 495, contra 1 (2.699); Albert *In 2 Sent* 20.2, obj 1 (B 27.342); Bonaventure *In 2 Sent* 20.1.1, sed contra 3 (2.478); Peter of Tarentaise *In 2 Sent* 20.1.1, arg 5 (2.168).

34 SFA 1-2 n 495, ad 1 (2.700). Bonaventure is more explicit about the Philosopher: 'The principal reason and according to the faith, which the Philosopher did not know, is on account of the multiplication of the number of the elect ...' (*In 2 Sent* 20.1.1, ad 3 [2.478]). On the repair of the ruin caused by the fallen angels being a cause of the creation of humans, see: Lombard *Sent* 2.1.5 (1.334) and *Sent* 2.9.7.2 (1.376); Thomas of Chobham *Summa confessorum* ed Broomfield 1; Bonaventure, *In 2 Sent* 9.1.5 (2.251); Aquinas *ST* 1.108.8; Aquinas *Quaestiones quodlibetales* 5.5.1 ed Spiazzi 101–2; Richard of Mediavilla 'but also on account of the multiplication of individuals in the same species so that in this way the number of the elect would be filled up' *In 2 Sent* 20.1.1, ad 2 (2.252).

35 Bonaventure *In 2 Sent* 20.1.1, ad 3 (2.478). Other reasons for God's granting the power of generation are to manifest divine glory and for the decor and completion (*perfectionem*) of the temporal universe.

36 Albert *In 2 Sent* 20.1 (B 27.341). The questions are: Would they have procreated through sexual union? Would there have been shameful concupiscence in the union? Would they have procreated with virginity intact or corrupted? Would they have come together for any reason other than the hope of offspring? Would there have been any resolution in them of tainted superfluous [matter]?

37 See Albert *In 2 Sent* 20.1, sed contra 2 (B 27.342); Aristotle *Generation of Animals* 1.2, 716a14–16; Avicenna *De natura animalium* 15.1 (f 59rb).

38 Albert *In 2 Sent* 20.1, ad 1 (B 27.342)

39 Albert *De homine* 2.77 (B 35.634)

40 Albert *In 2 Sent* 20.1, ad 4 (B 27.342)

41 See Albert *In 4 Sent* 26.10, ad 7 (B 30.113).

42 Aquinas *In 2 Sent* 20.1.1–2; see *ST* 1.98.2, sed contra 1.

43 Aquinas *In 2 Sent* 20.1.2, sed contra 1; *ST* 1.98.2, sed contra 1

44 Aquinas *ST* 1.98.2. See the definition in a medical work written about 1200: 'Coitus is the commingling of a man and a woman from the natural and voluntary act of union of both, with the emission of sperm; it is the procreation of a fetus with a great deal of concomitant pleasure ...' *The Prose Salernitan Questions* B 15: 9. The author says he will skip over many questions because of the subject matter, a hesitation not found in a classical work on the subject; see Constantinus Africanus *Liber de coitu*; Vincent of Beauvais *Speculum naturale* 31.2 (Douai 1624) 1.2291; *Speculum doctrinale* 13.93 (Douai 1624) 2.1230.

45 Aquinas *ST* 1.98.2. See Fuchs *Die Sexualethik des heiligen Thomas von Aquin* 22; Bonaventure *In 2 Sent* 20.1.1 (2.478).

46 Augustine *De Genesi ad litteram* 9.3 (CSEL 28.1, 271)

47 Augustine *De Genesi ad litteram* 9.5 (CSEL 28.1, 273)

48 *Ordinary Gloss* on Gen 2:18

49 See for example *SFA* 1-2 n 495, b (2.699); Albert *In 2 Sent* 20.1 (B 27.342); Bonaventure *In 2 Sent* 20.1.1 (2.477); Aquinas *ST* 1.92.1 and *ST* 1.98.2, sed contra 2; Peter of Tarentaise *In 2 Sent* 20.1.1, contra 3 (2.168); Richard of Mediavilla *In 2 Sent* 20.1.1, contra 1 (2.251). For this subject, see Børresen *Subordination and Equivalence* 17, 157.

50 See Aristotle *Generation of Animals* 1.18, 724b34–726a28; Avicenna *De natura animalium* 15.2–3 (f 60va); *SFA* 1-2 n 495, contra 5 (2.699).

51 *SFA* 1-2 n 495, ad 5 (2.700)

52 Ibid

53 Ibid (2.701)

54 Albert *In 2 Sent* 20.5 (B 27.345). See *SFA* 2-2 n 255–6 (3.268–71); Bonaventure *In 2 Sent* 20.1.2 (2.479–80); Aquinas *In 2 Sent* 20.1.2 ad 5 and ad 6; Peter of Tarentaise *In 2 Sent* 20.1.2, ad 1–4 (2.169–70).

55 *SFA* 1–2 n 495 (2.698)

56 See *SFA* 1-2 n 495, ad 6–7 (2.701). For a treatment of the process of seminal separation, see Aquinas *In 2 Sent* 30.2.2; *ST* 1.119.2.

57 'It must be said that as regards the commingling of the sexes the manner of propagation was the same then as it is now' (Albert *In 4 Sent* 26.6 [B 30.104–5]).

58 Peter of Tarentaise *In 2 Sent* 20.1.3 (2.170)

59 See text cited above, n 31.

60 *The City of God* 14.23–6 tr Levine 378–401

61 See Müller *Paradiesesehe* 25; Bonner 'Libido and Concupiscentia in St. Augustine' 311.

62 *SFA* 1-2 n 495, ad 8 (2.701)

63 Augustine *De Genesi ad litteram* 9.10.18 (CSEL 28.1, 279–80)

64 For Augustine see Müller *Paradiesesehe* 24; and see Augustine *Contra duas epistulas Pelagianorum* 1.15.31, cited by Bonner 'Libido and Concupiscentia in St. Augustine' 309 n2.

65 Albert *In 2 Sent* 20.2, obj 3 (B 27.342); see Aquinas *ST* 1-2.17.9, ad 3. For a summary statement of the causes of erection, see Vincent of Beauvais *Speculum doctrinale* 13.31 (Douai 1624) 2.1189.

66 See Peter Lombard *Sent* 2.20.1.3 (1.427–8), translated above, n 30.

67 'For, if man had not sinned, union would have been like the union of other bodily members and would have been without the fervour and itching of pleasure just like the union of the other members is. For [genital] member would have been joined to [genital] member without itching of the flesh just like any member would have been joined to another, or a slate to a slate' (Huguccio *Summa*, on Gratian *Decretum* 32.2.2 dp, ad v, *sine ardore* [Admont 7, ff 369va–vb]); for the Latin of the passage see Appendix 1, D.

68 See Albert *In 2 Sent* 20.2, obj 2–3 (B 27.342); Bonaventure *In 2 Sent* 20.1.3, arg 2 (2.480). Cf Aristotle *Generation of Animals* 1.18, 723b33–724a4, and Morsink *Aristotle on the Generation of Animals* 68–9. For William of Auxerre (*Summa aurea* 2.1 ed Ribaillier 2.1:252–3) there would have been natural pleasure, neither meritorious nor

demeritorious; and see William of Auxerre *Summa aurea* 4.17 ed
Ribaillier 4.382–3.

69 See above, n 42; and see 'Queritur quare tanta delectatio sit in coitu?
(Why should there be so much pleasure in coitus?)' (*The Prose Salernitan
Questions* q 16:10).

70 SFA 1-2 n 496 (2.703). The notion of the demands of human rectitude
suggests the hierarchical balance that would have characterized
humans in Paradise: persons subject to God, the lower powers subject
to reason in each person. This matter is discussed in the next chapter in
reference to original sin.

71 See Müller *Paradiesesehe* 70–2, 160–1 (Robert of Melun and Prepositinus
of Cremona) 275–9 (summary).

72 Albert *In 2 Sent* 20.2 (B 27.343). And see, 'I willingly grant that then
there would have been a greater and more unalloyed pleasure in the
activity, but under the command of reason' (Albert *In 4 Sent* 26.7
[B 30.106]).

73 Aquinas ST 1.98.2, ad 3. The 'those who say' perhaps refers to the position of the SFA and Bonaventure. See Fuchs *Die Sexualethik des heiligen
Thomas von Aquin* 26–7, 276.

74 SFA 1-2 n 496 (2.703); see Bonaventure *In 2 Sent* 20.1.3 (2.481).

75 SFA 1-2 n 496, contra a (2.702). In his *Commentary on the Sentences*,
Aquinas introduced a distinction between pleasure absolutely considered and pleasure according to a proportional relation to reason, a
position which seems closer to the view of the SFA: 'Therefore, speaking
absolutely, there would have been greater pleasure in coitus in the first
state than there is even now. But from the point of view of the proportioned relation to reason there would have been much less because
reason, while acting quite persistently, would have almost dominated
pleasure, and therefore pleasure would not have been as superabun-
dant and burning as it is now' (*In 2 Sent* 20.1.2, ad 2). This parallels
Albert's claim that there would be nothing *vehemens* in the state of
innocence (*In 4 Sent* 26.7 [B 30.106]).

76 Richard of Mediavilla *In 2 Sent* 20.1.3 (2.253)

77 See SFA 1-2 n 496, ad d (2.703).

78 Albert *In 4 Sent* 26.7 (B 30.106); see Peter Lombard *Sent* 4.26.2.1 (2.417);
Gratian *Decretum* C 32.2.2 dp, and the *Ordinary Gloss* on Gratian
Decretum C 32.2.2 dp, ad v *sine ardore*. See Appendix 1, E.

79 Albert *In 2 Sent* 20.4 (B 27.344)

80 The perfunctory treatment by Peter of Tarentaise depends on his Franciscan sources; *In 2 Sent* 20.1.1.2 (2.168–9).

81 SFA 1-2 n 497, ad 1 (2.705).

82 The *Summa* of Alexander (SFA 1-2 n 497, ad 1 [2.705–6]) gives five reasons why the reproductive system in the first parents would have been
under rational control: (1) Multiplication of the species in view of com-
pleting the number of the elect is a matter of rational orientation, and
so the reproductive system was more subject to reason; (2) since gener-

ation is oriented to producing a similar being (ie, human produces human), it is fitting that the act of generation be subject to what is most worthy in humans, namely, reason; (3) the act of generation is a sort of progressive motion and since progressive motion, in those having reason arises from practical understanding, in the first man who was perfectly ruled by reason the movement of his genitals ought to have been as subject to reason as the movement of his other bodily members; (4) in the act of generation there is a kind of taking away or subtraction (ie, sperm is released), so the reproductive system had to be ruled by reason to make sure there was not too much of this 'taking away'; (5) many organs serve the reproductive system in its functions, so it is fitting that that system more particularly be subject to reason, which had mastery over the whole body in the state of innocence.

83 SFA 1-2 n 497, ad 3 (2.706). See Richard of Mediavilla In 2 Sent 20.1.2, ad 1 and ad 2 (2.252).

84 See SFA 1-2 n 497, ad 4 and ad 5 (2.706-7).

85 'Tales quaestiones magis sunt stultae quam quod diu laboretur in eis; tamen inducuntur hic a quibusdam' (Albert In 2 Sent 20.3 [B 27.343]). See William of Auxerre Summa aurea 2.9 ed Ribaillier 2.1:252; SFA 1-2 n 498 (2.708).

86 Bonaventure In 2 Sent 20.1.4 (2.482)

87 Augustine The City of God 14.26. The Latin of the first part of the text is: 'et sine ardoris inlecebroso stimulo cum tranquillitate animi et corporis nulla corruptione integritatis infunderetur gremio maritus uxoris.' I translate 'infunderetur' by 'would have impregnated' and add [her], since the context calls for it. Augustine's point, as the rest of the text makes clear, is that there would have been penetration and impregnation and the hymen would have retained its physical integrity. Bettenson's translation ('the husband would have relaxed on his wife's bosom in tranquillity of mind and with no impairment of his body's integrity') seems to me to be mistaken; see Concerning the City of God against the Pagans tr Bettenson 591. Likewise, the Levine translation ('The husband ... could have come to rest on his wife's bosom with peace of mind undisturbed and pristine state of body intact') seems mistaken; see The City of God tr Levine 396-8. I believe both translators have been misled by the allusion to Virgil Aeneid 8.406 ('coniugis gremio infuso'), which may mean 'resting on her bosom.'

88 SFA 1-2 n 498 (2.708)

89 Albert In 2 Sent 20.3 (B 27.343-4). Albert seems to follow William of Auxerre, who speaks of a natural, non-violent breaking (fractio) in the sense of a separation; see William of Auxerre Summa aurea 2.9 ed Ribaillier 252.

90 Bonaventure In 2 Sent 20.1.4 (2.482-3)

91 Aquinas In 2 Sent 20.1.2, ad 1

92 Aquinas ST 1.98.2, ad 4. See Fuchs Die Sexualethik des heiligen Thomas von Aquin 97. Aquinas does not address the question of the destruction

of physical integrity through childbirth. Much earlier, St Jerome (*Adversus Iovinianum* 1.29 [PL 23.262D–263A]) had simply confessed that we do not know what would have been if there had been no sin in Paradise; but he implies that the normal state would have been that of virginity. See Pagels *Adam, Eve, and the Serpent* ch 4 'The "Paradise of Virginity" Regained'. See John Damascene *De fide orthodoxa* 97 ed Buytaert 367–71.

93 Peter of Tarentaise *In 2 Sent* 20.1.4 (2.171); see Richard of Mediavilla *In 2 Sent* 20.1.4 (2.254).

94 *SFA* 1-2 n 498 (2.707)

95 Ibid (2.709)

96 Aquinas *ST* 1.98.2, ad 3

97 Albert *In 2 Sent* 20.3 (B 27.344)

98 *SFA* 1-2 n 498 (2.708)

99 Ibid ad 8 (2.710)

100 See Peter Lombard *Sent* 2.20.2, rubric: 'Why did they not have intercourse in Paradise? Augustine answers in two ways in his commentary on Genesis (Quare in paradiso non coierunt. Duobus modis solvit Augustinus, Super Genesim)' (1.428); probably from the *Ordinary Gloss* on Gen 2:18.

101 Augustine *De Genesi ad litteram* 9.4 (CSEL 28.1, 272)

102 Ibid (CSEL 28.1, 273)

103 The interlinear gloss on Gen 4:1 emphasizes that there were no sexual relations in Paradise. *Adam* is glossed, 'already guilty'; *knew* has two glosses, 'not in Paradise' and 'virginity in Paradise, marriage outside.' For more ancient traditions in this regard see Anderson 'Celibacy or Consummation in the Garden?'

104 Bonaventure *In 2 Sent* 20.1, dubium 3 (2.488); see the parallel passage, *SFA* 1-2 n 498, ad 5 (2.710).

105 Milton followed the traditional Western view that there would have been sexual relations in Paradise; in fact, in several passages he presents Adam and Eve as having had sexual relations before the Fall (Milton *Paradise Lost* 4.492–504, 708–75; 8.510–20). See Lindenbaum 'Lovemaking in Milton's Paradise'; Le Comte *Milton on Sex* ch 6 'The Perfect Marriage.'

CHAPTER 2: THE FALL, ORIGINAL SIN, AND CONCUPISCENCE

1 See the question in Aquinas, 'Whether the devil tempted Eve out of envy and in the form of a serpent' (*In 2 Sent* 21.2.1). Peter Comestor (*Historia scholastica* Gen 21 [PL 198.1072]) reports a tradition that has the devil assuming the shape of a serpent with the countenance of a virgin (*vultus virgineus*), presumably to allay Eve's fears; see *SFA* 2-2 n 188, ad 12 (3.200); *Speculum morale* 3.9.1 (among the works of Vincent of Beauvais *Speculum maius* [Douai 1624] 3.1389). For a survey of accounts of the temptation and the Fall see Köster *Urstand, Fall und Erbsünde*

96–121. For an account of early Christian and gnostic interpretations of the Fall, see Pagels *Adam, Eve, and the Serpent*; for the views of Ambrosiaster, see Hunter '*On the Sin of Adam and Eve. A Little-Known Defense.*'

2 See Augustine *The City of God* 14.15 tr Levine 345. For an account of the progression of the temptation see Peter Lombard *Sent* 2.21.1–5 (1.433–6). The text associating gluttony, vainglory, and avarice with the temptation of Eve is attributed to Augustine by the Lombard but is from Gregory the Great XL *homiliarum in Evangelia libri duo* 1, homily 16.1–3 (PL 76.1135D–1136C).

3 Augustine *Sermo domini in monte* 1.12.34 (CCSL 35.36–8). This analysis lies behind similar analyses in Gregory the Great: XL *homiliarum in Evangelia libri duo* 1 homily 16.1 (PL 76.1135C); *Moralia in Job* 4.27.49 (CCSL 134.193–4). The Augustinian account is echoed in the 'Responses' of Gregory I to Augustine of Canterbury 9; see Bede *Bede's Ecclesiastical History of the English People* 1.27 ed Colgrave and Mynors 100–2; Gregory I 'Per dilectissimos meos filios' 343. For this text of the response of Gregory to Augustine of Canterbury see Gratian *Decretum* D 6.2. The text is summarized in the *Ordinary Gloss* on Gen 3:1: 'Tribus modis culpa perpetratur ... consensu ligamur.'

4 Augustine *De Genesi contra Manichaeos* 2.14.20–1 (PL 34.206); see Lombard *Sent* 2.24.12.5 (1.459–60); *Ordinary Gloss* on Gen 2:25.

5 Augustine was acquainted with a view that claimed that the first sin was of a sexual nature. For a discussion of this matter in Augustine and with references to scholars who claim to find a patristic tradition supporting the view that the first sin was sexual, see the note in Augustine *La Genèse au sens littéral en douze livres (VIII–XII)* tr Agaësse and Solignac 555–7; Pagels *Adam, Eve, and the Serpent* 27. The view was expressed in Cathar circles that sex was involved in the first sin; see Wakefield and Evans eds *Heresies of the High Middle Ages* 166, 172.

6 Alexander of Hales *Glossa in 2 Sent* 15.7 (2.140). This belief in a hierarchical, harmonious order was common teaching in the schools; see for example, Albert the Great *In 2 Sent* 30.1 (B 27.497); Aquinas ST 1.95.1 and 2-2.164.1; Richard of Mediavilla *In 2 Sent* 30.3.1–2 (2.376–7).

7 Aquinas ST 2-2.164.1. See Richard of Mediavilla *In 2 Sent* 30.3.1-2 (2.376–7).

8 See Aquinas ST 1-2.82.3; Richard of Mediavilla *In 2 Sent.*, 30.3.1-2 (2.376–7).

9 Bonaventure *In 2 Sent* 21.3.1 (2.505); the view is repeated by Aquinas: 'It is commonly held that Adam did not sin venially in the first state before he sinned mortally' (*De malo* 7.7 Leonine 23.177). See Peter Lombard *Sent* 2.22.4.3 (1.443, citing Augustine); Alexander of Hales *Glossa in 2 Sent* 22.6 (2.194) and 31.6 (2.299); SFA 2-2, n 199 (3.211–12). It does seem to have remained the common, but not unanimous, view; see the scholion in the edition of Bonaventure (2.505). Peter of Palude

(*In 2 Sent* 21.3 [BAV Vat lat 1073, ff 88rb–vb]) does not rule out the possibility of venial sin.

10 Aquinas ST 2-2.163.1. 'For in the first state the body was so subject to the soul that nothing could occur in the body that would have been contrary to the good of the soul in its being or operation' (Aquinas *In 2 Sent* 21.2.1 ad 2).

11 Rom 5:19; see Lombard *Sent* 2.30.3 and 2.30.11–13 (1.496 and 503).

12 See Alexander of Hales *Glossa in 2 Sent* 22.1a (2.192); SFA 2-2 n 193 (3.205); Aquinas ST 2-2.163.1. For a sensitive analysis of this point in Augustine see Watté *Structures philosophiques du péché originel* 27–65.

13 For Augustine and Aquinas see Børresen *Subordination and Equivalence* 51–5, 204–9. On the basis of this interpretation and fortified with the New Testament claim that 'Adam was not seduced; the woman, however, was seduced into deception' (1 Tim 2:14), it was believed that Eve had sinned more grievously than Adam; see Payer 'Eve's Sin, Woman's Fault.

14 See Jerome *Adversus Iovinianum* 1.29 (PL 23.262D); Lombard *Sent* 2.30.10.2 (1.501); SFA 2-2 n 228 (3.243); Bonaventure *In 2 Sent* 30.1.2 (2.720). See the sermon attributed to Peter Lombard (PL 171.845–53); for the attribution to Peter Lombard, see his *Sententiae in IV libris distinctae* 1. *Prolegomena* 102*.

15 Aquinas, ST 1-2.81.1. See SFA 2-2 n 228 (3.243); Albert *In 2 Sent* 30.1, ad 4 (B 27.498); Bonaventure *In 2 Sent* 30.1.2 (2.720).

16 Alexander of Hales *Glossa in 2 Sent* 15.7 (2.140)

17 The *Ordinary Gloss* (interlinear) comments on the expression 'no shame': 'because they felt no motion of the flesh,' 'because [they were] without stain or blemish.'

18 Augustine *The City of God* 13.13 tr Levine 178

19 Ibid. For extended treatments of this matter by Augustine see *The City of God* 14.17–18 tr Levine 354–62; *De Genesi ad litteram* 11.1, 31–5 (CSEL 28.1, 335, 364–9).

20 Albert *De bono* 3.3.14, ad 1 (C 28.178)

21 Roland of Cremona cited in Müller *Paradiesesehe* 197 n 42; see Albert the Great *Summa de creaturis* 1, 69.3 (B 34.710).

22 See SFA 2-2 n 220 (3.232); Bonaventure *In 2 Sent* 30.1.1 (2.719).

23 The history of this development is well documented by Dom Lottin in 'Les théories sur le péché originel.' For a summary treatment with reference to more recent literature see Gross *Geschichte des Erbsündendogmas*; Köster *Urstand, Fall und Erbsünde* 122–91. For the main treatment of original sin by Peter Lombard see *Sent* 2, dist 30–2 (2.496–517). For the clearest summary treatment by Augustine of original sin and its implications for human sexuality see *De nuptiis et concupiscentia* 207–319; this work is in French translation with excellent annotations in *Premières polémiques contre Julien. De nuptiis et concupiscentia. Contra duas epistulas pelagianorum.* Anselm of Canterbury develops his theory of original sin in *De conceptu virginali et de originali peccato.*

24 See Lottin 'Les théories sur le péché originel' 274; it is not clear why Gross attributes the first occurrence exclusively to John of Saint-Gilles, see *Geschichte des Erbsündendogmas* 3.185.
25 See the summary of Alexander of Hales: 'Original sin is the loss or deprivation of due justice effected through Adam's disobedience, which was accompanied by the loss of beatitude' (*Glossa in 2 Sent* 30.7a [2.287]). Cf SFA 2-2 n 221 (3.237), n 223 (3.238).
26 Aquinas ST 1-2.82.2. For Aquinas on original sin see: *In 2 Sent* dist 30–2; *De malo* q 4–5 Leonine 23.103–43; ST 1-2 81–3. For a philosophical treatment of original sin in Aquinas see Watté *Structures philosophiques du péché originel* 73–127.
27 Aquinas ST 1-2.82.3
28 Aquinas ST 1-2.82.2, ad 3; see ST 1-2.82.4, ad 1.
29 Aquinas ST 1-2.82.3
30 Ibid. See Gallagher 'Concupiscence.'
31 Albert *In 2 Sent* 30.1 (B 27.496–7); and see Albert *In 2 Sent* 30.3, ad 4 (B 27.505), and *In 2 Sent* 31.2 (B 27.514). The distinction is already found in Alexander of Hales *Glossa in 2 Sent* 31.6a (2.299); and see *Glossa in 2 Sent* 32.8 (2.310). Aquinas describes this habitual concupiscence: 'The disposition itself to desire inordinately, which is left over in the lower powers. It results from the fact that the halter of reason was removed from appetite by which appetite was held restrained from being able to tend to its own objects in an unbridled manner' (*In 2 Sent* 30.1.3, ad 2).
32 Lottin 'Les théories sur le péché originel' 267, 274–5. Gross raises the possibility that deference to Aquinas on the same point may have influenced Duns Scotus, *Geschichte der Erbsündendogmas* 3.335. For the use of the formal/material distinction see: SFA 2-2 n 221, II ad 2 (3.237); Albert the Great *In 2 Sent* 30.3 (B 27.504–5); Bonaventure *In 2 Sent* 32.1.1 (2.761); Thomas Aquinas *In 2 Sent* 30.1.3; ST 1-2.82.3; Peter of Tarentaise *In 2 Sent* 30.2.1 (2.258); Richard of Mediavilla *In 2 Sent* 30.4.1 (2.378).
33 Lombard *Sent* 2.31.3.2 (1.506), abbreviated from Augustine *De nuptiis et concupiscentia* 1.30–1, 34–5 (CSEL 42.245)
34 See Alexander of Hales *Glossa in 2 Sent* 30.11b (2.289); 32.1a (2.305); 32.2c (2.306); SFA 2-2 n 248 (3.262). Albert (*In 2 Sent* 30.4 [B 27.506]) attempts a more systematic articulation of the terms, as does Aquinas (*In 2 Sent* 30, expositio textus). Peter Lombard occasions this discussion, *Sent* 2.30.8.2 (1.500).
35 Albert *De homine* 66.1 (B 35.554). See Avicenna *De anima* 4.4 f 20rb.
36 Albert *De homine* 66.1, ad 2 (B 35.554). For a naturalistic account of the involuntary nature of erection see Albert *Liber de principiis motus processivi* 2.9 (C 12.68–70). Aquinas (ST 1-2.17.9, ad 3) links a theological explanation for the failure of the genitals to obey reason with a naturalistic account. For a detailed analysis (prepared for an examination of conscience) of the progression of concupiscence see Grosseteste *Speculum confessionis* 155–158.

37 See Bonaventure *In 2 Sent* 32.2.1 (2.765–6) and Peter of Tarentaise *In 2 Sent* 32.1.4 (2.277). Alexander of Hales assumes a distinction between concupiscence as an integral part of human beings and bestial concupiscence, which 'could not move human concupiscence before sin like it could after sin' (*Glossa in 2 Sent* 22.1.6b [2.194]).

38 See Albert *De homine* 66.2, ad 2 (B 35.555). 'And one definition is proposed by all, namely, that concupiscence is an appetite for sensual pleasure' (Albert *Super Ethica* 3, lect 14 [C 14.1, 209]). For a discussion of Albert on this matter see Michaud-Quantin *La psychologie de l'activité chez Albert le Grand* 77–89, particularly the note on terminology (88–9). For Aquinas see *ST* 1, q 77, 78, 80, and *ST* 1-2, q 23 and 30 (in particular *ST* 1-2.30.1). The schematic account of the divisions of the soul in Aristotle (*NE* 1.13, 1102a27–1103a4) influences these accounts.

39 Aquinas *In 2 Sent* 30.1.1. See Aquinas *ST* 1-2.85.3. For the term ordinability (*ordinabilitas*) see Aquinas *In 2 Sent* 30.1.2, ad 4.

40 Aquinas *ST* 1-2.85.1

41 Aquinas *ST* 1-2.85.2

42 See the interesting question of Godfrey of Fontaines, 'Whether, if man had been created with purely natural endowments ['in puris naturalibus'], there would have been opposition of sensuality to reason in such a man.' Quodlibetum 10 q 15 in *Le huitième Quodlibet de Godefroid de Fontaines* 384–7.

43 Lombard *Sent* 2.24.3.2 (1.453)

44 'Est enim sensualitas quaedam vis animae inferior ex qua est motus qui intenditur in corporis sensus, atque appetitus rerum ad corpus pertinentium' (Lombard *Sent* 2.24.3–4 [1.453])

45 Albert *Summa de creaturis* 1.69 (B 34.703); Albert *In 2 Sent* 24.8 (B 27.406); Aquinas *ST* 1.81.1 and 1-2.74.3

46 *SFA* 1-2 n 366 (2.444); see Bonaventure *In 2 Sent* 24, dubium 3 (2.589).

47 Michaud-Quantin *La psychologie de l'activité chez Albert le Grand* 183–6

48 'Primus motus est motus sensualitatis secundum impulsum fomitis tendens impetuose ad fruitionem creature delectabilis,' in Lottin 'Les mouvements premiers de l'appétit sensitif' 542. See James Weisheipl on the medieval efforts to distinguish the specifically human component of first movements from purely physiological and biochemical modifications of the body; *Friar Thomas d'Aquino* 74 n 79.

49 The period up to Aquinas is amply treated by Lottin: 'Les mouvements premiers de l'appétit sensitif' 493–589; for emphasis on sexual inclinations see, for example: 497 n 1 (Peter of Poitiers); 499 ll 15, 21, 33 (Peter of Capua); 505–13 *passim* (Stephen Langton); 514 l 12 (Godfrey of Poitiers); 517 l 8 (Simon of Tournai); 523, l 41, and 525 ll 104, 125, and 526, l 146 (Wm of Auxerre); 535 ll 70, 72, 87 (Collection of Douai 434); 561 l 99 (Guerric of Saint-Quentin); 568 l 146 (William of Meliton). Against Lottin's suggestion that Roland Bandinelli first raised the question of the sinfulness of first movements, Müller (*Paradiesesehe*, 93 n 154a) suggests it was Robert Pullen.

50 For Peter Lombard see *Sent* 2.24.9.3 (1.457); 2.24.12.2 (1.458); 2.24.12.6 (1.460), and the earlier statement, 'temptation that arises from the flesh does not occur without sin' *Sent* 2.21.6.3 (1.437). On the mistaken association of the view with Augustine, see Deman 'Le péché de sensualité' 266–7

51 Albert *Summa de creaturis* 1.69.3.2, ad 1 (B 34.711); see Deman 'Le péché de sensualité' 266–7.

52 Albert *Summa theologiae* 2.92.4 (B 33.197–9). See Lottin 'Les mouvements premiers de l'appétit sensitif' 572–8; Brandl *Die Sexualethik des heiligen Albertus Magnus* 48–56.

53 Aquinas *ST* 1-2.74.3, obj 2; text from Augustine *De libero arbitrio* 3.18.50 (CSEL 74.131). For Aquinas as codifier of the tradition see Lottin 'Les mouvements premiers de l'appétit sensitif,' 584.

54 Aquinas *ST* 1-2.74.3, ad 2; this reply owes much to William of Auxerre; see Lottin 'Les mouvements premiers de l'appétit sensitif' 523. See Alexander of Hales *Glossa in 2 Sent* 24.1 (2.213); Bonaventure *In 2 Sent* 24.3.1 (2.583–4); Aquinas *In 2 Sent* 24.3.2; *De malo* 7.6 Leonine 23.174–6.

55 See Lombard *Sent* 2.32.1.6 (1.513); Alexander of Hales *Glossa in 2 Sent* 32.1a (2.305); SFA 2-2 n 233 (3.249).

56 For the effects of baptism see Lottin 'Péché originel et baptême.'

57 For the period after Aquinas see Couture *L'imputabilité morale des premiers mouvements de sensualité*. See Henry of Ghent, Quodlibet 6 q 32 'Utrum primi motus sint peccata' in *Quodlibet VI*, 267–79. For Peter of Palude (omitted by Couture), who lends his voice to the number opposing the view that movements of sensuality are sinful, see *In 2 Sent* 24.3.2 (BAV Vat lat 1073, ff 96rb–97rb).

58 See Lombard *Sent* 2.31.7.1 (1.509); SFA 2-2 n 230 (3.247); SFA 2-2 n 617, ad 1 (3.597).

59 In a departure from this usage Robert Grosseteste makes *libido* a subdivision of *luxuria*; see Grosseteste 'Deus Est' 281.

60 Lombard *Sent* 2.31.7.2 (1.509–10); see Lombard *Sent* 2.30.7.3 (1.499). Text of Fulgentius of Ruspe *De fide ad Petrum* 2.16 (CCL 91A.721). This text was attributed to St Augustine throughout the Middle Ages; see Gross *Geschichte des Erbsündendogmas* 2.84.

61 See Aquinas *ST* 1-2.82.4, ad 3.

62 Augustine *De libero arbitrio* 1.4.10 (CSEL 74.10)

63 Augustine *De libero arbitrio* 3.18.48 (CSEL 74.130)

64 *City of God* 14.15 tr Levine 351; at 14.16 Augustine discusses the specifically sexual connotations of *libido*. For an excellent discussion of classical Latin usage and of Augustine's use of the term see Bonner 'Libido and Concupiscentia in St. Augustine'; and see Schmitt *Le mariage chrétien dans l'oeuvre de saint Augustin* 95. Alexander of Hales notes that, like Augustine, he too uses *libido* to mean 'desire'; see *Glossa in 2 Sent* 2.21.10b (2.188–9).

65 Augustine *Contra duas epistulas Pelagianorum* 1.16.34–5 (CSEL 60.450–2);

see Bonner 'Libido and Concupiscentia in St. Augustine' 304; Müller Paradiesesehe 25–6.

66 See Augustine Contra secundam Iuliani responsionem imperfectum opus 6.22 (PL 45.1553); Müller Paradiesesehe 26; Thonnard 'La notion de concupiscence en philosophie augustinienne' 85–95; Clark '"Adam's Only Companion"' 149.

67 Augustine, Letter 6* in Epistolae ex duobus codicibus nuper in lucem prolatae 32–8. For discussion of this letter see Peter Brown 'Sexuality and Society in the Fifth Century A.D.' 49–70.

68 Ordinary Gloss on Gratian Decretum C 32.2.2 dp, ad v sine ardore; for the Latin of this passage see Appendix 1, D.

69 See Roland of Cremona cited in Müller Paradiesesehe 195 n 38; Albert In 2 Sent 31.2 (B 27.514); In 2 Sent 42.5 (B 27.661); De homine 67.3, ad 4 (B 35.557); De bono 3.1.1, ad 4 (C 28.118); Bonaventure In 2 Sent 31.2.3 (2.754–5) and Breviloquium 3.6 (5.235); Peter of Tarentaise In 2 Sent 31.2.2 (2.270); Richard of Mediavilla In 2 Sent 31.7.2 (2.392). Cf Aquinas In 2 Sent 31.1.1, ad 3; De malo 4.6, ad 16 Leonine 23.114.

70 See the commentaries on the second book of the Sentences, dist 31 from previous note.

71 Albert In 2 Sent 31.2 (B 27.514)

72 Bonaventure In 2 Sent 31.2.3 (2.754)

73 Aquinas In 2 Sent 31.1.1, ad 3; see In 4 Sent 41.1.1.2, ad 2; ST 1-2.82.4, ad 3.

74 See Peter of Tarentaise In 2 Sent 31.2.2 (2.270); Richard of Mediavilla In 2 Sent 31.2.2 (2.392).

75 Aquinas ST 1-2.83.4, sed contra; see Alexander of Hales Glossa in 2 Sent 30.8 (2.288); 31.4 (2.297–8); SFA 2-2 n 239 (3.254); Albert De homine 67.3 (B 35.556–7) and Brandl Die Sexualethik des heiligen Albertus Magnus 93–9; Bonaventure In 2 Sent 31.1.3 (2.746); in the second doubt raised in regard to the text of the Lombard (2.755) Bonaventure calls the generative power the font of infection (fontalis infectio); Aquinas In 2 Sent 31.2.2; ST 1-2.83.4.

76 SFA 2-2 n 239 (3.254); see SFA 2-2 n 257 (3.271).

77 Lombard Sentences 2.31.4 (1.506). See Lombard In 4 Sent 26.2.3 (2.417), 31.5.1 (2.446). See the summary in Alexander of Hales: 'Out of the corruption of the flesh in Adam the flesh in those coming after is corrupted and this corruption or infection is punishment in the flesh of his successors. From this punitive infection a stain is contracted in the soul, which is original sin' (Glossa in 2 Sent 30.12a [2.289]).

78 See Lombard Sent 2.31.7.2 (1.510); Alexander of Hales Glossa in 2 Sent 31.13 (2.304); SFA 2-2 n 230 (3.247); Albert In 2 Sent 31.2 (B 27.514); Bonaventure In 2 Sent 31, dubium 3 (2.756); Aquinas In 2 Sent 31.1.2, ad 3; ST 1-2.81.4; Peter of Palude In 2 Sent 31.2 (BAV, Vat lat 1073 ff 126va–127ra).

79 For a textually rich account of the later debate see Martin La controverse sur le péché originel au début du XIVe siècle; for a useful summary, with

literature, see Gross *Geschichte des Erbsündendogmas* 3.268–343. Martin edits some texts from the end of the thirteenth century in 'Les questions sur le péché originel dans la *Lectura Thomasina* de Guillaume Godin, O. P.'

80 *SFA* 1-2 n 496 (2.703). See Peraldus *Summa de vitiis et virtutibus* 'De temperantia' (Schlägl 12 f 249ra). For differing views of the human condition after the Fall see Innocent III *Lotharii cardinalis (Innocentii III) De miseria humanae conditionis* 1.1–7 (7–15); Bromyard 'Hominis conditio' *Summa praedicantium* 1.347ra-vb. For a comment of Albert the Great on the appropriateness of the equestrian metaphor see below, ch 6 n 56.

CHAPTER 3: MARRIAGE AND SEX

1 The principal treatment of marriage by Gratian is in *Decretum* Causa 27 to 36 (Causa 33, q 3 is a digression dealing with penance and confession). Peter Lombard's substantial treatment of marriage is in *Sentences* bk 4, dist 26–42. There were treatises on marriage contemporaneous with Peter Lombard but his treatment in the *Sentences* supplanted all of them. Worthy of note is a work on which the Lombard himself relied, the *De sacramento coniugii* of Walter of Mortagne, found as tract 7 of *Summa sententiarum* (PL 176.153–74). See the works on marriage edited in Master Simon *Maître Simon et son groupe 'De sacramentis'*.

2 See the study of Gratian's use of Augustine in Gaudemet 'L'apport de la patristique latine au Decrèt de Gratien en matière de mariage.' The two most representative works by Augustine on marriage are: *De bono coniugali* (CSEL 41.185–231) and *De nuptiis et concupiscentia* (CSEL 42.2, 207–319). See Noonan's remarks about Aquinas' dependence on Augustine in *Contraception* 254 n 33.

3 The scholarly writing about medieval conceptions of marriage is immense. Taken together the following works provide an introduction to medieval thinking about marriage: Esmein *Le mariage en droit canonique*; Le Bras 'Mariage'; Lindner *Der usus matrimonii*; Müller *Paradiesesehe*; Noonan *Contraception*. The recent work of James Brundage, *Law, Sex, and Christian Society in Medieval Europe*, provides a wealth of information about the treatment of marriage and sex by the ecclesiastical law and its commentators.

4 My discussion of marriage and sex is restricted to generally accepted orthodox views. From the late twelfth century there was an alternative view of marriage associated with the Cathar or Albigensian heresy, which saw marriage as evil, the creation not of God but of the devil. Medieval theologians were conscious of this heretical view of marriage, and in their treatments of the goodness of marriage they sometimes went out of their way to draw attention to it. For a conveniently available discussion of Cathar views of marriage and sex see Noonan *Contraception* 179–99.

5 Gratian *Decretum* C 32.2.1 da, and canons 1 and 2

6 For the full text of Gratian's dictum see Appendix 1, A.

7 'et quod sanis est officium, egrotis est remedium'; Augustine *De Genesi ad litteram* 9.7 (CSEL 28.1, 275)

8 Master Roland *Summa* ed Thaner 165; Peter Lombard *Sent* 4.26.2.1 (2.417). See Aquinas ST 3.61.2, ad 3.

9 Lombard *Sent* 4.26.2.2–3 (2.417–18)

10 Gratian *Decretum* C 32.2.2 dp (see Appendix 1, A); Master Roland *Summa* ed Thaner 165; Peter Lombard *Sent* 4.26.2.1 (2.417); Raymond of Penyafort *Summa* 4.2.5 (514). Contrary to the general view, the *Ordinary Gloss* on Gratian claims that both institutions occurred *in* Paradise (see Appendix 1, E).

11 Albert *In 4 Sent* 26.1 (B 30.98); cf Synod of Exeter II (1287) n 7 Synodal Statutes (English) ed Powicke and Cheney 2.2, 996. Prepositinus of Cremona (cited in Müller *Paradiesesehe* 161 n 102) says that many make the untenable claim that now (*hodie*) marriage is only *ad remedium*. For signs of this view see Alan of Lille *Regulae* 114.2 ed Häring 216, and William of Auxerre 'Sed in tempore apostoli erat matrimonium ad remedium tantum et modo similiter' (*Summa aurea* 3.23 ed Ribaillier 3.1, 435), but cf *Summa aurea* 4.17 ed Ribaillier 4.383.

12 See Jerome, Letter 117.3 (CSEL 55.425). For the use of the image in regard to penance see Jerome, Letter 130.9 (CSEL 56.189); Gratian *Decretum, De penit* D 1.72; Peter Lombard *Sent* 4.14.1.1 (2.315). The first plank was baptism.

13 The original expression seems to originate with Cassian *Conlationes* XXIIII 19.14 (CSEL 13.547). See McNeill 'Medicine for Sin.'

14 See the question in Albert, 'Is matrimony a remedy and medicine against the disease [*morbum*] of concupiscence?' *In 4 Sent* 26.8 (B 30.106–8).

15 Aquinas *In 4 Sent* 26.2.3, ad 4 (ST Supplement 42.3, ad 4); see Albert *In 4 Sent* 26.8 (B 30.107).

16 Gratian *Decretum* C 32.2.2 dp (see Appendix 1, A).

17 See Huguccio *Summa* on Gratian, *Decretum* C 32.2.1 da, ad v *quod autem* (Admont 7, f 367ra); *Ordinary Gloss* on Gratian C 32.2.1 da, ad v *quod autem*; Hostiensis *Summa* 4.2.8 (ff 195ra, 196vb, 206rb); Raymond of Penyafort *Summa* 4.2.5 (513–14); SFA 1-2 n 495, ad 9 (2.701); Bonaventure *In 4 Sent* 26.1.1 (4.662–3).

18 William of Auxerre *Summa aurea* 4.17 ed Ribaillier 4.390–3. The appeal to God's dispensing with the requirement of monogamy is the characteristic response to objections based on the Old Testament examples. See, for example, Gratian *Decretum* C 32.4.2 dp; C 32.4.7; William of Auvergne 'De matrimonio' ch 9 (Opera omnia 1.526–7); SFA 2-2 n 616 (3.595–6); SFA 3 n 255 (4.2, 360–1); Albert *In 4 Sent* 26.10 (B 30.111); *In 4 Sent* 33.2 (B 30.291–3). However, while nothing contradictory to nature was seen in one man's having many wives, the same was not the case for one woman's having many husbands. See William of Auxerre *Summa aurea* 4.17 ed Ribaillier 4.396–7; Albert *In 4 Sent* 33.3 (B 30.294–6).

19 See Gratian *Decretum* D 1.1 da; Peter Lombard *Collectanea in epistolam ad Romanos* Rom 2:4 (PL 191.1345); Lombard *Sent* 3.37.5.5 (2.212).

20 William of Auxerre *Summa aurea* 4.17 ed Ribaillier 4.393

21 'Natural law is what nature has taught all animals, for this law is not proper to the human race but is common to all animals that are born on earth and in the sea and to birds also. From it there descends the union of male and female, which we call matrimony, and from it the procreation and education of children. We see other animals also, even wild animals, coming under this law' (Justinian *Digesta* 1.1.1.3 ed Mommsen and Kreuger 1.1); see Crowe *The Changing Profile of the Natural Law* 44–51. See Isidore *Etymologies* 5.4, recorded by Gratian *Decretum* D 1.7; William of Auxerre *Summa aurea* 4.17 ed Ribaillier 4.394. This is a characteristic Stoic view: 'The desire for union for the sake of procreation and the care of what is procreated is common to all living things' (Cicero *De officiis* 1.4.11).

22 William of Auxerre *Summa aurea* 4.17 ed Ribaillier 4.395. In addition to its being marked by monogamy and fidelity, marriage was also considered to be characterized by inseparability. William does not address this question here, but in the discussion of the sinfulness of simple fornication he claims that the perpetuity or individuality of cohabitation is dictated by natural reason (ed Ribaillier 4.398–9).

23 Aquinas *In 4 Sent* 26.1.1 (*ST* Supplement 41.1). Others will formulate the question in terms of natural law; see Peter of Tarentaise *In 4 Sent* 26.1.1 (4.283); Richard of Mediavilla *In 4 Sent* 26.1.1 (4.401). For the *Summa Fratris Alexandri* see Steinmüller 'Die Naturrechtslehre des Johannes von Rupella und Alexander von Hales' 393–404 ('Die Ehe im Naturgesetz').

24 See Justinian *Digesta* 1.1.1.3 ed Mommsen and Kreuger 1.1; Aristotle NE 8.12, 1162a17; 9.9, 1169b19. For Aquinas' use of Roman law definitions of natural law, and particularly his use of the definition from Ulpian ('what nature has taught all animals') that Thomas cites in his first objection, see Crowe 'St. Thomas and Ulpian's Natural Law' 1.261–82; Crowe *Changing Profile of the Natural Law* 145–55; Oscar J. Brown *Natural Rectitude and Divine Law in Aquinas* 38 n 22. In his commentary on the *Nicomachean Ethics* (on 8.12, 1162a16-33), Albert the Great offers a philosophical account of the naturalness of marriage, monogamy, and inseparability; see *Super Ethica* bk 8 lect 12 (C 14.2, 641–3).

25 See Aristotle NE 8.11, 1161a17.

26 See Dedek 'Premarital Sex.'

27 What I translate as 'a union of man and woman' is not entirely accurate. The Latin is *'quaedam associatio viri ad mulierem,'* which literally means 'a union of man (male) to woman,' with the apparent implication that nature moves a male in the first instance towards an association with a woman, resulting in marriage.

28 Aquinas *In 4 Sent* 26.2.2. Richard of Mediavilla (*In 4 Sent* 26.1.2 [4.402]) will have none of this multiplication of institutions, holding for the traditional division into *ad officium* and *ad remedium*.

29 Synod of Angers n 129 Synodal Statutes (French) ed Pontal 232–4. See the Statutes of Salisbury I (ca 1217–19) n 35 Synodal Statutes (English) ed Powicke and Cheney 2.1, 72; Statutes of Coventry (ca 1224–37) *Tractatus de confessione* Synodal Statutes (English) ed Powicke and Cheney 2.1, 222.

30 Council of Lambeth (1281) c 9 Synodal Statutes (English) ed Powicke and Cheney 2.2, 902–3. See *Speculum christiani* 29.

31 See Peter Lombard *Sent* 4.26.5.2 (2.429). An expanded list is provided by Peraldus *Summa de vitiis et virtutibus* 'De temperantia' Schlägl 12 ff 260va–261rb. Peraldus provides a lengthy account of marriage in his treatise on the virtue of temperance. The Venice (1497) edition of Peraldus omits a substantial amount of that treatise (Schlägl 12 f 261rb l 11, to f 262ra, four lines from the bottom is omitted in the 1497 edition). The first reason given by Peraldus presents marriage as an order like other religious orders: 'While some saint such as Augustine or Benedict founded other orders, God, who cannot err, founded the order of matrimony (Cum alios ordines instituerit aliquis sanctus ut Augustinus vel Benedictus, ordinem matrimonii instituit Deus qui errare non potest)' (Schlägl 12 f 260vb). See the account of the idea of marriage as an order in Bériou and D'Avray 'Henry of Provins.' An outline of Peraldus' treatise on temperance is given in Appendix 2. See the sermon on marriage by Peraldus 'Notandum quod triplex est matrimonium'; see Schneyer *Repertorium der lateinischen Sermones des Mittelalters* 535.

32 Jerome *Adversus Iovinianum* (PL 23.221–352). For a fuller treatment of this dispute see below, ch 7.

33 In his discussion of the goods of marriage in *De Genesi ad litteram* (9.7 [CSEL 28.1, 275–6]), Augustine reminds his readers of the themes of *De bono coniugali*. For Augustine's own account of the occasion for writing *De bono coniugali* see *Retractationes* 2.22 (CCSL 57.107–8).

34 Augustine *De bono coniugali* 9.9 (CSEL 41.200). This text on goods in general is used by both Philip the Chancellor (*Summa de bono* 'De temperantia' ed Wicki 2.935) and the *Summa Fratris Alexandri* (SFA 2-2 n 240, contra c [3.255]) in their accounts of the goods of marriage.

35 Augustine *De peccato originali* 34.39 (PL 44.404). See *De nuptiis et concupiscentia* 1.17.19 (CSEL 42.231–2).

36 This is the order given in *De bono coniugali* 24.32 (CSEL 41.227). The first two are reversed in *De Genesi ad litteram* 9.7 (CSEL 28.1, 275). The usual scriptural warrants advanced by Augustine are: offspring (1 Tim 5:14), fidelity (1 Cor 7:4), inseparability (Matt 19:6).

37 Augustine *De Genesi ad litteram* 9.7 (CSEL 28.1, 275–6). See *Ordinary Gloss* on Gen. 2:18; Lombard *Sent* 4.31.1 (2.442). And see, 'Whoever wishes to praise marriage, praises these marital goods' (Augustine *De nuptiis et concupiscentia* 1.17.19 [CSEL 42.231–2]).

38 See Lombard *Sent* 4.31.4 (2.443–4).

39 Discussion of the goods can be found in commentaries on the *Sentences*, bk 4, dist 31.

40 Albert *In 4 Sent* 31.4 (B 30.233–4).
41 Albert *In 4 Sent* 31.4, ad 1 (B 30.233–4)
42 See Aquinas *In 4 Sent* 31.1.1 (*ST* Supplement 49.1); Peter of Tarentaise *In 4 Sent* 31.1.1 (4.320); Richard of Mediavilla *In 4 Sent* 31.1.1 (4.448).
43 See *SFA* 2-2 n 616 (3.595–6); 3 n 255 (4.2, 360–1); Albert *Super Ethica* bk 8 lect 12 (C 14.2, 641–3); *In 4 Sent* 33.2–3 (B 30.294–6); Bonaventure *In 4 Sent* 26.2.2 (4.668); Aquinas *In 4 Sent* 33.1.1 (*ST* Supplement 65.1).
44 Bonaventure *In 4 Sent* 26.1.3 (4.665)
45 See below, ch 5.
46 Impotence alone receives formal and extended treatment in the canon law and theology.
47 Lombard *Sent* 4.31.2.5 (2.445)
48 Lombard *Sent* 4.31.3 (2.445), from Gratian *Decretum* C 32.2.7. See Noonan *Contraception* 136–7, 174–9. The text itself originates with Augustine *De nuptiis et concupiscentia* 1.15.17 (CSEL 42.230; tr Noonan *Contraception* 136).
49 Grosseteste 'Deus est' 282. For methods of contraception discussed in the Middle Ages see Noonan *Contraception* 200–11.
50 Grosseteste <*De modo confitendi et paenitentias iniungendi*> 102 (bk 2.52); Albert the Great *In 4 Sent* 31.18 (B 30.250)
51 Raymond of Penyafort *Summa* 4.16.1 (558). See Brundage 'The Problem of Impotence.'
52 Aquinas *In 4 Sent* 34.1.2, ad 1 (*ST* Supplement 58.1, ad 1)
53 Noonan *Contraception* 290
54 See the *Ordinary Gloss* on Gratian *Decretum* C 32.7.25: 'Or say that there is marriage if he has an erect member whether sperm is resolved or not, for such satisfies the woman, just as the woman satisfies the man whether she resolves [semen] or not (Vel dicas quod si si [*sic*] habet virgam arrectam sive resolvat sperma sive non, quod sit matrimonium, nam talis satisfacit mulieri, sicut mulier satisfacit viro sive resolvat sive non).' See Peter of Palude *In 4 Sent* 34.2.1 (ff 170va–171ra). The principal canonical texts regarding impotence: Gratian *Decretum* C 27.2.15–16, 28–9; 32.7.18, 25; 33.1.1–4; and X 4.15.1–7; for a summary of the legal tradition to his day see Raymond of Penyafort *Summa* 4.16 (558–64). The principal theological texts are found in commentaries on Peter Lombard *Sent* 4.34.2–3 (2.463–5).
55 For discussion of female *arctatio* see Peter of Tarentaise *In 4 Sent* 34.1.3 (4.343); Richard of Mediavilla *In 4 Sent* 34.2.2 (4.476).
56 John of Freiburg *Summa confessorum* 4.16 q 1–25 (ff 234ra–236va); see Astesanus *Summa* 8.20–3 (2.614–20).
57 Belief in impotence through sorcery was an important element of later discussions of witchcraft; see the late fifteenth-century handbook on witchcraft, Kramer and Sprenger *Malleus maleficarum* 1.8 (1.54–9). Such concerns were not exclusive to the Middle Ages; see the fascinating account of the fear of impotence through sorcery in Le Roy Ladurie 'The Aiguillette.'

58 On the expression 'by the seventh hand' (*septima manu*) see Albert the Great *In 4 Sent* 34.5 (B 30.333); Bonaventure *In 4 Sent* 34, dubium 4 (4.777); Aquinas *In 4 Sent* 34, expositio textus. In the case of disagreement in the reports, the husband's word is to be taken, unless he claimed to have had intercourse and his wife could be shown from physical inspection to be a virgin. For the possibility of the physical verification of virginity see Lastique and Lemay 'A Medieval Physician's Guide to Virginity' (edition of fifteenth-century text 71–2).

59 For court cases over impotence see Brundage *Law, Sex, and Christian Society* 456–8. For the use of professional and practical experts in such cases see Jacquart and Thomasset *Sexuality and Medicine in the Middle Ages* 171–2; Murray 'On the Origins and Role of "Wise Women."'

60 *Commentarius Cantabrigiensis in epistolas Pauli* ed Landgraf 242–3. See Noonan *Contraception* 289–92.

61 In a passage not exactly on the point, Augustine (*De bono coniugali* 3.3 [CSEL 41.190–1]) speaks of old age when the value of the natural association of the sexes is a premium, when ardour wanes, and charity flourishes with the free choice of continence.

62 Aquinas *In 4 Sent* 32.1.2 (2), ad 3

63 'Maledicta erit sterilis quae non relinquebat semen super terram.' Cited by Peter Lombard as 'in Lege' (*Sent* 4.33.1.3 [2.457]). The idea of the text is in the Bible, however; see Exod 23:26; Deut 7:14. See Gratian *Decretum* C 32.4.3 da. It seems that sterility was invariably associated with women.

64 See Bonaventure *In 4 Sent* 33, dubium 1 (4.762); Aquinas *In 4 Sent* 33, expositio textus; Gratian *Decretum* C 32.5.18; C 32.7.27. Sterility as the result of some evil is mentioned by William of Auvergne *De universo* 2.3.24 (Opera omnia 1.1068).

65 An exception to this is the tolerance shown by some to withdrawal before (and without) seminal emission (*amplexus reservatus*). The reasoning is that there is no obligation to complete the act if it can be interrupted without danger of extra-vaginal ejaculation and if it is done by mutual consent. Where there is ejaculation (*coitus interruptus*) the act is seriously sinful, the act for which Onan was struck down by God. See Noonan *Contraception* 161–2, 222–7, 296–9. The Latin expressions *amplexus reservatus* and *coitus interruptus* are not medieval in origin. A reader of my manuscript observes: 'Throughout the discussion of impotence and sterility the author assumes that medieval writers were so naive as to think that couples did not have premarital intercourse. That unlikely assumption renders this discussion highly abstract, to the point of being unreal.' I make no such assumption. Medieval theologians were well aware of the frequency of premarital intercourse, but their concerns with impotence and sterility were prompted by considerations of the necessary conditions for marriage, annulment, separation, and the possibility of remarriage. These are issues that must be discussed in the abstract before being brought to bear on 'reality.'

66 'Nature teaches that the proper manner is that the woman be on her
   back with the man lying on her stomach' (Albert the Great *In 4 Sent*
   31.24 [B 30.263]).
67 The penitential literature prior to the twelfth century was far more
   explicit in its descriptions of oral and anal heterosexual relations. See
   Payer 'Early Medieval Regulations Concerning Marital Sexual Relations' 357–9; Brundage 'Let Me Count the Ways'; Payer *Sex and the
   Penitentials* 29–30.
68 'For while the natural use, when it slips beyond the marriage pact, that
   is beyond the necessity of procreation, is forgiveable in a wife, it is
   damnable in a prostitute; the use that is against nature is cursed in a
   prostitute, but more cursed in a wife' Augustine *De bono coniugali* 11.12
   (CSEL 41.203–4). This text was known to the Middle Ages through a text
   in Gratian (*Decretum* C 32.7.11) that is a composite of *De bono coniugali*
   8.8 and 11.12 (CSEL 41.198, 203–4). In the original, Augustine continues,
   'Indeed, when a man wishes to use a woman's organ not provided for
   that use ...' This passage is transposed in Gratian to make the connection with *contra naturam*.
69 'Quinta est peccatum contra naturam quod fit duobus modis.
   Quandoque enim est contra naturam quo ad modum ut cum mulier
   supergreditur vel cum fit bestiali modo opus illud, tamen in vase
   debito. Quandoque vero est contra naturam quantum ad substantiam
   cum quis procurat vel consentit ut semen alibi quam in loco ad hoc a
   natura deputato effundatur' (Peraldus *Summa de vitiis et virtutibus* 'De
   luxuria' Schlägl 12 f 8vb). For other distinctions see: Master Roland
   Summa on Gratian *Decretum* C 35.2/3.11, ad v *extraordinaria* ed Thaner
   210–12; Rufinus *Summa* on Gratian *Decretum* C 35.2/3.11, ad v
   extraordinaria ed Singer 518.
70 Albert the Great *In 4 Sent* 31.24 (B. 30.263)
71 'De quo vitio cum magna cautela loquendum est et predicando et in
   confessionibus interrogationes faciendo ut nichil hominibus reveletur
   quod eis prestat occasionem peccandi' *Summa de vitiis et virtutibus* 'De
   luxuria' Schlägl 12 f 8vb. See Peter of Poitiers <*Summa de confessione*>
   19 ed Longère CCCM 51.22; Synod of Angers n 95 Synodal Statutes
   (French) ed Pontal 204; an unedited confessional summa (incipit, 'Cum
   ad sacerdotem') advises the confessor to take the following approach:
   'For he can inquire thus: "The natural manner is that, if a man has
   intercourse with a woman, he always take the superior position, with
   the woman lying below. Have you acted otherwise? If you have, don't
   be ashamed to speak up." If he says no, go on to something else.
   (Potest enim querere sic: "Modus naturalis est ut si vir coheat cum
   muliere semper sit superior, mulier iacendo inferior. Fecisti aliter? Si
   fecisti, non erubesces dicere." Si dicit non, transeat ultra.)' (J. Goering
   and P. Payer have edited this work, based on Dublin, Trinity College,
   MS 326.) Ziegler deals with this matter in the confessional literature (*Die
   Ehelehre der Pönitentialsummen von 1200–1350* 227–31).

72 Albert the Great *In 4 Sent* 31.24 (B 30.263). Since departure from the basic form is intrinsically evil, there can be no justifying reasons for it and so it must be refused in all circumstances. It is certainly not covered by the mutual obligations arising from the marital debt (see *SFA* 2-2 n 656, ad 2 [3.637]). Peter of Palude is uncompromising in this regard (*In 4 Sent* 31.3.2 [f 160vb]).

73 Albert's view is perhaps derived from Roland of Cremona: 'For no spouse can ever sin in paying the debt ... as long as it is paid in the proper manner, which nature itself teaches' (cited in Müller *Paradiesesehe* 194 n 35). The canonist Hostiensis relies on nature to teach and expound this matter, confessing an unwillingness to write about it (*Summa* 5, De penitentiis et remissionibus, n 49 [f 278va]).

74 Among his objections Albert describes the position from behind in this way: 'And they would have properly united if the woman were bent over facing away from the man (Et bene coniungerentur si mulier retrorsum contra virium incurvata disponeretur)' (*In 4 Sent* 31.24 [1], obj 3 [B 30.262]). For the older expression, see Burchard of Worms: 'Have you had intercourse with your wife or any other woman from behind, in dog-like fashion? If you have, you should do penance for ten days on bread and water' (Burchard *Decretum* 19.5 [PL 140.959D]).

75 See Roland of Cremona cited in Müller *Paradiesesehe* 194 n 35 (Müller notes that Roland counsels seeking medical help in the case of obesity); William of Rennes on Raymond of Penyafort *Summa* 4.2.13, ad v *nihil fedius* (520); *Summa* in Munich, Clm 22233, cited in Müller *Paradiesesehe* 206 n 77; *SFA* 2-2 n 676 (3.655–6), introduced as a special moral case (*casus*). Albert envisages the situations of obesity, a tumour on the woman's stomach, and pregnancy. He replies that deviation is allowed in such cases, since otherwise couples would not be able to have sex at all (Albert *In 4 Sent* 31.24, ad 2 and 3 [B 30.263]).

76 Peraldus *Summa de vitiis et virtutibus* 'De temperantia' Schlägl 12 f 262rb. See Astesanus *Summa* 8.5.2 (2.553–4).

77 Peter Comestor *Historia scholastica* (Genesis) 31 (PL 198.1081C). See Methodius in Sackur *Sibyllinische Texte* 59–63. This text is cited throughout the Middle Ages and beyond; see Sanchez (d 1610) *De sancto matrimonii sacramento* 2.219. Although I know of no author who makes the point, a possible source of the horror of this position may also be that it is a reversal of the natural roles of the active male and the passive female (see Aristotle *De generatione animalium* 1.2, 716a3–26; 1.20, 729a22–34). Although Albert does not include this position in his grading of deviations from the natural position, he does mention it as an objection ('if the husband is underneath') and appears to allow it for cause (Albert *In 4 Sent* 31.24, obj 2 [B 30.262]).

78 Aquinas *In 4 Sent* 31, expositio textus. See Aquinas *ST* 2-2.154.11; John of Freiburg *Summa confessorum* 4.2, q 47 (ff 220vb–221ra); Peter of Palude *In 4 Sent* 31.3.2 (f 160va).

79 See Lombard *Sent* 4.26.5.1 (2.419). When William Peraldus begins to

deal with the subject of marriage in his tract on temperance he says he must first destroy the evil of the Cathars (*Summa de vitiis et virtutibus* 'De temperantia' Schlägl 12 f 259vb). Albert has two lengthy discussions of the reasons heretics might have to condemn marital intercourse: *In 4 Sent* 26.9 (30.108–10), a 13 (30.117–19). See Noonan *Contraception* ch 6.

80 Aquinas *In 4 Sent* 26.1.3 (*ST* Supplement 41.3)

81 Aquinas *In 4 Sent* 31.2.1 and 2 (*ST* Supplement 49.4–5)

82 Early commentaries on Peter Lombard's *Sentences* tended to deal with the moral character of marital intercourse in the different contexts in which the subject was introduced by the Master. Peter of Palude, who wrote in the early fourteenth century, departed from this approach by gathering the various issues together under three questions: When is intercourse meritorious? When is it a mortal sin? When is it a venial sin? (*In 4 Sent* 31.3 [f 160rb–161ra]).

83 Philip the Chancellor in summary form and the *Summa Fratris Alexandri* follow the account of Augustine on goods in general and on the derivation of the goods of marriage from that account. See Philip the Chancellor *Summa de bono* 'De temperantia' ed Wicki 2.935–6; *SFA* 2-2 n 240 (3.255); 2-2 n 617 (3.596–8); 3 n 370, ad 2 (4.2, 555). It is not unusual to encounter arguments based on the naturalness of marriage and on the natural finality of the reproductive system. However, such arguments ultimately appeal to the goods of offspring and fidelity.

84 See Bonaventure *In 4 Sent* 31.2.1, ad 7 (4.723).

85 Aquinas *In 4 Sent* 31.2.1, sed contra (1) (*ST* Supplement 49.4)

86 For example: 'But the third good does not pertain to the use of matrimony' (Aquinas, *In 4 Sent* 31.2.2 [*ST* Supplement 49.5]). There is some dispute whether Albert the Great allowed 'for the good of the sacrament' to be a legitimate subjective reason for marital intercourse; see Noonan (*Contraception* 286–7) for a summary of the issue, with literature. What is overlooked in this dispute is that the idea of *rememoratio* of the sacramental good is not peculiar to Albert. He would have been familiar with the notion from William of Auvergne, who certainly did not allow for the motive of 'recalling the sacrament' to be a legitimate subjective intention for intercourse; see William of Auvergne *De sacramento matrimonii* 6, Opera omnia 1.519a.

87 See Peter of Palude *In 4 Sent* 31.2.1 (f 159rb).

88 Peter of Palude *In 4 Sent* 31.1 (f 159rb). This view was not shared universally; Peter of Tarentaise (*In 4 Sent* 31.1.1, ad 5 [4.320]), for example, denies that marriage before the Fall needed excusing. The reasons given by Aquinas suggest that he too considered that only marriage after the Fall required to be excused. However, from a response to an objection in the same context it is clear that Aquinas saw the excuse extending to before the Fall (*In 4 Sent* 31.1.1, ad 2 and ad 3 [*ST* Supplement 49.1]).

89 For example, see *SFA* 2-2 n 617, ad 1 (3.598); Albert *In 4 Sent* 26.9

(B 30.108–10); *In 4 Sent* 26.13 (B 30.117–19); Aquinas *In 4 Sent* 26.1.3
(ST Supplement 41.3); *In 4 Sent* 31.2.1 (ST Supplement 49.4).

90 Augustine, Sermon 162.2 (PL 38.887). See Ambrosiaster *Commentarius in
ep. Pauli ad Corinthios primam* 1 Cor 6:18 (CSEL 81.2, 67–8); Robert of
Melun *Questiones [theologice] de epistolis Pauli, De epistola 1 ad Corinthios*
ed Martin 201–2; Peter Lombard *Collectanea in epistolam 1 ad Corinthios* 1
Cor 6:18 (PL 191.1583C–1584B); see the question 'Quare fornicatio
dicatur esse peccatum in corpus' SFA 2-2 n 619 (3.600–1); Aquinas *Super
epistolam 1 ad Corinthios* ch 6 lect 3 n 306–7 ed Cai 1.292–3.

91 Aristotle *Nicomachean Ethics* 7.11, 1152b18 tr Rackham. Although often
presented as a view of Aristotle, it is not his own view but is introduced by him as one of the arguments used by those who claim that
pleasure is an evil. See Aquinas on this passage: 'Prudence is not
impeded by anything good. However, it is impeded by pleasures, the
more so the greater the pleasures. It is clear that sexual pleasure, which
is the greatest, impedes reason so much that no one experiencing pleasure is able to actually understand anything. The whole intention of the
soul is drawn to the pleasure' (Aquinas *Sententia libri Ethicorum* bk 7, 11
[1152b16] Leonine 47.2, 425).

92 Aquinas *In 4 Sent* 31.2.1, ad 3 (ST Supplement 49.4, ad 3). See Aquinas
In 4 Sent 26.1.3, ad 6 (ST Supplement 41.3, ad 6). Bonaventure (*In 4 Sent*
31.2.1, contra 1-6 [4.723]) provides a convenient summary of traditional
arguments that claimed that marital relations, even for the sake of
offspring, could not be excused from sin. The arguments are from the
point of view of: pleasure, absorption of reason, shame, lust, original
sin, and first movements (of sensuality). A particularly troublesome
text from Origen (attributed to Jerome) rules out the presence of the
Holy Spirit at the time of intercourse, suggesting that the act must be
evil and certainly not meritorious. See Gratian *Decretum* C 32.2.4 (from
Origen *In Numeros* 6.3; PG 12.610C); Lombard *Sent* 4.32.3.3 (2.455). The
usual interpretation notes that the text simply rules out the ability to
prophesy at such times and does not imply that the act of intercourse
is evil or lacks merit; see Huguccio *Summa* on Gratian *Decretum* C
32.2.4, ad v *presentia* (Admont 7, f 370ra); *Ordinary Gloss* on Gratian
Decretum C 32.2.4, ad v *presentia*; Alexander of Hales *Glossa in 4 Sent*
32.13 (4.513); SFA 2-2 n 617 (3.598); Albert the Great *In 4 Sent* 9.10, ad 8
(B 29.233); Aquinas *In 4 Sent* 26.1.3, ad 2 (ST Supplement 41.3) and
ST 2-2.172.3, ad 3. Note that a certain Master Martin (cited in Müller
Paradiesesehe 145 n 58) and Peter of Tarentaise (*In 4 Sent* 31.3.1.3, obj 2
[4.323]) correctly name Origen as the author of this text.

93 See Lombard *Sent* 4.31.5.1–2 (2.446–7).

CHAPTER 4: LEGITIMATE REASONS FOR MARITAL RELATIONS

1 Peter Lombard *Sent* 4.31.5.1 (2.446)
2 For examples of this terminology see: (Pseudo) Peter of Poitiers, gloss

on the *Sentences*, cited in Müller *Paradiesesehe* 131 n 18 (and see Müller 131–64); Alan of Lille *Liber poenitentialis* 1.26 ed Longère 2.34–5; John of La Rochelle, cited in Müller *Paradiesesehe* 213 n 93, which is virtually identical with an account in *SFA* 3 n 406 (4.2, 595); *SFA* 3 n 76 (4.2, 113–14).

3 For what follows see Rufinus *Summa* ed Singer 479–80.

4 To this type Rufinus relates *Decretum* C 27.2.24 and C 33.5.1.

5 With this Rufinus associates Gratian *Decretum* C 32.7.11.

6 Rufinus distributes the texts of Gratian in the following way: (1) Offspring: C 33.4.7, where mention is made of the procreative purpose. This text, however, is traditionally associated with the question of pleasure, as will be seen. (2) Avoidance of incontinence: D 13.2, § 4; D 25.3 dp § 7; C 33.4.7; (3) To satisfy lust: C 33.4.5; C 32.4.14.

7 See Huguccio *Summa* on Gratian *Decretum* C 32.2.2 dp, ad v *quod enim* (Admont 7, f 369va; see Appendix 1, D); *Ordinary Gloss* on Gratian C 32.2.3, ad v *ab adulterio*.

8 Raymond *Summa* 4.2.13 (519). At the end of his discussion of the reasons Raymond adds: 'Everything I have said about the goods of marriage you will find in (*Decretum*) 32, all of q. 2, q. 4, c. 5 and in the fourth book of the *Sentences* in the tract on marriage' (520). Raymond, thus, grounds himself on the two fundamental sources for medieval views about marital intercourse.

9 William of Rennes on Raymond *Summa* 4.2.13, ad v *veniale* (519)

10 Albert the Great agrees with the theory of the four reasons expounded by his contemporaries. However, in his developed position on the question of reasons he is inclined to approach the issue from the point of view of what he calls the *moventia* (things that move) to intercourse (nature, lust, and grace). See the emergence of this approach: *De sacramentis* 9.2.2, ad 2 (C 26.160–61); *In 4 Sent* 26.11 (B 30.113–15); *In 4 Sent* 31.21 (B 30.254–8).

11 Raymond of Penyafort *Summa* 4.2.13 (519), citing Peter Lombard *Sent* 4.31.5.1 and 4.31.7.2 (2.446, 449); Augustine *De bono coniugali* 6.6 (CSEL 41.195)

12 In Gratian *Decretum* C 33.4.7

13 Raymond of Penyafort *Summa* 4.2.12 (518), citing Lombard *Sent* 4.31.2.4 (2.444). See Lombard *Sent* 4.31.1 (2.442).

14 See Philip the Chancellor *Summa de bono* 'De temperantia' ed Wicki 2.938; John of La Rochelle *Summa de preceptis* cited in Müller *Paradiesesehe* 213; *SFA* 'Brevis explanatio preceptorum' 12 (4.2, 595–6); Albert *In 4 Sent* 26.11 (30.114); Aquinas *In 4 Sent* 26.1.4 (*ST* Supplement 41.4) and *Super epistolam 1 ad Corinthios* ch 7 lect 1 n 329 ed Cai 1.298; Astesanus *Summa* 8.5.2 (2.553).

15 See Albert *In 4 Sent* 26.11 (B 30.114); *In 4 Sent* 26.1, sol and ad 5 (B 30.98). The position is suggested by Philip the Chancellor (*Summa de bono* 'De temperantia' ed Wicki 2.936). Marriage that is granted by way of indulgence will be discussed in the next chapter.

16 Aquinas *Super epistolam 1 ad Corinthios* ch 7 lect 1 n 329 ed Cai 1.298

17 Aquinas *In 4 Sent* 31.2.2, ad l (*ST* Supplement 49.5, ad 1)

18 Richard of Mediavilla provides an example of these ideas as they apply to parties contracting to marry and the kind of intention required of them in regard to the three goods of marriage (*In 4 Sent* 31.2.1 [4.449–50]).

19 Bonaventure, *In 4 Sent* 31.2.1 (4.723). See Peter Lombard, 'Scarcely can any be found experiencing carnal embraces to the point that they do not sometimes come together without the intention of procreation' (*Sent* 4.31.8.3 [2.451]).

20 Aquinas *In 4 Sent* 31.2.2 (*ST* Supplement 49.5); Peter of Tarentaise *In 4 Sent* 31.3.1 (2) (4.324). Richard of Mediavilla (*In 4 Sent* 26.2.2 [4.404]) requires that the intention be direct and exclusive (*directe et tantum*), and cf *In 4 Sent* 31.3.2 (4.451–2).

21 Peter of Palude *In 4 Sent* 31.2.1 (f 159va); cf Durandus of St Pourcain *In 4 Sent* 31.4.8 (2.374vb) who seems to be the source of Peter's view.

22 The text is from Caesarius of Arles (d 542) Sermon 177 (*Sermones* ed Morin [CCSL 104.725]), but was attributed to Augustine in Gratian (*Decretum* D 25.3 dp § 7). See Payer *Sex and the Penitentials* 24 n 28.

23 *Ordinary Gloss* on Gratian *Decretum* D 25.3 dp § 7, ad v *desiderio*

24 See Brundage 'Carnal delight' 381.

25 For accounts of the debt see Makowski 'The Conjugal Debt'; Ziegler *Die Ehelehre der Pönitentialsummen* 104–6, l24–7, 211–13. The article by Vaccari ('La tradizione canonica del "debitum" coniugale') is not on the debt as such but deals with the question of the constitutive role of sexual intercourse in the creation of a complete and perfect marriage.

26 Parmisano 'Love and Marriage in the Middle Ages' 657 (author's emphasis)

27 For reflections on the notion of love in marriage see J. Leclercq *Love in Marriage in Twelfth-Century Europe* and *Monks on Marriage* ch 2 'Conjugal Love as a Doctrinal Issue'; Duby *Que sait-on de l'amour ...?*

28 Raymond of Penyafort *Summa* 4.2.13 (519). See Gratian *Decretum* C 33.5.1; Lombard *Sent* 4.32.2.1 (2.453), from Augustine *Enarrationes in Psalmos* 149.8.15 (CCSL 40.2189). The text is used by Paul of Hungary *De confessione* 198; the editors entitle this work *Liber de poenitentia*; a manuscript rubric introduces the work as 'rationes penitentie.' In the prologue, however, Paul himself speaks of the work as *Tractatus brevis de confexione*; this is the basis for my title, *De confessione*. See SFA 2-2 n 654, sed e contra a (3,632).

29 See *Ordinary Gloss* (to 1 Cor 7:4); Lombard *Collectanea in epistolam 1 ad Corinthios* (PL 191.1588A); Aquinas on 1 Cor 7:4 in *Super epistolam 1 ad Corinthios* lect 1 n 322 ed Cai 1.297.

30 See Raymond of Penyafort *Summa* 4.2.9 (515–16) who refers to Gratian *Decretum* C 27.2.19 and 26; C 33.5.1–4. For the two-month period see X 3.33.2 and 7; *Decretum* C 27.2.39, *Ordinary Gloss* ad v *institutum*;

C 27.2.27, *Ordinary Gloss* ad v *monasterium*; Alexander of Hales *Glossa in 4 Sent* 27.1.d (4.464–5); 27.4.a (4.468–9); 3l.1 (4.488).

31 Aquinas *In 4 Sent* 27.1.3 (2), ad 2 (*ST* Supplement 61.2, ad 2); see Bonaventure *In 4 Sent* 32.1.3 (4.733). In the words of Richard of Mediavilla, 'a stay of two months from paying the debt is granted by the law' (*In 4 Sent* 27.2.2, ad 1 [4.416]).

32 William of Rennes gloss on Raymond of Penyafort *Summa* 4.2.9, ad v *secreta* (pp. 515–16); Alexander of Hales *Glossa in 4 Sent* 27.4.c (4.469). See the early comment of William of Auxerre *Summa aurea* 4.17 ed Ribaillier 4.387, 388.

33 See Bonaventure *In 4 Sent* 32.1.2, ad 4 (4.733).

34 The same views are expressed by Aquinas (*In 4 Sent* 27.1.3 [2]) and Richard of Mediavilla (*In 4 Sent* 27.2.2 [4.415–16]).

35 See *Ordinary Gloss* on Gratian *Decretum* C 32.5.20, ad v *conditione*. The gloss continues with examples of male superiority taken from Roman and ecclesiastical law. Canons 12–20 of this question provide an important collection of texts on the superiority of man over woman, husband over wife. For an account of the types of female servitude before and after the Fall see Aquinas *ST* 1.92.1, ad 2.

36 See Alexander of Hales *Glossa in 4 Sent* 32.8 (4.510); Albert *In 4 Sent* 28.7, ad 4 (B 30.196), 32.1 (B 30.269–70); Bonaventure *In 4 Sent* 32, dubium 1 (4.742); Brundage 'Carnal delight' 380–1.

37 Aquinas *In 4 Sent* 33.1.3 (*ST* Supplement 64.3).

38 See Albert *In 4 Sent* 32.1 (B 30.270).

39 *Commentarius Porretanus* 92. See Lombard *Collectanea in epistolam 1 ad Corinthios* 1 Cor 7:3 ad v *uxori vir debitum reddat* (PL 191.1588A), and his *Sent* 4.32.1 (2.451–2), which incorporates much of the material from his own commentary on St Paul; *Commentarius Cantabrigiensis* ad v *uxori* 241; other glosses on Gilbert in Müller *Paradiesesehe* 61 n 67; 64 n 78; Aquinas *Super epistolam 1 ad Corinthios* ch 7 lect 1 n 321–2 ed Cai 1.296–7.

40 See Peter of Tarentaise *In 4 Sent* 32.1.1 (2) (4.327); Richard of Mediavilla *In 4 Sent* 32.1.2 (4.455–6).

41 Richard of Mediavilla (*In 4 Sent* 32.1.2 [4.455–6]) refers to *Decretals* 3.31.16.

42 Aquinas *In 4 Sent* 32.1.3, ad 2 (*ST* Supplement 64.3) and *In 4 Sent* 32.1.2 (1), ad 2. See Albert *In 4 Sent* 32.4 (B 30.273); Peter of Tarentaise *In 4 Sent* 32.1.1 (2) (4.327); Richard of Mediavilla *In 4 Sent* 32.1.2 (4.455–6); John of Freiburg *Summa confessorum* 4.2, q 40 (f 220rb); Astesanus *Summa* 8.6.1 (2.555)

43 Albert *In 4 Sent* 32.12 (B 30.281). Albert's use of the term 'opportunity' perhaps depends on a comment on a text of Gratian (*Decretum* D 31.13) dealing with married priests in the Eastern Church. The text lays down the rule that priests are not to be deprived of familiarity with their wives 'when the time is opportune' (*in tempore opportuno*). At the word *opportuno* the *Ordinary Gloss* comments that the regulation is against

those who incorrectly claim that the husband is bound to pay the debt in any place and at any time his wife asks. The claim is not true any more than it is true that a debtor must always come with his purse ready (to pay his debts). Note that this text of the *Ordinary Gloss* seems to contradict the unconditioned statement of the gloss at *Decretum* C 33.4.1 da, ad v *quod autem*.

44 Albert *In 4 Sent* 32.2 ad 3 (B 30.272); see Aquinas *In 4 Sent* 32.1.1, ad 3 (ST Supplement 64.1, ad 3); John of Freiburg *Summa confessorum* 4.2, q 36 (f 220ra); Richard of Mediavilla *In 4 Sent* 32.1.1, ad 1 (4.455); Astesanus *Summa* 8.6 (2.555); Peter of Palude *In 4 Sent* 32.1.2 (f 161va).

45 Albert *In 4 Sent* 32.2, ad 3 (B 30.272)

46 Albert *In 4 Sent* 32.2, ad 3 (B 30.272)

47 Gratian *Decretum* C 27.2.24; Huguccio *Summa* on *Decretum* C 27.2.24, ad v *licentiam* (Admont 7, f 344rb); *Ordinary Gloss* ad v *licentiam* and ad v *imputabitur*

48 Aquinas *In 4 Sent* 32.1.1 (ST Supplement 64.1). The Latin, 'salva tamen prius personae incolumitate,' is underlined in the translation.

49 Peter of Tarentaise *In 4 Sent* 32.1.1 (4.327); Richard of Mediavilla *In 4 Sent* 32.1.1 (4.455). See John of Freiburg *Summa confessorum* 4.2, q 35 (f 220ra); Peter of Palude *In 4 Sent* 32.1.2 (f 161va).

50 Durandus of St Pourcain *In 4 Sent* 32.1 n 6 (2.375rb); his expressions are: 'sistendo in terminis generalibus' and 'descendendo ad casum singularem.'

51 Gratian *Decretum* C 33.5.5; see C 32.2.2 dp; C 33.5.1; and *Ordinary Gloss* on Gratian *Decretum* D 31.13, ad v *apostolicae*. See Augustine, Letter 262 n 2 (CSEL 52.622); Lombard *Sent* 4.32.2.2 (2.453).

52 *Ordinary Gloss* on Gratian *Decretum* C 33.4.1 da, ad v *quod autem*

53 Lombard *Sent* 4.32.3.1 (2.454). See a commentary on the *Sentences* incorrectly attributed to Peter of Poitiers *In 4 Sent* 32.3, ad v *Et licet debitum*, quoted in Müller *Paradiesesehe* 132 n 20. Müller cites the source as Paris BN lat 14428; Landgraf (*Introduction* 137) cites it as Paris BN lat. 14423.

54 Robert of Flamborough *Liber poenitentialis* 2.71 ed Firth 97

55 Cited in Müller *Paradiesesehe* 190 n 28

56 Pseudo-Peter of Poitiers cited in Müller *Paradiesesehe* 132 n 20; Peter of Palude *In 4 Sent* 32.1.1 (f 161ra)

57 Sicard of Cremona on Gratian (*Decretum* C 32.2), cited in Müller *Paradiesesehe* 108 n 15

58 Grosseteste *Templum Dei* 17.9 (ed Goering and Mantello 60)

59 SFA 2-2 n 651, Introduction (3.629); see SFA 2-2 ante n 654 (3.631); SFA 3 n 372 (4.2, 557–8); SFA 3 n 406 (4.2, 596).

60 SFA 2-2 n 655, d (3.633)

61 For the penitentials see Payer *Sex and the Penitentials, passim.* Flandrin's *Un temps pour embrasser* purports to be a study of sexual regulations in the penitentials from the sixth to the eleventh century. As a study of the penitentials claiming chronological, geographical, and textual accu-

racy, the work is marred by serious errors and so is quite untrustworthy. If one abstracts from the treatment of the penitentials, however, the book can be read with profit for the insights it offers into the early history of the regulation of marital sexual relations.

62 A version of Peter the Chanter *Verbum abbreviatum* (Munich, Clm 17458) cited by Müller (*Paradiesesehe* 150 n 74). For the version and manuscript see Baldwin *Masters, Princes and Merchants* 2: 254.

63 Robert of Courson cited in Müller *Paradiesesehe* 160 n 98. See Payer 'Early Medieval Regulations'; Brundage *Law, Sex, and Christian Society*. These works provide adequate discussion of sexual regulations concerning times, places, conditions of persons, and sexual positions for the centuries prior to the twelfth century.

64 Gratian *Decretum* C 33.4.1 da

65 *Ordinary Gloss* on Gratian *Decretum* C 33.4.1 da, ad v *quod autem*; see Huguccio *Summa* on *Decretum* C 33.4 prol (Admont 7, f 385va).

66 Gratian *Decretum, De consec* 2.21. The original text regarding communion cites Jerome who refers to the biblical incident (1 Sam 21:4–5) when the holy bread was promised to relieve hunger on condition that those who would receive it would have abstained from their wives beforehand. Similar biblical support for requirements of sexual abstinence is frequently encountered in the literature: for the eucharist, Exod 19:15 (abstain from wives so as to be ready to meet the Lord); Eccles 3:5 (general idea that there is a time for sex and a time to abstain from sex); Tobit 6:18, 8:4 (to support the requirement of abstinence immediately after marriage); 1 Cor. 7:5 (general in regard to abstinence for prayer).

67 Huguccio *Summa* on Gratian *Decretum* 33.4.1 da, ad v *quod autem* (Admont 7, f 385va). See Synod of Paris n 99 Synodal Statutes (French) ed Pontal 88.

68 *Ordinary Gloss* on Gratian *Decretum* 33.4.4, ad v *processionis*; and see Rufinus *Summa* ed Singer 504.

69 *Ordinary Gloss* on Gratian *Decretum* C 33.4.2, ad v *festivitates*. See Gratian *Decretum, De consec* 3.1.

70 This list was still relevant in the early thirteenth century; see Synod of Angers n 62 Synodal Statutes (French) ed Pontal 176–8.

71 Huguccio *Summa* on Gratian *Decretum* 33.4.1 da, ad v *quod autem* (Admont 7, f 385vb)

72 Synod of Paris n 39 Synodal Statutes (French) ed Pontal 65. Several years later the Synod of Angers (n 60 ibid 176) specifies the vigils.

73 In some cases texts attributed to Ambrose (C 33.4.4) and Augustine (C 33.4.5) are actually from the elusive Ambrosiaster. For the source of C 33.4.2 (attributed to Augustine) see the editorial note in Peter Lombard *Sent* 4.32.3.1 (2.455 n 1).

74 The earliest Irish penitentials that proposed times for sexual abstinence did not attach penances to the non-observance of these times. See *Penitential of Vinnian* 46 (*The Irish Penitentials* ed Bieler 90–3); *Penitential of Cummean* 2.30–1 (ibid 116–17).

75 'In demanding at such a time, namely the time of prayer, there is always sin even if the coitus is for the sake of offspring (In exigendo vero tali tempore, scilicet tempore orationis, semper est peccatum etiam ipse coitus quamvis sit causa filiorum)' (Huguccio on Gratian *Decretum* 33.4.1 da, ad v *quod autem* [Admont 7, f 385va]). See Raymond of Penyafort 4.2.10 (516); Albert the Great *In 4 Sent* 31.23 (B 30.261).

76 *Ordinary Gloss* on Gratian *Decretum* 33.4.1 da, ad v *quod autem*

77 *Ordinary Gloss* on Gratian *Decretum, De consec* 2.21, ad v *abstinere*

78 *Ordinary Gloss* on Gratian *Decretum* D 23.33, ad v *in virginitate*. One has to wonder whether Gratian incorporated these canons into his own collection because they were so frequently encountered in the collections he used. The requirement itself originates in one of the earliest collections of ecclesiastical law, the *Statuta ecclesiae antiqua*; see Payer 'Early Medieval Regulations' 364–5.

79 Peter Lombard *Sent* 4.32.3.1–2 (2.454–5)

80 Alexander of Hales *Glossa in 4 Sent* 32.9 (4.510). Philip the Chancellor (*Summa de bono* 'De temperantia' ed Wicki 2.940) says much the same, adding that the authorities are to be understood as applying to the one asking.

81 Bonaventure *In 4 Sent* 32.3.2 (4.738–9). In this same discussion Bonaventure makes it a condition for the sinlessness of the one paying that the payment be made 'with displeasure and regret.' See Peter of Palude *In 4 Sent* 31.3.3 (f 161ra).

82 Albert *In 4 Sent* 31.23 (B 30.261); *In 4 Sent* 32.6 (B 30.275); *In 4 Sent* 32.10 (B 30.278–9)

83 Albert *In 4 Sent* 32.11, ad 1 (B 30.279). Albert answers an objection that claims that there ought to be intercourse on feast days. Intercourse is a sign of the spiritual union of Christ with the Church, and the soul with God, symbols that should be celebrated on feast days. Albert does not dispute the point about intercourse being a sign but denies the conclusion because of the 'foul concupiscence' connected with the act of intercourse (*In 4 Sent* 32.11, ad 2 [B 30.280]).

84 Aquinas *In 4 Sent* 32.1.5 (1) (*ST* Supplement 64.5). And see, 'but he is bound to hold himself worthy for prayer the whole day' (ibid ad 2). See Durandus of St Pourcain *In 4 Sent* 32 n 9 (2.375va).

85 See ch 3 n 90.

86 See ch 3 n 92.

87 Gratian *Decretum* C 32.2.4 da. See Gratian *Decretum, De penit* D 2.11 for an account of when the spirit is present and absent.

88 Huguccio *Summa* on Gratian *Decretum* C 32.2.4, ad v *presentia spiritus sancti* (Admont 7, f 370ra). See 'Or say that the Holy Spirit is not given in all circumstances because there is a certain dullness there and man becomes completely carnal' (*Ordinary Gloss* on Gratian *Decretum* C 32.2.4, ad v *presentia*).

89 See Ambrosiaster on 1 Cor 7:5 (CSEL 81.2, 71), and Peter Lombard on 1 Cor 7:5 (PL 191.1588C).

90 See Huguccio *Summa* on Gratian *Decretum* C 33.4 prol, ad v *quod autem* (Admont 7, f 385va). The *Ordinary Gloss* (on Gratian *Decretum* C 33.4.12, ad v *fraudari*) claims that Gratian says the debt must be paid, but I do not know where Gratian says this. Here and in D 31.13, ad v *opportuno*, the gloss takes the view that the debt is not to be paid everywhere, adducing in support a text of the Justinian *Digesta* 46.3.105 (2.721) that claims that a debtor does not have to carry around a sack of money ready to pay his debts at a moment's notice.

91 Huguccio *Summa* on Gratian *Decretum* C 33.4 prol, ad v *quod autem* (Admont 7, f 385va); see William of Rennes on Raymond of Penyafort *Summa* 4.2.10, ad v *abstinendum* (517).

92 See Gratian *Decretum, De consec* D 1.20, and see *Decretum* D 68.3; X 3.40.10.

93 See Gratian *Decretum, De consec* D 1.19; SFA 2-2 n 655, ad 7 (3.634); SFA 2-2 n 855 (3.813); Albert *In 4 Sent* 32.12, ad 3 (B 30.282); Aquinas ST 2-2.99.2, obj 2.

94 Albert *In 4 Sent* 32.12, sed contra (B 30.281)

95 Albert *In 4 Sent* 32.12, ad 2 (B 30.281); Richard of Mediavilla *In 4 Sent* 32.3.1 (4.457–8); John of Freiburg *Summa confessorum* 4.2 q 43 (f 220va); Astesanus *Summa* 8.6.4 (2.560–1). Peter of Palude (*In 4 Sent* 31.3.2 [f 160va]) reports a stricter opinion that he seems to regard as 'truer' but does not follow. According to this view intercourse in a church is a mortal sin and a sacrilege even in necessity because the necessity is not absolute like the necessity to urinate, about which people have no choice.

96 William of Auvergne *De matrimonio* 9 (Opera omnia 1.526). See Noonan *Contraception* 284 n 7.

97 Gratian *Decretum* C 33.4.4; attributed to Ambrose but from Ambrosiaster *Commentarius in epistolas ad Corinthios* 1 Cor 7:5 (CSEL 81.2, 72)

98 See Gratian *Decretum* C 32.7.15.

99 William of Auvergne *De sacramento matrimonii* 9 (Opera omnia 1.526). These nature analogies are encountered in the sermon literature of Jacques de Vitry and Guibertus de Tornaco; see D'Avray and Tausche 'Marriage Sermons' 96–101.

100 *Ordinary Gloss* on Gratian *Decretum* C 33.4.4, ad v *conceptus*

101 Jerome *Adversus Iovinianum* 1.49 (PL 23.294A), in Gratian *Decretum* C 32.4.5

102 Huguccio *Summa* on Gratian *Decretum* C 32.4.5, ad v *non perdant* (Admont 7, f 373va); *Ordinary Gloss* on Gratian *Decretum* C 32.4.5, ad v *non perdant*

103 Robert of Flamborough *Liber poenitentialis* 4 n 226 ed Firth 197–8. See Synod of Angers n 98 Synodal Statutes (French) ed Pontal 206.

104 See Jacques de Vitry in *The Exempla* n 229 (95); D'Avray and Tausche 'Marriage Sermons' 99 n 30.

105 Albert *In 4 Sent* 31.22 (B 30.258); Aquinas *In 4 Sent* 31, expositio textus. I am unable to locate this reference; see Avicenna *Liber canonis* 3.21.2.8 (f 366va).

106 Albert *In 4 Sent* 31.32, ad 2 (B 30.258)
107 See *SFA* 2-2 n 655, ad 8 and ad 9 (3.634); *SFA* 2-2 n 656, ad 6 (3.637); Aquinas *In 4 Sent* 31, expositio textus; Peter of Tarentaise *In 4 Sent* 32.1.3 (2) (4.329); Peter of Palude *In 4 Sent* 31.3.2 (f 160rb); *In 4 Sent* 32.1.3 (f 161vb).
108 Albert *De animalibus* 10.2.3 n 56 ed Stadler 15.753; ibid 18.2.4 n 72 ed Stadler 16.1228; Albert *In 4 Sent* 31.22, obj 1 (B 30.258); Richard of Mediavilla *In 4 Sent* 32.4.2 (4.458). Peter of Palude invokes the views of the medical doctors in support of this opinion, *In 4 Sent* 32.1.3 (f 161vb).
109 Albert *In 4 Sent* 31.22, ad 1 (B 30.258); Peter of Palude *In 4 Sent* 32.1.3 (f 161vb)
110 Lev 12:2–8; Gratian *Decretum* C 33.4.4; Lombard *Sent* 4.32.3.1 (2.455)
111 Bede *Bede's Ecclesiastical History* 1.27 ed Colgrave and Mynors 88
112 'Responses' of Gregory I to Augustine in Bede *Bede's Ecclesiastical History* 1.27 ed Colgrave and Mynors 90–4; Nicholas I ('Ad consulta vestra') 591; Gratian *Decretum* D 5.4; Innocent III in X 3.47. For the contrary custom see Rufinus *Summa* on Gratian *Decretum* D 5 ed Singer 16; *Ordinary Gloss* on Gratian D 5.2, ad v *pondere peccati*. For discussion of the subject see Browe *Beiträge zur Sexualethik* 15–35. See the twelfth-century ritual 'Benedictio ad introducendam post partum mulierem' Franz *Die kirchlichen Benediktionem im Mittelalter* 2.224–6.
113 See Bede *Bede's Ecclesiastical History* 1.27 ed Colgrave and Mynors 90–4; Gratian *Decretum* D 5.4.
114 Synod of Angers n 96–7 Synodal Statutes (French) ed Pontal 204–6; see Robert of Flamborough *Liber poenitentialis* 5 n 296 ed Firth 243.
115 Robert of Flamborough *Liber poenitentialis* Appendix B n 385 ed Firth 297. Rufinus offers a curious reason for post-partum abstinence. There is supposed to be sexual abstinence from the time of conception, but this time cannot be known precisely. The abstinence required after birth makes up for the time when the woman was pregnant but her pregnancy was unknown. Rufinus *Summa* on Gratian *Decretum* D 5.1 da, ad v *in lege namque* ed Singer 17. See *Ordinary Gloss* on Gratian *Decretum* D 5.1 da, ad v *quadraginta*.
116 See Flandrin *Un temps pour embrasser* 12–20, 77–82.
117 *Ordinary Gloss* on Gratian *Decretum* D 5.4 ad v *ablactetur*; Astesanus *Summa* 8.6.4 (2.562)
118 See *Ordinary Gloss* on Gratian *Decretum* D 5.4, ad v *ablactetur*; Richard of Mediavilla *In 4 Sent* 32.4.1 (4.459); John of Freiburg *Summa confessorum* 4.2 q 45 (f 220vb).
119 Peter of Palude *In 4 Sent* 32.1.3 (ff 161vb–162ra)
120 See Gratian *Decretum* D 5.4. In the original response of Gregory I to Augustine of Canterbury the question about menstruation concerns only church entry and reception of communion; see Bede *Bede's Ecclesiastical History* 1.27 ed Colgrave and Mynors 88, 92–4.
121 Pliny *Natural History* (Bks 3–7) 7.15.66 tr Rackham 548

122 Pliny *Natural History* (Bks 27–32) 27.23.77 tr Jones 54
123 Ibid 27.23.81 (58)
124 See Solinus C. *Iulii Solini collectanea rerum memorabilium* 1.54–6 (13);
    Isidore *Etymologies* 11.1.140–2; Browe *Beiträge zur Sexualethik* 1–14.
125 Rufinus *Summa* on Gratian *Decretum* D 5 ed Singer 16
126 Jerome *Commentariorum in Hiezechielem* 6 Ezech 18:6 (CCSL 75.235).
    Flandrin (*Un temps pour embrasser* 74–5) suggests that the idea of peril
    to the offspring conceived during menstruation is perhaps of Christian
    origin. It is possible, but further research would be required to estab-
    lish this, given the accounts of Pliny we have seen and the almost uni-
    versal cross-cultural evidence of menstruation taboos. Jerome does not
    simply affirm the effects of intercourse during menstruation but claims
    that the effects 'are said' to occur.
127 Jerome *Commentariorum in Hiezechielem* 6 Ezech 18:6 (CCSL 75.235–6).
    Although this passage from Jerome is not in Gratian or Peter Lombard,
    it is in the *Ordinary Gloss* on the Bible (see gloss on Is 64:6 [and see
    Haimo of Halberstadt *Commentariorum in Isaiam* 3, on Is 64:6; PL
    116.1063B] and Ezech 18:6) and is encountered in commentaries on
    Gratian and Peter Lombard. The passage from Sextus is discussed
    below, ch 5.
128 Rufinus *Summa* on Gratian D 5 ed Singer 16. Innocent III in his gloomy
    treatise on the human condition weaves together the traditional texts of
    Isidore, Jerome, and Leviticus in his account of menstruation; *Lotharii
    cardinalis (Innocentii III)* 1.4 ed Maccarrone 11–12; the editor does not
    pick up on the Jerome reference and the reference to Leviticus is
    incorrect.
129 Huguccio *Summa* on Gratian *Decretum* D 5.4, ad v *ad eius* (Admont 7,
    f 8ra)
130 *Ordinary Gloss* on Gratian *Decretum* D 5.4, ad v *ablactetur*, and C 33.4.4,
    ad v *conceptus*. William of Rennes on Raymond of Penyafort *Summa*
    4.2.10, ad v *abstinendum* (516)
131 See for example: SFA 2-2 n 651 (3.629); 2-2 n 655, ad 10 (3.636); Albert
    the Great *In 4 Sent* 9.11, ad 2 (B 29.238); Bonaventure *In 4 Sent* 32.3.1
    (4.735–7); Aquinas *In 4 Sent* 32.1.2 (2) (3) (these sub-questions are not in
    the Supplement to the *Summa of Theology*).
132 See Richard of Mediavilla *In 4 Sent* 32.4.1 (4.458–9); Astesanus *Summa*
    8.6.4 (2.561–2).
133 Peter of Palude *In 4 Sent* 32.1.3 (ff 161ra–rb)
134 Peter of Poitiers <*Summa de confessione*> 12 ed Longère (CCCM 51.16–17)
135 A fragment of the school of Anselm of Laon illustrates how in inter-
    course the couple become two in one flesh from the facts about the
    spread of leprosy; Anselm of Laon 'Les écrits d'Anselme de Laon' ed
    Lottin PEM 5.101–2 n 127. *Handlyng Synne* speaks of contracting measles
    from prostitutes, but the original French has leprosy (*Robert of Brunne's
    'Handlyng Synne'*, 238). See Synod of Angers n 88 Synodal Statutes
    (French) ed Pontal 200; Robert of Sorbonne 'Cum repetes a proximo

tuo' (among the works of William of Auvergne, Opera omnia 2 Supplement 235).

136 Hildegard of Bingam *Physica* 1.144 (PL 197.1177), cited in Browe *Beiträge zur Sexualethik* 1 n 2. For a treatment of leprosy in medieval literature see Brody *Disease of the Soul.*

137 Lateran Council III (1179), canon 23 in *Conciliorum oecumenicorum decreta* 222–3

138 See X 4.8.1–3. For the treatment of leprosy in the canon law see Merzbacher 'Die Leprosen im alten kanonischen Recht' (regarding sex and the married, 32–40).

139 X 4.8.3. There is an old canon of a council of Compiègne (c 19) that seems to allow for divorce and remarriage if leprosy occurs after a marriage (*Capitularia regum francorum* ed Boretius 1.39).

140 X 4.8.1. This text does speak of non-sexual concerns, but the Pope seems also to have in mind the problems of sex that such a situation can create. Noonan ('Marital Affection' 502–3) argues that the text is not related to sexual matters. This is difficult to reconcile with the idea developed in it that the healthy person is to minister to the unhealthy with conjugal affection, but if they cannot be induced to this *they are to observe continence.* This continence can be none other than sexual continence.

141 X 4.8.2

142 Albert *In 2 Sent* 30.1, obj to fourth way (B 27.496). Continence as an option underlies X 4.8.1 and 2.

143 The following are representative of the theological view: Alexander of Hales *Glossa in 4 Sent* 32.1a–e (4.505–6); Bonaventure *In 4 Sent* 32.2.1 (4.733–4); Aquinas *In 4 Sent* 32.1.1, ad 4; Peter of Palude *In 4 Sent* 32.1.2 (f 161rb). For the canon law see: *Ordinary Gloss* on X 4.8.1, ad v *ministrent;* Geoffrey of Trani *Summa super titulos decretalium* 4.8 (f 179vb–180ra). Hostiensis *Summa* 4 (on X 4.8) n 2 (f 206rb); Joannes Andreae *Commentarium in quartum decretalium* (on X 4.8) ff 33vb–34vb.

144 Durandus of St Pourcain *In 4 Sent* 32.1 n 6–8 (2.375rb). Peter of Palude (*In 4 Sent* 32.1.2 f 161rb) follows the opinion of Durandus in this matter, adding that lepers are said to have a great desire for intercourse because of the internal heat generated by the disease. On leprosy and contamination see Jacquart and Thomasset *Sexuality and Medicine in the Middle Ages* 183–93.

CHAPTER 5: PROBLEMATIC REASONS FOR MARITAL RELATIONS

1 The older terms for this type of intercourse are 'fragile' (*fragilis*) and 'carnal' (*carnalis*) intercourse.

2 Huguccio *Summa* on Gratian *Decretum* C 32.2.2 dp, ad v *quod autem* (Admont 7, f 369vb), see below n 31. For the term 'spontaneous' see Rufinus *Summa* on Gratian *Decretum* C 32.2.2 dp ed Singer 479.

3 The term 'fornication' is used in a non-specific sense. A married person

cannot commit fornication in the technical sense of the term; extramarital heterosexual delicts are acts of adultery.

4 'Hoc autem dico secundum indulgentiam, non secundum imperium' (1 Cor 7:6). Modern English translations such as the Revised Standard Version, the New English Bible, and the New American Bible render the phrase 'by way of concession.' The King James version uses the phrase 'by permission' and the Douai-Rheims 'by indulgence.' For a modern interpretation of 1 Cor 7 see Chadwick '"All things to all men"' 261–70.

5 See for example Jerome *Adversus Iovinianum* 1.8 (PL 23.232B); Ambrosiaster *Commentarius in epistolas ad Corinthios* 1 Cor 7:6 (CSEL 81.2, 72).

6 Robert of Melun *Oeuvres de Robert de Melun*. 2. *Questiones* 196

7 Text of Gilbert cited in Müller *Paradiesesehe* 63 n 74

8 Augustine *De gratia Christi* 2.38.43 (CSEL 42.201). See Augustine *De bono coniugali* 6.6 and 13.15 (CSEL 41.194–5, 207–8); *De continentia* 12.27 (CSEL 41.177); *Contra Iulianum* 3.14.28, 3.16.30, 3.21.43 (PL 44.716–17, 718, 724). On Augustine's use of the 'secundum veniam' version of 1 Cor 7:6, see Müller *Paradiesesehe* 31 n 61, and in particular, Lodovici 'Sessualità, matrimonio e concupiscenza' 243–7.

9 Lodovici believes that Augustine does not mean a venial sin in the modern sense of the term; see 'Sessualità, matrimonio e concupiscenza' 245 n 144 and 247.

10 This is the text as in Gratian *Decretum* D 13.2, § 4; for the original see Gregory *Moralia in Job* 32.39 (CCSL 143B.1658). The same kind of conceptual slide from indulgence to venial sin is seen in the twelfth century in a commentary from the school of Gilbert de la Porrée *Commentarius Porretanus* 94–6. In the thirteenth century we find Albert the Great even formulating a question in terms of 'venia': 'Quae sunt illa quae Apostolus secundum veniam concessit?' *In 4 Sent* 31.26 (B 30.264).

11 Lombard *Sent* 4.26.3 (2.418). Much of the material in the *Sentences* on the matter of indulgence was taken over by the Lombard from his own commentary on 1 Cor 7:6; see his *Collectanea in epistolam 1 ad Corinthios* (PL 191.1588D–1589C).

12 Lombard *Sent* 4.31.6.2 (2.447–8). In this account Peter Lombard refers to his earlier attempt in the *Sentences* (4.26.4 [2.418–19]) to clarify the idea of indulgence. The first attempt is confusing, since the language of concession is used there to describe what is granted by way of permission.

13 For the use of 'forgiveness' see Lombard *Sent* 4.31.6.1 (2.447); 4.31.6.3 (2.448); 4.31.7.3 (2.449).

14 See Albert the Great *In 4 Sent* 26.11 (B 30.113–15); 26.12 (B 30.115–16); 31.26 (B 30.264); Bonaventure *Questiones disputatae de perfectione evangelica* 3.1, ad 6 (5.170); Aquinas *In 4 Sent* 26.1.4, ad 2 (ST Supplement 41.4, ad 2); 31.2.2 (ST Supplement 49.5); *Super Epistolam 1 ad*

Corinthios 1 Cor 7:6 ch 7 lect 1 n 328–9 ed Cai 1.297–8; Peter of
Tarentaise *In 4 Sent* 31.3.1 (3) and contra 3 (4.324).

15 Master Roland mentions a wife, fear of youthful incontinence, one's
own or one's wife's incontinence (*Summa* on Gratian *Decretum* C 33.4
prol [ed Thaner 195–6]); for Omnebene see Müller *Paradiesesehe* 75
n 162.

16 Philip the Chancellor *Summa de bono* ed Wicki 2.937, 939

17 *Ordinary Gloss* on Gratian *Decretum* C 32.2.3, ad v *adulterio*: 'Again, by
reason of incontinence when he is predisposed (*preventus*) by pleasure;
then it is a venial sin. But some say that in this case there is no sin
because of the authority of the apostle, "each should have his own
[wife]" etc.' Paul of Hungary: 'or to avoid incontinence when he is
predisposed by pleasure, and then it is a venial sin according to some.
But I do not believe there is any sin because of the authority of the
apostle where he says "each should have" etc.' (*De confessione* 4.198).
Noonan (*Contraception* 249) mentions a few writers who hold the sinlessness of coitus to avoid fornication: Alexander of Hales (really
Summa Fratris Alexandri), Hugh of St Cher, and Robert of Sorbonne as
referred to by Lindner (*Der usus matrimonii* 123, 129). As Lindner himself correctly points out, however (129 n 42), Robert of Sorbonne does
not explicitly mention the third reason. See the work of Robert of
Sorbonne, incipit: '"Honorabile conjugium et thorus immaculatus" (Heb
13:4), etc. Verbum istud pertinet.' A text of this work was prepared by
Hauréau in *Notices et extraits* 188–202; see the editor's warning: 'on ne
trouvera dans le texte que nous allons donner au publique la transcrip-
tion fidèle d'aucun des manuscrits cités' (188). Alexander of Hales himself seems to have the distinction in mind when he claims that intercourse to avoid fornication is not a sin (*Glossa in 4 Sent* 30.11 [4.487]),
but this is later clarified as referring to forestalling fornication in one's
spouse (*Glossa in 4 Sent* 31.10e [4.496]). One could add the following
who hold the minority view that sex to avoid fornication in oneself is
not a sin: Robert of Courson (cited in Müller *Paradiesesehe* 153 n 84);
Roland of Cremona (cited in Müller *Paradiesesehe* 190 n 28); John of La
Rochelle (cited in Müller *Paradiesesehe* 213 n 93). The text of John of La
Rochelle was used in a pastoral summary of the ten commandments in
SFA 3 n 406 (4.2, 595).

18 Albert *In 4 Sent* 26.1, ad 1 (B 30.98); 26.11, ad sed contra (1) (B 30.114);
31.26 (B 30.264). See Brandl *Die Sexualethik des heiligen Albertus Magnus*
226–9.

19 Bonaventure *In 4 Sent* 31.2.2 (4.724–5); Aquinas *In 4 Sent* 31.2.2, ad 2
(*ST* Supplement 49.5); Peter of Tarentaise *In 4 Sent* 31.3.2 (2), contra 2
(4.324). See Fuchs *Die Sexualethik des heiligen Thomas von Aquin* 224. Of
the account of Aquinas, Lindner says, 'Am klarsten hat diesen Beweis
der Aquinate formuliert' (*Der usus matrimonii* 131).

20 Richard of Mediavilla *In 4 Sent* 31.3.2 (4.452). A similar objection follows based explicitly on 1 Cor 7:2 and Paul's censure of those who do

evil to produce good (Rom 3:8). The reasoning is that, since Paul allows marriage 'propter fornicationem' and says that one must not do evil that good may come of it, knowing one's wife to avoid fornication is not evil in any way. Richard agrees as far as another is concerned, but he claims that when the focus is on avoiding one's own fornication alone the act becomes evil because of the omission of a proper end of the act. A similar view is reflected in the confessional literature: John of Freiburg *Summa confessorum* 4.2 q 37 (f 220rb) and Astesanus *Summa* 8.5.2 (2.553); see Ziegler *Die Ehelehre der Pönitentialsummen* 213–18.

21 Durandus of St Pourcain *In 4 Sent* 31.4 n 6–7, 9 (2.374rb–vb). Durandus also notes that the good of fidelity embraces more than simply paying the debt. To keep oneself faithfully within the bounds of marriage is also an act of fidelity. However, Durandus requires that when offspring is possible it must be intended (2.374vb). See Peter of Palude *In 4 Sent* 31.2.3, ad 2 (f 160rb).

22 Alexander of Hales *Glossa in 4 Sent* 31.15 (4.501)

23 William of Rennes on Raymond of Penyafort *Summa* 4.2.6, ad v *veniale* (519)

24 Peter of Palude *In 4 Sent* 31.2.2 (f 159va).

25 Peter of Palude *In 4 Sent* 31.2.2–3 (f 159vb–160rb). See Noonan *Contraception* 249. For an earlier example of the idea of cooling off ('refrigeratio in proprio vase') see Robert of Courson cited in Müller *Paradiesesehe* 153 n 84.

26 Lombard *Sent* 4.31.5.2 (2.447)

27 In a text attributed to Peter of Poitiers (cited in Müller *Paradiesesehe* 131 n 18). I suspect the text in question is cited from Paris BN lat 14423 and not 14428 as in Müller (see Landgraf *Introduction* 137). For the influence of this text see Müller *Paradiesesehe* 132 n 22; 144 n 55; 167 n 121.

28 John of La Rochelle *Summa de preceptis* (cited in Müller *Paradiesesehe* 213 n 93): 'Impetuous [intercourse], proceeding from lust alone, transcends the limits of uprightness and reason and so is always mortal.'

29 See *SFA* 3 n 406 (4.2, 596); *SFA* 3 n 372 (4.2, 557–8). Müller (*Paradiesesehe* 213 n 93) incorrectly notes that in his *Confessionale* Bonaventure uses the modes of John of La Rochelle but ascribes them to Alexander of Hales. The *Confessionale* was not written by Bonaventure, although it is found among his works. It is attributed to an early fourteenth century author (Marchesinus of Reggio Emelia) by Michaud-Quantin (*Sommes de casuistique et manuels de confession* 55). See Payer 'The Humanism of the Penitentials' 354 n 63. The text in question is from the interrogatory in regard to the sixth commandment; see Bonaventure *Confessionale* 8.365. The passage concludes: 'Haec sunt verba magistri Alexandri,' a likely indication that the source was *SFA* 3 n 406 (4.2, 596). The Latin version of the *Speculum Christiani* uses a description of impetuous coitus that seems to have originated with John of La Rochelle; see '*Speculum Christiani*' 29.

30 Similar to the third reason, there are really two formulations of the

fourth reason, which are not synonymous. 'To satisfy lust' is a broader category than 'for the sake of pleasure.'

31 Huguccio *Summa* on Gratian *Decretum* C 32.2.2 dp, ad v *quod enim* (Admont 7, f 369vb; Latin found in Appendix 1, D); see *Ordinary Gloss* on Gratian *Decretum* C 32.2.3, ad v *quicquid*; Paul of Hungary *De confessione* (4.198–9); William of Rennes on Raymond of Penyafort *Summa* 4.2.13, ad v *nihil foedius* (520); SFA 3 n 371, ad a (4.2, 556).

32 Lombard *Sent* 4.31.5.2 (2.447)

33 Lombard *Sent* 4.31.5.2 (2.447). The Sextus text and the text from Jerome betray a curious use of texts by Peter Lombard. The 'origo' passage from Jerome is excerpted from Gratian (*Decretum* C 32.4.5). In that text Jerome himself cites the saying of Sextus. For some reason the Lombard did not quote the Sextus passage as in Gratian, but he cites it according to another version from Jerome's commentary on Ezechiel, where Jerome calls Sextus a Pythagorean, a characterization missing in Gratian; see Jerome *Commentariorum in Hiezechielem* 6 Ezech 18:6 (CCSL 75.235). The note in the edition of Peter Lombard needs correction on this matter. The same note suggests that the Sextus passage in the prologue to the Lombard's commentary on 1 Cor 7, which has been newly edited and included in the recent edition of the *Sentences* as 'Tractatus de coniugio' n 11 (2.87*), is cited anonymously and is also from Gratian (*Decretum* 32.4.5). It is cited anonymously, but not according to either version of Jerome, and is not from Gratian.

34 Recall that this is Raymond's authority for the sinfulness of the fourth reason; see below, n 49.

35 See Jerome *Adversus Iovinianum* 1.49 (PL 23.293A–294B). For the effects of love Jerome seems to depend on the speech of Lysias in Plato (*Phaedrus* 230E–234C). The canonist Rufinus (*Summa* on Gratian *Decretum* C 32.4.5, ad v *origo* ed Singer 486) relates the text to the broader context of the *Adversus Iovinianum*.

36 In the division of the text I follow the view of Bickel (*Diatribe*) on the fragments of Seneca's lost work on marriage. Bickel (393, ll 11–21) provides an edition of the text. There is little variation between Bickel's edition and the version in Gratian. Where there is variation, the reading of the *Decretum* will be followed in the translation. I believe Gratian was the first to incorporate this text into a collection of canon law.

37 See Bickel *Diatribe* 357–60 for commentary.

38 See Bickel *Diatribe* 357–8.

39 See Bickel *Diatribe* 361–3. This is the text cited by the Lombard (*Sent* 4.31.5.2 [2.447]) beginning at 'The wise man' and running to the end of the passage.

40 Recall that in his commentary on Ezechiel Jerome uses the Sextus part of the text to confirm his censure of intercourse during menstruation; see above, ch 4 n 127.

41 Noonan says of this text, 'Symbolic of Stoic influence, the epigram, in a variation of it by St. Jerome, was destined to echo through a thousand

years of Christian writing on marriage' (*Contraception* 47). D'Avray
speaks of 'the topos of the "too ardent lover of his wife"' (D'Avray and
Tausche 'Marriage Sermons' 100).

42 On the work in general, see Sextus *Sentences of Sextus* ed Chadwick; for
Jerome's attacks on Rufinus, see in particular Sextus 117–37. The Greek
text: 'moikos tes heautou gunaikos pas ho akolastos' (Sextus 38 n 231);
the translation of Rufinus: 'Adulter etiam propriae uxoris omnis
impudicus' (Sextus 39 n 231). The source of Jerome's idea that this
Sextus was a Pythagorean may have come from Jerome's acquaintance
with the *Chronicon* of Eusebius, a work that Jerome himself translated;
see under the entry for the one hundred and ninety-fifth Olympiad,
'Sextus pythagoricus philosophus agnoscitur' (Eusebius *Chronicon* 169).
This text, which was perhaps the most notable of the sayings of Sextus
in the Middle Ages, is not mentioned by Burley among the *notabilia* of
Sextus (*De vita et moribus philosophorum* ed Kunst 350–4).

43 Jerome *Adversus Iovinianum* 1.49 (PL 23.293C). This is the version used
by Gratian in the *Decretum* C 32.4.5. I have found no evidence of the
use of this text in any other collection before Gratian. Somewhat contemporaneous with Gratian, Abelard cited the text, *Theologia christiana*
2.47 ed Buytaert 15.

44 Jerome *Commentariorum in Hiezechielem* 6 Ezech 18.6 (CCSL 75.236).
Found as early as Hrabanus Maurus *Commentariorum in Ezechielem libri
viginti* bk 8 (PL 110.706D); it made its way into the *Ordinary Gloss* on
Ezech 18:6. This is the version of the text used by Peter Lombard
(*Sentences* 4.31.5.2 [2.447]).

45 I am unaware of the source of this version. Its most noteworthy use is
by Peter Lombard in the introductory essay on marriage in his commentary on 1 Cor 7. This essay has been recently edited as 'Tractatus
de coniugio' in Lombard *Sententiae* (2.84*–7*).

46 Jerome *Adversus Iovinianum* 1.49 (PL 23.294A); Gratian *Decretum* C 32.4.5;
Lombard *Sent* 4.31.5.2 (2.447)

47 Seneca *De constantia* 7.4 tr Basore 68–70. This text is found in a medieval florilegium of texts ascribed to Seneca, see Meersseman 'Seneca
maestro di spiritualità' 76 n 117. For Seneca's censuring of a double
sexual standard for husbands and wives and his condemnation of adultery, see Letter 94 *Ad Lucilium epistulae morales* tr Gummere 3:29.

48 Augustine *Contra Iulianum* 2.7.20 (PL 44.687). For the *De philosophia* of
Ambrose see Madec *Saint Ambroise et la philosophie* chs 4–5, esp 259,
311–17.

49 Aside from anonymous citations, I have encountered the text attributed
to: Jerome, Sextus, Ambrose, Augustine, Fulgentius, Gregory the Great,
and Hesychius. Raymond of Penyafort (*Summa* 4.2.13 [519]) attributes it
to 'the [a ?] philosopher,' an attribution that confused Martin Le Maistre
at the end of the fifteenth century. Le Maistre (*De temperantia liber* f 44rb)
notes that he had not read this in the Philosopher (ie, Aristotle).

50 On Gratian *Decretum* C 32.4.5, ad v *adulter*, see: Master Roland *Summa*

ed Thaner 172; Huguccio (Admont 7, f 373rb); *Ordinary Gloss* ('similitudine adulterine libidinis'). In spite of the precise technical meaning that the term 'adultery' acquired, there were numerous traditional texts inherited from the past in which the term was used in a broad sense. See Brundage 'Adultery and Fornication' 131.

51 Master Roland *Summa* on Gratian *Decretum* C 32.4.5, ad v *nichil fedius* ed Thaner 172; *Summa Parisiensis* on Gratian *Decretum* C 32.4.5, ad v *deformis* ed McLaughlin 243, and see on Gratian *Decretum* D 5.2, ad v *si mulier* ed McLaughlin 5; and on Gratian *Decretum* C 32.2.3, ad v *immoderatus* (241); Huguccio *Summa* on Gratian *Decretum* C 32.4.5, ad v *amator* (Admont 7, f 373rb); the *Ordinary Gloss* on Gratian *Decretum* C 32.4.5, ad v *amator* reproduces Master Roland.

52 'Dicendum quod ardentior hic vocatur ardor excedens totius matrimonii concessionem et honestatem' (Albert *In 4 Sent* 31.20 [B 30.253]). This is a consistent position of Albert: *De sacramentis* 9.2.2, ad 2 (C 26.160–1); *In 4 Sent* 26.8, ad 5 (B 30.108); *In 4 Sent* 31.21 (B 30.256); *Super Ethica commentum* 5 lect 16 (C 14.1, 385, l 12). In his late theological summa, Albert spells the matter out in some detail, concluding that the too-ardent lover is one who respects neither the measure of nature nor the good of marriage (*ST* 2.22 q 133 m 2 [B 33.450]).

53 'Vehemens amator proprie uxoris adulter est et grauiter peccat maxime si indifferenter non habito respectu ad uinculum coniugale irreuerenter ad suam tamquam ad alienam accedit' (Richard Wetheringsett [ca 1215–22?] 'Qui bene presunt' British Library, Royal 9.A.XIV, f 99rb [transcription obtained from Prof J. Goering]).

54 The usual expressions are *infra* and *extra limites matrimonii*.

55 Roland of Cremona cited in Müller *Paradiesesehe* 192 n 32; Aquinas *In 4 Sent* 26.1.4 (*ST* Supplement 41.4); Peter of Tarentaise *In 4 Sent* 31.3.2 (4.324)

56 See: Bonaventure 'Whether having intercourse with your wife to satisfy concupiscence is always a mortal sin' (*In 4 Sent* 31.2.3 [4.725]); Aquinas 'Whether a person sins mortally if he knows his wife without intending the good of matrimony, but pleasure alone' (*In 4 Sent* 31.2.3 [*ST* Supplement 49.6]).

57 Peter of Tarentaise *In 4 Sent* 31.3.2 (4.324). See Richard of Mediavilla *In 4 Sent* 31.2.2–3 (4.451–3). Abstracting from the theological notion of mortal sin, one can find the same problematic in the Stoic Musonius Rufus: 'Men who are not wanton or immoral are bound to consider intercourse justified only when it occurs in marriage and is indulged in for the purpose of begetting children, since that is lawful, but unjust and unlawful when it is mere pleasure-seeking, even in marriage' (*Reliquiae* 12 tr Lutz 86–7).

58 An early example is seen in Willliam of Auxerre *Summa aurea* 4.17 ed Ribaillier 4.401–10; Bonaventure provides a convenient summary of traditional objections along these lines (*In 4 Sent* 31.2.1, contra 1–6 [4.722]).

59 Aquinas speaking about concupiscence as remaining after baptism: 'although it does not dominate, it particularly prods men to sexual acts because of the vehemence of the pleasure' (*Super epistolam 1 ad Corinthios* ch 7 lect 1 n 316 ed Cai 1.296.

60 See Bede *Bede's Ecclesiastical History* 1.27 ed Colgrave and Mynors 94–9. It is unfortunate that in this case the editors of Bede chose the *voluntas* reading for *voluptas* in this section of the response, I assume for palaeographical reasons. For the text with the *voluptas* readings, see Gregory the Great 'Per dilectissimos filios meos' 2.338–42 (Letter XI, 56a [601]). Gratian *Decretum* C 33.4.7; Peter Lombard *Sent* 4.31.8 (2.450–1).

61 Gregory to Augustine in Bede *Bede's Ecclesiastical History* 1.27 ed Colgrave and Mynors 88

62 Other texts in Gratian explicitly mention pleasure: pleasure of the flesh, not the pain of childbirth, is what is faultworthy (D 5.2); the impetus of pleasure does not rule in a wise man (C 32.4.5); pleasures out of the ordinary and shameful acts with one's wife are looked upon by God as lechery and uncleanness (C 32.4.12); the kinds of pleasures wrested from the embraces of prostitutes are condemned in relation to one's wife (C 32.4.14; see Lombard *Sent* 4.31.5.2).

63 Gratian *Decretum* C 33.4.7. The text in Gratian omits several sections of the response but nothing substantially germane to the argument.

64 Huguccio *Summa* on Gratian *Decretum* C 33.4.7, ad v *nullatenus potest* (Admont 7, f 386rb)

65 'In no way can it be without fault: that is, it cannot be without there being fault and a sin. And from this it is obviously gathered that the conjugal act cannot be exercised without sin, although it itself is not a sin, because there is always itching of the flesh and pleasure in the emission of sperm which is always a sin although very minor ... Whence it is that Christ did not wish to be born through coitus because it cannot be exercised without sin, even if it were a saint who was having intercourse (*nullatenus potest esse sine culpa*, id est non potest esse quin ipsa sit culpa et peccatum. Et hinc expresse colligitur quod opus coniugale non potest exerceri sine peccato, licet ipsum non sit peccatum quia semper est ibi quidam pruritus carnis et quedam voluptas in emissione spermatis que semper est peccatum licet venialissimum ut hic dicitur et [Gratian *Decretum* D 5]. Et hinc est quod christus nolluit nasci de coitu quia sine peccato exerceri non potest etiam si sanctus sit qui coeat ut [Gratian *Decretum* C 27.2.10; C 32.2.4])' (Huguccio *Summa* on Gratian *Decretum* C 33.4.7, ad v *nullatenus potest* [Admont 7, f 386rb]).

66 See Huguccio *Summa* on Gratian *Decretum* C 33.4.7, ad v *cum vero* (Admont 7, f 386va). He offers no reasons, but refers the reader to his commentary on Gratian (*Decretum* C 32.2.2 dp) for when conjugal intercourse is a sin and when not, when it is mortal and when it is venial.

67 *Ordinary Gloss* on Gratian *Decretum* C 33.4.7, ad v *quod defleant*

68 *Ordinary Gloss* on Gratian *Decretum* C 32.2.3, ad v *ab adulterio*
69 See above, ch 4 n 8.
70 See the early summa of Godfrey of Poitiers: 'The laity are not to be judged as sinning mortally if they love their wives somewhat too much or are sometimes excessive in knowing their wives; but [they are to be so judged] when they act too immoderately or against nature or when acting in an improper manner' (cited in Müller *Paradiesesehe* 177 n 150). Landgraf (*Introduction* 171) dates this work to ca 1212–19.
71 William of Rennes on Raymond of Penyafort *Summa* 4.2.6, ad v *adulter* 420. In interpreting the fourth reason along the lines of Huguccio's account of provoking arousal, Paul of Hungary claims that intercourse to give an outlet to lust is a mortal sin (*De confessione* 4.198).
72 Lombard *Sent* 4.31.8.1 (2.450). In the list of chapter headings he is non-committal: 'Whether or not carnal pleasure is a sin' (2.18).
73 Lombard *Sent* 4.31.8.3 (2.451)
74 Bonaventure *In 4 Sent* 31.2.3 (4.726); Aquinas *In 4 Sent* 31.2.3 (*ST* Supplement 49.6)
75 Bonaventure *In 4 Sent* 31.2.3 (4.726)
76 Aquinas *In 4 Sent* 31.2.3. See Aristotle *NE* 10.5 in general; in particular see *NE* 10.5, 1175b24–8 and Aquinas *Sententia libri Ethicorum* 10 (Leonine 47.2, 575). The question of the moral character of sexual relations that were motivated by a desire for pleasure had been asked and answered for almost a hundred years before the scholastics had at their disposal a sophisticated account of the nature of pleasure. With the complete Latin translation of Aristotle's *Nicomachean Ethics* (ca 1248), two accounts of pleasure became accessible (bk 7 chs 11–14; bk 10 chs 1–5). Both Albert the Great and Thomas Aquinas discuss the nature of pleasure in their respective commentaries on Aristotle, and Aquinas has two independent accounts of pleasure (*In 4 Sent* 49.3.1–5; *ST* 1-2.31–4). While mention of the sense of touch and sex is made in these discussions of pleasure, nowhere is the traditional question of sex for pleasure broached in a formal manner. Furthermore, discussion of the fourth reason for marital relations is conducted virtually independently of *ex professo* accounts of pleasure. This suggests that the issue was not seen to arise from the pleasure as such but from the manner in which it was sought, from the intention in seeking the pleasure.
77 Bonaventure *In 4 Sent* 31.2.3 (4.726); Aquinas *In 4 Sent* 31.2.3 (*ST* Supplement 49.6). See Aquinas *In 4 Sent* 33.1.3 (1) (*ST* Supplement 65.3); Peter of Tarentaise *In 4 Sent* 31.3.2 (1) (4.324–5); Richard of Mediavilla *In 4 Sent* 31.2.3 (4.452–3); Peter of Palude *In 4 Sent* 31.3 (f 161ra). Earlier, Peter of Palude had discussed the question of pleasure that is consciously provoked. He takes the opportunity to comment on cases where the provocation constitutes a form of sexual foreplay with its attendant risk of premature ejaculation. The assessment of such cases is determined according to the principle: 'Therefore, in married people for whom the act would not be mortal, incitement to the act is not mortal

(Ergo in coniugatis in quibus actus non esset mortalis, nec incitatio ad ipsum est mortalis)' (*In 4 Sent* 31.3.2 f 160vb).

78 Durandus of St Pourcain *In 4 Sent* 31.4 n 5 (2.374va)

79 Noonan *Contraception* 251. Parmisano provides a plausible interpretation of the principle that stipulates that a man would sin mortally in approaching his wife with the readiness to have sex with this woman even if she were not his wife: 'Here is the lover who loves only himself and is after his own solitary pleasure. He is not interested in society at large, for he has no desire to procreate. He is not concerned for his partner, for he does not consider her person or needs. This is brute, and perhaps brutal sexuality' (Parmisano 'Love and Marriage in the Middle Ages – II' 657).

80 Antoninus of Florence *Summa confessionalis* 3.2 f 156v

81 Noonan *Contraception* 251

82 Antoninus of Florence *Summa confessionalis* 1.2 f 35r. Antoninus does not hesitate to use the principle in his theological work (*Summa theologica* 3.1.20 col 81).

83 Robert of Courson cited in Müller *Paradiesesehe* 159 n 96. Godfrey of Poitiers provides a similar account, noting that when Augustine proposes the four reasons he is speaking *doctrinaliter* (which I take to mean that Augustine was understood to be making an academic point, not to be giving advice to ordinary people or to confessors for their penitential practice). See Müller *Paradiesesehe* 177 n 150; Lindner *Der usus matrimonii* 114 n 79.

84 See Introduction, n 2, and Conclusion, n 6.

CHAPTER 6: THE VIRTUE OF TEMPERANCE

1 Rosemond Tuve notes the different authors who contributed to the medieval conception of the virtues: Cicero, Macrobius, Pseudo-Seneca (ie, Martin of Braga), and Aristotle; see her 'Notes on the Virtues and Vices.' For the Stoic contribution see Stelzenberger *Die Beziehungen der frühchristlichen Sittenlehre zur Ethik der Stoa* 355–78. The work on the passions by Pseudo-Andronicus of Rhodes (ΠΕΡΙ ΠΑΘΩΝ. *Edition critique* ed Glibert-Thirry) should be added to the list of Tuve, since it played a role in the account of Aquinas. The reference to Pseudo-Seneca (Martin of Braga) is to the popular *Formula vitae honestae* by Martin, based on Seneca, which circulated under the name of Seneca in the Middle Ages; see Martin of Braga *Martini episcopi Bracarensis opera omnia* 204–50. For an excellent introduction to medieval apocryphal works attributed to Seneca, see Meersseman 'Seneca maestro di spiritualità.' For the early philosophy of the virtue of temperance see North *Sophrosyne*.

2 See Cicero *De officiis* 1.26.93 and 1.27.96. For 'Ne quid nimis' (Nothing in excess) see Terence *Andria* 61 in *The Lady of Andros*; Jerome, Letter

130.11 (CSEL 56.191). For Cicero, see North *Sophrosyne* 268–85.

3 Ambrose *De officiis ministrorum* (PL 16.25–194; temperance in 1.43 [PL 16.92–110]); Coyle 'Cicero's *De officiis*'; Deman 'Le *De officiis* de saint Ambroise'; Nelson *Cicero's 'De officiis'*; North *Sophrosyne* 360–70.

4 'Temperantia est modus vitae in omni verbo et opere' (Isidore *Differentiae* 2.39.158 [PL 83.95]). See the *Formula vitae honestae* of Martin of Braga (*Martini Episcopis Bracarensis* ed Barlow 242–6, 248–9). Martin uses the term *continentia*, but its setting in the context of the other three cardinal virtues and the content of the discussion make it clear that he means the cardinal virtue of temperance.

5 'Temperantia est totius vitae modus ne quid nimis homo vel amet vel odio habet, sed omnes vitae huius varietates considerata temperet diligentia' (Alcuin *De virtutibus et vitiis* ch 35 [PL 101.637]). On the sources of Alcuin's work see Wallach 'Alcuin on Virtues and Vices.'

6 Bernard of Clairvaux *De consideratione* 1.8.9 ed Leclercq and Rochais 404–5

7 Bernard of Clairvaux *De consideratione* 1.8.10 and 1.8.11 ed Leclercq and Rochais 405 and 406. This view of Bernard marks the culmination of a long Christian tradition in which temperance is conceived almost as an intellectual virtue, equivalent in function to *discretio*. See texts in Dingjan *Discretio*: Cassian (25, 35–6, 71–5), Isidore (107), Smaragdus (117, 119), Alcuin (122), Hrabanus Maurus (126), Paschasius Radbertus (126). When the thirteenth-century masters began to develop a theory of the cardinal virtues this tradition, which they found in Bernard, posed considerable problems for them, particularly when cast against the Aristotelian background that saw the establishment of a mean and measure as an act of reason (prudence) operating in the area of appetites (temperance and fortitude). Much of Philip the Chancellor's discussion of the definition of temperance is taken up with the problem posed by Bernard's remarks. Albert deals with the same problem in his treatise on prudence.

8 'The safest general characterization of the European philosophical tradition is that it consists of a series of footnotes to Plato' (Whitehead *Process and Reality* 39).

9 'Temperantia est rationis in libidinem atque in alios non rectos impetus animi firma et moderata dominatio' (Cicero, *De inventione* 2.5.164). Cicero's account of the cardinal virtues was lent considerable authority by Augustine, who incorporated it into one of his own works; see *De diversis quaestionibus octoginta tribus* q 31.1 (CCSL 44A.43). The definition, sometimes with slight modifications, can be found throughout the Middle Ages: eg, Alcuin *Dialogus de rhetorica et virtutibus* (PL 101.945); *Moralium dogma philosophorum* ed Holmberg 41 l 10; Abelard *Dialogus inter Philosophum* ed Thomas 120 l 2113; Philip the Chancellor *Summa de bono* 'De temperantia' ed Wicki 2.862; Albert *De bono* 3.1.1 (C 28.114 l 15; omits *rationis*).

10 See Cicero *De officiis* 1.28.101–3; 1.36.132; 1.39.141.

11 For Augustine on the term *libido* see above, ch 2. See Papias *Vocabulista* sv *libido*; Balbus *Catholicon* sv *libido*.

12 Isidore *Etymologies* 2.24.6 (see Aquinas ST 2-2.141.3, sed contra); Hermannus *Epitome* ch 32 (PL 178.1752C); William of Auxerre 'Temperantia enim domat rebellionem carnis et cohibet motus eius illicitos' (*Summa aurea* 3.21 ed Ribaillier 3.1, 396). See the twelfth-century theological collection *Sententiae Parisienses* 3 ed Landgraf 53, 54, and *Ysagoge in theologiam* 1 ed Landgraf 75.

13 See Seneca, who associates temperance with restraining desires: (Letter 120.11 *Ad Lucilium epistulae morales* 3:388).

14 *Ordinary Gloss* on Matt 15:38; this text probably entered the gloss from Augustine through Bede (see Augustine *De diversis quaestionibus octoginta tribus* q 61.4 [CCSL 44A.127]; Bede *In Matthaei evangelium expositio* [Matt 15:38] PL 92.77C). See Hugh of St Victor *Scala celi* ed Baron 243; Alexander of Hales *Glossa in 3 Sent* 33.3c (3.385); Philip the Chancellor *Summa de bono* 'De temperantia' ed Wicki 2.862; Albert *De bono* 3.1.1 (C 28.114 l 18).

15 'Temperantia in coercendis delectationibus pravis' (Augustine *De trinitate* 14.9.12 [CCSL 50A.439]); Peter Lombard *Sent* 3.33.1.2 (2.188). See William of Auxerre *Summa aurea* 3.19 ed Ribaillier 3.1, 388; Alexander of Hales *Glossa in 3 Sent* 33.7e (3.389), 7n (3.392). It is the view of Bonaventure that the Lombard's definition is given from the standpoint of the state of fallen nature 'in which depraved pleasures arise and are bridled by the virtue of temperance' (*In 3 Sent* 33, dubium 4 [3.729]). Although not as popular as his division of temperance, one of the definitions by Macrobius, which captures the spirit of Cicero, is frequently encountered: 'It befalls to temperance to seek nothing that will be regretted, not to exceed the law of moderation in anything, to curb cupidity under the yoke of reason' (Macrobius *Commentarii in Somnium Scipionis* 1.8.7). Albert (*De bono* 3.1.1 [C 28.114 l 26]) adds this definition to those he took from Philip the Chancellor. Much of the Macrobian treatment is incorporated by Hugh of Strasbourg into his popular *Compendium theologicae veritatis* (Neukloster, Stift Cod A 1 f 70va); see Kaeppeli *Scriptores Ordinis Praedicatorum* 2.260–9. The work of Hugh of Strasbourg is printed among the works of Albert the Great (B 34) and Bonaventure *Confessionale* 8.61–246.

16 Cicero *De inventione* 2.54.164

17 These terms were not unknown to readers of the Vulgate: *continentia* – Wis 10:2; Ecclus 26:20; Gal 5:22, 23; Titus 1:7; *modestia* – Prov 22:4; 2 Cor 10:1; Philip 4:5; Col 3:12; 2 Tim 2:25; 1 Pet 3:16. St Augustine wrote a work entitled *De continentia* (CSEL 41). For the terms associated with temperance see North *Sophrosyne* 262–8.

18 Macrobius *Commentarii in Somnium Scipionis* 1.8.7 (definition and parts). I have not followed to the letter the translation of Stahl *Macrobius. Commentary on the Dream of Scipio* 122.

19 *Moralium dogma philosophorum* ed Holmberg 41–52 (in PL 171.1034–42).

The temporal relationships, questions of authorship, lines of depend-ence, and borrowing among many of the twelfth-century accounts of the virtues are still not clear, even after a rather heated debate of some years ago between R.A. Gauthier and Philippe Delhaye. For a summary of this debate (somewhat biased in favour of the author's own views) see Williams 'The Quest for the Author of the *Moralium Dogma Philosophorum*, 1931–1956.' For charts illustrating different divisions of temperance at this time see Baron 'A propos des ramifications des vertus au XIIe siècle' 26, 29. For a brief discussion of temperance in the *Moralium* see Delhaye 'Une adaptation de *De officiis* au XIIe siècle' 17–20. The work is cited by John of La Rochelle in the thirteenth cen-tury *Tractatus de divisione multiplici potentiarum animae* 175–8.

20 Continence in the context of lechery (*Sententiae* 2.40; PL 83.643–5); conti-nence and chastity (*Synonyma* 2.9–10; PL 83.847); three states of life (*De ecclesiasticis officiis* 2.18–20; PL 83.804–14).

21 Alcuin *De virtutibus et vitiis* ch 18 (PL 101.626–7).

22 Abelard *Dialogus* ed Thomas 126 ll 2259–61.

23 *De fructibus carnis et spiritus* ch 15 (PL 176.1003D); for the attribution to Conrad of Hirschau see Bultot 'L'auteur et la fonction littéraire de *De fructibus carnis et spiritus*' 148–54; Goy *Die Uberlieferung der Werke Hugos von St. Victor* 488. Perhaps Albert has this work in mind in his refer-ence to a book he calls *De diffinitionibus virtutum et vitiorum*; see *De bono* 3.3.1 (C 28.155 l 14).

24 *De fructibus carnis* chs 16 and 17 (PL 176.1004).

25 In those who adopt the Macrobian division the definitions for the terms are closely related; see *Ysagoge in theologiam* 1 ed Landgraf 77–8; Hugh of St Victor *De contemplatione et eius speciebus* (I used the provisional edition in Baron 'A propos des ramifications des vertus au XIIe siècle' 20–1; see Goy *Die Uberlieferung* 279–80 [probably authentic or by one of his students]); *Moralium dogma philosophorum* ed Holmberg 41–52; Alan of Lille *De virtutibus et de vitiis* ed Lottin 6.56–7.

26 Alan of Lille *De virtutibus et vitiis* ed Lottin 6.57 l 1; see *Ysagoge in theologiam* 1 ed Landgraf 78.

27 'Castitas, sub iugo rationis solum libidinis impetum conprimens' (*De contemplatione* ed Baron 21 l 69). For *castitas* in the Vulgate: Judith 15:11, 16:26; 2 Cor 6:6; Gal 5:23; 1 Tim 2:2, 3:4, 4:12, 5:2

28 Alan of Lille *De virtutibus et vitiis* ed Lottin 6.57 l 3; cf *Ysagoge in theologiam* 1 ed Landgraf 78.

29 Alan of Lille *De virtutibus et vitiis* ed Lottin 6.57 l 27. For shame (*verecundia*) see Alan of Lille *De virtutibus et vitiis* ed Lottin 6.57 l 26. See Hugh of St Victor *De contemplatione* ed Baron 21 ll 64–6. With the entry of the translation of John Damascene a new account of sense of shame was introduced that distinguished between *erubescentia* and *verecundia*; see *De fide orthodoxa* 2.29 ed Buytaert 122.

30 See *Ysagoge in theologiam* 1 ed Landgraf 78; *De contemplatione* ed Baron 21 l 70; Alan of Lille *De virtutibus et vitiis* ed Lottin 6.57 l 9.

31 *De fructibus carnis* ch 15 (PL 176.1003D–1004A)

32 Hugh of St Victor *Scala celi* ed Baron 238–9. Considered a probably genuine work by Goy *Die Uberlieferung* 481

33 This division will be dealt with in the discussion of virginity in the next chapter.

34 Alan of Lille *De virtutibus et vitiis* ed Lottin 6.57 ll 9–15. Paul of Hungary (ca 1221) adopts this division of Alan of Lille; see his *De confessione* 4.214. In his work on preaching, Alan of Lille provides sermon types for each of the three states under the rubric of temperance; see *Summa de arte praedicatoria* chs 29 and 45 (the married; PL 210.185C 193–4); chs 29 and 46 (widows; PL 210.185D, 194); chs 29 and 47 (virgins; PL 210.185D, 194–5).

35 Papias *Vocabulista* sv *castitas*

36 Ibid sv *castus*; cf Isidore *Etymologies* 10.33. The term 'lust' (*libido*) is used to indicate conscious sexual desire and perhaps even the carrying out of that desire in the sense of Isidore's account of the lustful person: 'Libidinosus, ab eo quod facit quod libet' (*Etymologies* 10.160). This is the sense of lust in Robert Grosseteste's division of lechery (*luxuria*) into lust (*libido*) and lasciviousness (*lascivia*); see his 'Deus est' ed Wenzel 281.

37 Papias *Vocabulista* sv *continens*. Isidore (*Etymologies* 10.35) is more detailed in his description of continence.

38 Paul of Hungary *De confessione* 4.210–14 (temperance 213–14); Grosseteste *Templum Dei* ch 10 ed Goering and Mantello 49–50; Grosseteste 'Deus est' ed Wenzel 248–50; the virtues are then dealt with in a wider context of confessional interrogation about their contrary vices (for temperance see 281–6); Hugh of Strasbourg *Compendium theologicae veritatis* (Neukloster, Stift A 1 ff 70va–71ra); *Speculum morale* 1.3.91–5 (among the works of Vincent of Beauvais *Speculum maius* 3:479–93). See Bloomfield et al *Incipits of Latin Works on the Virtues and Vices*.

39 Dondaine 'Guillaume Peyraut' 162. For an updated list of manuscripts, see Kaeppeli *Scriptores* 2.133–52. For a use made of Peraldus, see Evans 'An Illustrated Fragment of Peraldus' *Summa* of Vice' (pl 1–9).

40 This is a point made by Dondaine (162). Too much should not be made of it, however, since Peraldus does show an acquaintance with the new learning. The apparent neglect of this new learning should probably be attributed more to the purpose Peraldus had in writing than to his own intellectual capacities.

41 Dondaine 'Guillaume Peyraut' 162

42 Reference to Peraldus will be made to the manuscript, Schlägl, Stift 12, Cpl 88.

43 Dondaine ('Guillaume Peyraut' 191 n 93) indicates some uses made of Peraldus. One might add the *Speculum morale*, attributed to Vincent of Beauvais; *The Book of Vices and Virtues*, the English version of *La somme roi*. On Chaucer's use of Peraldus see *Summa virtutum de remediis animae*

ed Wenzel. See the commendation by Jean Gerson of what is likely the work of Peraldus, in Gerson *De remediis contra recidivum peccati* ed Glorieux 70.

44 For the plan of Peraldus' treatment of temperance see Appendix 2. The inclusion of clerical celibacy in relation to widowhood is prompted by the need to have the three states cover all possibilities of the Christian life. To accommodate the category of clerics and other classes that did not fit readily into the threefold division, widowhood was sometimes given a broad interpretation; see the remarks of Philip the Chancellor *Summa de bono* 'De temperantia' ed Wicki 2.932–3, and the later remarks of John Bromyard about the penitential state being a state of spiritual widowhood; *Summa predicantium* 'Luxuria' f 459ra.

45 For a summary of the entry of Aristotle see Payer 'Prudence and the Principles of Natural Law' 55 n 2.

46 The virtue of temperance in NE 3.10, 1117b24–3.12, 1119b18. I follow the chapter numbers of the Rackham edition in the Loeb Classical Library. Note that 1119a34–b18 was not part of the text of the *Ethica vetus* but was added later (1240–4) by Herman the German; see Gauthier and Jolif *L'Ethique à Nicomaque* 1.1, 114.

47 See NE 3.10, 1118a23, 26, 30, b9–11 (*Ethica vetus* ed Gauthier 45–6).

48 NE 3.11, 1119a6–11 (*Ethica vetus* ed Gauthier 47); see NE 2.7, 1107b7. See North *Sophrosyne* 196–211.

49 See Philip the Chancellor *Summa de bono* 'De temperantia' ed Wicki 2.889–93; Albert *De bono* 3.3.1, ad 6–8 (C 28.155). Note that no less a linguist than St Jerome suggests that *castitas* is a proper Latin translation of *sophrosune* (*Adversus Iovinianum* 1.27 [PL 23.260B]), but see 1.37 (PL 23.274C), where *pudicitia* is also suggested as a legitimate translation. For Cicero's ideas about the translation of this term see Dingjan *Discretio* 171 n 3; North *Sophrosyne* 268–9.

50 See Gauthier and Jolif *L'Ethique à Nicomaque* 1.1, 123 and 120–46, for discussion of medieval commentaries.

51 William of Auxerre *Summa aurea* 3.19–23 ed Ribaillier 3.1, 395–437: temperance divided into sobriety and continence; continence divided according to the three states; virginity. For an early precedent for a narrowing of the field to food, drink, and sex and a consequent shortened list of parts, see Hermannus *Epitome* ch 32 (PL 178.1752C: *continentia, castitas, sobrietas*). Philip the Chancellor *Summa de bono* 'De temperantia': temperance ed Wicki 2.861–942), divided into sobriety, continence, modesty (2.861), continence divided according to the three states (2.890–908), virginity (2.911–32), conjugal continence (2.932–42). Albert the Great *De bono* temperance (Tract 3; C 28.114–94), parts according to Cicero, Macrobius, *sancti* announced (3.2 prol; C 28.134), continence divided according to the three states (3.3.1 prol; C 28.154), virginity (3.3.4–11; C 28.157–71), continence in marriage (3.3.13; C 28.175–6). Somewhat similar divisions are had in pastoral works attributed to Robert Grosseteste: *Templum Dei* divides temperance into

abstinence, continence, modesty (ed Goering and Mantello 30); 'Deus est' in one passage relates modesty, sense of shame, abstinence, and purity to temperance (ed Wenzel 249); in another passage temperance is divided into the three species of modesty, sense of shame, and purity (ed Wenzel 290); the threefold division of continence according to states of life is mentioned (ed Wenzel 281).

52 Albert *De bono* 3.1.1 (C 28.114); see *De bono* 1.6.1 (C 28.80); for Albert's preference for Cicero, see *De bono* 3.1.1, sol (C 28.117). The first eighteen objections deal with Cicero's definition. The source of the first four definitions is Philip the Chancellor *Summa de bono* 'De temperantia' ed Wicki 2.861, 864).

53 'It is harder to fight against pleasure than against anger ... but virtue like art is constantly dealing with what is harder, since the harder the task the better is success' (Aristotle *NE* 2.3, 1105a8 tr Rackham, *Ethica vetus* ed Gauthier 9–10). Albert frequently invokes this idea *De bono* 1.2.4, obj 4 (C 28.28); 1.4.1 (C 28.44 l 11); 3.1.3, ad 4 (C 28.127).

54 *De bono* 3.1.1, ad 1 (C 28.118); cf Albert *Super Ethica* 3 lect 12 (C 14.1, 199 l 61)

55 See Albert *De bono* 3.1.1, ad 4 (C 28.118); 3.1.2 (C 28.122–4); 3.2.3, ad 1 (C 28.137); 3.3.1, ad 1 and ad 2 (C 28.157); 3.3.1, ad 5 (C 28.155).

56 Albert *De bono* 3.1.1, ad 19 and ad 21 (C 28.120); cf 3.3.3, ad 3 (C 28.157). See Aristotle *Historia animalium* 6.22, 575b30–1; Bonaventure *In 2 Sent* 20.1.3 (2.481); Aquinas *De malo* 4.2, ad 7 ed Leonine 23.112. For the depiction of temperance with bit and bridle see Tuve 'Notes on the Virtues and Vices' 278 (pl 33a); Mâle *L'art religieux* 313 (fig 168). North (*Sophrosyne* 381) comments on the antiquity of the image: 'The imagery of the bridle or the bit – foreshadowed by Aeschylus' references to bridle or yoke in connection with Prometheus' need to learn moderation ... constitutes the favorite symbol for sophrosyne in ancient literature: the mastery of a wild or unruly beast.'

57 Philip the Chancellor *Summa de bono* 'De temperantia' ed Wicki 2.882

58 Ibid 2.886

59 Ibid 2.881

60 Ibid 2.891

61 Albert *De bono* 3.1.1, ad 7 (C 28.118); 3.1.1, ad 9 (C 28.119); 3.1.1, ad 4 (C 28.122)

62 Ibid 3.2.1, ad 4 (C 28.155)

63 Ibid 3.3.14, ad 1 (C 28.178)

64 Albert *Super Ethica* 3 lect 13 (C 14.1, 207)

65 See Albert *De bono* 3.1.1 (C 28.114 l 15). A manuscript adds *rationis* in the margin, but the absence of any commentary on the term points to the addition as a correction against the text of Cicero, not against the text of Albert.

66 See *ST* 2–2 prol.

67 Thomas Aquinas deals with temperance in his *Commentary on the Sentences* (*In 3 Sent* 33.1–3), but nowhere does he provide as ample an

account as in his *Summa of Theology*, which shall be the principal source here.

68 Alan of Lille *De virtutibus et de vitiis* 1.2 ed Lottin 6.56. Albert's views are sketchy and not well developed in the *De bono* or in later works. I deal with the subject in my doctoral dissertation, 'Prudence in the Writings of Albert the Great.' For texts in Albert see: *De bono* 2.2.10 (C 28.112); 2.2.1, ad 6 (C 28.100); 3.2.2 (C 28.136); 3.4.5 (C 28.194).

69 Aquinas *ST* 2–2.48.1 and 143.1

70 Ibid 2–2.48.1

71 Ibid 2–2.48.1 and 143.1

72 Ibid 2–2.48.1

73 Ibid 2–2.143.1

74 Ibid 2–2.48.1

75 The Latin terms in Pseudo-Andronicus are: *austeritas, continentia, humilitas, simplicitas, ornatus, bona ordinatio, per se sufficientia*; see Andronicus *De passionibus* ed Glibert-Thirry 250–2. In his account of the parts of temperance in the commentary on the *Sentences* Aquinas uses the division of Cicero and Pseudo-Andronicus ('quidam philosophus grecus') but does not deal with the Macrobian division; instead, he takes up a division ('a quibusdam' = Wm of Auxerre?) into sobriety and chastity; see *In 3 Sent* 33.3.2.1–3.

76 In following Aquinas, Richard of Mediavilla (*In 3 Sent* 33.5.7 [3.407]) does not slavishly adopt his division. He accepts the integral parts but argues that sense of shame (*verecundia*) is a virtue; he accepts the subjective parts, but argues that *pudicitia* is more closely related to the essence of chastity than Aquinas allows; he departs considerably in his account of the potential parts.

77 See Dionysius the Areopagite *De divinis nominibus* 4.32 ed Chevalier 1.309, and PG 3.734; Aquinas *ST* 1-2.24.1, obj 2; 1-2.24.3; 1-2.34.1, obj 1; 2-2.23.12; 2-2.141.1; 2-2.142.1, obj 2; 2-2.155.1, ad 2.

78 Aquinas *ST* 2-2.141.1

79 Ibid 2-2.123.12

80 Ibid 2-2.141.3, ad 2

81 Ibid 2-2.141.2

82 Ibid 2-2.141.2, ad 3. Recall Albert's use of the expression 'cattle-like' nature, above n 54.

83 See Aquinas *ST* 1-2.61.2, ad 3.

84 Ibid 1-2.61.4. See a more formal definition in John Buridan: 'Temperance, however, is the habit inclining to the maintenance of the mean in regard to such pleasures so that we might hold ourselves in their regard neither more nor less than we ought, but wholly as right reason dictates in accord with a good and upright life (Temperantia autem est habitus inclinans ad medium tendendum circa huiusmodi delectationes, scilicet ut non habeamus nos circa eas plus vel minus debito sed omnino sicut recta ratio dictat secundum decentem vitam et bonam)' (*Questiones super decem libros Ethicorum* 3 question 26 [f 62va]).

85 Aquinas ST 2-2.141.6
86 Ibid 2-2.141.6, ad 2
87 Ibid 2-2.141.5. See Aquinas, 'However, the end that nature intends in intercourse is the procreation and rearing of offspring; it placed pleasure in intercourse so that this good would be sought, as Constantinus says' (*In 4 Sent* 33.1.3 [1] [ST Supplement 65.3]). See Constantinus Africanus, 'So for animals he fashioned natural organs that would be properly suited for this undertaking, and inserted such marvellous power and attractive pleasure into them that there would be no animal that would not take great pleasure in intercourse (Ideoque conplasmavit animalibus naturalia membra que ad hoc opus apta forent et propria, eisque tam mirabilem virtutuem et amabilem delectationem inseruit ut nullum sit animalium quod non pernimium delectetur coitu)' (*De coitu* ed Cartelle 76).
88 Aquinas ST 1-2.60.5
89 'It is clear that all commingling of male and female outside the law of matrimony, which rules out promiscuous intercourse, is disordered in and of itself. However, this is not the place to deal with the questions whether the specification is to have one or several wives or whether they are to be had in a divisible or indivisible manner. These questions belong to the treatment of marriage; but whatever the situation is, it is necessarily the case that every commingling of male and female outside the law of matrimony is disordered' (Aquinas *De malo* 15.1 Leonine 23.271).

CHAPTER 7: CONTINENCE, CHASTITY, AND VIRGINITY

1 Aquinas ST 2-2.151.4. Philip the Chancellor (*Summa de bono* 'De temperantia') divides temperance into *sobrietas, castitas, modestia*. In arguing for a division of temperance based on the reproductive powers, he uses the term *castitas*, but he deals with sexual matters under the rubric of *continentia* (ed Wicki 2.900), dividing it into the three states (ibid 2.903). In the latter context *castitas* is restricted to marriage (ibid). For Philip's account of the usage of *pudicitia* see ibid. The *Ordinary Gloss* on Gratian betrays some uncertainty about the terms *castitas* and *pudicitia*: see Gratian *Decretum* C 31.1.12, ad v *nuptiali castitate*; C 32.5.1, da, ad v *quod autem*; C 32.6.5, ad v *castitas*.
2 See Gauthier and Jolif *L'Ethique à Nicomaque* 2.579–81 for the Aristotelian setting of the problem.
3 Aristotle NE 7.9, 1151b34–1152a3 tr Rackham. See the Latin text: 'Et enim continens potens nichil preter racionem propter corporales delectationes facere, et temperatus. Set hic quidem habens, hic autem non habens pravas concupiscencias; et hic quidem talis qualis non delectari preter racionem, hic autem qualis delectari, set non duci' (*Ethica Nicomachea. Translatio Roberti Grosseteste* ed Gauthier). Cf NE 4.9, 1128b34–5.

4 See Albert *Super Ethica* 7 lect 11 (C 14.2, 566–8); Aquinas *Sententia libri Ethicorum* bk 7 Leonine 47.2, 419 and bk 4 Leonine 47.2, 261.

5 Aquinas *Sententia libri Ethicorum* bk 8 Leonine 47.2, 442. See Aquinas *In 3 Sent* 33.3.2.1, ad 1; *ST* 2-2.155.1; 2–2.143.1, ad 1; Peter of Tarentaise *In 3 Sent* 33.3.2, ad 1 (3.261). Bonaventure uses continence in the traditional sense in *Quaestiones disputatae de perfectione evangelica* q 3 (5.166–79).

6 Gauthier and Jolif *L'Ethique à Nicomaque* 2.579. I am not sure why *essentialiter* is omitted, but it is present in the printed texts of the original. The condemnation is n 208 in Mandonnet's thematic rearrangement of the list of condemned propositions, Siger of Brabant *Siger de Brabant et l'averroisme latin au XIIIme siècle* 190. It is n 168 in *Chartularium universitatis Parisiensis* ed Denifle and Chatelain 1.553. For a survey of the condemned propositions see Hissette *Enquête sur les 219 articles condemnés à Paris le 7 mars 1277*; see the bibliography for later studies by Hissette.

7 'It must be said that something can be called a virtue in two ways. Either according to the essence of virtue, like temperance is a virtue, and taken in this way these [continence and heroic virtue] are not virtues, but continence is below virtue because it does not abstain from passions with joy ...' (Albert *Super Ethica* 7 lect 1 [C 14.2, 515]). William de la Mare seems to have thought that remarks of Aquinas (*ST* 2-2.185.6 and 189.3) came under the condemnation; see *Declarationes magistri Guilelmi de la Mare O.F.M. de variis sententiis S. Thomae Aquinatis* ed Pelster 24–5. In none of the *correctoria* edited at present is such a view of Aquinas singled out for censure.

8 In 1298 Raymond Lull wrote a commentary in dialogue form on the condemned propositions, see Lull *Declaratio* ed Keicher 7.4–5, 95–221. The proposition under consideration here is ch 168 (202). See Hissette *Enquête* 298.

9 Gauthier 'Trois commentaires' 300. See Aquinas *ST* 2-2.186.4.

10 See Hissette *Enquête* 298, citing Gauthier.

11 Buridan *Questiones Joannis Buridani super decem libros Ethicorum* f 141vb–142va

12 Aquinas *ST* 2-2.155.1. See Cassian *Conlationes XXIIII* ed Petschenig (CSEL 13).

13 Philip the Chancellor *Summa de bono* 'De temperantia' ed Wicki 2.863

14 Bonaventure *In 3 Sent* 33, dubium 4 (3.729). Gauthier ('Trois commentaires' 335) suggests an interesting contrast between Albert and Thomas, on the one hand, and Franciscan authors, on the other. The Dominican authors saw the possibility of a true humanism in Aristotle, but never addressed the question of how it could arise in pagan Greece and be dropped from the Christian tradition. The Franciscans, with their historical sense of the Fall, understood the latter problem but were unable to account for a true humanism. This is a valuable insight that gains some credence from a reading of Thomas Aquinas on tem-

perance whose *Summa* account develops as if there was no historical
Fall to be taken into account.

15 Aquinas *ST* 2–2.151.2
16 Ibid 2-2.143.1
17 Ibid 2-2.151.3, ad 2
18 See ibid 2-2.151.1; Aristotle *NE* 3.12, 1119a34–b15 (*Ethica vetus* ed
   Gauthier 134–5). In his commentary on the *Ethics*, Aquinas introduces
   castitas as a species of temperance (*Sententia libri Ethicorum* bk 3 Leonine 47.1, 192). Albert, using Grosseteste, explains Aristotle's point by
   reference to the Greek term, *Super Ethica* 3 lect 15 (C 14.1, 219, and note
   to l 45). See Gauthier and Jolif *L'Ethique à Nicomaque* 2.1, 249 (on
   1119a34).
19 Aquinas *ST* 2-2.143.1
20 Ibid 2-2.151.4. And see, 'Among the vices of intemperance sexual sins
   are particularly subject to reproach both because of the disobedience of
   the genitals and because reason is especially absorbed by them [ie, by
   sexual sins]' (ibid 2–2.151.4, ad 3). In the body of the article Aquinas
   refers to Augustine's mention of the shame attached to sexual matters
   and to the disobedience of the genitals; see above, ch 2 n 19. This passage is as close as Aquinas comes in his discussion of temperance to
   referring to the effects of the Fall and their consequences for a proper
   understanding of chastity.
21 Ibid 2-2.151.4; Richard of Mediavilla *In 3 Sent* 33.5.7 (3.407)
22 Aquinas *ST* 2-2.152.3, ad 5
23 Ibid 2-2 prol (*sermones universales*).
24 Ibid (my emphasis).
25 Alexander of Hales *Quaestiones disputatae* q 58 (recension Ao, n 39
   [2.1133]). See Radulph Ardens on how each of the states deals with
   lust, cited in Müller *Paradiesesehe* 139 n 41.
26 *The Book of Vices and Virtues* 243 ll 22–4. See Bromyard *Summa
   praedicantium* 'Matrimonium' 2.15rb; Chaucer *Canterbury Tales* 'The
   Parson's Tale': marriage (ll 916–42), widowhood (ll 943–6), virginity
   (ll 947–9), and see *Summa virtutum de remediis anime* ed Wenzel 279.
   Jean Gerson 'Je regarde que chastete prant trois logis selond trois estas,
   et selon ce elle a trois noms. Elle se loge en l'estat de virginite: c'est
   chastete virginale; de mariage; de viduite' (Sermon 'Poenitemini. De la
   chastete' 842 n 372).
27 *Speculum morale* 1.3.95 (Douai 1642) 3.493C
28 For the idea of widowhood see Rosambert *La veuve en droit canonique*.
29 See Camelot 'Les traités *De virginitate*'; Bugge *Virginitas*; but see the
   review of Bugge in *Speculum* 52 (1977) 938–41.
30 See below, n 62.
31 See for example a very late (1471) dialogue on virginity, Bernardine of
   Florence *Dialogus*, and Gal 'Bernardini de Florentia Dialogus de
   laudibus castitatis atque virginitatis.' In the thirteenth century, Albert
   the Great writes with verve in defence of the virginity of Mary (*De bono*

3.3.9 [C 28.167–71]). See Bernards *Speculum virginum; Hali Meidhad* ed Millet xxiv–xxvi (literature).

32 'Virginalis autem integritas et per piam continentiam ab omni concubitu inmunitas angelica portio est et in carne corruptibili incorruptionis perpetue meditatio' (Augustine *De sancta virginitate* ch 13 [CSEL 41.245]). According to Lewis and Short (sv *meditatio*) the cognitional connotation of *meditatio* is rare in classical Latin. There is nothing in Augustine's context to suggest that he means the term to have that connotation; thus my translation, 'exercise.' However, from medieval discussions of the definition it is clear that the term was understood in its cognitional sense in the thirteenth century. In the text of Augustine, 'perpetual' is in the genitive case governing 'incorruption'; in the definitions in Alexander of Hales, Philip the Chancellor, Albert, Aquinas, and Peter of Tarentaise, 'perpetual' is in the nominative case governing 'meditation.' The editors of the SFA note that in a disputed question on virginity Alexander of Hales says that he believes the reading ought to be in the genitive: 'melius credimus, quod debeat dici "incorruptionis perpetue meditatio"' (SFA *Prolegomena* [4.1 CLXXXI]); however, in two edited passages where Alexander cites Augustine, he follows the nominative reading; see *Glossa in 4 Sent* 33.3.1.a (4.521) and *Quaestiones disputatae 'antequam esset frater'* 57.3.2 n 68 (2.1122). Bonaventure (*In 4 Sent* 33.2.1, arg 2 [4.753]) has the genitive reading. With few exceptions the reference is incorrectly made to Augustine's *De nuptiis et concupiscentia*. This fact makes Albert's reference to the *originalia* suspect or at least puzzling. In response to the question whether some form of dedication to God is part of the concept of virginity, Albert says: 'if one inspects the original works (*originalia*) of the saints [Ambrose, Augustine, Jerome] they will be seen only to speak of virgins who profess virginity for the sake of God' (*De bono* 3.3.4, ad 9 [C 28.159]). Now, if Albert had checked the original of Augustine (*De nuptiis et concupiscentia*), he would not have found the definition he claims to be from that work; if Albert had checked Augustine's *De sancta virginitate*, he would have found the definition and known his own reference was wrong. Besides, Albert's immediate predecessors (Alexander of Hales and Philip the Chancellor) both cite the correct work of Augustine, and he himself claims later to have read the *De sancta virginitate* (see *De bono* 3.3.8 [C 28.167 l 46]). A similar puzzle occurs in Aquinas who in one passage (ST 2-2.152.1, obj 1) attributes Augustine's definition to the *De nuptiis et concupiscentia* and shortly afterwards (ibid obj 4) cites the first part of Augustine's text, attributing it correctly to the *De sancta virginitate*!

33 See similar divisions pointing to much the same conclusion: William of Auxerre *Summa aurea* 3.23 ed Ribaillier 3.1, 422–3; Philip the Chancellor *Summa de bono* 'De temperantia' ed Wicki 2.917–18; Aquinas *In 4 Sent* 33.3.1 and ST 2-2.152.1; Peter of Tarentaise *In 4 Sent* 33.4.1 (4.338); Richard of Mediavilla *In 4 Sent* 33.4.1 (4.471).

34 Albert *De bono* 3.3.6 (C 28.163)
35 Ibid 3.3.6 (C 28.163); and see ibid 3.3.1 (C 28.158)
36 Ibid 3.3.6 (C 28.163 l 69)
37 See Deut 22:23–4.
38 Albert *De bono* 3.3.6, ad 2 (C 28.164 l 55). For a discussion of chastity and virginity in Albert see Brandl *Die Sexualethik des heiligen Albertus Magnus* 268–98.
39 Aquinas *In 4 Sent* 4.33.1, ad 4
40 Aquinas *ST* 2-2.152.1; *Quaestiones quodlibetales. Quodlibetum 6*, q 10 (Utrum scilicet aliquis possit esse naturaliter vel miraculose simul virgo et pater [Whether one can naturally or miraculously be a virgin and father at the same time]) ed Spiazzi 129–30
41 Albert *De bono* 3.3.6, obj 3 (C 28.163). See above, ch 3 n 70 for similar remarks in regard to hesitation about dealing with the question of the proper manner of marital sexual intercourse.
42 Albert *De bono* 3.3.7 (C 28.165 l 77, my emphasis)
43 'Si invitam me feceris violari, castitas michi duplicabitur ad coronam' (Gratian *Decretum* C 32.5.1 da). See the Office of St Lucy (Dec 13), second nocturne, lesson 6, in *Breviarium ad usum insignis ecclesiae Sarum. 3. Proprium sanctorum* ed Procter and Wordsworth 57, and *Passio sanctae Luciae virginis et martyris* in *Sanctuarium seu vitae sanctorum* ed Mombritius 2.108. A sample of the use of the text: William of Auxerre *Summa aurea* 3.23 ed Ribaillier 3.1, 430, 432; Philip the Chancellor *Summa de bono* ed Wicki 2.917–19; Peraldus *Summa* 'De temperantia' Schlägl 12 f 255ra; Bonaventure *In 4 Sent* 33.2.3, sed contra 3 (4.756); Aquinas *In 4 Sent* 33.3.1; John of Freiburg *Summa confessorum* 3.3 q 18 (f 98rb). See the series of texts in Gratian *Decretum* C 32.5.1–12. For the implications of this position – ie, you cannot tell if a woman is a virgin by simple bodily inspection – see the texts of Cyprian in Gratian *Decretum* C 27.1.4–5.
44 See Astesanus *Summa* 2.45.2 (1.216–17).
45 Ibid 2.45.4 (1.218); cf. Albert *De bono* 3.3.6, ad 1 (C 28.164). Albert's position is more nuanced, suggesting that the tradition encouraged (*suadet*) such abstention, while Astesanus uses legal language (*statutum est*), citing Gratian (*Decretum* C 32.5.14 and gloss, and C 15.1.13). Neither Albert nor Astesanus says there is a presumption in favour of consent to the pleasure, but see Aquinas *In 4 Sent* 33.3.1, ad 7. Another situation taxed the ingenuity of these authors, namely, the case of a woman who had lost virginity in secret and who was still thought to be a virgin. The problem here seems to have been posed by this woman's being a member of a group or class in a convent who would normally be consecrated as virgins. How can she not be consecrated without causing scandal by revealing her true status? See Albert *De bono* 3.3.7, ad 2 (C 28.166); Astesanus *Summa* 2.45.4 (1.217–18).
46 *ST* 2-2.152.3 and see 2–2.152.5. Durandus of St Pourcain goes so far as to say that virginity is not a good in itself (*per se bona*), *In 4 Sent* 33.4

n 6 (2.378va), prompting a reply from Peter of Palude *In 4 Sent* 33.2.3 (f 167va–vb).

47 See Aquinas *In 4 Sent* 33.3.2; *ST* 2-2.152.3; Albert *De bono* 3.3.5 (C 28.160–2).

48 Aquinas *ST* 2-2.152.3, ad 5. See above, n 22.

49 Richard of Mediavilla *In 4 Sent* 33.4.1 (4.471)

50 Aquinas *ST* 2-2.152.2; Peter of Palude *In 4 Sent* 33.2–3 (f 167ra–vb); Buridan *Questiones Joannis Buridani* bk 3 q 13 ff 67va–68va

51 See above, ch 1.

52 Aquinas *ST* 2-2.152.2, ad 1. Richard of Mediavilla has an interesting comment on the imaginary situation of a need to procreate arising and virgins having to shoulder that responsibility on divine command, all the while wanting to be virgins. After fulfilling their obligations to procreate could they still be said to be virgins? In a sense they could but according to common linguistic usage they could not (*In 4 Sent* 33.4.1 [4.472]).

53 Aristotle *NE* 2.2, 1104a22–5, in Aquinas *ST* 2-2.152.2, obj 2. Aristotle's definition of virtue *NE* 2.6, 1106b36–1107a2

54 'Quod perfecta abstinentia ab actu carnis corrupit virtutem et speciem' *Siger de Brabant* ed Mandonnet n 210 (190); see *Chartularium universitatis Parisiensis* n 169 1.553. Raymund Lull has no comment on this proposition, referring the reader to his remarks on the question whether continence is a virtue (see above, n 8, for the work of Raymond Lull).

55 Hissette *Enquête* 300. For Siger of Brabant see the question 'Quis status magis competit philosophis?' *Quaestiones morales* q 2 in Siger of Brabant *Ecrits de logique, de morale et de physique* ed Bazan 100–1; Siger of Brabant *Siger de Brabant d'après ses oeuvres inédites. 2. Siger dans l'histoire de l'aristotélisme* 663–7.

56 See Gauthier and Jolif *L'Ethique à Nicomaque* 2.1, 246. For judicious comment on Aristotle's views of sex see ibid 238, 242–4, 246–8.

57 Commentary on the *Nicomachean Ethics* (Vat lat 2172), cited in Gauthier 'Trois commentaires' 298 nn 1, 5. For the reference to Bonaventure (*Collationes in Hexaëmeron* 5.5 [5.355]) see Gauthier and Jolif *L'Ethique à Nicomaque* 2.1, 246. For a careful analysis of this question by a member of the Arts Faculty in the fourteenth century who quite consciously attempts to follow the route of reason and not theology ('In this process we intend only to undertake what can be concluded from the scope of human reason [In hoc processu nichil intendimus aggredi nisi quod et inquantum ex humana ratione precise concludi potest]' [f 67vb]), see Buridan *Questiones Joannis Buridani* bk 3 q 13 ff 67va–68va.

58 See Sebastian 'William of Wheteley's (Fl. 1309–1316) Commentary' 351–6, in particular 355–6. For the account of lechery in the *De disciplina scolarium*, see the recent edition, *Pseudo-Boèce. De disciplina scolarium*, ed Weijers. William of Wheteley's account is a far cry from an anonymous commentary published among the works of Aquinas *Commentarium super lib. Boethii De scholarium disciplina* 24.166–8.

59 Bonaventure *In 4 Sent* 33.2.1, ad 1 (4.754)
60 See Aquinas *In 4 Sent* 33.3.2, ad 1; *Sententia libri Ethicorum* 2 Leonine
    47.1, 281; see Gauthier and Jolif *L'Ethique à Nicomaque* 2.1, 126 (on
    1104a24); *ST* 2-2.152.2, ad 2. See Peter of Tarentaise *In 4 Sent* 33.4.1, ad 1
    (4.338); Richard of Mediavilla *In 4 Sent* 33.4.1, ad 1 (4.471).
61 Aquinas *ST* 2-2.152.2. For Aquinas on the comparative values of the
    contemplative and active life see ibid 2-2.182. There is a genre of lit-
    erature that bypasses academic debate, concentrating simply on singing
    the praises of virginity. For example see Peraldus *Summa de vitiis et
    virtutibus* 'De temperantia' on the commendation of virginity (Schlägl
    12 ff 255rb–256vb); and the large body of texts following the lengthy
    citation of Aquinas (*ST* 2-2.152) in *Speculum morale* 1.3.96 (Douai 1624)
    3.502–21 (ie, vol 3 of the *Speculum maius* of Vincent of Beauvais).
62 Albert *De bono* 3.3.8 (C 28.167 l 26); Aquinas *Summa contra Gentiles*
    3.137; *ST* 2-2.152.4. See Augustine *De haeresibus* 82 (CCSL 46.337);
    Gennadius *Liber ecclesiasticorum dogmatum* 34 in Turner 'The *Liber
    ecclesiasticorum dogmatum* Attributed to Gennadius' 96.
63 For Jovinian see: Haller *Jovinianus*; Valli *Gioviniano*. See Hagendahl
    Latin Fathers and the Classics; Wiesen *St. Jerome as a Satirist*.
64 See Siricius, Letter 7 'Optarem semper' (PL 13.1168–72); Ambrose, Letter
    42 'Recognovimus litteris' (PL 16.1172–8); Jerome *Adversus Iovini-
    anum* (PL 23.221–352); Jerome, Letter 49 (48) 'Apologeticum ad
    Pammachium' (CSEL 54.350–87). For Kelly's chronology see Kelly *Jerome*
    182, and more generally, ch 17. Biographies of St Ambrose tend to
    cluster the writings around 393, but Dudden has Ambrose writing after
    the *Adversus Iovinianum* (Dudden *Life and Times of St. Ambrose* 2.393n 1);
    see Paredi *Saint Ambrose* 355. See Clark 'Heresy, Asceticism, Adam, and
    Eve' 104–9.
65 'Dicit virgines, viduas, et maritatas, quae semel in Christo lotae sunt, si
    non discrepent caeteris operibus, eiusdem esse meriti' Jerome *Adversus
    Iovinianum* 1.3 (PL 23.224B). It seems that Jovinian also denied the per-
    petual virginity of Mary, an item missing from Jerome's list. See
    Ambrose, Letter 42 (PL 16.1173B); Augustine *De haeresibus* n 82 (CCSL
    46.337). On the first proposition of Jovinian see Valli *Gioviniano*
    75–92; Hunter 'Resistance to the Virginal Ideal in Late Fourth-Century
    Rome.'
66 See Augustine *De haeresibus* 82 (CCSL 46.337); *Retractationes* 2.22 (CCSL
    57.107–8).
67 In his application of the parable of the sower to the three states, Jerome
    finds significance in the ancient method of finger counting. Jerome was
    one of the first to apply the thirtyfold to the married, the sixtyfold to
    widows, and the hundredfold to virgins, an application that became
    standard for the later Middle Ages; see the useful collection of texts in
    Quacquarelli *Il triplice frutto delle vita cristiana*.
68 Jerome *Adversus Iovinianum* 1.3 (PL 23.223A). See 'from Zacharia and
    Elizabeth John was born, that is, a virgin from marriage' (257B), and

'Then a woman will be saved if she gives birth to children who will remain virgins' (260C).

69 Augustine *Retractationes* 2.22.1 (CCSL 57.107–8). On the use made of the latter part of the *Adversus Iovinianum* see: Bickel *Diatribe in Senecae philosophi fragmenta*; Delhaye 'Le Dossier anti-matrimonial de l'*Adversus Iovinianum*.' For a twelfth-century attack on some of Jerome's reasoning see Berengarius of Poitiers *Apologeticus pro Abaelardo* (PL 178.1869B–70A). On Berengarius see Luscombe *The School of Peter Abelard* 29–49. For an analysis of the structure of Jerome's dispute see Opelt *Hieronymus' Streitschriften* 37–63; for a reflective critique of Jerome's handling of sexual questions against the background of his own apparent problems, see Nodet 'Positions de saint Jérôme en face des problèmes sexuels.'

70 Lambert notes the extant manuscripts of the *Adversus Iovinianum*: sixth century (1), seventh century (1), eighth century (3), ninth century (8), ninth to tenth centuries (1), later – whole or excerpts (238)! Lambert *Bibliotheca Hieronymiana manuscripta* 2.276–93 (n 252). Even if one allows for the fact that very early manuscripts were less likely to survive, these figures point to a considerable presence of *Against Jovinian* from the eleventh century onwards. Some texts from the *Adversus Iovinianum* in Gratian, on virginity: 1.12 (*Decretum* C 33.5.9), 1.13 (D 27.5), 1.13 (D 27.9), 1.27 (C 33.5.7), 1.40 (C 33.5.8), 2.4 (C 32.4.6); on marriage: 1.14–15 (C 31.1.10), 1.16 (C 32.1.12), 1.49 (C 32.4.5)

71 See Alexander of Hales *Questiones disputatae* q 57 n 77 (2.1125).

72 'virtus perfectissima est in iis in quibus secundum totum et semper continent' (Albert *De bono* 3.3.13, ad 7 [C 28.176])

73 Ibid 3.3.13, ad 2 and ad 16 (C 28.176, 181)

74 Aquinas *In 4 Sent* 49.5.3 (1) (*ST* Supplement 96.5)

75 Bonaventure *In 4 Sent* 33.2.2 (4.755); see Alexander of Hales *Questiones disputatae* q 57 n 72 (2.1123).

76 Aquinas *ST* 2-2.152.4. This argument is used by Durandus of St Pourcain *In 4 Sent* 33.4 n 7 (2.378va) and by Peter of Palude *In 4 Sent* 33.6 concl 3 (f 179ra).

77 Augustine *De bono coniugali* 1.2.26 (CSEL 41.221). See Lombard *Sent* 4.33.2.1 (2.459–60) and a similar text in Gratian *Decretum* C 32.4.6 (in Lombard *Sent* 4.33.2.1 [2.460]).

78 See Alexander of Hales *Glossa in 4 Sent* 33.3.II.1 (4.528); Albert *De bono* 3.3.8 (C 28.167), 3.3.10, ad 9 (C 28.173). Bonaventure (*In 4 Sent* 33.2.2 [4.755]) uses Albert's expression 'excedentia et excessa.'

79 Bonaventure *In 4 Sent* 33.2.2 (4.755). See Aquinas *ST* 2-2.152.4, ad 1; Peter of Tarentaise *In 4 Sent* 33.4.2 (4.339); Durandus of St Pourcain *In 4 Sent* 33.4, ad 2 (2.378vb).

80 Aquinas *ST* 2-2.152.4, ad 1; Bonaventure *In 4 Sent* 33, dubium 3 (4.763). Richard of Mediavilla goes even further, suggesting that the term 'virginity' could apply to Abraham, but common linguistic usage would not allow it (*In 4 Sent* 33.4.2, ad 1 [4.473]).

81 See Alexander of Hales *Questiones disputatae* q 57 n 78 (2.1126); Aquinas

In 4 Sent 49.5.1 (*ST* Supplement 96.1). Although this matter is treated in commentaries on the *Sentences* (4.49), the categories are not found in Peter Lombard.

82 See William Peraldus *Summa de vitiis et virtutibus* 'De luxuria' (Schlägl 12 f 10ra), 'De temperantia' (Schlägl 12 ff 256vb, 258vb).

83 Jerome *Adversus Iovinianum* 1.3 (PL 23.223C–224A). This text was used by Bede, see *De temporum ratione* 1.1 (CCSL 123B.268–9); *In Lucae evangelium expositio* 8.15 (CCSL 120.177). The theme is reworked in a late-medieval preface to Bede; see Stock and Synan 'A Tenth-Century Preface to Bede's *De temporum ratione*.' The notes to the translation might have paid closer attention to Jerome's account and the tradition of counting. For a discussion of the first chapter of the *De temporum ratione* see Cordoliani 'A propos du chapitre premier du *De Temporum ratione*, de Bede.' See the anonymous *De flexibus digitorum* ed Jones (CCSL 123C) 671–2.

84 See the note to Juvenal *Thirteen Satires of Juvenal* 10.249 ed Mayor 2.142–3; Quacquarelli *Il triplice frutto* ch 3 ('Il modo degli antichi di contare con le dita') 37–42 (drawings 35); Meyer *Die Zahlenallegorese im Mittelalter* 75, 156–7, 167, 177, 178. See the illustration of this method of counting in a reproduction from Bede's *De temporum ratione* in Beaujouan 'The Transformation of the Quadrivium' fig 12 (Rouen, Bibliothèque municipale MS 3055).

85 See Albert *De bono* 3.3.16 (C 28.181 ll 57–65 and 183 l 68); Aquinas *In 4 Sent* 49.5.2.3, obj 4 (*ST* Supplement 96.4); Henry of Ghent *Quodlibeta* Quodl 1 q 36 and Quodl 7 q 12 f 24v (question enunciated at f 23r), f 265r–267v (question enunciated at f 263v).

86 Albert *De bono* 3.3.16 (C 28.184 l 8). The account of Aquinas is strikingly dependent on Albert here; Aquinas *In 4 Sent* 49.5.2 (3). See Alexander of Hales *Glossa in 4 Sent* 33.3.III.e–g (4.531–3); *Questiones disputate* q 58 n 79 (2.1157–8).

87 See Albert *De bono* 3.3.14, obj 1 (C 28.177).

88 Aquinas *In 4 Sent* 49.5.2 (1) (*ST*, Supplement 96.2). One of the most complete discussions of the fruits is provided by Alexander of Hales *Questiones disputate* q 58 (2.1128–58); the first part is in two different recensions, which are edited separately. See Albert *De bono* 3.3.14–16 (C 28.176–84); Aquinas *In 4 Sent* 49.5.2 (1); Peter of Palude *In 4 Sent* 49.8 (ff 245ra–rb).

89 Aquinas *In 4 Sent* 49.5.5 (1) (*ST* Supplement 96.11). This is very close to a text in Bonaventure: 'Again, a crown is owed to a contestant; but the greatest fight is against the flesh; therefore, whoever conquers it perfectly and in a notable fashion ought to be crowned in a notable fashion. But virgins conquer perfectly; therefore, they ought to be notably crowned. Therefore, they will have a crown not had by the married' (*In 4 Sent* 33.2.3, arg 4 [4.756]). See Alexander of Hales *Glossa in 4 Sent* 33.3.II.g (4.526); *Questiones disputate* q 57 n 78 (2.1126); Richard of Mediavilla *In 4 Sent* 49.5.3 (4.687); Peter of Palude *In 4 Sent* 49.8

(f 244va–245ra). For the coronet see Nikolaus Wicki *Die Lehre von der himmlischen Seligkeit* 198–318.

90 See Alexander of Hales *Glossa in 4 Sent* 33.3.II.m (4.528); *SFA* 2–2 n 627 (3.606–7); Bonaventure dubs the refusal a hard saying, *In 4 Sent* 33.2.5 (4.757 *alia opinio*); Aquinas *In 4 Sent* 49.5.5 (1), ad 4 (*ST* Supplement 96.5, ad 4); Peter of Palude *In 4 Sent* 49.8 (f 244vb). See the *Ordinary Gloss* on Gratian *Decretum* C 32.5.1 da, ad v *simpliciter*; C 32.5.2, ad v *caro*; C 32.5.11, ad v *suscitare*; C 32.5.14, ad v *comparare*.

CONCLUSION

1 Speaking of pagan concerns Foucault says, 'The accent was placed on the relationship with the self that enabled a person to keep from being carried away by the appetites and pleasure, to maintain a mastery and superiority over them, to keep his senses in a state of tranquility, to remain free from interior bondage to the passions, and to achieve a mode of being that could be defined by the full enjoyment of oneself, or the perfect supremacy of oneself over oneself' (Foucault *The History of Sexuality* 2. *The Use of Pleasure* 31). Aside from the mode of being to be achieved, these concerns were as central to the Christian ideal as to the pagan ideal.

2 Ibid 5

3 Ibid 7

4 See 'The word "game" can lead you into error: when I say "game" I mean an ensemble of rules for the production of the truth. It is not a game in the sense of imitating or entertaining ... it is an ensemble of procedures which lead to a certain result, which can be considered in function of its principles and its rules of procedures, as valid or not, as winner or loser' (Foucault 'The Ethic of Care for the Self as a Practice of Freedom' 16).

5 Aquinas *Collationes in decem preceptis* 25 ed Torrell 251–2

6 A sample of concern that was expressed about the belief that fornication was not a mortal sin: Bartholomew of Exeter *Penitential* ch 69 ed Morey 236–7; Thomas of Chobham *Summa confessorum* ed Broomfield 342; Thomas of Chobham *Summa de arte praedicandi* ed Morenzoni (CCCM 82.255–6); Aquinas *Summa contra Gentiles* 3.122 (Ex hoc); Albert the Great *ST* 2 q 122.1.2 (B 33.395–7); Bromyard *Summa predicantium* 'Luxuria' ff 457vb–463rb. In 1277 the following was listed among the propositions condemned by Archbishop Tempier: 'That simple fornication, that is, an unattached man with an unattached woman, is not a sin' (number 183 in the official list of condemned propositions in *Chartularium universitatis Parisiensis* ed Denifle and Chatelain 1.553; number 205 in Siger of Brabant *Siger de Brabant et l'averroisme latin* 190. See above, Introduction n 2.

7 See Aquinas *ST* 1-2.31.7.

Bibliography

SOURCES

Abelard, Peter *Dialogus inter Philosophum, Judaeum et Christianum* ed Rudolf Thomas. Stuttgart-Bad Cannstatt 1970
- *Theologia christiana. Theologia scholarium, Recensiones breviores. Capitula haeresum Petri Abaelardi* ed E.M. Buytaert. CCCM 12. Turnhout 1969
Alan of Lille *De virtutibus et de vitiis et de donis Spiritus Sancti* In O. Lottin 'Le traité d'Alain de Lille sur les vertus, les vices et les dons du Saint-Esprit' *Psychologie et morale* 6.27–92
- *Liber poenitentialis. 2. La tradition longue* ed Jean Longère. Analecta mediaevalia Namurcensia 18. Louvain 1965
- *Regulae caelestis iuris* In N. Häring 'Magister Alanus de Insulis. Regulae caelestis iuris' *Archives d'histoire doctrinale et littéraire du moyen âge* 48 (1981) 97–226
- *Summa de arte praedicatoria.* PL 210.109–98
Albert the Great *De animalibus libri XXVI nach der Cölner Urschrift* ed Hermann Stadler. 2 vols. Beiträge zur Geschichte der Philosophie des Mittelalters 15 (bks 1–12). Münster Westf 1916. Beiträge zur Geschichte der Philosophie des Mittelalters 16 (bks 13–26). Münster Westf 1921
- *De bono* ed H. Kühle, C. Feckes, B. Geyer, W. Kübel. Opera omnia 28. Münster Westf 1951
- *De sacramentis* ed A. Ohlmeyer. Opera omnia 26. Cologne 1958
- *Commentarii in II Sententiarum* ed S.C.A. Borgnet. Opera omnia 27. Paris 1894
- *Commentarii in IV Sententiarum (Dist. XXIII–L)* ed S.C.A. Borgnet. Opera omnia 27. Paris 1894
- *Liber de principiis motus processivi* ed B. Geyer. Opera omnia. Münster Westf 1955
- *Opera omnia* ed S.C.A. Borgnet. 38 vols. Paris 1890–99
- *Summa de creaturis 1* ed S.C.A. Borgnet. Opera omnia 34. Paris 1895
- *Summa de creaturis 2. De homine* ed S.C.A. Borgnet. Opera omnia 35. Paris 1896

- *Summa theologiae pars secunda (Quaest. LXVIII–CXLI)* ed S.C.A. Borgnet. Opera omnia 33. Paris 1895
- *Super Ethica commentum et quaestiones* ed W. Kübel. (Bks 1–5) opera omnia 14.1. Münster Westf 1968, 1972. (Bks 6–10) opera omnia 14.2. Münster Westf 1987

Alcuin *De virtutibus et vitiis.* PL 101.615–39
- *Dialogus de rhetorica et virtutibus.* PL 101.919–50.

Alexander of Hales *Glossa in quatuor libros Sententiarum Petri Lombardi* 4 vols. Quaracchi 1951–7
- *Quaestiones disputatae 'Antequam esset frater'* Vol 2. Quaracchi 1960

Ambrose *De officiis ministrorum.* PL 16.25–194
- Letter 42 'Recognovimus litteris.' PL 16.1172–8
- *Rescriptum episcoporum Ambrosii et cet. ad Siricium papam.* PL 16.1121–9

Ambrosiaster *Commentarius in epistolas Pauli ad Corinthios* ed H.J. Vogels. CSEL 81.2. Vienna 1968

Andreas Capellanus *De amore libri tres* ed E. Trojel. 2d edn. Munich 1972, orig edn. 1892

Andronicus of Rhodes (Pseudo) ΠΕΡΙ ΠΑΘΩΝ *[De passionibus]. Edition critique du texte grec et de la traduction latine médiévale.* ed A. Glibert-Thirry. Corpus latinum commentariorum in Aristotelem graecorum, Supp 2. Leiden 1977

Anselm of Canterbury *De conceptu virginali et de originali peccato* ed F.S. Schmitt. Opera omnia 2. Rome 1940

Anselm of Laon 'Les écrits d'Anselme de Laon' ed O. Lottin. *Psychologie et morale* 5.9–188

Antoninus of Florence *Summa confessionalis* Venice 1584
- *Summa theologica* 4 vols. Verona 1740

Aristotle *Ethica Nicomachea. Translatio antiquissima lib. II–III sive 'Ethica vetus' et Translationis antiquioris quae supersunt sive 'Ethica nova', 'Hoferiana', 'Borghesiana'* ed R.A. Gauthier. Aristoteles Latinus 26.1–3, Fasc 2. Leiden 1972
- *Ethica Nicomachea. Translatio Roberti Grosseteste Lincolniensis sive 'Liber Ethicorum' B. Recensio Recognita* ed R.A. Gauthier. Aristoteles Latinus 26.1–3, Fasc 4. Leiden 1973
- *L'Ethique à Nicomaque. Introduction, traduction et commentaire* tr R.A. Gauthier and J.Y. Jolif. 2d edn. 2 vols. Louvain 1970
- *Generation of Animals* tr A.L. Peck. LCL. Cambridge Mass 1979
- *The Nicomachean Ethics* tr H. Rackham. LCL. Cambridge Mass 1962

Astesanus *Summa Astensis* Vol 1. Rome 1728. Vol 2. Rome 1730

Augustine *The City of God against the Pagans (Books 8–11)* tr David S. Wiesen. LCL. Cambridge Mass 1968
- *The City of God against the Pagans (Books 12–15)* tr Philip Levine. LCL. Cambridge Mass 1966
- *Concerning the City of God against the Pagans* tr H. Bettenson. Penguin Books 1972
- *Contra duas epistulas Pelagianorum libri quattuor* ed C.F. Urba and J. Zycha. CSEL 60. Vienna 1913

- *Contra Iulianum libri sex.* PL 44.641–874
- *Contra secundam Iuliani responsionem opus imperfectum.* PL 45.1049–1608
- *De bono coniugali* ed J. Zycha. CSEL 41.185–231. Vienna 1900
- *De continentia* ed J. Zycha. CSEL 41.139–83. Vienna 1900
- *De diversis quaestionibus octoginta tribus* ed Almut Mutzenbecher. CCSL 44A. Turnhout 1975
- *De Genesi ad litteram libri duodecim* ed J. Zycha. CSEL 28.1. Vienna 1894. See also *La Genèse au sens littéral en douze livres (I–VII). De Genesi ad litteram libri duodecim* tr, intro, et notes P. Agaësse et A. Solignac. Oeuvres de saint Augustin. Bibliothèque augustinienne 48. Paris 1972. *La Genèse au sens littéral en douze livres (VIII–XII). De Genesi ad litteram libri duodecim* tr, intro, et notes P. Agaësse et A. Solignac. Oeuvres de saint Augustin. Bibliothèque augustinienne 49. Paris 1972
- *De Genesi contra Manichaeos.* PL 34
- *De gratia Christi et de peccato originali* ed C.F. Urba and J. Zycha. CSEL 42. Vienna 1902. See also: *La crise pelagienne. II. De gratia Christi et de peccato originali libri II. De natura et origine animae libri IV* intro, tr, et notes J. Plagnieux et F.J. Thonnard. Oeuvres de saint Augustin. Bibliothèque augustinienne 22. Paris 1975
- *De haeresibus* ed R. Vander Plaetse and C. Beukers. CCSL 46. Turnhout 1969
- *De libero arbitrio libri tres* ed W.M. Green. CSEL 74. Vienna 1956
- *De nuptiis et concupiscentia* ed C.F. Urba and J. Zycha. CSEL 42, 2.207–319. Vienna 1902. See also: *Premières polémiques contre Julien. De nuptiis et concupiscentia. Contra duas epistulas pelagianorum* intro, tr, et notes F.J. Thonnard, E. Bleuzen, et A.C. de Veer. Oeuvres de saint Augustin. Bibliothèque augustinienne 23. Paris 1974
- *De sancta virginitate* ed J. Zycha. CSEL 41.233–302. Vienna 1900
- *De sermone domini in monte* ed Almut Mutzenbecher. CCSL 35. Turnhout 1967
- *De trinitate (libri XIII–XV)* ed W.J. Mountain and Fr Glorie. CCSL 50A. Turnhout 1968
- *Enarrationes in Psalmos CI–CL* ed E. Dekkers and J. Fraipont. CCSL 40. Turnhout 1956
- *Epistolae ex duobus codicibus nuper in lucem prolatae* ed J. Divjak. CSEL 88. Vienna 1981
- *Retractationum libri II* ed Almut Mutzenbecher. CCSL 57. Turnhout 1984
Avicenna *De anima* Opera philosophica. Venice 1508
- *Liber canonis* Venice 1507
- *Liber de animalibus* Opera philosophica. Venice 1508
Balbus, John *Catholicon* Mainz 1460
Bartholomew of Exeter *Penitential* In *Bartholomew of Exeter, Bishop and Canonist. A Study in the Twelfth Century. With the Text of Bartholomew's Penitential from the Cotton MS. Vitellius A.XII* ed Adrian Morey. Cambridge 1937

Bede *Bede's Ecclesiastical History of the English People* ed and tr Bertram Colgrave and R.A.B. Mynors. Oxford 1969
– *De temporum ratione* ed Charles W. Jones. CCSL 123B. Turnhout 1977
– *In Lucae evangelium expositio. In Marci evangelium* ed D. Hurst. CCSL 120. Turnhout 1960
– *In Matthaei evangelium expositio.* PL 92
Berengarius of Poitiers *Apologeticus pro Abaelardo.* PL 178.1869–70
Bernard of Clairvaux *De consideratione ad Eugenium papam* ed J. Leclercq and H.M. Rochais. Opera omnia 3: Tractatus et opuscula. Rome 1963
Bernardine of Florence *Dialogus de laudibus castitatis* In G. Gal 'Bernardini de Florentia Dialogus de laudibus castitatis atque virginitatis' *Franciscan Studies* 23 (1963) 140–78 (text 149–78)
Biblia sacra cum glossa ordinaria ed Nicholas of Lyra. 6 vols. Vol 1 (Genesis–Deuteronomy) Paris 1590. Vol 5 (Gospels) Lyons 1545. Vol 6 (Epistles) Paris 1590
Biblia sacra iuxta Vulgatam Clementinam new edn. Biblioteca de autores cristinaos. Madrid 1965
Bonaventure *Breviloquium* Opera omnia 5. Quaracchi 1891
– *Collationes in Hexaëmeron* Opera omnia 5. Quaracchi 1985
– *Commentaria in quatuor libros Sententiarum* Opera omnia 1–4. Quaracchi 1882–9
– *Questiones disputatae de perfectione evangelica* Opera omnia 5. Quaracchi 1891
The Book of Vices and Virtues. A Fourteenth Century English Translation of the 'Somme le Roi' of Lorens d'Orleans ed W. Nelson Francis. Early English Text Society os 217. London 1968
Breviarium ad usum insignis ecclesiae Sarum. 3. Proprium sanctorum ed F. Procter and C. Wordsworth. Canterbury 1886
Bromyard, John *Summa praedicantium* Venice 1586
Burchard of Worms *Decretum.* PL 140.537–1058
Buridan, J. *Questiones Joannis Buridani super decem libros Ethicorum Aristotelis ad Nicomachum* Paris 1513
Burley, Walter *De vita et moribus philosophorum* ed Hermann Künst. Tübingen 1886
Caesarius of Arles *Sermones* ed Dom G. Morin. 2d edn. 2 vols. CCSL 103–4. Turnhout 1953
Capitularia regum francorum ed A. Boretius. MGH. Legum sectio 1. Hannover 1883
Cassian, John *Conlationes XXIIII* ed M. Petschenig. CSEL 13. Vienna 1886
Chartularium universitatis Parisiensis Vol 1 (1200–86). ed H. Denifle and E. Chatelain. Paris 1899
Chaucer, Geoffrey *The Works of Geoffrey Chaucer* ed F.N. Robertson. 2d edn. Boston 1957
Cicero. *De inventione* tr H.M. Hubbell. LCL. Cambridge Mass 1949
– *De officiis* tr Walter Miller. LCL. Cambridge Mass 1913
Commentarium super lib. Boethii De scholarium disciplina Among the works of Thomas Aquinas. Opera omnia 24. Parma 1869

Commentarius Cantabrigiensis in episolas Pauli e schola Petri Abaelardi: 2. In epistolam ad Corinthios Iam et IIam, ad Galatas et ad Ephesios ed Artur Landgraf. Publications in Mediaeval Studies 2. Notre Dame 1939

Commentarius Porretanus in primam epistolam ad Corinthios ed Artur Landgraf. Studi e testi 117. Vatican City 1945

Conciliorum oecumenicorum decreta ed J. Alberigo, J.A. Dossetti, P. Joannou, C. Leonardi, P. Prodi. 3d edn. Bologna 1973

Confessionale ed A.C. Peltier. Among the works of Bonaventure. Opera omnia 8. Paris 1866

Conrad of Hirschau *De fructibus carnis et spiritus.* PL 176.997–1010

Constantinus Africanus *Liber de coitu. El tratado de andrología de Constantino el Africano* Estudio y Edicion critica. ed Enrique Montero Cartelle. Monografias de la Universidad de Santiago de Compostela 77. Santiago de Compostela 1983

Correctorium: Les premières polemiques thomistes: 1. Le Correctorium corruptorii 'Quare' ed P. Glorieux. Bibliothèque thomiste 9. Kain 1927

De disciplina scolarium: Olga Weijers ed *Pseudo-Boèce. De disciplina scolarium* Studien und Texte zur Geistesgeschichte des Mittelalters 12. Leiden 1976

De disciplina scolarium: Commentum super librum Boethii De scholarum disciplina Among works of Thomas Aquinas. Opera omnia 24.148–216. Parma 1869

De flexibus digitorum ed C.W. Jones. In Bede, Opera didascalia. CCSL 123C.671–2. Turnhout 1980

Dionysius the Areopagite *De divinibus nominibus* In *Dionysiaca* ed P. Chevalier. np 1937

Durandus of St Pourcain *In Petri Lombardi Sententias theologicas commentariorum libri IIII.* 2 vols. Venice 1571

Eusebius *Chronicon* 7 *Die Chronik des Hieronymus. 1. Text* ed R. Helm. Die griechischen christlichen Schriftsteller der ersten drei Jahrhundert. Leipzig 1913

Fulgentius of Ruspe *De fide ad Petrum* ed J. Fraipont. CCSL 91A. Turnhout 1968

Gennadius *Liber ecclesiasticorum dogmatum* In C.H. Turner 'The *Liber ecclesiasticorum dogmatum* Attributed to Gennadius' *The Journal of Theological Studies* 7 (1906) 78–99

Geoffrey of Trani *Summa super titulis decretalium* Lyons 1519

Gerson, Jean *De remediis contra recidivum peccati* ed P. Glorieux. Oeuvres complètes 8. Paris 1971

– Sermon 'Poenitemini. De la chasteté' ed P. Glorieux. Oeuvres complètes 7.2. Paris 1968

Godfrey of Fontaines *La huitième Quodlibet de Godefroid de Fontaines* ed J. Hoffmans. Les philosophes Belges. Textes et études 4. Louvain 1924

Gratian *Corpus iuris canonici, pars prior. Decretum Gratiani* ed A. Friedberg. Leipzig 1879

– [*Ordinary Gloss*] *Decretum Gratiani, seu verius, Decretorum canonicorum collectanea ab ipso auctore Gratiano primum inscripta concordia discordantium canonum ... additi sunt insuper ab eodem passim ad marginem, librorum et capitum ex quibus ista Decretorum farrago compacta est, numeri indicatorii ...* Paris 1561

Gregory I (the Great) XL *homiliarum in Evangelia libri duo.* PL 76
- *Moralia in Iob (libri I–X)* ed Marc Adriaen. CCSL 143. Turnhout 1979
- *Moralia in Iob (libri XXIII–XXXV)* ed M. Adriaen. CCSL 143B. Turnhout 1985
- 'Per dilectissimos filios meos' (Letter of Gregory to Augustine of Canterbury; Register, Book 11, letter 56a) *Gregorii I papae registrum epistolarum* Libri VIII–XIV. Ed L.M. Hartmann. MGH. Epistolae 2.331–43. Berlin 1899

Gregory IX. *Decretales* In *Corpus iuris canonici. Pars secunda: Decretalium collectiones* ed A. Friedberg. Leipzig 1879
- [*Ordinary Gloss*] *Decretales Gregorii IX. Pont. max. suis commentariis illustratae* Paris 1561

Gregory of Nyssa *De hominis opificio.* PG 44.123–256

Grosseteste, Robert. <*De modo confitendi et paenitentias iniungendi*> In J. Goering and F.A.C. Mantello 'The Early Penitential Writings of Robert Grosseteste' *Recherches de théologie ancienne et médiévale* 54 (1987) 52–112
- 'Deus est' In Siegfried Wenzel 'Robert Grosseteste's Treatise on Confession, "Deus Est"' *Franciscan Studies* 30 (1970) 218–93
- *Hexaëmeron* ed Richard C. Dales and Servus Gieben. Auctores Britannici Medii Aevi 6. London 1982
- *Speculum confessionis* In J. Goering and F.A.C. Mantello 'The "Perambulavit Iudas ..."* (Speculum confessionis)* Attributed to Robert Grosseteste' *Revue Bénédictine* 96 (1986) 125–68
- *Templum Dei, edited from* MS. *27 of Emmanuel College, Cambridge* ed J. Goering and F.A.C. Mantello. Toronto medieval Latin texts 14. Toronto 1984

Haimo of Halberstadt *Commentariorum in Isaiam, libri tres.* PL 116.713–1086

Hali Meidhad ed B. Millet. Early English Text Society os 284. London 1982

Handlyng Synne. Robert of Brunne's 'Handlyng Synne,' A.D. 1303 ed Frederick J. Furnivall. Early English Text Society os 119. London 1901

Henry of Ghent *Quodlibet I* ed R. Macken. Opera omnia 5. Leuven 1979
- *Quodlibet VI* ed G.A. Wilson. Opera omnia 10. Leuven 1987
- *Quodlibeta* Paris 1518

Hermannus *Epitome christianae theologiae [Sententiae Hermanni].* PL 178.1695–1758

Hostiensis *Summa, una cum summariis et adnotationibus Nicolai Superantii* Lyons 1537

Hrabanus Maurus *Commentariorum in Ezechielem libri viginti.* PL 110.495–1084

Hugh of St Victor *Scala celi* In R. Baron *Etudes sur Hugues de Saint-Victor* Bruges 1963
- *De contemplatione et eius speciebus* In R. Baron 'A propos des ramifications des vertus au XIIe siècle' *Recherches de théologie ancienne et médiévale* 23 (1956) 20–1

Hugh of Strasbourg *Compendium theologicae veritatis* Neukloster,

Stiftsbibliothek MS A 1. Among works of Albert the Great B 34 and
Bonaventure ed A.C. Peltier. Opera omnia 8. Paris 1866
Huguccio *Summa decretorum* Admont, Stiftsbibliothek 7
Innocent III. *Lotharii cardinalis (Innocentii III) De miseria humanae conditionis* ed
Michele Maccarrone. Lucca 1955
The Irish Penitentials ed Ludwig Bieler. Scriptores Latini Hiberniae 5. Dublin
1975
Isidore *De ecclesiasticis officiis*. PL 83.737–826
– *Differentiae*. PL 83.9–98
– *Etymologiarum sive originum libri* XX. ed W.M. Lindsay. Oxford 1911
– *Sententiae*. PL 83.557–738
– *Synonyma de lamentatione animae peccatricis*. PL 83.825–68
Jacques de Vitry *Sermons* In *The Exempla or Illustrative Stories from the
Sermones Vulgares of Jacques de Vitry* ed, with intro, analysis, and notes
T.F. Crane. New York 1971
Jerome *Adversus Iovinianum, libri duo*. PL 23.221–352
– *Commentariorum in Hiezechielem libri* XIV. ed F. Glorie. CCSL 75. Turnhout
1964
– *Epistolae (*LXXI–CXX*)*. ed I. Hilberg. CSEL 55. Vienna 1912
– *Epistolae (*CXXI–CLIV*)*. ed I. Hilberg. CSEL 56. Vienna 1918
– *In Hieremiam libri* VI. ed S. Reiter. CSEL 59. Vienna 1913. Reproduced with-
out preface in CCSL 74. Turnhout 1960
Joannes Andreae *In quinque Decretalium libros novella commentaria* intro S.
Kuttner. 6 vols. Venice 1581 repr 1963–6
John Damascene *De fide orthodoxa* Versions of Burgundio and Cerbanus. ed
Eligius M. Buytaert. Franciscan Institute Publications. Text Series 8. St
Bonaventure NY 1955
John of Freiburg *Summa confessorum* Rome 1518
John of La Rochelle *Tractatus de divisione multiplici potentiarum animae* Texte
critique avec intro, notes, et tables. ed P. Michaud-Quantin. Textes
philosophiques du moyen âge 11. Paris 1964
John Scottus Eriugena *De divisione naturae*. PL 122.441–1022
Justinian *Digesta* ed Th. Mommsen and P. Kreuger. 2d edn. 2 vols. Berlin
1870
Juvenal *Thirteen Satires of Juvenal* ed J.E.B. Mayor. 2d edn. London 1878
Kramer, Henry and James Sprenger *Malleus maleficarum* In *Malleus
maleficarum, maleficas et earum haeresim framea conterens ...* Vol 1.1–305.
Lyons 1669
Lull, Raymond *Declaratio* In *Raymundus Lullus und seine Stellung zur
arabischen Philosophie. Mit einem Anhang, enthaltend die zum ersten Male
veröffentlichte 'Declaratio Raymundi per modum dialogi edita'* ed O. Keicher.
Beiträge zur Geschichte der Philosophie des Mittelalters 7.4–5. Münster
1909
Macrobius *Commentarii in Somnium Scipionis* ed J. Willis. Bibliotheca
scriptorum graecorum et romanorum teubneriana. Leipzig 1963. English
translation: *Macrobius. Commentary on the Dream of Scipio* tr, intro, and

notes W.H. Stahl. Records of Civilization. Sources and Studies 48. New York 1952

Martin Le Maistre *De temperantia liber* Paris 1511

Martin of Braga *Martini episcopi Bracarensis opera omnia* ed Claude W. Barlow. Papers and Monographs of the American Academy in Rome 12. New Haven 1950

Master Roland *Die Summa magistri Rolandi nachmals Papstes Alexander III nebst einem Anhange incerti auctoris quaestiones.* ed Friedrich Thaner. Innsbruck 1874

Master Simon *Maître Simon et son groupe 'De sacramentis'. Textes inédits* ed H. Weisweiler. Appendix 'Pierre le Mangeur. *De sacramentis.* Texte inédit' intro V*–XXVIII*, text 1*–105* ed R.M. Martin. Spicilegium sacrum Lovaniense. Etudes et documents 17. Louvain 1937

Maurice of Sully *Maurice of Sully and the Medieval Vernacular Homily with the Text of Maurice's French Homilies from a Sens Cathedral Chapter Ms* ed C.A. Robson. Oxford 1952

Methodius: In Ernst Sackur *Sibyllinische Texte und Forschungen con premessa di Raoul Manselli* Torino 1963

Milton, John *Paradise Lost* ed Merritt Y. Hughes. New York 1962

Moralium dogma philosophorum: Das moralium dogma philosophorum des Guillaume de Conches, lateinisch, altfranzösisch und mittelniederfränkisch ed J. Holmberg. Uppsala 1929. PL 171.1034–42

Musonius Rufus *Reliquiae* In Cora E. Lutz *Musonius Rufus 'The Roman Socrates'* Yale Classical Studies 10. New Haven 1947

Neckam, Alexander *De naturis rerum, libri duo* ed Thomas Wright. Rerum Britannicarum medii aevi scriptores 34. London 1863

Nicholas I 'Ad consulta vestra' ed E. Perels, MGH. Epistolae Karolini aevi 6 (no. 99). Berlin 1925

Origen *In Numeros homilia.* PG 12.585–806

Papias *Vocabulista* Milan 1476

Paul of Hungary *De confessione* Bibliotheca casinensis 4.191–215 Monte Cassino 1880

Peraldus, William 'Notandum quod triplex est matrimonium' Sermon 26 in works of William of Auvergne. Opera omnia 2.187. Paris 1674

– *Summa aurea de virtutibus et vitiis* Venice 1497

– *Summa viciorum* Schlägl, Stiftsbibliothek, Cod 12 (453 a 88) ff 1ra–16orb. *Summa virtutum* Schlägl, Stiftsbibliothek, Cod 12 (453 a 88) ff 161ra–341vb

Peter Comestor. *Historia scholastica.* PL 198.1055–1722

– *Tractatus de sacramentis* see above, Master Simon *Maître Simon et son groupe* Appendix

Peter Lombard *Collectanea in epistolam ad Romanos.* PL 191.1301–1534

– *Collectanea in epistolam 1 ad Corinthios.* PL 191.1533–1696

– *Sententiae in IV libris distinctae* 3d edn. Spicilegium Bonaventurianum 4 and 5. 2 vols. Grottaferrata [Rome] 1971–81

– Sermon '"In Egyptum descendit" [Is 52:4]. Dolendum est primi hominis casum'. PL 171.845–53

Peter of Palude *In secundum Sententiarum* Vatican City. Biblioteca Apostolica
  Vaticana. Vat lat 1073 ff 1ra–189rb
– *In quartum Sententiarum* Paris 1514
Peter of Poitiers <*Summa de Confessione*> 'Compilatio praesens' ed Jean
  Longère. CCCM 51. Turnhout 1984
Peter of Tarentaise *In IV libros Sententiarum commentaria* 4 vols. Toulouse
  1649–51
Peter the Chanter *Verbum abbreviatum*. PL 205.21–554
– *Verbum abbreviatum* British Library Add MSS 19767
Philip the Chancellor *Summa de bono* Pars posterior. Ed N. Wicki. Corpus
  philosophorum medii aevi. Opera philosophica mediae aetatis selecta 2.
  Berne 1985
Pliny. *Natural History* (Bks 3–7) tr H. Rackham. LCL. Cambridge Mass 1942
– *Natural History* (Bks 27–32) tr W.H.S. Jones. LCL. Cambridge Mass 1963
The Prose Salernitan Questions. Edited from a Bodleian Manuscript (Auct. F.3.10)
  ed Brian Lawn. Auctores Britannici medii aevi 5. London 1979
Raymond of Penyafort *Summa ... de poenitentia et matrimonio* Rome 1603
Richard of Mediavilla *Quaestiones super 4 libros Sententiarum* 4 vols. Brescia
  1591
Robert of Flamborough *Liber poenitentialis* A Critical Edition with Introduction and Notes. Ed J.J. Francis Firth. Studies and Texts 18. Toronto 1971
Robert of Melun *Oeuvres de Robert de Melun. 2. Questiones [theologice] de
  epistolis Pauli* ed R.M. Martin. Spicilegium sacrum Lovaniense 18. Louvain
  1938
Robert of Sorbonne. '"Cum repetes a proximo tuo" [Deut 24:10–11]. Ex hac
  authoritate magnus clericus' In works of William of Auvergne. Opera
  omnia 2. Suppl 233–6. Paris 1674
– *Honorabile coniugium (De conditionibus matrimonii)* In B. Hauréau *Notices et
  extraits de quelques manuscrits latins de la Bibliothèque nationale* 1 (1890)
  187–203
Rufinus *Die Summa decretorum des Magister Rufinus* ed H. Singer. Paderborn
  1902
Sanchez, T. *De sancto matrimonii sacramento* Vol 2. Venice 1619
Seneca *Ad Lucilium epistolae morales* tr Richard M. Gummere. 3 vols. LCL.
  Cambridge Mass 1917–25
– *De constantia* In *Moral Essays* tr John W. Basore. Vol 1:48–105. LCL. Cam-
  bridge Mass 1963
– In Gilles G. Meersseman 'Seneca maestro di spiritualità nei suoi opuscoli
  apocrifi dal XII al XV secolo' *Italia medioevale e humanistica* 16 (1973) 43–135
Sententiae Parisienses In *Ecrits théologiques de l'école d'Abélard* ed A. Landgraf.
  Spicilegium sacrum Lovaniense 14:1–60. Louvain 1934
Sextus [Pythagoricus] *The Sentences of Sextus. A Contribution to the History of
  Early Christian Ethics* ed Henry Chadwick. Cambridge 1959
Siger of Brabant *Ecrits de logique, de morale et de physique* ed Bernardo Bazan.
  Philosophes médiévaux 14. Paris 1974
– *Siger de Brabant d'après ses oeuvres inédites* Vol 1 *Les oeuvres inédites* Vol 2

Siger dans l'histoire de l'aristotélisme ed F. Van Steenberghen. Louvain 1931, 1942

– *Siger de Brabant et l'averroisme latin au XIIIme siècle* 2 *Textes inédits* ed P. Mandonnet. 2d edn. Louvain 1908

Siricius Letter 7 'Optarem semper.' PL 13.1168–72

Solinus C. *Iulii Solini collectanea rerum memorabilium* ed Th. Mommsen. From the 2d edn. of 1895. Berlin 1958

Speculum Christiani. A Middle English Religious Treatise of the 14th Century (ca 1360/70) ed G. Holmstedt. Early English Text Society os 182. London 1933

Speculum morale Vol 3 of *Speculum maius* of Vincent of Beauvais. Douai 1624

Summa Duacensis P. Glorieux ed *La 'Summa Duacensis' (Douai 434)* Textes philosophiques du moyen âge 2. Paris 1955

Summa Fratris Alexandri: Summa theologica, seu sic ab origine dicta 'Summa Fratris Alexandri' 4 vols. Quaracchi 1928–48

Summa Parisiensis: The Summa Parisiensis on the Decretum Gratiani ed T.P. McLaughlin. Toronto 1952

Summa virtutum de remediis anime ed Siegfried Wenzel. The Chaucer Library. Athens GA 1984

Synodal Statutes (English): F.M. Powicke and C.R. Cheney eds *Councils and Synods with Other Documents Relating to the English Church* II *A.D. 1205–1313. Part I. 1205–1265. Part II. 1265–1313* 2 vols. Oxford 1964

Synodal Statutes (French): O. Pontal ed *Les statuts synodaux français du XIIIe siècle précédés de l'historique du synode diocésain depuis ses origines* 1 *Les statuts de Paris et le Synodal de l'oeust (XIIIe siècle)* Collection de documents inédits sur l'histoire de France. Section de philologie et d'histoire jusqu'à 1610. Serie 8 vol 9. Paris 1971

Tancred *Tancredi Summa de matrimonio* ed Agathon Wunderlich. Göttingen 1841

Terence *The Lady of Andros. The Self-Tormentor. The Eunuch* tr John Sargeaunt. LCC. London 1931

Thomas Aquinas *Collationes in decem preceptis* In Jean-Pierre Torrell 'Les *Collationes in decem preceptis* de saint Thomas d'Aquin. Edition critique avec introduction et notes' *Revue des sciences philosophiques et théologiques* 69 (1985) 5–40, 227–63

– *In 4 Sententiarum (D. 13–50)* Opera omnia 7. Parma 1858

– *Quaestio disputata de virtutibus cardinalibus* ed A. Odetto. In *Quaestiones disputatae* Vol 2 ed B. Bazzi, M. Calcaterra, T.S. Centi, E. Odetto, P.M. Pession. 9th rev edn. Turin 1953

– *Quaestio disputata de virtutibus in communi* ed A Odetto. In *Quaestiones disputatae* Vol 2 ed B. Bazzi, M. Calcaterra, T.S. Centi, E. Odetto, P.M. Pession. 9th rev edn. Turin 1953

– *Quaestiones disputatae de malo* Opera omnia. Leonine 23. Rome 1982

– *Quaestiones quodlibetales* ed Raymund Spiazzi. 9th edn. Torino 1956

– *Scriptum super libros Sententiarum Magistri Petri Lombardi* Bks 1–2 ed

P. Mandonnet. 2 vols. Paris 1929. *Scriptum super Sententiis Magistri Petri Lombardi* Bks 3–4 (distinctions 1–22) ed Maria Fabianus Moos. 2 vols. Paris 1937, 1947
– *Sententia libri Ethicorum* ed R.A. Gauthier. 2 vols. Opera omnia 47. Rome 1969
– *Summa contra Gentiles* editio Leonina manualis. Rome 1934
– *Summa theologiae* 2d edn. Ottawa 1953
– *Super epistolas s. Pauli lectura* ed R. Cai. Vol 1. Rome 1953
Thomas of Chobham *Summa confessorum* ed F. Broomfield. Analecta mediaevalia Namurcensia 25. Louvain 1968
– *Summa de arte praedicandi* ed Franco Morenzoni CCCM 82. Turnhout 1988
Vincent of Beauvais *Speculum maius: Speculum quadruplex sive Speculum maius* Vol 1 *Speculum naturale* Vol 2 *Speculum doctrinale* Douai 1624
Walter of Mortagne *De sacramento coniugii* In *Summa sententiarum*. PL 176.153–74
William de la Mare *Declarationes magistri Guilelmi de la Mare O.F.M. de variis sententiis S. Thomae Aquinatis* ed F. Pelster. Opuscula et textus. Series scholastica 21. Münster Westf 1956
William of Auvergne *De sacramento matrimonii* Opera omnia 1.512–28. Paris 1674
– *De universo* Opera omnia 1.593–1074. Paris 1674
William of Auxerre *Summa aurea. Introduction générale* ed Jean Ribaillier. Spicilegium Bonaventurianum 20. Paris 1987
– *Summa aurea* Bks 1–4 ed Jean Ribaillier. Spicilegium Bonaventurianum 16, 17, 18, 19. Paris 1980–5
William of Rennes *Gloss* in edition of Raymond of Penyafort
Ysagoge in theologiam In *Ecrits théologiques de l'école d'Abélard* ed A. Landgraf. Spicilegium sacrum Lovaniense 14:63–289. Louvain 1934

STUDIES

Allegro, Calogero *Giovanni Scoto Eriugena. II. Antropologia* Rome 1976
Anderson, Gary 'Celibacy or Consummation in the Garden? Reflections on Early Jewish and Christian Interpretations of the Garden of Eden.' *Harvard Theological Review* 82 (1989) 121–48
Baldwin, John W. 'Five Discourses on Desire: Sexuality and Gender in Northern France around 1200' *Speculum* 66 (1991) 797–819
– *Masters, Princes and Merchants. The Social Views of Peter the Chanter and His Circle* 2 vols. Princeton 1970
Baron, Roger 'A propos des ramifications des vertus au XIIe siècle' *Recherches de théologie ancienne et médiévale* 23 (1956) 19–39
Beaujouan, Guy 'The Transformation of the Quadrivium' In *Renaissance and Renewal in the Twelfth Century* 463–87. See Benson and Constable
Benedek, Thomas G. 'Beliefs about Human Sexual Function in the Middle Ages and Renaissance' In *Human Sexuality in the Middle Ages and Renaissance* 97–119. See Radcliff-Umstead

Benson, Robert L. and Giles Constable with Carol D. Lanham eds *Renaissance and Renewal in the Twelfth Century* Cambridge Mass 1982

Bériou, N. and David L. D'Avray 'Henry of Provins, O.P.'s Comparison of the Dominican and Franciscan Orders with the "Order" of Matrimony' *Archivum Fratrum Praedicatorum* 49 (1979) 513–17

Bernards, M. *Speculum virginum. Geistigkeit und Seelenleben der Frau im Hochmittelalter* 2d edn. unchanged. Cologne 1982

Bickel, E. *Diatribe in Senecae philosophi fragmenta. Vol. 1. Fragmenta de matrimonio* Leipzig 1915

Bloomfield, Morton W., B.-G. Guyot, D.R. Howard, T.B. Kabealo *Incipits of Latin Works on the Virtues and Vices, 1100–1500 A.D. Including a Section of Incipits of Works on the Pater Noster* Cambridge Mass 1979

Bonner, G.I. '*Libido* and *Concupiscentia* in St. Augustine' *Studia Patristica* 6 (1962) 303–14

Børresen, Kari E. *Subordination and Equivalence. The Nature and Role of Woman in Augustine and Thomas Aquinas* tr from the revised French original by Charles H. Talbot. Washington 1981

Boswell, J. *Christianity, Social Tolerance, and Homosexuality. Gay People in Western Europe from the Beginning of the Christian Era to the Fourteenth Century* Chicago 1980

Brandl, P.L. *Die Sexualethik des heiligen Albertus Magnus. Eine moralgeschichtliche Untersuchung* Regensburg 1955

Brody, S.N. *The Disease of the Soul: Leprosy in Medieval Literature* Ithaca NY 1974

Browe, Peter *Beiträge zur Sexualethik des Mittelalters* Breslauer Studien zur historischen Theologie 23. Breslau 1932

Brown, Oscar J. *Natural Rectitude and Divine Law in Aquinas. An Approach to an Integral Interpretation of the Thomistic Doctrine of Law* Studies and Texts 55. Toronto 1981

Brown, Peter *The Body and Society. Men, Women and Sexual Renunciation in Early Christianity* New York 1988

– 'Sexuality and Society in the Fifth Century A.D.: Augustine and Julian of Eclanum' In *Tria corda. Scritti in onore di Arnaldo Momigliano* ed E. Gabba 49–70. Biblioteca di Athenaeum 1. Como 1983

Brundage, J.A. 'Adultery and Fornication: A Study in Legal Theology' In *Sexual Practices and the Medieval Church* 129–34. *See* Bullough and Brundage

– 'Allas! That Evere Love was Synne! Sex and the Medieval Canon Law' *The Catholic Historical Review* 72 (1986) 1–13

– 'Appendix: Medieval Canon Law and Its Sources' In *Sexual Practices and the Medieval Church* 219–23. *See* Bullough and Brundage

– 'Carnal Delight: Canonistic theories of sexuality' *Proceedings of the Fifth International Congress of Medieval Canon Law. Salamanca, 21–25 September 1976* 361–85. Ed Stephan Kuttner and Kenneth Pennington. Monumenta iuris canonici. Series C Subsidia 6. Vatican 1980

– *Law, Sex, and Christian Society in Medieval Europe* Chicago 1987

- 'Let Me Count the Ways: Canonists and Theologians Contemplate Coital Positions' *Journal of Medieval History* 10 (1984) 81–93
- 'The Problem of Impotence' In *Sexual Practices & the Medieval Church* 135–40. *See* Bullough and Brundage
Bugge, John *Virginitas: An Essay in the History of a Medieval Ideal* International Archives of the History of Ideas, Series Minor 17. The Hague 1975
Bullough, Vern L. and James Brundage eds *Sexual Practices and the Medieval Church* Buffalo NY 1982
Bultot, R. 'L'auteur et la fonction littéraire du *De fructibus carnis et spiritus*' *Recherches de théologie ancienne et médiévale* 30 (1963) 148–56
Camelot, T. 'Les traités *De virginitate* au IVe siècle' *Etudes carmélitaines* 31 Suppl (1952) 273–92
Cantalamessa, Raniero ed *Etica sessuale e matrimonio nel cristianesimo delle origini* Studia Patristica Mediolanensia 5. Milan 1976
Cappuyns, M. *Jean Scot Erigène. Sa vie, son oeuvre, sa pensée* Louvain 1933
- 'Le "De imagine" de Grégoire de Nysse traduit par Jean Scot Erigène' *Recherches de théologie ancienne et médiévale* 32 (1965) 205–62
Chadwick, H. '"All Things to All Men" (1 Cor IX:22)' *New Testament Studies* 1 (1954–5) 261–75
Chenu, M.D. 'Les "Philosophes" dans la philosophie chrétienne médiévale' *Revue des sciences philosophiques et théologiques* 26 (1937) 27–40
- *Toward Understanding Saint Thomas* tr with authorized corrections and bibliographical additions by A.M. Landry and D. Hughes. Chicago 1964
Clark, Elizabeth A. '"Adam's Only Companion": Augustine and the Early Christian Debate on Marriage' *Recherches augustiniennes* 21 (1986) 139–62
- 'Heresy, Asceticism, Adam, and Eve. Interpretations of Genesis 1–3 in the Later Latin Fathers' In *Genesis 1–3 in the History of Exegesis. Intrigue in the Garden* 99–133. *See* Robbins
Cloes, H. 'La systématisation théologique pendant la première moitié du XIIe siècle' *Ephemerides theologicae Louvaniensis* 34 (1958) 277–329
Cohen, Jeremy *Be Fertile and Increase* Ithaca NY 1989
Cole, William G. *Sex in Christianity and Psychoanalysis* New York 1966
Cordoliani, A. 'A propos du chapitre premier du *De Temporum ratione*, de Bède' *Le Moyen Age* 54 (1948) 209–23
Couture, Roger A. *L'imputabilité morale des premiers mouvements de sensualité de saint Thomas aux Salmanticenses* Analecta Gregoriana, vol 124, series facultatis theologicae: sectio B n 41. Rome 1962
Coyle, A.F. 'Cicero's *De officiis* and *De officiis ministrorum* of St. Ambrose' *Franciscan Studies* 15 (1955) 224–56
Crowe, Michael B. *The Changing Profile of the Natural Law* The Hague 1977
- 'St. Thomas and Ulpian's Natural Law' In *St. Thomas Aquinas, 1274–1974. Commemorative Studies* ed Armand A. Mauer 1.261–82. Toronto 1974
D'Avray, David L. and M. Tausche 'Marriage Sermons in *ad status* Collections of the Central Middle Ages' *Archives d'histoire doctrinale et littéraire du moyen âge* 47 (1980) 71–119

De Ghellinck, J. *Le mouvement théologique du XIIe siècle* Museum Lessianum, Section historique 10. 2d edn. Bruges 1948

De Rougemont, D. *Love in the Western World* tr M. Belgion. Rev ed. Princeton 1983

Dedek, John 'Premarital Sex: The Theological Argument from Peter Lombard to Durand' *Theological Studies* 41 (1980) 652–6

Delhaye, Philippe 'Une adaptation du *De officiis* au XIIe siècle, le *Moralium dogma philosophorum*' *Recherches de théologie ancienne et médiévale* 16 (1949) 227–58; 17 (1950) 5–28

– 'Le Dossier anti-matrimonial de l'*Adversus Jovinianum* et son influence sur quelques écrits latins du XIIe siècle' *Mediaeval Studies* 13 (1951) 65–86

– *Pierre Lombard. Sa vie, ses oeuvres, sa morale* Conférence Albert-le-Grand 1960. Montreal 1961

Deman, T. 'Le *De officiis* de Saint Ambroise dans l'histoire de la théologie morale' *Revue des sciences philosophiques et théologiques* 37 (1953) 409–24

– 'Le péché de sensualité' *Mélanges Mandonnet* 1.265–83

Dietrich, Paul A. and Donald F. Duclow 'Virgins in Paradise: Deification and Exegesis in *Periphyseon* V' In *Jean Scot écrivain* Actes du IVe Colloque international, Montreal, 28 aout–2 septembre 1983 ed G.H. Allard 29–40. Cahiers d'études médiévales. Cahier spécial 1. Montreal and Paris 1986

Dingjan, F. *Discretio. Les origines patristiques et monastiques de la doctrine sur la prudence chez Saint Thomas d'Aquin* Van Gorcum's theologische bibliotheek 38. Assen 1967

Doherty, D. *The Sexual Doctrine of Cardinal Cajetan* Studien zur Geschichte der katholischen Moraltheologie 12. Regensburg 1966

Dondaine, A. 'Guillaume Peyraut. Vie et oeuvres' *Archivum Fratrum Praedicatorum* 18 (1948) 162–236

Duby, G. *Que sait-on de l'amour en France au XIIe siècle?* Zaharoff Lecture for 1982–3. Oxford 1983

Dudden, F.H. *The Life and Times of St. Ambrose* 2 vols. Oxford 1953

Esmein, A. *Le mariage en droit canonique* 2d edn. Vol 1 R. Génestal. Paris 1929. Vol 2 R. Génestal and Jean Dauvillier. Paris 1935

Evans, M. 'An Illustrated Fragment of Peraldus's *Summa* of Vices: Harleian MS 3244' *Journal of the Warburg and Courtauld Institutes* 45 (1982) 14–68

Faral, E. 'Jean Buridan. Notes sur les manuscrits, les editions et le contenu de ses ouvrages' *Archives d'histoire doctrinale et littéraire du moyen âge* 15 (1946) 1–53

Feckes, C. 'Die Behandlung der Tugend der Keuscheit im Schriftum Alberts des Grossen' Beiträge zur Geschichte der Philosophie und Theologie des Mittelalters. Supplementband 4. Studia Albertina. Festschrift für Bernhard Geyer zum 70. Geburstage 90–111. Ed H. Ostlender. Münster Westf 1952

Festugière, A.J. *Aristote. Le plaisir (Eth. Nic. VII 11–14, XI 1–5)* intro, tr et notes. Paris 1936

– 'La doctrine du plaisir des premiers sages à Epicure' *Revue des sciences philosophiques et théologiques* 25 (1936) 233–68

Flandrin, J.L. 'La doctrine chrétienne du mariage. A propos d'un livre de John T. Noonan' In *Le sexe et l'Occident* 101–8. *See* Flandrin
– *Le sexe et l'Occident. Evolution des attitudes et des comportements* Paris 1981
– *Un temps pour embrasser. Aux origines de la morale sexuelle occidentale (VIe–XIe siècle)* Paris 1983
Floeri, F. 'Le sens de la "division des sexes" chez Grégoire de Nysse' *Revue des sciences religeuses* 27 (1953) 105–11
Foucault, Michel 'The Ethic of Care for the Self as a Practice of Freedom. An Interview' tr J.D. Gauthier. In *The Final Foucault* ed James Bernauer and David Rasmussen 1–20. Cambridge Mass 1988
– *Histoire de la sexualité. 1. La volonté de savoir* Gallimard 1976. English translation: *The History of Sexuality. 1. An Introduction* tr Robert Hurley. New York 1978
– *Histoire de la sexualité. 2. L'usage des plaisirs* Gallimard 1984. English translation: *The History of Sexuality. 2. The Use of Pleasure* tr Robert Hurley. New York 1986
– *Histoire de la sexualité. 3. Le souci de soi* Gallimard 1984. English translation: *The History of Sexuality. 3. The Care of the Self* tr Robert Hurley. New York 1988
Fournier, P. 'Pierre de la Palu. Théologien et canoniste' *Histoire littéraire de la France* 37.39–84. Paris 1938
Franz, Adolph *Die kirchlichen Benediktionen im Mittelalter* 2 vols. Freiburg i B 1909 repr Graz 1960
Freisen, J. *Geschichte des canonischen Eherechts bis zum Verfall der Glossenlitteratur* 2d edn. Paderborn 1893
Fuchs, J. *Die Sexualethik des heiligen Thomas von Aquin* Cologne 1949
Gallagher, C. 'Concupiscence' *The Thomist* 30 (1966) 228–59
Gaudemet, J. 'L'apport de la patristique latine au Décret de Gratien en matière de mariage' *Studia Gratiana* 2 (1954) 49–81
Gauthier, R.A. 'Trois commentaires "averroistes" sur l'Ethique à Nicomaque' *Archives d'histoire doctrinale et littéraire du moyen âge* 16 (1947–8) 187–336
Gauthier, R.A. and J.Y. Jolif *L'Ethique à Nicomaque. Introduction, traduction et commentaire* 2d edn. with new intro. 2 vols. Louvain 1970
Glorieux, P. *La 'Summa Duacensis' (Douai 434)* Paris 1955
Goy, Rudolf *Die Uberlieferung der Werke Hugos von St. Viktor. Ein Beitrag zur Kommunikationsgeschichte des Mittelalters* Monographien zur Geschichte des Mittelalters 14. Stuttgart 1976
Grevy-Pons, N. *Célibat et nature. Une controverse médiévale. A propos d'un traité du début du XVe siècle* Centre d'Histoire des Sciences et des Doctrines, Equipe de Recherche sur l'Humanisme Français des XIVe et XVe siècles. Textes et Etudes 1. Paris 1975
Gross, J. *Geschichte des Erbsündendogmas. Ein Beitrag zur Geschichte des Problems vom Ursprung des Ubels. 3. Entwicklungsgeschichte des Erbsündendogmas im Zeitalter der Scholastik (12–15. Jahrhundert)* Munich and Basel 1971
Hagendahl, H. *Latin Fathers and the Classics. A Study on the Apologists, Jerome*

and Other Christian Writers Studia Graeca et Latina Gothoburgensia 6.
Göteborg 1958

Haller, W. *Iovinianus. Die Fragmente seiner Schriften, die Quellen zu seiner
Geschichte, sein Leben und seine Lehre* Texte und Untersuchungen zur
Geschichte der altchristlichen Literatur 17.1. Leipzig 1897

Halperin, David M. 'Is There a History of Sexuality?' *History and Theory* 28
(1989) 257–74

Häring, N.M. 'Commentary and Hermeneutics' In *Renaissance and Renewal in
the Twelfth Century* 173–200. See Benson and Constable

Heynck, Valens 'Zur Datierung des Sentenzenkommentars des Petrus de
Palude' *Franziskanische Studien* 53 (1971) 317–27

Hieatt, A. Kent 'Eve as Reason in a Tradition of Allegorical Interpretation of
the Fall' *Journal of the Warburg and Courtauld Institutes* 43 (1980) 221–6

Hissette, R. 'Albert le Grand et Thomas d'Aquin dans la censure parisienne
du 7 mars 1277' *Miscellanea Mediaevalia* 15. Studien zur mittelalterlichen
Geistesgeschichte und ihren Quellen 226–46. Berlin 1982

– 'André le Chapelain et la double vérité' *Bulletin de philosophie médiévale* 21
(1979) 63–7

– 'Une "duplex sententia" dans le *De amore* d'André le Chapelain?'
Recherches de théologie ancienne et médiévale 50 (1983) 246–51

– *Enquête sur les 219 articles condamnés à Paris le 7 mars 1277* Philosophes
médiévaux 22. Louvain and Paris 1977

– 'Etienne Tempier et ses condamnations' *Recherches de théologie ancienne et
médiévale* 47 (1980) 231–70

– 'Etienne Tempier et les menaces contre l'éthique chrétienne' *Bulletin de
philosophie médiévale* 21 (1979) 68–72

Hocedez, E. *Richard de Middleton. Sa vie, ses oeuvres, sa doctrine* Spicilegium
sacrum Lovaniense. Etudes et documents 7. Louvain 1925

Hunter, David G. 'On the Sin of Adam and Eve: A Little-Known Defense of
Marriage and Childbearing by Ambrosiaster' *Harvard Theological Review*
82 (1989) 283–99

– 'Resistance to the Virginal Ideal in Late Fourth-Century Rome: The Case
of Jovinian' *Theological Studies* 48 (1987) 45–64

Jacquart, Danielle and Claude Thomasset *Sexuality and Medicine in the
Middle Ages* tr Matthew Adamson. Cambridge 1988

Jeauneau, Edouard 'La division des sexes chez Grégoire de Nysse et chez
Jean Scot Erigène' In *Eriugena. Studien zu seinen Quellen. Vorträge des III.
Internationalen Eriugena-Colloquiums* ed Werner Beierwaltes 33–54.
Heidelberg 1980

Kaeppeli, T. *Scriptores Ordinis Praedicatorum medii aevi* 3 vols to date. Rome
1970–80

Kelly, J.D.D. *Jerome. His Life, Writings, and Controversies* 1975

Köster, Heinrich *Urstand, Fall und Erbsünde. In der Scholastik* In *Handbuch der
Dogmengeschichte. Vol. 2. Der Trinitarische Gott. Die Schöpfung. Die Sünde*
Fasc 36. Ed M. Schmaus et al. Freiburg 1979

Kuttner, S. 'The Father of the Science of Canon Law' *The Jurist* 1 (1941) 2–19

- *Harmony from Dissonance. An Interpretation of Medieval Canon Law* Latrobe Pa 1960
- 'The Revival of Jurisprudence' In *Renaissance and Renewal in the Twelfth Century* 299–323. *See* Benson and Constable
Ladner, G.B. 'The Philosophical Anthropology of Saint Gregory of Nyssa' In G.B. Ladner *Images and Ideas in the Middle Ages. Selected Studies in History and Art* Storia e letteratura. Raccolta di studi e testi 156: 825–65. Rome 1983
Lambert, Bernard *Bibliotheca Hieronymiana manuscripta. La tradition manuscrite des oeuvres de saint Jérôme* Vol 2. Instrumenta patristica 4. The Hague 1969
Landgraf, A. *Introduction à l'histoire de la littérature théologique de la scolastique naissante* Fr ed A.M. Landry. Tr L.B. Geiger. Publications de l'Institut d'études médiévales 22. Montreal and Paris 1973
- ed *Ecrits théologiques de l'école d'Abélard* Spicilegium sacrum Lovaniense 14. Louvain 1934
Lastique, Esther and Helen Rodnite Lemay 'A Medieval Physician's Guide to Virginity' In *Sex in the Middle Ages* 56–79. *See* Salisbury
Le Bras, G. 'Mariage. III. La doctrine du mariage chez les théologiens et les canonistes depuis l'an mille' *Dictionnaire de théologie catholique* 9.2123–2223
Leclercq, Jean *Love in Marriage in Twelfth-Century Europe* Hobart, Tasmania 1978
- *Monks on Marriage. A Twelfth-Century View* New York 1982
- 'The Renewal of Theology' In *Renaissance and Renewal in the Twelfth Century* 68–87. *See* Benson and Constable
Le Comte, Edward *Milton and Sex* New York 1978
Le Roy Ladurie, Emmanuel 'The Aiguillette: Castration by Magic' In *The Mind and the Method of the Historian* 84–96. Tr Sian Reynolds and Ben Reynolds. Chicago 1981
Lindenbaum, Peter 'Lovemaking in Milton's Paradise' *Milton Studies* 6 (1974) 277–306
Lindner, D. *Der usus matrimonii. Eine Untersuchung über seine sittliche Bewertung in der katholischen Moraltheologie alter und neuer Zeit* Munich 1929
Lodovici, E.S. 'Sessualità, matrimonio e concupiscenza in sant' Agostino' In *Etica sessuale e matrimonio nel cristianesimo delle origini* 212–72. *See* Cantalamessa
Lottin, O. 'Les mouvements premiers de l'appétit sensitif de Pierre Lombard à saint Thomas d'Aquin' *Psychologie et morale* 2.493–589
- 'Péché originel et baptême de saint Anselme à saint Thomas d'Aquin' *Psychologie et morale* 4.1, 283–305
- 'Les premières définitions et classifications des vertus au moyen âge' *Psychologie et morale* 3.99–150
- *Psychologie et morale aux XIIe et XIIIe siècles* 6 vols. Louvain 1942–60
- 'Les théories sur le péché originel de saint Anselm à saint Thomas d'Aquin' *Psychologie et morale* 4.1, 11–280
- 'Les vertus cardinales et leurs ramifications chez les théologiens de 1230 à 1250' *Psychologie et morale* 3.153–94

Luscombe, D.E. *The School of Peter Abelard. The Influence of Abelard's Thought in the Early Scholastic Period* Cambridge Studies in Medieval Life and Thought ns 14. Cambridge 1969

Lynch, K.F. 'The Theory of Alexander of Hales on the Efficacy of the Sacrament of Matrimony' *Franciscan Studies* 11 (1951) 69–139

McCall, A. *The Medieval Underworld* London 1979

McNeill, John 'Medicine for Sin as Prescribed in the Penitentials' *Church History* 1(1932) 14–26

Madec, Goulven *Saint Ambroise et la philosophie* Paris 1974

Makowski, E.M. 'The Conjugal Debt and Medieval Canon Law' *Journal of Medieval History* 3 (1977) 99–114

Mâle, Emile *L'art religieux de la fin du moyen âge en France*. 3d edn. Paris 1925

Marchisa, S.E. 'Saggio sull'antropologia filosofico dei Pietro da Tarentaise (Beatus Innocentius V) nel commento alle Sentenze di Pier Lombardo' *Divus Thomas* (Piacenza) 71 (1968) 210–70

Martin, Raymond *La controverse sur le péché originel au début du XIVe siècle. Textes inédits* Spicilegium sacrum Lovaniense. Etudes et documents 10. Louvain 1930

– 'Les questions sur le péché originel dans la *Lectura Thomasina* de Guillaume Godin, O.P.' In *Mélanges Mandonnet* 1.411–21. See *Mélanges Mandonnet*

Mélanges Mandonnet. Etudes d'histoire littéraire et doctrinale du moyen âge 2 vols. Bibliothèque thomiste 13, 14. Paris 1930

Merzbacher, F. 'Die Leprosen im alten kanonischen Recht' *Zeitschrift der Savigny-Stiftung für Rechtgeschichte. Kanonistische Abteilung* 53 (1967) 27–45

Meyer, Heinz *Die Zahlenallegorese im Mittelalter. Methode und Gebrauch* Münstersche Mittelalter-Schriften 25. Munich 1975

Michaud-Quantin, P. *La psychologie de l'activité chez Albert le Grand* Bibliothèque thomiste 36. Paris 1966

– *Sommes de casuistique et manuels de confession au moyen âge (XII–XVIe siècles).* Analecta mediaevalia Namurcensia 13. Louvain 1962

Mitterer, A. 'Mann und Weib nach dem biologischen Weltbild des hl. Thomas und dem der Gegenwart' *Zeitschrift für katholische Theologie* 57 (1933) 491–556

Moorehead, J. 'Adam and Eve and the Discovery of Sex' *Parergon* ns 1 (1983) 1–12

Morsink, Joannes *Aristotle on the Generation of Animals. A Philosophical Study* University Press of America np nd

Müller, M. *Die Lehre des hl. Augustinus von der Paradiesesehe und ihre Auswirkung in der Sexualethik des 12. und 13. Jahrhunderts bis Thomas von Aquin* Regensburg 1954

Murray, Jacqueline 'On the Origins and Role of "Wise Women" in Causes for Annulment on the Grounds of Male Impotence' *Journal of Medieval History* 16 (1990) 235–49

Mystique et continence Travaux scientifiques du VIIe congrès international d'Avon. *Etudes carmélitaines* 31 Supp (1952)

Nelson, N.E. *Cicero's 'De officiis' in Christian Thought* Ann Arbor Mich 1933

Nietzsche, Friedrich *Philosophy and Truth. Selections from Nietzsche's Notebooks of the Early 1870's* ed and tr Daniel Breazeale. Atlantic Highlands NY 1990

Nodet, C.H. 'Positions de saint Jérôme en face des problèmes sexuels' *Mystique et continence. Etudes carmélitaines* 31 Supp (1952) 308–56

Noonan, J.T. *Contraception. A History of Its Treatment by the Catholic Theologians and Canonists.* Cambridge Mass 1965

– 'Gratian Slept Here. The Changing Identity of the Father of the Systematic Study of Canon Law' *Traditio* 35 (1979) 145–72

– 'Marital Affection in the Canonists' *Studia Gratiana* 12 (1967) 481–509

– 'Who was Rolandus?' In *Law, Church and Society: Essays in Honor of Stephan Kuttner* ed Kenneth J. Pennington and R. Somerville 21–48 Philadelphia 1977

North, Helen *Sophrosyne. Self-Knowledge and Self-Restraint in Greek Literature* Cornell Studies in Classical Philology 35. Ithaca NY 1966

Opelt, Ilona *Hieronymus' Streitschriften* Bibliothek der klaşsischen Altertumswissenschaften NF 2 Reihe 44. Heidelberg 1973

Padgug, Robert A. 'Sexual Matters: On Conceptualizing Sexuality in History' *Radical History Review* 20 (1979) 3–23

Pagels, Elaine *Adam, Eve, and the Serpent* New York 1988

Paredi, A. *Saint Ambrose. His Life and Times* tr M.J. Costelloe. Notre Dame 1964

Parmisano, F. 'Love and Marriage in the Middle Ages. I and II' *New Blackfriars* 50 (1968–9) 599–608, 649–60

Payer, Pierre J. 'The Doctrine of Prudence in the Writings of Albert the Great' PH D diss, University of Toronto 1968

– 'Early Medieval Regulations concerning Marital Sexual Relations' *Journal of Medieval History* 6 (1980) 353–76

– 'Eve's Sin, Woman's Fault: A Medieval View' *Atlantis* 2 (1977) 2–14

– 'Foucault on Penance and the Shaping of Sexuality' *Studies in Religion* 14 (1985) 313–20

– 'The Humanism of the Penitentials and the Continuity of the Penitential Tradition' *Medieval Studies* 46 (1984) 340–54

– 'Prudence and the Principles of Natural Law: A Medieval Development' *Speculum* 54 (1979) 55–70

– 'Sex and Confession in the Thirteenth Century' In *Sex in the Middle Ages. A Book of Essays* 126–42. *See* Salisbury

– *Sex and the Penitentials. The Development of a Sexual Code, 550–1150* Toronto 1984

Plus, R. and A. Rayez 'Chasteté. 1. Chasteté et perfection' *Dictionnaire de spiritualité* 2 (1953) 777–97

Quacquarelli, A. *Il triplice frutto della vita cristiana: 100, 60 e 30 (Matteo XIII–8, nelle diverse interpretazioni)* Rome 1953

Quinn, J.F. 'Saint Bonaventure and the Sacrament of Matrimony' *Franciscan Studies* 34 (1974) 101–43

Radcliff-Umstead, Douglas ed *Human Sexuality in the Middle Ages and*

Renaissance University of Pittsburgh Publications on the Middle Ages and Renaissance 4. Pittsburgh 1978

Ramsey, Paul 'Human Sexuality in the History of Redemption' *Journal of Religious Ethics* 16 (1988) 56–86

Robbins, Gregory Allen ed *Genesis 1–3 in the History of Exegesis. Intrigue in the Garden* Studies in Women and Religion 27. Queenston Ont 1988

Rosambert, André *La veuve en droit canonique jusqu'au XIVe siècle* Paris 1923

Rouse, Richard H. and Mary A. Rouse 'Statim invenire: Schools, Preachers, and New Attitudes to the Page' In *Renaissance and Renewal in the Twelfth Century* 201–25. *See* Benson and Constable

Salisbury, Joyce E. ed *Sex in the Middle Ages. A Book of Essays* New York 1991

Schlösser, F. *Andreas Capellanus. Seine Minnelehre und das christliche Weltbild um 1200* Abhandlungen zur Kunst-, Musik- und Literaturwissenschaft 15. Bonn 1960

Schmitt, E. *Le mariage chrétien dans l'oeuvre de saint Augustin. Une théologie baptismale de la vie conjugale* Paris 1983

Schneyer, J.B. *Repertorium der lateinischen Sermones des Mittelalters für die Zeit von 1150–1350 (Autoren: E-H)* BGPTM 43.2. Münster Westf 1970

Sebastian, H.F. 'William of Wheteley's (Fl. 1309–1316) Commentary on the Pseudo Boethius' Tractate *De disciplina scolarium* and Medieval Grammar School Education' PH D diss, Columbia University 1970

Sheehan, M.M. 'Marriage and Family in English Conciliar and Synodal Legislation' In *Essays in Honour of Anton Charles Pegis* ed J.R. O'Donnell 205–14. Toronto 1974

Skinner, Quentin 'Language and Social Change' In *Meaning and Context. Quentin Skinner and His Critics* ed James Tully 119–32. Princeton 1988

Smalley, B. 'The Bible in the Medieval Schools' In *The Cambridge History of the Bible. Vol. 2: The West from the Fathers to the Reformation* ed G.W. Lampe 197–220. Cambridge 1969

– *The Study of the Bible in the Middle Ages* 3d edn. Oxford 1983

Steinmüller, Wilhelm H. 'Die Naturrechtslehre des Johannes von Rupella und des Alexander von Hales in der 'Summa fratris Alexandri' III, q. 26–29, q. 39 (n. 224–286, 395–399) und in der neuaufgefundenen Sentenzenglosse des Alexander von Hales' *Fraziskanische Studien* 41 (1959) 310–422

Stelzenberger, Joannes *Die Beziehungen der frühchristlichen Sittenlehre zur Ethik der Stoa. Eine moralgeschichtliche Studie* Munich 1933

Stock, Brian 'The Philosophical Anthropology of Johannes Scottus Eriugena' *Studi medievali* 3d ser, 8 (1967) 1–57

Stock, Brian and Edward A. Synan 'A Tenth-Century Preface to Bede's *De temporum ratione*' *Manuscripta* 23 (1979) 113–15

Strohm, H. 'Der Begriff der *natura vitiata* bei Augustin' *Theologische Quartalschrift* 135 (1955) 184–203

Tannahill, R. *Sex in History* New York 1981

Taylor, G. Rattray *Sex in History* London 1953

Tentler, Thomas N. *Sin and Confession on the Eve of the Reformation* Princeton 1977

Tessitore, Aristide 'A Political Reading of Aristotle's Treatment of Pleasure in the *Nicomachean Ethics' Political Theory* 17 (1989) 247–65

Thomasset, Claude 'La représentation de la sexualité et de la génération dans la pensée scientifique médiévale' In *Love and Marriage in the Twelfth Century* 1–17. See Van Hoecke and Welkenhuysen

Thonnard, F.J. 'La notion de concupiscence en philosophie augustinienne' *Recherches augustiniennes* 3 (1965) 59–105

Tuchman, B.W. *A Distant Mirror: The Calamitous 14th Century* New York 1978

Tuve, Rosemond 'Notes on the Virtues and Vices' *Journal of the Warburg and Courtauld Institutes* 26 (1963) 264–303; 27 (1964) 42–72

Vaccari, P. 'La tradizione canonica del "debitum" coniugale e la posizione di Graziano' *Studia Gratiana* 1 (1952) 533–47

Valli, F. *Gioviniano. Esame delle fonti e dei frammenti* Pubblicazioni dell'Universita di Urbino. Serie di Lettere e Filosofia 2. Urbino 1953

Valois, N. *Guillaume d'Auvergne Evêque de Paris (1228–1249). Sa vie et ses ouvrages* Paris 1880

Van Hoecke, W. and A. Welkenhuysen eds *Love and Marriage in the Twelfth Century* Mediaevalia Lovaniensia, Ser 1, Studia 8. Louvain 1981

Van Oort, J. 'Augustine on Sexual Concupiscence and Original Sin' *Studia Patristica* 22 (1989) 382–6

Verbraken, P.P. *Etudes critiques sur les sermons authentiques de saint Augustin* Instrumenta patristica 12. Steenbrugge 1976

Vinaty, T. 'Sant' Alberto Magno, embriologo e ginecologo' *Angelicum* 58 (1981) 151–80

Wakefield, Walter and Austin P. Evans eds and trs *Heresies of the High Middle Ages. Selected Sources Translated and Annotated* Records of Civilization. Sources and Studies 81. New York 1969

Wallach, L. 'Alcuin on Virtues and Vices. A Manual for a Carolingian Soldier' *Harvard Theological Review* 48 (1955) 175–95

Walsh, J. 'Buridan and Seneca' *Journal of the History of Ideas* 27 (1966) 23–40

Watté, P. *Structures philosophiques du péché originel. S. Augustin, s. Thomas, Kant* Recherches et synthèses, section de dogme 5. Gembloux 1974

Weigand, R. 'Die Lehre der Kanonisten des 12. und 13. Jahrhunderts von den Ehezwecken' *Studia Gratiana* 12 (1967) 443–78

– 'Magister Rolandus und Papst Alexander III' *Archiv für katholisches Kirchenrecht* 149 (1980) 3–44

Weisheipl, James A. *Friar Thomas d'Aquino. His Life, Thought, and Works* Garden City NY 1974

Whitehead, Alfred North *Process and Reality. An Essay in Cosmology* Gifford Lectures Delivered in the University of Edinburgh during the Session 1927–8. Ed David Ray Griffin and Donald W. Sherburne. Corrected edn. New York 1979

Wicki, Nikolaus *Die Lehre von der himmlischen Seligkeit in der mittelalterlichen*

Scholastik von Petrus Lombardus bis Thomas von Aquin Studia Friburgensia NF 9. Freiburg, S 1954

Wiesen, D.S. *St. Jerome as a Satirist. A Study in Christian Latin Thought and Letters* Cornell Studies in Classical Philology 34. Ithaca NY 1964

Williams, J.R. 'The Quest for the Author of the *Moralium Dogma Philosophorum*, 1931–1956' *Speculum* 32 (1957) 736–47

Wood, C.T. 'The Doctor's Dilemma: Sin, Salvation, and the Menstrual Cycle in Medieval Thought' *Speculum* 56 (1981) 710–27

Ziegler, J.G. *Die Ehelehre der Pönitentialsummen von 1200–1350. Eine Untersuchung zur Geschichte der Moral- und Pastoraltheologie* Regensburg 1959

Index

Adam, as embodiment of human
    nature 44–5
Alan of Lille 139
Albert the Great: on gender
    difference 26–7; on the limits of
    marriage 123; on manner of inter-
    course 77–9; on paying the debt
    93; on pleasure in Paradise 32; on
    temperance 144–5, 146–7; on
    virginity 162–4
Alcuin 134, 137
Alexander III (Pope) 109
Alexander of Hales 43, 44, 46, 91–2;
    on concupiscence 48
Ambrose, *On Philosophy* 122
amplexus reservatus 218n65
Andronicus of Rhodes 150
Anselm of Canterbury 46
Antoninus of Florence 128–9
Ardour 31, 34, 56, 123
Aristotle 12–13, 25–6, 28, 82, 133,
    167; on continence 155; on
    temperance 141–2
Astesanus of Asti 10, 106
Augustine of Hippo 45, 52, 113,
    122, 136; on concupiscence 56; on
    Eve as helpmate 28; on gender
    difference 23–4; on the good of
    marriage 69–70; on lust 54–6; on
    manner of intercourse 76–7; on
    no sex in Paradise 39; on rational
    control 30–1; on temptation 43;

on virginity in Paradise 35–6
Avicenna 48, 104

Baptism, effects of 53
Bernard of Clairvaux 134
Bible (references in text only): 1
    Corinthians (6:18) 82; (7:2) 84,
    112, 114, 115; (7:3) 90, 93;
    (7:5) 98, 113; (7:6) 112, 113, 114;
    (7:7) 113; (7:9) 113; (7:28) 69;
    (7:38) 161; Esther (14:16) 106;
    Ezechiel (18:6) 106, 107; Genesis
    (1:27) 21, 25, 27, 38; (1:28) 8, 21,
    22, 23, 25, 61, 114, 167, 172;
    (2:18) 26, 28; (2:22) 27; (2:24) 19,
    68; (2:25) 45; (3:7) 45; (3:10) 45;
    (4:1) 39; (9:1) 8, 38, 114; Hebrews
    (13:4) 18, 24, 58, 63, 172, 183;
    Isaiah (64:6) 106; John (2:2–10) 68;
    Leviticus (15:24) 106; (18:19) 106;
    (20:18) 106, 108; Matthew (5:32)
    68, 95; (7:12) 66; (13:8) 172,
    175; (13:23) 172, 175; (15:38) 136,
    144, 145; (19:10) 38; (19:19) 68;
    Psalms (50:7) 54; (77:39) 82;
    Romans (7:23) 133; 1 Thessa-
    lonians (4:4) 107
Biblical gloss 5
Bonaventure 39–40; on forced
    intercourse 92; on pleasure 127–8;
    on virginity 36
Book of Vices and Virtues 160